Language, Society and Power

Language, Society and Power is an accessible introduction to studying language in a variety of social contexts.

This book examines the ways language functions, how it influences the way we view society and how it varies according to age, ethnicity, class and gender. It considers whether representations of people and their language matter, explores how identity is constructed and performed and considers the creative potential of language in the media, politics and everyday talk.

The **fifth edition** of this popular textbook features:

- Updated chapters with new activities;
- Examples that include material related to youth language, computer-mediated communication, texting and electronic communication;
- New material on online mass media, fake news and Twitter as a form of political agency;
- More discussion of social media, social networking, memes and mobile communication;
- An introduction to the concepts of translanguaging and superdiversity;
- An expanded *Gender* chapter that explores binary gender identities;
- A companion website which includes more video material to support learning as students make their way through the book.

Language, Society and Power assumes no linguistic background among readers and is a must-read for all students of English language and linguistics, media, communication, cultural studies, sociology and psychology who are studying language and society for the first time.

Annabelle Mooney is Professor of Language and Society at the University of Roehampton, UK.

Betsy Evans is Associate Professor of Linguistics at the University of Washington, USA.

Language, Society and Power

An Introduction

Fifth Edition

Annabelle Mooney and Betsy Evans

Routledge
Taylor & Francis Group

LONDON AND NEW YORK

Fifth edition published 2019
by Routledge
2 Park Square, Milton Park, Abingdon, Oxon, OX14 4RN

and by Routledge
711 Third Avenue, New York, NY 10017

Routledge is an imprint of the Taylor & Francis Group, an informa business

First edition published by Routledge 1999
Fourth edition published by Routledge 2015

British Library Cataloguing-in-Publication Data
A catalogue record for this book is available from the British Library

Library of Congress Cataloging-in-Publication Data
Names: Mooney, Annabelle, 1974– author. | Evans, Betsy, 1966– author.
Title: Language, society and power : an introduction / Annabelle Mooney and Betsy Evans.
Description: Fifth edition. | Milton Park, Abingdon, Oxon ; New York, NY :
    Routledge, 2019. | Includes bibliographical references.
Identifiers: LCCN 2018019738 | ISBN 9780415786225 (hbk) |
    ISBN 9780415786249 (pbk) | ISBN 9780429447006 (ebk)
Subjects: LCSH: Language and languages. | Sociolinguistics. |
    BISAC: LANGUAGE ARTS & DISCIPLINES / Linguistics / Sociolinguistics. |
    LANGUAGE ARTS & DISCIPLINES / Linguistics / General. |
    LANGUAGE ARTS & DISCIPLINES / Communication Studies.
Classification: LCC P40 .L29987 2019 | DDC 306.44—dc23
LC record available at https://lccn.loc.gov/2018019738

ISBN: 978-0-415-78622-5 (hbk)
ISBN: 978-0-415-78624-9 (pbk)
ISBN: 978-0-429-44700-6 (ebk)

Typeset in Akzidenz Grotesk
by Apex CoVantage, LLC

Visit the companion website: www.routledge.com/cw/mooney

For Debbie and Jen

Contents

Figures

Images

Tables

Transcription conventions

Detailed transcription conventions are as follows:

{laughter}	non-verbal information
<u>xxxxxx</u>*{laughing}*	paralinguistic information qualifying underlined utterance
[. . . .]	beginning/end of simultaneous speech
(xxxxxxxx)	inaudible material
(. . . .)	doubt about accuracy of transcription
'. . . .'	speaker quotes/uses words of others
CAPITALS	increased volume
%. . . . .%	decreased volume
bold print	speaker emphasis
>. . .<	faster speed of utterance delivery
/	rising intonation
?	question intonation
yeah:::::	lengthened sound
–	incomplete word or utterance
=	latching on (no gap between speakers' utterances)
(.)	micropause
(-)	pause shorter than one second
(1); (2)	timed pauses (longer than one second)

Preface to the fifth edition

As in the past, we have sought to maintain the structure and focus of previous editions while being mindful of changes in the field and in society. To that end, this edition provides updated examples of several concepts and includes more material on online communication throughout the book. Nevertheless, given the fast-moving nature of technology, aspects of online communication presented here will have already changed by the time this book is in press.

Given the broad reach of language, the complexity of society and the vagaries of power, it's important to remember that there are many possibilities for interpreting the way that language is used. In fact, when we work on the text, we have animated discussions about the concepts and examples we provide. Even though we are both native English speakers and linguists, our understanding of different issues and events does not always coincide. It is our intention that you, the readers, will also have these kinds of stimulating discussions inside and outside of the classroom as you encounter the topics in this book and try your hand at analysing them.

Links to further information about specific topics can be found where ⊕ is indicated in the margin of the text. In addition to these links, the companion website provides chapter-specific links that we hope will inspire further discussion, debate and exploration of language, society and power.

Preface to the fourth edition

In this fourth edition, we have sought to maintain the structure and focus of previous editions while making some revisions in response to the changing nature of linguistic research and feedback from our students and readers. We have added a new chapter on Linguistic Landscapes, focusing on the language and semiotics found in both the physical and virtual worlds. We have also included a chapter on Global Englishes, to highlight the variation in meaning, use and perceived values of Englishes used around the world.

This book introduces readers to some of the key concepts and issues in the exploration of language, society and power. We have maintained some of the analytic tools used in previous editions, as these approaches are applicable to a range of texts, utterances and linguistic uses despite constant changes to the way language is used in the world. The issues related to language, society and power are so complex and extensive it's difficult to give every issue comprehensive treatment. As such there is much more that could be covered in each chapter. We have chosen examples from scholars in the field that we hope are both accessible and illuminating. It is impossible to do justice to this research in the space available, however, and we encourage the consultation of the original work where possible. We have also maintained the tradition of including classic texts and studies while also using more recent research and approaches to show continuity and change in the field. Ongoing debates about standard language, sexism and discrimination on the basis of age or ethnicity all show that while a great deal of research has identified the key issues and questions, and provided solutions, some ideological views are extremely firmly entrenched. Ideology, the construction and maintenance of power and the performance of identity remain central in this edition. These topics recur throughout the book as they underpin our central concerns.

Chapters 1 and 2 introduce ideology and representation as well as some tools for analysing linguistic meaning at the level of the sign and sentence. We focus on the difference between description and prescription in Chapter 1 to make clear the connection between power and language ideologies. The attitudes that people hold about language use are intensely ideological and this can be seen in this and later chapters. Chapter 3 examines language and politics. While we touch on issues that are associated with routine meanings of 'politics', the emphasis in this edition is on the notion that a wide range of issues are, in fact, political. Thus, we employ a broad understanding of politics and cover topics such as the ideologies suggested by children's toys and the politics inherent in the relationship between students and higher education providers.

Chapter 4 focuses on mass news media. While this might seem to be a narrow focus, given changes in technology, especially in relation to social media and the World Wide Web, taking this approach allows us to explore various dimensions of representation, ideology and the construction and reception of news. Chapter 5 is a new chapter exploring linguistic landscapes. This has become an important area of research in sociolinguistics, and because it examines our everyday environment, it forces us to consider important aspects of ideology and how we are positioned by it through the use of signs, language and other semiotics.

The following chapters deal with the classic sociolinguistic variables of gender, ethnicity, age and class. We have tried to balance coverage of classic work in these fields with new issues and research in order to show that while identity is always performed, it is nevertheless understood through ideologies that expect identity to be essential and fixed. Chapter 10 deals with Global Englishes. As with all other linguistic variation, the effect of language ideology, power and politics are significant here. While linguists are clear that all varieties of English are equal as languages, the political, social and ideological structure of the world means that not all varieties are treated equally.

Chapter 11 contains some resources for further exploration, including suggestions for student projects and lists of texts and websites that may assist in seeking out and analysing language in relation to power and ideology.

In keeping with the last edition, a book symbol 📖 is included against texts that appear in the companion reader to this text. We have also included 🌐 to indicate where material is included on the website. In addition, suggestions for further reading are included at the end of each chapter, and we encourage consultation of works cited in the chapters as well. We hope readers find these resources, and the issues covered in the text, interesting, illuminating and challenging.

Preface to the third edition

In this third edition, we have sought to continue the traditions so well established in the first and second editions. The course, out of which this book grew, is still running as required for students on the English Language and Linguistics programme at Roehampton University. While we have kept the structure and tone of previous editions, there have been some changes. The previous editions were authored by academics who had at some time taught at Roehampton. We have kept to this in as much as all of the authors of the present edition have either worked or studied at Roehampton. Indeed, some have done both. What we all have in common is an enthusiasm for the course.

As previously, authors come from all over the world. While we have continued to include material about global Englishes, in this edition we have sought to include examples from other languages. We have also tried to include material from internet sources. The internet is indeed a global phenomenon; we hope you will be able to find your own 'local' examples of the kind of material which we have indicated.

This book introduces students to the central concepts around the topics of language, society and power. Since the previous edition, things have changed in the world of sociolinguistics, and we have tried to capture some of these changes as well as indicate where the field has come from. It is our belief that it is impossible to understand some of the current issues in the field of sociolinguistics without having a sense of how the various topics developed. Certainly the material is only indicative of these changes; we have tried to keep material accessible to students without a background in linguistics, while also wanting to whet the appetite of students and encourage them to take forward their studies in the area.

The importance of language is something that will never go away. The increasingly mediated nature of contemporary society means that it is important to be aware of issues related to representation and ideology. This critical stance is common in many disciplines; we understand it as crucial for meaningful engagement with the world in all areas. Because of this, in the first four chapters, we spend time on the concepts of ideology and representation.

The first two chapters set out our approach to language, society and power. The tools and concepts introduced in these chapters recur throughout the book. While we have indicated, by way of cross-referencing, particular topic links between chapters, the core ideas of ideology and discourse are relevant throughout the text. We have kept to the structure of the book from previous editions with some minor changes. In the chapters on politics (Chapter 3) and media (Chapter 4) we have worked with a broad understanding of these concepts, in order to highlight the importance of power and the ideological choices that are made with any representation. We hope that such a broad focus will assist in developing critical skills and the 'making strange' of the familiar. The other topics we cover were chosen as we understand them to be the 'classic' sociolinguistic variables. We start with gender (Chapter 5), moving on to ethnicity (Chapter 6), age (Chapter 7) and class (Chapter 8). While each of these are areas of change in terms of the questions they ask, they have all, to some degree, also become implicated in a more general discussion of identity. We cover this in Chapter 9 and hope that the topics and issues from previous chapters will be borne in mind when thinking about identity. The final chapter has been altered slightly to address the issue of standard languages and attitudes towards language. While standard English is still an important area, and is included in this section, we thought it important to highlight the work conducted in the area of language attitudes. Further, we see this discussion as bringing the discussion back to where we start, that is, the question of what 'language' means and what ideas we already have about language.

A new addition is the projects chapter. We have sought to provide ideas for investigation of real language, building on the areas covered in the chapters. Included in this chapter is material to encourage students to think about research, issues around gathering and analysing data, as well as information about ongoing research and resources that may be useful in exploring some of the concepts introduced in this book.

As there is a companion Reader for the textbook (*Language, Society and Power: A Reader*, Routledge, 2011), we have indicated in the Further Reading sections any texts which are included in the Reader. The book icon ▢ is placed next to these readings.

Many of the changes have come about as a result of teaching the course. We would like to thank the students we have taught for their engagement, the sharing of their own thoughts and language and their questions. The latter especially have helped us enormously in the writing of this book. Part of the reason for continuing to address our readers as 'you' is to try to capture the dialogue that we experience when teaching the course. Thinking about language is, for us, something which benefits from conversation, discussion and debate. We all have our own biases (something you should bear in mind when reading the book); reflecting on these in the company of others is, for us, an essential part of learning. In this spirit, as authors, we have benefited from the input of a number of people. Thus, alterations, at various stages, were prompted by incredibly helpful suggestions from current users of the second edition as well as reviewers of the draft of this edition. This detailed and constructive advice has been very useful and we are grateful for it.

We hope you enjoy thinking about language. While it can be challenging to develop the critical skills we believe are central to working with language, there is also a great deal of fun to be had.

Preface to the second edition

The first edition of *Language, Society and Power* was published in 1999, when the majority of the contributing authors were lecturers at Roehampton University of Surrey (then Roehampton Institute London). The book had evolved out of an identically titled course on which we had all taught and which is still running as a required course for students on the English Language and Linguistics programme, and as a popular option for students in other departments. Since that first edition, several of us have moved to other universities and colleges, but we have all maintained an interest in studying language as a social entity. Thus, even though producing this second edition has required a great deal more co-ordination than the last time, we were all willing to be involved in revising and updating a project which has not only been enjoyable for us but which has also had a favourable reception from its intended audience.

The second edition has remained faithful to the first in many ways. We have maintained a focus on English (primarily British and American varieties). The first edition's glossary of terms potentially new to the reader (printed in bold in each chapter) has been retained but also updated. We have continued to make use of personal reference (something not typically found in academic texts), addressing the reader as you, and referring to ourselves as I or we as appropriate. We have also continued to assume that our readers are generally not, or not yet, specialists in the areas of language study and linguistics and therefore need an introduction to the kinds of topics which feed into a broader examination of language and society. As such, the book does not offer comprehensive coverage of every possible issue within this vast subject area but, instead, provides a stepping-stone to exploring and thinking about at least some of them. Thus, each of the chapters deals with a topic that has been the subject of academic sociolinguistic investigation and is supplemented with references to useful reading and other sources of material. There are substantial activities throughout the text to help the reader engage more actively with the ideas being presented.

We have maintained the distinctive authorial 'voices' of the first edition, since they make for a more varied and interesting approach to analysis and discussion. One of the things that the majority of the chapters do have in common, though, is that they seek to interpret the ways in which language and language issues can be deconstructed to reveal underlying ideologies, or beliefs. While all of the chapters have a solid academic grounding, it is important to bear in mind that any interpretation of what people do and say is necessarily going to contain a certain measure of bias. Thus, while we can justifiably analyse a newspaper headline about immigration, for example, and state that its 'slant' reveals an affiliation to politically left- or right-wing principles, it must be remembered that any such approach is in itself ideologically determined: it reveals the analyst's belief that language is not a neutral tool of communication but instead a channel for how we see and construct the world around us. This tenet will become clearer as you read through the text.

Each chapter of this book deals with a different area of language, although there are connections between many of the chapter topics. We have designed the book so that it can be read from cover to cover as a continuous text, but also so that individual chapters can stand alone and be read in their own right. We have divided chapters into subsections, partly to indicate the structure clearly with subtitles and partly to help you find the sections you need to read if you don't need to read the whole chapter.

Chapter 1 interrogates the notion of 'language' and raises some of the underlying questions and ideas that will be relevant as you move into the other chapters. Chapters 2–4 all concentrate on the ideological properties of language and on how it can be used to influence the ways in which people think and behave. Chapter 2 is concerned with the connections between language, thought and representation and considers the extent to which language can be said to shape and perpetuate our worldviews. Chapter 3 moves on from the conclusions of Chapter 2 to consider whether, and how, language can be used in politics, and in other fields, to persuade people of particular points of view. Chapter 4 considers how language is used, and to what effects, in media such as newspapers and television with particular reference to news reporting and advertising. Chapters 5–7 deal with language use in connection with particular subgroups within a population. The terms or 'labels' that can be or are applied to members of those groups, and the effect of those labels, are considered. The chapters also look at the kinds of language choices members of those groups sometimes make. Chapter 5 focuses on language and gender; Chapter 6 deals with language and ethnicity and Chapter 7 with language and age. Chapter 8 considers how a further set of subgroup divisions, namely those which go into the construction of social class, affect language use. The last three chapters, 9–11, are concerned with attitudes towards language and the relationship between language and identity. Chapter 9 deals with language and social identity and Chapter 10 with the debates that surround the use of standard English. Chapter 11 provides a conclusion to the whole book with an overview of attitudes towards language.

Finally, we hope that you will enjoy reading and using this second edition and that it will add another dimension to how you think about language and language use. We have certainly enjoyed putting it together, and we hope that at least some measure of our passion and interest in this everyday but extraordinary faculty will prove infectious!

Preface to the first edition

This book is based on a course of the same name that runs in the English Language and Linguistics Programme at Roehampton Institute London and on which all the authors have taught. It began life as Language, Power, Politics and Sexuality, a short (five-week) introduction to language issues for students studying literature. Over the years, the course has grown as interest in language study has grown, and it is now an introductory course for students studying language and linguistics, while continuing in popularity with students of literature. Many of the students taking the course are combining their studies with subjects such as sociology, media studies, women's studies, education and history, where they find that the issues raised are also relevant.

In preparing this book, we have assumed no prior knowledge of linguistics. We hope that students taking courses on the social and political dimensions of language use will find this a useful foundation text. Students of disciplines that include the study of language use, discourse and ideology, power relations, education, the rights of minority groups and equal opportunities should also find this a helpful text. Learners of English may find this a useful route to a better understanding of language use. Since we see language use as being central to many, or most, human activities, we hope that students studying apparently unrelated disciplines may also find it helpful to have a book which covers the range of issues we deal with here. And we have tried to make the text appropriate and interesting for the general reader.

The ideas covered in this book have been explored and developed with groups of students since the early 1980s. They are presented here as eleven topics, currently covered in a modular course on a week-by-week basis. Although they may look it, the topics are not discrete but have overlapping themes and common threads which we have tried to bring out. Nor are they exclusive. As you read, you may well think of other areas of language use which are worthy of investigation or consideration, such as the relationship between language and health or language and the law. Issues such as these are not omitted because we think that they are unimportant but because in a book of this length, there is not space to cover everything. We hope what we have covered will assist your thinking about the relationship between language and the different dimensions of the societies in which we live.

The authors have taught as a team the course from which this book was generated. We felt that as a group, we shared common values both about the topics we taught and our approach to teaching and that this provided us with a solid foundation for writing this book also as a team. We distributed the topics amongst the six of us, according to our areas of special interest, and met regularly to review the drafts of our chapters and to discuss revisions. Our aim was to produce a coherent text that still reflected the ideas and writing styles of individual team members. To some extent, the different 'voices' of the authors should still be apparent.

Amongst other decisions we had to make as a team of authors, we had to decide on how we would use pronouns such as *I, we* and *you*. We could, for example, have decided to write impersonally and avoid using personal pronouns as much as possible, which is quite common in academic writing. We had to decide whether we should refer to ourselves in the chapters as *I* (the individual writing the chapter) or *we* (the team of writers). We also had to decide whether we should use *you* to address our readers. The conventional, impersonal academic style is often criticised by people with an interest in the social and political functions of language because, as is discussed in Chapter 3, it can be used to make ideas seem less accessible than they need be and to increase the apparent status of the writers by making them seem 'cleverer' than the readers. In the end, we felt the most honest and sensible thing to do would be to use *we* to refer to the team of authors, to acknowledge the input we have all had in each other's thinking and writing, but to use *I* if we write about our personal experiences. We have addressed you the readers as *you*.

Throughout the book, we concentrate on the English language, although we occasionally use another language to illustrate a particular point. The main varieties of English looked at are British and American English.

There is a glossary of terms with brief explanations at the back of the book. Words which appear in the glossary are printed in bold the first time they occur in a chapter. You will also find at the end of each chapter recommended further reading, which you can follow up if you want to learn more about a topic. If you want to check whether a topic is covered in this book, and where, the index at the back gives page numbers.

We have included activities throughout the text. Some ask you to reflect on your own use of, or feelings about, language. Some ask you to talk to other people, to elicit their language use or thoughts on certain issues. Some require you to collect data from other sources around you, such as the newspapers or television. Some you will be able to do alone, and some need group discussion. One of the main reasons we have included activities is that we believe that the ideas we are discussing in this book really come alive when you begin to look for them in the language which goes on around you. We have seen students' attitudes change from mild interest, or even a lack of interest, to absolute fascination when they have started to investigate language use for themselves.

If the ideas we have presented here are ones you have come across before, we hope we have presented them in such a way as to provoke further thought or make connections you hadn't previously made. If you haven't thought about some of the ideas we raise here before, we hope that you also find them exciting and spend the rest of your life listening to what people say, reading newspapers and watching television commercials differently.

Acknowledgements

As this book is now in its fifth edition, the list of people involved in reaching this point is lengthy. We would like to thank Deborah Cameron and Jennifer Coates, who designed the course that led to this book. We retain the dedication to them as a tribute to their extensive work in establishing the programme and the course. We hope to have continued the traditions they established in a way that would please them.

Our students on all our courses have also provided invaluable feedback and information about particular issues and also in terms of giving us a clearer idea of our audience. We'd like to thank readers who have provided reports and reviews, as well as those who contacted us about the book. While it hasn't always been possible to cover what was requested, this input has been very useful in honing our ideas about content, structure and focus. Our editors at Routledge, Nadia Seemungal and Elizabeth Cox, have been unstinting in their enthusiasm, support and patience.

Both of us have benefited from the support of our colleagues, family, friends and readers. They have our heartfelt thanks. We have also looked to previous editions for material, ideas and sensibility; this has been of great importance, and we would like thank our colleagues who worked on these texts.

Image 2.1 on p. 30 is reproduced with the kind permission of Russell Hugo © 2014 *russ@portnw.com*.

Example 2.1 on p. 31 is reprinted from Andres Romero-Figueroa, 'OSV as the basic order in Warao', from *Lingua*, volume 66, Issues 2–3, July 1985, with permission from Elsevier.

Image 3.1 on p. 62 is reproduced with the kind permission of Russell Hugo © 2014 *russ@portnw.com*.

Example 4.1 on p. 74 is reproduced with the permission of © Telegraph Media Group Limited 2010.

Example 4.5 on p. 81, extracts from Tammy Boyce (2006) "Journalism and expertise", *Journalism Studies*, 7:6,889–906 are reprinted by permission of the publisher.

Figure 4.2 on p. 86 'A typology of online journalisms' is from Mark Deuze (2003) "The web and its journalisms: considering the consequences of different types of newsmedia online", *New Media & Society*, 5(2): 202–230. Reprinted by permission of SAGE Publications, Ltd.

Image 5.1 on p 101 and Image 5.2 on p 101 are reproduced under terms of the Open Government Licence v1.0.

Image 5.7 on p. 108 is reproduced with the permission of the photographer, Nyssa Lilovich.

Image 5.8 on p. 109 is reproduced with the permission of the Orpheum Theatre and Vancouver Civic Theatres.

Image 5.10 on p. 111 is reproduced with the permission of the photographer, © Dr. Sarah Pasfield Neofitou.

Image 5.11 on p. 111 is reproduced with the kind permission of Ryan Laughlin © http://rofreg.com.

Image 5.13 on p. 123 is reproduced with the kind permission of James Scott.

Tables 6.1 and 6.2 on pp. 131 and 133 are from Motschenbacher, Heiko (2013) "Gentlemen before ladies? A corpus-based study of conjunct order in personal binomials", *Journal of English Linguistics*, 41(3): 212–42. Reprinted by permission of SAGE Publications, Inc.

Example 6.5 on p. 140 is from Deborah Cameron (1997) "Performing Gender Identity: Young men's talk and the construction of heterosexual masculinity". Originally published in *Language and Masculinity*, eds. Sally Johnson and Ulrike Hanna Meinhof. Copyright © Blackwell Publishers Ltd. 1997. Reprinted by permission of John Wiley & Sons Ltd.

Table 6.6 on p. 150 is from Hazenberg, E. (2016) "Walking the straight and narrow: linguistic choice and gendered presentation", *Gender & Language*, 10(2): 270–94. Reprinted by permission of the publisher. Copyright © Equinox Publishing Ltd. 2016.

Figure 7.3 on p. 166 is from Natalie Schilling-Estes (2004) "Constructing ethnicity in interaction", *Journal of Sociolinguistics*, 8(2): 163–95. Reprinted by permission of John Wiley and Sons.

Example 7.6 on p. 168 is from Norma Mendoza-Denton (1996) "'Muy macha:' gender and ideology in gang girls' discourse about makeup", *Ethnos: Journal of Anthropology*, 61(1–2): 47–63.

Example 7.7 on p. 170 is from Petra Scott Shenk (2007) "I'm Mexican, remember? Constructing ethnic identities via authenticating discourse", *Journal of*

Sociolinguistics, 11(2): 194–220. Reprinted by permission of John Wiley and Sons.

Example 7.8 on p. 172 is from Cecilia A. Cutler (1999) "Yorkville Crossing: white teens, hip-hop and African American English", *Journal of Sociolinguistics*, 3(4): 428–42. Reprinted by permission of John Wiley and Sons.

Examples 8.4 and 8.5 on p. 197 and p. 198 are reprinted from Marsden, S., & Holmes, J. (2014) "Talking to the elderly in New Zealand residential care settings", *Journal of Pragmatics*, 64: 17–34 with permission from Elsevier.

Example 8.6 on p. 199 is from Virpi Ylänne-McEwan (1999) "'Young at heart': discourse of age identity in travel agency interaction", *Aging and Society* 19(4): 417–40. Copyright © 1999 Cambridge University Press.

Examples 8.7 and 8.8 on p. 201 and p. 203 are from David Divita (2012) "Online in later life: age as a chronological fact and a dynamic social category in an Internet class for retirees", *Journal of Sociolinguistics*, 16(5): 586–612. Reprinted by permission of John Wiley and Sons.

Figure 8.1 on p. 189 is reprinted from Sali Tagliamonte (2005) "So who? Like how? Just what?: Discourse markers in the conversations of young Canadians", *Journal of Pragmatics*, 37(11): 1896–1915, with permission from Elsevier.

Table 8.2 on p. 193 is from Sali Tagliamonte, Derek Denis (2008) "Linguistic ruin? LOL! Instant messaging and teen language", *American Speech*, 83(1): 3–34. Copyright 2008, the American Dialect Society. All rights reserved.

Example 9.2 on p. 219 is from Stuart-Smith, J., Timmins, C. and Tweedie, F. (2007) "'Talkin' Jockney'? Variation and change in Glaswegian accent", *Journal of Sociolinguistics*, 11(2): 221–260. Reprinted by permission of John Wiley and Sons.

Example 9.3 on p. 220 is reprinted from Ben Rampton (2011) "Style contrasts, migration and social class", *Journal of Pragmatics*, 43(5): 1236–50, with permission from Elsevier.

In Chapter 10, data extracts on p. 246 and p. 247 are from R. Tupas, and A. Salonga, A. (2016) "Unequal Englishes in the Philippines", *Journal of Sociolinguistics*, 20(3): 367–81. Reprinted by permission of John Wiley and Sons.

Image 10.1 on p. 235 is reproduced with the kind permission of Russell Hugo © 2014 russ@portnw.com.

Figure 10.2 on p. 233 is reproduced from Tom McArthur (1987) "The English languages?", *English Today*, 3(3): 9–13. Reproduced with permission of Cambridge University Press.

While every effort has been made to trace and contact the copyright holders of material used in this volume, the publishers would be grateful to hear from any they were unable to contact.

CHAPTER 1

Language?

1.1 INTRODUCTION

Even though we use language constantly, we usually take it for granted. When we pay attention to it, it's usually because something has gone wrong or because we're passionate about the topic or speaker. While we will consider cases where things go wrong, in this book, we focus more often on how language works successfully, in common situations, in different ways, for different people. We also consider the effects that language can have, especially in relation to power, representations and control. Before we do this, we need to think about what 'language' is. This is not an easy task. What counts as a language is a political, cultural and technical question. As will be discussed in this and the following chapters, there are well-established languages that are often not considered to be 'proper' languages by people in general. To make matters even more complicated, individuals don't always use language in the same way. The language we use when we talk to our friends is not the same as the language we use to write a letter of complaint. Language varies depending on the people using it, the task at hand and the society in which it all takes place.

Linguists study language for many different reasons, with various questions that they want to answer. Whatever path this research takes, it always treats language as a system. Studying systems might sound tedious, but linguists do more than that – they *describe* the systems. Linguists describe the construction of these complex and changing systems, working with examples of language from the everyday world. And this is not just any set of rules for construction – language is a system that enables people to tell jokes, write poetry, make an arrest, sell you washing powder, pay a compliment and wish you good night.

1.2 WHY STUDY LANGUAGE?

It's important to study language because *language matters*. For example, the choice of words to describe a person or event reveals the attitude of the person writing or speaking. One such example concerns US CIA contractor Edward Snowden, who, in 2013, released classified material relating to British and American surveillance programmes. How he was described in the subsequent media coverage is instructive. Those who saw his actions as bravely exposing secret and harmful state actions call him a 'whistleblower' or 'patriot'. Those who argue that he was obligated to protect the confidentiality of this material label him a 'traitor'. This example shows how one word can serve as a shorthand for a belief system and position on Snowden's actions. Paying attention to these choices is part of having a critical awareness of language. This is a skill that this book will help you develop.

Because the choice of words – and how things are said – is so important, it's worth looking at two more examples. The first is similar to the Snowden example in that it concerns what is and is not labelled as 'terrorism'. In September 2016, an explosive device went off in Chelsea, New York. Governor Andrew Cuomo and New York City Mayor Bill de Blasio both commented on the event, but they did so in very different ways. Governor Cuomo described it as an act of 'terrorism', while Mayor de Blasio refused to use this word. The governor pointed out that he and de Blaiso agreed about what had happened. He continued:

> 'I think it becomes a question of semantics, if anything', Cuomo said. 'Yes, it was an intentional act. It was a violent act. It was a criminal act. And it was an act that frightened, hurt and scared many, many people. And generically, you call that terrorism'.
>
> (Figueroa, 2016)

This news report is perhaps unusual in that it recounts an explicit disagreement about how to label a set of events. As the quote from Governor Cuomo makes clear, both men agree about what happened, and both evaluate the act very negatively. At the level of who did what to whom (see Chapter 2), they agree. But to call something an act of 'terrorism' invokes a specific set of associations. This is where they do not agree. Terrorists are generally represented as being an other, a 'them' that is seeking to destroy 'us'. That is, once the word 'terrorist' or 'terrorism' is used, people are inclined to see events through a very particular lens: one that makes a distinction between us and them. More generally, the language used to describe acts of terrorism is the language of war, where *we* must fight *them* with force. Such naming, however, is not just a matter of choosing between two words. A 'terrorist' act is viewed by the media and the public in a different way to other violent acts; it attracts different legal punishments, and it shapes our views of who 'we' are. Choosing (or not choosing) 'terrorist' in this context reflects the belief system of the speaker. The words we use to describe people and events have consequences. This is precisely why we should pay attention to language and the way people use it.

The next example also shows a set of beliefs but of a very different kind. In July 2017, the *Economist* posed an interesting question. What do we call people who are older but not yet retired? (*The Economist*, 2017). They ask 'WHAT do you call someone who is over 65 but not yet elderly? This stage of life, between work and decrepitude, lacks a name'. A series of possibilities are then given.

These are some of the words that the *Economist* lists as being possible candidates for this group of people.

Geriactives
Sunsetters
Nightcappers
Nyppies (Not Yet Past It)
Owls (Older, Working Less, Still Earning)
Pretirees

Are you familiar with all of them? What do they mean to you? Are there others that you can think of?

Activity 1.1

We will see in Chapter 8 that the representation of age and life stages is complicated (e.g., the use of 'decreptitude' in the preceding quotation). Here, the *Economist* have identified a gap in our language. They suggest that change in society has outpaced the language that we use to represent people. Language is always changing. For example, they report that the term 'teenager' was coined around 1940. It is not the case that people in this age group did not exist before, but rather, it had not seemed necessary to identify them specifically until then.

Thinking about how we talk about age and life stage and how we think about terrorism and traitors are all good examples of what Norman Fairclough calls developing a 'critical awareness of language'. He writes that a 'critical awareness of language . . . arises within the normal ways people reflect on their lives as part of their lives' (1999: 73). Such reflection is well worth encouraging; Fairclough argues that the ability to understand how language functions, to think about it in different ways, is crucial to understanding society and other people. Critical awareness isn't important because it makes us more accomplished or more intelligent; there is much more at stake. Fairclough argues that to understand power, persuasion and how people live together, a conscious engagement with language is necessary. That is, critical thinking about language can assist in resisting oppression, protecting the powerless and building a good society. Ferdinand de Saussure, sometimes referred to as the founder of modern linguistics, puts it rather more starkly. He writes: '[I]n the lives of individuals and societies, speech is more important than anything else. That linguistics should continue to be the prerogative of a few specialists would be unthinkable – everyone is concerned with it in one way or another' (1966: 7). People often say that quibbling over word choice, such as in the Edward Snowdon case, is 'just semantics'. But it is much more than this. It is about the meaning of the words used (**semantics**) but also the context in which the words are used.

Semantics is just one of the areas of linguistics that explores how we understand and construct meaning. But there are many others. Some linguists work to describe the construction of word order (**syntax**) or the sounds that make up words (**phonetics**, **phonology** and **morphology**). Looking closely at language can tell us about

- how our brains understand and process language (psycholinguistics)
- how we learn languages and so how best to teach them (applied linguistics)
- how social factors (age, gender, class, ethnicity, and so on) affect the way people use language (sociolinguistics)
- how it might be possible to have a realistic conversation with a computer (artificial intelligence)
- what it is distinctive about literature and poetry (stylistics)
- how people in different cultures use language to do things (anthropology)
- the relationship between words and meaning and the 'real' world (philosophy)
- whether someone is guilty of a criminal offence (forensic linguistics)
- the structure of non-verbal languages (e.g. sign languages)

This is far from a full account of the various kinds of linguistics. The subfields here are much richer and further reaching than the bullet points suggest. The important thing is to realise that language can be examined in a variety of ways with diverse and specific concerns in mind. It's also important to point out that these areas aren't completely separate. We may want to know something about how brains process language if we're interested in finding good teaching methods, for example. The way linguists in these areas go about studying language may also overlap. For example, the kind of analysis that is done in stylistics will be similar in some ways to the work done by forensic linguistics because there is a similar attention to the detail of language and some of the same tools of analysis are used. In this book, we'll be exploring what language can tell us about people as individuals and as members of groups and about how people interact with other people. This is called sociolinguistics. The subject of our attention here is the way that language is used in normal life, by all kinds of people, to accomplish all manner of goals.

1.3 WHAT IS LANGUAGE?

As we noted earlier, language matters, and in this book, we'll be exploring the way different groups of people are represented by and use language. To be able to do this, we need to understand how linguists study language and what it means to say that language is a system.

1.3.1 Language: a system

If we look closely at language, we find that it is in fact a rule-governed system. This may make it sound like language is *controlled* by rules that prevent it from changing. However, this is not what we mean by system; we need to be clear about what kind of rules we're talking about. These 'rules' are more like inherent 'building codes' that enable speakers to use their language. The building codes in language tell users of the language how to combine different parts of that language. This includes inherent building codes about which sounds and words can be combined together. For example, we all know inherently, if English is our first language, that 'ngux' is not a word that is possible in English. The building codes of English sounds (**phonemes**) tell us that we can't have 'ng' at the start of a word. In the same way, if I tell you that I recently bought a 'mert', you would be able to form the question, 'What is a mert?'. Even though you don't know what a 'mert' is, from the way the sentence is constructed, you know 'mert' is a noun. You would already know how to make its plural ('merts'). This is because of the building codes in English about where certain kinds of words go in sentences (**syntax**) and how to form plurals (**morphology**). Theoretical linguists work at discovering these building codes for particular languages, including sign languages. Although sign language uses a different **modality**, that is, manual, facial and body movements, it is composed of the same components we've described for spoken language. Linguists' research on spoken and sign language can be used to say something about language in general, that is, linguists can come to conclusions about all languages, grouping them according to certain structural criteria, and even make arguments about how the language faculty itself works.

Linguists don't decide on building codes and then try to make everyone follow them. Rather, linguists examine language to discover what the building codes are that make it work, that is, the things that make communication possible. This means that linguistics is **descriptive** (we'll come back to this important concept). As language changes, new building codes are discovered and described by linguists. Even the variation that sociolinguists examine is systematic, that is, it appears to be amenable to description in terms of building codes.

The set of all the building codes that need to be followed in order to produce well-formed utterances in a language is referred to as 'the grammar' of a language. It is important to note that the meaning of 'grammar' for linguists is different from what 'grammar' refers to outside of the field of linguistics. Non-linguists typically use the term to refer to prescriptive rules of how to use language (prescriptive rules are described in Section 1.4). The theoretical linguist Noam Chomsky made an important distinction between **competence** in and **performance** of a grammar. To have competence in a language means to have knowledge of the grammar. Performance refers to the way individual speakers actually use the grammar. It is possible, therefore, for a speaker to have grammatical competence of a language but lack **communicative competence** of that same language because they are unaware of rules of social relationships, taboos or other cultural conventions. Knowing how to greet someone or what constitutes appropriate 'small talk' are examples of this competence. Communicative competence has also been called 'sociolinguistic competence' or 'pragmatic competence'.

David Crystal provides a list of some of the things we can do with language (2005: 462–468):

- expressing emotion
- expressing rapport
- expressing sounds
- playing
- controlling reality
- recording facts
- expressing thought processes
- expressing identity
- meeting technological demands

As Crystal's list makes clear, we can accomplish a range of things when we use language.

Activity 1.2

In order to see the different ways language can be used, consider a single word: 'fine'. Try to come up with a number of exchanges between two people in which one person uses the word 'fine'. Can it be used to do different things? How can we tell what the word is doing in each context?

In Activity 1.2, you might have come up with examples like the following:

a   I'm fine (in response to the question 'How are you?')
b   What fine weather we are having today (an attempt to start a conversation).
c   I hope you feel fine soon (to someone who is sick).
d   He's a fine man (positively evaluating a person's character).
e   He looks fine (very positively evaluating a person's appearance).

This makes clear that the same word can be used to do very different things. It can be used to engage in small talk about the weather, express concern about someone's health, and provide an assessment of a person's character or appearance. Moreover, knowing that these are appropriate things to say is a part of communicative competence. In many cultures, for example, the question 'How are you?' is not a real question. The person asking doesn't really want to know how you are. Rather, asking the question is a routine part of greeting someone. And the appropriate response is something like 'I'm fine; how are you?'. Communicative competence can also be articulated in terms of rules. But these rules are not commands. Rather, the rules that describe communicative competence constitute a shorthand for setting out what people actually do and what they find acceptable.

It is also worth remembering that not only language has 'rules'. Other systems of communication have inherent 'rules' too. The light that tells us when it's safe to cross the road is generally green. Around the world, there are differences in the shape of the light. Sometimes a word is given, like 'WALK' and sometimes a picture shape that suggests a person moving. The red light (in whatever shape it happens to be) tells pedestrians to stop. This signal varies from place to place. Some countries have a flashing red light, for example, indicating that you shouldn't start crossing the road. While there are differences in the way different countries configure their traffic signals, there is one thing that is the same: the traffic lights can't tell you to 'skip' or to 'watch out for the tiger'. They tell us only about whether or not we can proceed (either on foot or in our car). Even a new combination would not of itself provide a new message. For example, if both red and green lights were illuminated at the same time, you would probably conclude that the light was faulty, not that a new message was being communicated. Such lights are very limited in what they can communicate. The structure of spoken and written language, however, makes it possible to invent new words, exploit existing structures and repurpose existing spoken and written **texts**. This is true in all manner of contexts, from interaction with friends and family to more public interactions in the realm of politics and media. This key component of human language is called recursivity. This is what makes human language different from other kinds of communication like traffic lights.

1.3.2 Language: a system with variation

We tend to talk about English as though it is the same everywhere. But even in one city, the English that people use varies widely. Of course, this is true of any language. When we talk about 'a' language, we are referring to something that is rather abstract and elusive. Variation in language is a challenge, as it prompts us to think about how we can classify different varieties in relation to each other. How we choose to classify these varieties can vary according to linguistic and political considerations. We might think that a language variety can be identified geographically, such that everyone in England speaks English, while everyone in the United States speaks American English. But if you listen to someone from Liverpool in England and then to someone from Brighton, it's clear that there are some important differences.

There are differences in the way that people pronounce words, which varies systematically and often on the basis of geography. Such differences are often referred to in terms of **accent**. There are other differences between speakers of English in relation to the words they use for particular things (vocabulary) and even the order in which words are placed (syntax); we can talk about this collection of features in terms of **dialect** or **variety**. We will use the neutral term 'variety' because very often non-linguists use the term 'dialect' in a pejorative way. To say, for example, that Australian English is not a variety in its own right but merely a 'dialect' of British English immediately places Australian English in a subordinate position to British English.

Most speakers perceive that different varieties of a language exist on a hierarchy that awards a lot of prestige to those varieties at the top of the hierarchy and very little prestige or even stigmatisation to those at the bottom. How decisions are taken about what is 'correct', 'standard' or even attractive and desirable for a language is very often related to power (there are many different kinds of power, a topic that we consider in later chapters). For example, research has shown that speakers of English in Western countries believe that British English is the most correct variety of English in the world (Evans, 2005). The most likely reason is that speakers perceive British English to be the 'original' English and other varieties as 'spin-offs' of the original. In addition, the longstanding historical position of the United Kingdom as a powerful country plays a role in this perception. By contrast, Indian English, in spite of it being a first language for some (Sailaja, 2009: 2), is not perceived as having the same status as Englishes spoken in the West (the issues of 'world Englishes' are taken up in Chapter 10). As we described earlier, linguists value all varieties equally regardless of their origins, so this perception of a hierarchy of Englishes is not a descriptive one.

1.3.3 The potential to create new meanings

It is certainly possible to use existing words in a new way. For example, the verb 'to ghost' has long been a term to describe ghost writing (when the named author employs someone else to write their book). Now, however, it is being used to describe the disappearance of an individual from a person's life and especially their online social network. While it is often used to describe a way of ending a romantic relationship, it can also be used more generally to refer to the disappearance of a friend. Predegrast observes that

> Being 'ghosted' is one of the toughest ways to be dumped.

She then explains what it means:

> It's when someone you've been seeing suddenly ceases all contact with you. They defriend you on Facebook, stop following you on Twitter and avoid responding to calls, texts and emails. They just disappear; fade out of your life mysteriously.
>
> (Prendergast, 2015)

As we will see more in Chapters 4 and 5, social media provides interesting examples of language use. Some of this is related to the activities people can undertake using social media. For example, before Twitter, 'tweeting' was something that birds did, and the idea that you can 'inbox' someone would not have made much sense before email and indeed other alternative forms of electronic communication. While 'inbox' as a verb is not yet in the online Oxford English Dictionary, the verb 'tweet' is.

It is also possible for the function of a word to change. For example, US scholars have noticed that the word 'because' has recently been used in a new way (Zimmer, Solomon and Carson, 2014). This word has been used in the English language for hundreds of years as a conjunction (usually followed by 'of') as shown in Example 1.1.a.

Example 1.1
  a   The picnic was cancelled because of the rain.
  b   The picnic was cancelled because rain.
  c   Fido ate too many biscuits because delicious.

More recently, 'because' has been turning up in sentences as a sort of preposition, as in Examples 1.1.b. and c. New uses for old words and changes to the kind of word it is (noun, verb, and so on) are far from unusual. The use of a conjunction as a word to serve new functions, as in the 'because' example, is unusual. This new use is particularly interesting to linguists, and they are still studying this new usage in order to ascertain just what the additional linguistic role of 'because' might be.

It is also possible to add entirely new words to the language. Not only is this possible, it is essential as new objects, practices and ways of doing things develop. As these words enter the language, they conform to the building codes (see Section 1.3.1) about how to construct an acceptable word in whatever language we're using. For example, the September 2016 update of the Oxford English Dictionary included (among many other new words) 'clickbait'. They provide the following definition:

> Internet content whose main purpose is to encourage users to follow a link to a web page, esp. where that web page is considered to be of low quality or value.
>
> (Oxford English Dictionary)

It is marked as colloquial and citations (that is, key examples) of the term are documented back to 1999.

Very new uses or unconventional uses of language aren't often found in dictionaries. Many people believe that because something cannot be found in 'the dictionary', it's not a legitimate use of the language. However, the lack of a dictionary entry is not evidence for the new word's illegitimacy. It is important to understand that dictionaries are descriptive, but they are also conservative in that they tend to include new meanings of words only when they have demonstrated some longevity. The *Oxford English Dictionary* won't amend their content every time you and your friends come up with a new use for a word. The compilers of dictionaries, **lexiocographers**, make a judgement about whether to include a word based on how widely it is used (in terms of both time and number of people). The fact that the role of dictionaries is to describe language and not to dictate use is often misunderstood.

1.4 THE 'RULES' OF LANGUAGE: PRESCRIPTION VERSUS DESCRIPTION

Linguists understand that language change, such as new word formation, is a fundamental part of language. However, linguists aren't the only people interested in language. Most people have opinions about language and language use. We refer broadly to all the types of opinions and underlying belief systems that people have about language as 'language regard' (Preston, 2010). Looking at comments people make online, on television and in general conversation, we notice that people have very strong ideas about language. There may be particular words or expressions that are commented on, perhaps because they cause offence or because they are considered to be 'grammatically wrong'. This idea that some things are 'grammatically wrong' is a significant belief for many speakers. For example, a magazine called *The Idler* hands out annual bad grammar awards. They identify examples of what they believe to be bad usage of English. They argue the purpose of the awards is not to ridicule people but instead to have a discussion about language, but their position is clear when they claim 'we reckon grammar is more like the law' (The *Idler*, n.d.). The very idea that there is a right or wrong way to use language is a prescriptivist position (see Section 1.4). *The Idler* have devoted considerable time to this endeavour by recruiting readers to contribute nominations and selecting high-profile judges. The 'winner' is sent a copy of a well-known prescriptive grammar book.

What do you think about these words in Example 1.2? Do you think they are useful additions to English? What do you suppose someone from *The Idler* might say about them?

Example 1.2
a   slaktivist (noun): 'A person who supports a political or social cause via the Internet (e.g., by signing an online petition) and whose actions are characterised as requiring little time, effort, or commitment, or as providing more personal satisfaction than public impact' (Oxford English Dictionary).
b   glam-ma (noun): 'A glamorous grandmother, esp. one who is relatively young or fashion-conscious. Also used as a form of address' (Oxford English Dictionary).
c   Squee (verb): 'Of a person: to utter a high-pitched squealing sound expressive of delight or excitement' (Oxford English Dictionary).

For linguists, and for lexicographers, meaning is determined by use. That is, we don't judge a use of a word as 'correct' or 'incorrect' because our concern is mutual understanding. This can be captured more precisely by talking about the difference between **description** and **prescription**. Linguists are concerned with describing what people do with language (description) while people who want to say that a certain use is incorrect are setting down rules for proper language use (prescription), quite apart from what people actually do. Prescriptivists have very strong ideas about how language should be used. They have clear ideas about what is 'correct' and what isn't. This is an example of language regard. Prescriptivists seem to think that if language changes, if 'rules' are broken, that the heart of language will be torn out. As we've pointed out, for linguists, these changes are an inherent feature of language and very interesting. As languages are used, they change naturally. Although language changes, it is always systematic; that is, language changes are always consistent with the building codes of that language. The difference between prescriptive and descriptive perspectives might take some getting used to, but it is fundamental for any study of language.

Many prescriptivist requests to respect the 'rules' also come with some kind of warning: breaking the rules will lead to breaking the language itself. 'The crisis is imminent', we are told; 'things have never been this bad, it's all the fault of young people, foreigners and poor schooling'. The themes of prescriptivist arguments remain strikingly consistent over time. Disapproval of the way some people use language, especially in relation to grammar and the meaning of words, has a very long history known as 'the complaint tradition' (Milroy and Milroy, 1999, see also Beal, 2009). The idea that language is in decline and that this is someone's fault dates back to at least the 14th century (Boletta, 1992; see also Crowley, 2003). You can find many contemporary examples of the complaint tradition in newspapers and on the internet.

The concept of correctness and 'standard English' is a tricky one (Trudgill, 1999). 'Standard English' (or 'standard' in any other language) is defined by speech communities and not linguists. Therefore, 'standard' refers to many varieties that speakers believe to be correct. In this book, we use the expression 'standard English' to refer to this popular definition. This term is intended to acknowledge that non-linguists believe that there are varieties that are more correct than others, a belief that is predicated on prescriptivist ideas but that we do not endorse.

In contrast, prescriptivists believe it's important to have guidelines or 'rules' for the best way of speaking. So they assert the importance of the 'rules' by recording them in books and teaching them to students. It's very important to consider who 'makes' these rules for language use and why they insist everyone follow them. These rules for language use (remember: we are *not* talking about the 'building codes') are dictated and maintained by educated members of the higher social echelons of society. They are the members of society who have the power to sanction members of the speech community for not 'following the rules'. These sanctions might take the form of a poor mark in school, a failed job interview, or lack of a promotion at work. So, knowing the prescriptive rules of language clearly has consequences. Because prescriptive ideas about language circulate in our culture, it is not uncommon to form judgements about other people because of their use of language. Writing in the *Baltimore Sun*, Lynne Agress asks, 'Why can't Americans speak/write English correctly?' (2016).

She provides a number of examples of 'errors' that are commonly made.

- confusion of singular and plural
  - O There's many people on the train versus There are many people on the train.
  - O The media is misinformed versus The media are misinformed.
- using 'good' as an adverb
  - O I'm good versus I'm well.
- using 'between' instead of 'among'
  - O I will divide the cake between my three friends versus I will divide the cake among my three friends.

While Agress is not particularly damning of people who make these mistakes, there is a clear negative judgement here. She writes: 'There are hundreds of grammar mistakes people make daily, and I cringe every time I hear just one. I am certain my readers have their own lists of pet peeves' (2016).

One longstanding complaint in the domain of written language relates to the use of apostrophes. One man is so upset by this, that he corrects them. He has developed a tool called 'the apostrophiser', which allows him to cover up 'incorrect' apostrophes on signs in his local Bristol (UK). While many of us do have our own 'pet peeves' about how language is used (linguists included), the idea that there is a single 'correct' way to use language is mistaken. The internet has also enabled a thriving community of individuals expressing their concern about 'falling' standards in language. Advice about how to use language 'properly' can be easily found on social media. As Vriesendorp observes, 'the standard language ideology seems to have established itself firmly on these new platforms, adapting itself in the process' (2016: 18).

Activity 1.4

Consider the following example sentences. Decide which ones would be considered 'correct' from a descriptive or prescriptive position. What features of the examples make you think so?

Table 1.1 Prescriptive/descriptive activity

	Prescriptive	Descriptive
Example: *Mary don't usually be at church.*	*Not correct: it does not follow prescriptive rules for negation in English.*	*Correct: it consists of a structure allowed by the building codes of English.*
1. If I was you, I'd study harder for exams.		
2. Yesterday, I was conversating with my friend.		
3. Dog the up quickly ran road.		
4. The ring was very unique.		
5. It was an argument between my friend and I.		
6. He took less days off than his colleagues.		
7. I book read yesterday the have.		
8. Steve and me went to the cinema yesterday.		

Examples 3 and 7 are 'not correct' from either a prescriptivist or descriptivist perspective because they don't conform to the building codes of English and therefore don't communicate a clear message. A reader can probably rearrange the words to find an acceptable message, but all speakers of English would agree that something here isn't right. The other examples, however, seem to communicate a clear message and are 'correct' from the descriptive perspective. From the prescriptive perspective, though, they are 'incorrect' because they don't follow prescriptive rules.

All of these examples contain elements that prescriptivists might find very objectionable. The use of 'conversating' (in 2) and 'less' (in relation to a countable noun) annoy some people. Using 'unique' as a comparative rather than absolute description is also troubling to some people. You may feel like the example *Mary don't usually be at church* doesn't conform to the building codes of English. In fact, there are varieties of English where this form is used. There are so many different kinds of English that some constructions might actually sound impossible to you. We'll encounter this again in Chapter 10.

1.5 POWER

Finding a full definition of power with respect to language is not straightforward. The many functions of language mean that there are different ways in which power can be exercised. While there are some examples of power being used to change language directly, the relationship is generally more subtle. We saw earlier that speaking a particular variety of English (e.g., British English) may make it possible to perform particular actions or influence particular groups of people. But even small variation in language use can bring benefits to speakers. People who speak the standard variety of British English, for example, will be thought to be more educated and more capable than others. This may give them access to better employment, institutions with power or even a better education. This is because of the attitudes that people have about language. While the speakers gain from being able to speak the standard language and so have a degree of power, it is not the case that they – as individuals – are controlling others. Rather, having competence in a prestigious language is in itself beneficial.

We noted earlier that language change is an inherent part of language, yet some people feel that language should stay the same. Some nations even have institutions which attempt to regulate the form of their language by stipulating which forms are 'correct' (the Académie Française in France, for example). There are many ways that nations seek to control what people do with language. Many countries regulate what people can say and write, or at least punishments exist for certain kinds of linguistic activity. The most common areas of 'regulation' relate to threats, encouraging others to commit crimes, protection of intellectual property and damaging someone's reputation. This kind of regulation can be understood in relation to the connection between language and actions. That is, sometimes saying something is doing something, and the restriction is not so much about the fact that language is used but that it is used to do something that should be prohibited. It is generally accepted that some speech acts should be prohibited: encouraging a person to murder someone else or shouting 'Fire!' in a crowded fire-free theatre are common prohibitions. Recently, a woman was sent to prison for involuntary manslaughter for encouraging her boyfriend to kill himself by sending him text messages (Bever and Phillips, 2017). The text messages did not directly instruct her boyfriend to kill himself, but they were understood by the court as encouraging him to do so.

Laws regulate language use in other ways. At a general level, many countries have designated one or more official languages. Wales, for example, has both Welsh and English as official languages (though this has not always been the case). Once a language is 'official', this has many potential consequences for education, interaction with government bodies and public signage. And while being an official language is good for the languages that are so identified, it can result in the stigmatisation of other languages. Nevertheless, the choice of an official language is usually connected to who holds power (the elite) and their attitudes about languages.

Do you think some kinds of language use should be regulated by law? Which ones? Why?

Activity 1.5

As already mentioned, some language use is prohibited by law and is generally accepted as being appropriate for the protection of individuals and public safety. But other examples of attempted language regulation are less straightforward, even though they may seem to be connected with the public good.

In March 2016, Salford City Council in the UK banned swearing in a part of the city known as Salford Quays (Boult, 2016). Some people were unhappy about the ban, but Salford defended it, pointing out that they held a public consultation. The presentation of the consultation results included the following:

> 118 (94%) of respondents agree with no causing general disturbance including being abusive to other persons, using foul language, being rowdy and inconsiderate.
>
> (Salford City Council, n.d.)

It is surprising that 6% of people did *not* think that being abusive and inconsiderate is bad. Perhaps this was because these 6% did not believe it is a particular problem in this area. But if the wording of the quotation above represents the actual question that people were asked, this presents a problem for the respondent. That is, perhaps people were asked, 'Do you think that we should ban people causing general disturbance, including being abusive to other persons, using foul language, being rowdy and inconsiderate?' If a person did agree that abusive behaviour causes 'general disturbance' but swearing does not, how should they respond? Thus the list would force a respondent to answer a question which actually includes a number of issues, which they may have different views on. Further, it is not certain a respondent would consider 'foul language' to be synonymous with 'swearing'. Here, the writers of the consultation may have used the power of the list (combined with the power of the questionnaire) in order to gather evidence to ban swearing.

The many ways in which language is used and the contexts in which it occurs means that there are different ways in which power can be exercised. Indeed, sometimes language is regulated in other, less predictable ways. In 2014, China banned wordplay in the media and advertisements (Branigan, 2014; Walker, 2014). The country's governmental print and media watchdog argues that this is to prevent 'cultural and linguistic chaos' (Branigan, 2014).

> [T]he order from the State Administration for Press, Publication, Radio, Film and Television says: 'Radio and television authorities at all levels must tighten up their regulations and crack down on the irregular and inaccurate use of the Chinese language, especially the misuse of idioms'.
> (Branigan, 2014)

China is certainly not alone in banning these kinds of language use. In 2016, North Korea was reported as banning sarcasm in relation to their leader (Agerholm, 2016). While this can be interpreted as a restriction on freedom of speech, others (e.g., Balantrapu, 2016) argue that it actually protects people. Nevertheless, the reference to 'inaccurate use' of Chinese in the preceding example clearly indicates a concern with prescriptivism.

Influence over language, and influence over people through language, is far more commonly achieved in less obvious and direct ways than passing a law. Of course there are situations where physical or institutional power has a direct influence on how language is understood. When a police officer asks you to stop your car, for example, the institutional power (and perhaps even their weapon) lends a particular force to the spoken request (Shon, 2005). In fact, such a request would more likely be understood as a command, because of the context in which the speech takes place.

Activity 1.6

Consider the following utterance:

'Nice dress.'

Does this look like an exercise of power?
Now consider the same utterance used in these contexts:

a female friend to a female friend
a male friend to a male friend
a male boss to a much younger female employee
a male stranger to a young woman walking alone

The same utterance can change its meaning and effect depending on who is saying it and in what context. In the male boss example, the way in which the phrase 'nice dress' is said will also be relevant (as will any previous interactions they have had).

A person doesn't need to have an obvious position of power in order for this to be exploited linguistically. When a manager uses a particular form of language, the power comes partially from their position (as your boss) but perhaps also from the kind of language that is used. We can think about this not as physical power, or even institutional power, but as 'symbolic power' (Bourdieu, 1991). Calling it symbolic power draws our attention to the link between power and symbols, that is, between power and language. To call it 'symbolic power' is not to say that the power is ineffective (we'll come back to Bourdieu's notion of symbolic power in Chapter 6). In many ways, it is more effective because it doesn't appear to be an exercise of power. It's also worth remembering that language can be used to do things. Sometimes saying something it is doing something (Austin, 1975). It is possible to insult, persuade, command, compliment, encourage or make a promise using language. While these can be seen as individual acts, when repeated over time, the culmination of such linguistic acts might change the way a person sees an issue.

Thus, while language is important in the exercise of power at particular moments, we also need to understand that language can work across long stretches of time. We can be commanded to do something now, but we can also be influenced to think and behave in a certain way pretty much all the time. This certainly involves language, but we need something more in order to understand how power can work across long stretches of time. Fairclough puts it as follows:

> It is important to emphasise that I am not suggesting that power is *just* a matter of language. . . . Power exists in various modalities, including the concrete and unmistakable modality of physical force . . . It is perhaps helpful to make a broad distinction between the exercise of power through *coercion* of various sorts including physical violence, and the exercise of power through the manufacture of *consent* to or at least acquiescence towards it. Power relations depend on both, though in varying proportions. Ideology is the prime means of manufacturing consent.
>
> (2001: 3)

Fairclough explains the difference between power working to make you do something (coercion) and power working to make you think you want to do something (consent). While a person can be ordered to speak in a particular language (coercion), they can also be conditioned to accept that the particular language is the correct way of speaking (consent). Once they believe that the language is the correct one, they will use of their own volition. This belief can be connected to the concept of ideology. The concept of **ideology** is a difficult one to come to terms with and we'll keep coming back to it in this book.

1.5.1 Ideology

Examining language closely allows us to pick out these ideologies. In the same way that we can deduce the structure of a language by studying the way people use it, we can also describe the structure and content of an ideology. Power, and especially symbolic power, is supported by ideologies. Because scholars have many approaches to defining ideology, we don't cover them all here. Rather, we'll describe a few key ideas that will provide you with the tools you need to help you understand language and power.

The linguists Gunther Kress and Robert Hodge define ideology 'as a systematic body of ideas, organised from a particular point of view' (1993: 6). In everyday contexts, the word 'ideology' is something negative or at the very least **marked**. We think that only groups like terrorists have an ideology. But as an ideology is a set of beliefs, a world view, we all have ideologies. While they might seem natural, normal and commensensical, they are ideologies nevertheless. It is common to think that ideology is bad and that only other people have ideologies. But this is not the case. In a similar way, we don't tend to notice our own language as one with an 'accent' when we are among people who speak like us. We mostly only notice other accents. Our perception of our own ideologies is the same. Our ideologies seem normal, and we tend to label the world views of people who see the world differently as 'ideological'. It is this common sense, this seemingly natural and normal way of thinking and acting which we can talk about in terms of the dominant ideology, or **hegemonic** ideology. So, ideology is a way of talking about a whole set of ways of thinking and acting.

As world views, ideologies help us to make sense of the world and the people in it. Earlier, we referred to prescriptivism. This is the belief that there are correct ways of using language. As we discussed, these correct ways are defended as protecting a language, promoting clarity and mutual comprehension. As you can see now, prescriptivism is an ideology, sometimes referred to as **standard language** ideology. But as we have also seen, ideologies have consequences. The standard language ideology results in negative judgements being made about people who do not use the 'correct' forms of language.

Ideologies also have structures. The beliefs that constitute the ideology can be identified (for example, that there is a standard language and that people should always use it). Moreover, these beliefs, and so the structure of the ideology, can be mapped and understood by paying attention to the way the choices are made in language. Consider the two sentences from Agress quoted earlier:

> There are hundreds of grammar mistakes people make daily, and I cringe every time I hear just one. I am certain my readers have their own lists of pet peeves.
>
> (2016)

The identification of 'mistakes' and the account of her 'cringing' clearly shows the negative regard she has for those who don't follow this standard language ideology. Moreover, she includes her readers in this ideology as she is 'certain' that they have their 'own lists of pet peeves'.

The French sociologist Pierre Bourdieu points out that, in addition to individuals having their own ideologies, ideology also exists on the group level:

> [I]deologies serve particular interests which they tend to present as universal interests, shared by the group as a whole.
>
> (1991: 167)

Given that all groups have a particular point of view, everyone has ideologies. However, we tend to only talk about 'ideology' when we want to draw attention to the power or the particular interests ideologies have. To label another group's values as 'ideology' is common; to talk about one's own values in the same way is not common at all. A group's ideology will be unmarked for that group. However, thinking about our own 'taken for granted' values, as members of groups or as individuals, is an important task for critical thinking.

The way language is used is not the only evidence of ideology, but it is an important one. Language use creates and represents ideological concerns, as we saw in the examples about terrorism and traitors at the start of this chapter. The more general idea is that because language is connected to ideology in this way, we can be encouraged to do things, not because someone has commanded us at a particular point in time but because we have internalised certain values that mean we *want* to do certain things. This internalising of values takes place over longer stretches of time. Language is crucial to the creation and maintenance of 'common sense' ideology. You can think about ideology as a way of structuring the way language is used to communicate a more general message involving values and beliefs, in short, a world view. In summary, some key things to remember about ideology are that they are held by individuals *and* groups and they are often not recognised by the individual or group as a powerful influence on their own behaviour.

1.6 'POLITICAL CORRECTNESS'

As we've already seen, people tend to have strong views about their own language and may fervently resist any changes made to it, especially if it means that they have to change their own linguistic behaviour. In relation to language, this is sometimes called 'political correctness'.

'Political correctness' is a contested term and a contested practice. What it refers to, who uses and it and why people label practices in this way are far more complex than may first seem apparent. Generally, however, it is a reaction *against* people arguing for equal and non-discriminatory treatment. As Talbot writes: 'Anti-PC discourse is a response to the direct interventions into sexist and other discriminatory practices' (2010: 240). For some, it seems reasonable to think that language can be used in a way that doesn't discriminate or demean. Linguists often refer to this practice as 'language reform' because it has at its heart a concern with what we could call representational justice. Suppose there were a group that is discriminated against (let's call them 'Martians') and suppose that the term 'Martian' is pejorative. If a new term to refer to them were suggested, for example 'Marsites', would Martians cease to be a marginalised group? Would people think about Martians differently if they were known as 'Marsites'?

Activity 1.7

O'Neil (2011) argues that language reform in pursuit of political correctness will be unending. He argues that if we focus on the *form* of language rather than the *intent*, then the negative attitudes we seek to eliminate will simply attach to the new 'correct' word. We then need to invent yet another new term and the process starts again.

What do you think of this argument? Do you think language reform is futile?

One of the reasons people resist what they see as 'politically correct' language reform is connected to the reluctance to view language as political. Specifically, Cameron notes that people seem to object to their language choices being seen as political choices; 'Choice has altered the value of the terms and removed the option of political neutrality' (1995: 119). Burridge (1996) argues that there are three main reasons that people do not like language reform. The first is that people don't like linguistic change (see discussion above). The second is people resent being told what to do with their language because it seems like censorship. That is, critics argue that political correctness is an imposition of authority, a command to speak (and perhaps think) in a particular way. In this sense, they argue, it breaches rights to freedom of thought and speech. The third objection stems from the fact that people are uncomfortable when told that a term they thought was neutral or inoffensive is actually laden with meanings they did not intend. When someone is told their language use is offensive, it feels very much like their character is under attack (they are a bigot, racist, misogynist and so on). Resistance to 'political correctness' is carried out by asserting such changes are trivial and pointless. Thus, language reform is a kind of language change that is resisted using the accusation that these changes are frivolous and about 'political correctness'. Thus, the term 'political correctness' and what we understand it to mean is a direct result of more or less conscious effort directed at discrediting certain kinds of language reform and those who advocate it.

Cameron notes that the circulating definitions of PC all come from people denouncing a particular 'politically correct' change or attacking the concept as a whole. This tends to be political too: '[T]he way right wing commentators have established certain presuppositions about "political correctness" over the past few years is a triumph – as a sociolinguist I cannot help admiring it – of the politics of definition, or linguistic intervention' (1995:

123). But the choices that are available in a language have significant consequences. Cameron points out that language reform 'changes the repertoire of social meanings and choices available to social actors' (Cameron, 2014 [1990]: 90). This means that language reform provides social actors and people with particular ways of representing themselves and being represented by others. Language reform can provide people with positive terms in which to construct their identity. This is particularly important where no such positive terms previously existed.

The following are some examples of 'politically correct' language; some are actually in common use, and some have been reported by the media but are not actually used at all. Which ones are 'real' examples? What social meanings are being created by the new terms?

a   chairperson
b   living impaired
c   ethnic minorities
d   thought showers
e   snow figure
f   differently abled
g   seniors
h   herstory

Activity 1.8

In recent years, political correctness has become closely associated with terms that regulate speech in public domains at educational institutions (especially universities). Some examples include 'no platforming', 'trigger warnings' and 'safe spaces'. No platforming refers to the practice of not allowing people with particular views to speak at an event. Trigger warnings refers to statements made before a public discussion to alert the participants that the discussion topics may be upsetting or offensive. Safe spaces refers to spaces where a person will be free from discrimination of any kind. As these practices are seen by some as impediments to free speech or worse, a prevention of the truth being told, they are criticised and rejected.

The discussion of 'terrorism' can also be understood as an example of the idea that political correctness is a barrier to truth. President Barack Obama has also been criticised in relation to his rejection of the phrase 'Islamic terrorist', instead using simply 'terrorist'. Critics argue that to refuse to say 'Islamic terrorist' denies a link between Islam and terrorism. Obama argued that it is important to remember that while some terrorists are Muslim, they do not represent all of Islam and the phrase 'Islamic terrorist' suggests that they do (Diaz, 2016).

Considering our discussion of prescriptive and descriptive perspectives, you may be wondering how prescriptive rules are different from language reform and how it is that linguists don't agree with prescriptive rules but they do agree with language reform. Anne Curzan, a linguist at the University of Michigan, explains in her 2014 book *Fixing English* that there are different types of prescriptivism based on the aims of the prescriptive rules:

- standardising prescriptivism, which aims to enforce 'standard' usage;
- stylistic prescriptivism, which aims to distinguish between points of style;
- restorative prescriptivism, which aims to restore earlier usages, thus preserving the language from decline and decay;
- politically responsive prescriptivism, which aims to promote inclusive, non-discriminatory or 'politically correct' usages [what we referred to as language reform above].

(Curzan, 2014: 24)

So, many of the so-called ungrammatical sentences in Activity 1.4 reflect a kind of standardising prescriptive rule. In contrast, the 'not referring to terrorists as "Islamic"' is a politically responsive one. Linguists, generally, do not object to 'politically responsive prescriptivism' / language reform because its aim is representational justice to promote non-discriminatory usage, and it can have a positive effect on society. Standardising, stylistic or restorative prescriptivism, in contrast, can have negative effects (e.g., hindering social mobility).

Linguists do acknowledge that not everyone shares their point of view about prescriptivism (of any type) and are realistic about the need to follow prescriptive rules in many contexts. Our goal is to understand what prescriptivism is and how it affects society even if we, ourselves, follow prescriptive rules.

1.7 SUMMARY

In this book, we consider how language, ideology and power all come together. Sometimes the power that language has is difficult to observe. The notion that there is a correct form of English, discussed above, is an ideology that has substantial repercussions (Lippi-Green, 2011), and those repercussions can be seen as the effects of the power of language. For example, scholars have shown that attitudes to accented language can prevent a person from getting hired for a job (e.g., Carlson and McHenry, 2006), interfere with their education (e.g., Labov, 1982), and prevent a person from finding housing (e.g., Purnell, Idsardi and Baugh, 1999). Employment, education and housing are three essential aspects of life.

Using language in a particular way sends a message about the things you think are important and communicates something about who you are. We draw conclusions about people because of the language they use. For example, the language used by people with high status will generally garner more respect than language associated with marginalised people. While this may seem to some to be entirely unproblematic, it is also ideological. Whether a language variety reflects something positive or negative depends very much on what or who that variety is associated with.

In this chapter, we've introduced some of the themes and issues that are taken up throughout this book. Understanding language as a system, with inherently understood structure, is important in exploring the kinds of variation that we find. The rules that we're interested in are those which explain what people actually do (descriptive), rather than those about what people should do (prescriptive). While some people are uncomfortable with language change, it is inescapable and unstoppable. It is also exciting, as such change is possible exactly because of the creative possibilities that language provides. This adaptability is an important language function, but there are others. Studying language also allows us to understand the way people exercise power with language and, in turn, ways this can be resisted. We introduced the relationship between language and power. The complexity of this relationship can be seen in the case of 'political correctness'. It is a relationship we continue to explore in the following chapters, as it can take some time for this complex interaction to make sense. Studying language allows us to think critically about power and helps us see that what we might think of as 'common sense' is nevertheless ideological. In the next chapter, we consider the tools we need to analyse some of these questions in more depth.

FURTHER READING

Crystal, D. (2007) *The Fight for English: How Language Pundits Ate, Shot, and Left.* Oxford: Oxford University Press.

Curzan, A. (2014) *Fixing English: Prescriptivism and Language History.* Cambridge: Cambridge University Press.

Fairclough, N. (1999) Global capitalism and critical awareness of language, *Language Awareness*, 8(2): 71–83.

Milroy, J. and Milroy, L. (1999) *Authority in Language: Investigating Standard English.* London: Taylor & Francis Ltd.

Montgomery, M. (2008) *An Introduction to Language and Society*, 3rd ed. London: Routledge.

O'Neill, B. (2011) A critique of politically correct language, *The Independent Review*, 16(2): 279–291.

Trudgill, P. (1999) Standard English: What is isn't, in Bex, T. and Watts, R. J. (eds.) *Standard English: The Widening Debate.* London: Routledge: 117–128.

CHAPTER 2

Language, thought and representation

2.1 INTRODUCTION

In the last chapter, we began to discuss the way that linguists understand the structure and functions of language and key concepts like ideology. In this chapter, we explore Ferdinand de Saussure's theory of signs, which will provide a way of discussing how meaning is constructed at the level of the word, how this can change, how words fit together into larger structures (sentences) and what happens when we make choices in sentences. Thinking about words as signs may take a while to get used to; likewise, the use of 'sign' in the technical sense introduced in this chapter can also take some time to feel familiar. These models of meaning are important though, as they help articulate the way small changes can have significant consequences for the meaning communicated.

2.2 LANGUAGE AS A SYSTEM OF REPRESENTATION

Language is one way of representing reality. It is possible to analyse how language does this. There are other ways to represent reality. A person might take a photograph, make a drawing or write some music. The elements of these representations can also be analysed. A black-and-white photograph might be understood differently to one that is in colour; this difference is meaningful. When thinking about visual representations, it is clear that there is always a point of view. A photographer, for example, takes an image while

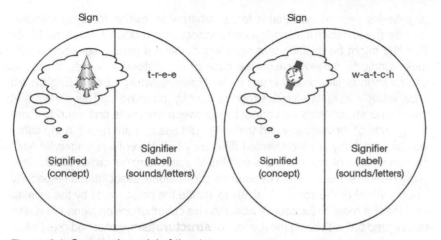

Figure 2.1 Saussure's model of the sign

standing in a particular place. They choose what to include in the visual frame, what to focus on and so on. When it comes to language, even though we have building codes to follow, there is always more than one way of representing a person, event or situation. In this chapter, we provide some tools that will help identify the choices that language users can make and also their significance. We begin with the concept of the sign.

In the definition that we're working with, all 'signs' have two parts: a concept and an object or marker that is connected to the concept. For example, the pedestrian signals at a crosswalk that tell you when to walk or not are signs because of the connection between the red light (the object) and the concept of stopping. Without these two parts, the red light would just be a red light. When we know that red means 'stop', the red light becomes a sign.

Words in language are also signs. For Saussure, a **sign** is made up of two things: a **signifier** and **signified**. His definition of the sign makes a distinction between the sound we hear (the **signifier**) and the concept this makes us think of (the **signified**). So, for example, when you hear the sounds represented by the letters d-o-g, you think of the concept 'canine mammal'. Together, the word sound and the concept it invokes form a sign. It is important to note 'A linguistic sign is not a link between a thing and a name, but between a concept and a sound pattern' (Saussure, 1966: 66). These cannot be separated in the sign; to try to do so would be like trying to cut only one side of a piece of paper (Saussure, 1966: 113). A signifier needs at least one signified for there to be a sign. If there is no such signified, the alleged signifier is merely a sound that *could* be a word; it is not a sign by Saussure's definition.

The connection between words and their meaning is accidental: there is no reason why bread should be called 'bread'. This can be seen clearly if one considers other languages. In French, bread is 'pain', and in Welsh, it is 'bara'. The arbitrary connection between words and their meaning was one of Ferdinand de Saussure's great insights. Nevertheless, saying that the connection between the signifier and the signified is arbitrary doesn't suggest that words can mean whatever we like. 'The term [arbitrary] simply implies that the signal [signifier] is *unmotivated*: that is to say arbitrary in relation to its signification [signified], with which it has no natural connection in relation' (Saussure, 1966: 69). You might be thinking that signifiers do have a natural connection with their signifieds, for example, in the case of onomatopoeic words, those we use for sounds, like what animals make. However, while a bee in English will buzz, in Japanese, its sound is represented by 'boon boon'. This shows that there is no straightforward connection between concepts and sounds. Even the sounds of the natural world that we might assume are heard in the same way by everybody are represented differently by different languages. At best, such examples of animal noises and the like are marginal cases of how language reflects meaning and depend on conventional associations (especially when written) or the speaker's ability to imitate the noise made by the animal.

There is more to Saussure's work than his contributions on signs. He is also usually credited with being the founder of **structuralism**, which had great influence on linguistics, literary criticism and the social sciences. We'll look at structuralism when we consider signs later in the chapter. But recall that in Chapter 1 we established that language is a system; systems have rules, and these rules structure the language. The system of language allows us to talk about and represent the world around us. But just as the relationship between word and meaning is arbitrary, so too is the way that language divides up the world.

2.2.1 Different kinds of language

Saussure distinguishes three kinds of language. Recall in Chapter 1 we discussed the difficulties of knowing exactly what we mean when we talk about 'language'. The three aspects Saussure identifies help with some of these difficulties. The first of these is '*langage*', which has been translated as 'human speech', including its psychological and physical aspects, belonging both to the individual and to societies. It is the most general category and is composed of the following two aspects, which will be our focus here. These two parts of 'langage' are '**langue**' and '**parole**'. You can think of langue as competence and parole as performance (both in Chomsky's terms that we discussed in Chapter 1). The former is the overarching language system, the latter being individual use of language. While they are treated as separate by Saussure, they are also closely linked.

Langue is the system that makes parole possible. In so far as langue makes speech possible, it has a social element. As we'll see when we look more at definitions of signs, the social and conventional agreement on how signs are constructed is crucial. You can think of langue as the rules of the game, the entire system, including the building codes discussed in Chapter 1 together with communicative competence. Saussure provides a musical metaphor. He compares langue to a symphony written for an orchestra and parole to the performance of the symphony. The quality or nature of the composition is not related to how a particular orchestra may perform it (1966: 18).

While individuals draw on langue every time they use language, they don't have direct access to langue. Langue is 'not complete in any speaker;

it exists perfectly only within a collectivity' (Saussure, 1966: 12). We can only talk about langue sensibly if we have a community of speakers. You can't have a language all by yourself. This is why there is a social aspect to langue.

Every instance of language in the world, all actual utterances, is parole. As speakers, we perform parole acts. While as speakers of a language we rely on shared understanding (accounted for by langue), as individuals, we can do things with language that haven't been done before. You can construct a sentence that is so odd that you can be pretty confident that no one else has ever said or written it. For example, 'The surly clouds gathered their amusing faces and spat furiously on my new chartreuse-coloured coat'. While this is a slightly poetic example (representing clouds as people, with faces and moods), because of langue, the system we all share, you should be able to understand this original parole act.

It is the relationship between langue and parole that is important. The system and rules of langue can change. These changes are very slow and may take hundreds of years. Individuals start using a new word, or an existing word in a new way (all these usages are parole), and other language users understand and adopt this. When this new linguistic behaviour is well established, we can say that the new form has become part of langue, one that we all understand. The last part is important; the new behaviour has to become recognised and conventional, such that other people understand it. That is, acts of parole draw on *and* contribute to the abstract system of langue. As Saussure puts it, 'Language has an individual aspect and a social aspect. One is not conceivable without the other' (1966: 8). The distinction between langue and parole, however, allows us to think through their differences, while understanding that they are linked. It allows us to understand how language use can be individual and original and yet still be communicative.

While this is only a model, it is a useful one, as it helps us understand how language enables us to communicate and how language changes. It is the level of parole that we are normally most concerned with in this book, at least as a starting point. There are a number of reasons for this. The first, and most important, is that we don't have direct access to langue. While it would be very convenient if it were the case, langue is not a big book somewhere with all the codes written down. These codes are the same 'building codes' we referred to in Chapter 1. The only access that we have to the codes of langue is through the particular uses of language, that is, parole. From this evidence, we can try to map what the code is.

The second reason we focus on parole is that as sociolinguists, we're primarily interested in how people use language. The creative aspect of language means that speakers will always do things that are different, new and surprising. The concept of langue and its relationship with parole allows us to describe and account for this.

Because instances of parole both draw on and contribute to langue, as individual speakers, we have some power over what langue contains. Were we all to decide to call 'bread' 'dice', for example, eventually that would become part of langue. Yet, while many speakers might not make conscious decisions to change linguistic signs, change nevertheless occurs (see Section 1.3.3).

2.2.2 Signs and structure

We have described how a sign needs both a signifier and a signified to be a sign. In this model of meaning, Saussure postulates that a sign needs other signs in order to have meaning. He suggests 'Signs function, then, not through their intrinsic value but through their relative position' (Saussure, 1966: 118). That is, the meaning of a linguistic sign depends on its relation to other signs. It may be useful to think of this relation using a spatial metaphor, where the meaning of each sign is contained in a space. The space that signs occupy fits together, such that if a space is occupied by one sign, it means that same space can't be occupied by another. In the example of traffic signs earlier, we could say that 'red' means 'stop' because 'green' means 'go' and amber/yellow means something else. In this context, the meaning of 'red' depends on what it does not mean ('go').

Consider, for example some linguistic signs that are related, that are in the same semantic field:

COLLEAGUE, ASSOCIATE, FRIEND, ACQUAINTANCE, MATE, COMPANION

All of these linguistic signs say something about a relationship. While these might all be considered synonyms to some degree, which word a person would use to refer to another person depends on the kind of relationship they have. Further, referring to someone as an 'acquaintance' will be interpreted in light of the fact that the word 'friend' was not used. Likewise, we can say that 'mate' means what it does because it does *not* mean 'friend', 'associate', 'colleague' or 'companion'. We can say that the space a sign occupies that is, what it means, is delineated by the spaces all other signs leave behind: 'In language ... whatever distinguishes one sign from the others constitute it' (Saussure, 1966: 121).

Understanding that this is how words have meanings is important, as it demonstrates the importance of which choices are made. Because 'friend' and 'acquaintance' occupy different spaces and mean different things, it matters if we describe someone as one or the other. It changes the representation we are making of the world and the people in it.

The way we've been talking about langue may seem all encompassing and monolithic as if we're talking about the langue of the whole English language. If we included the whole English language, we'd be considering all the different varieties of English: British, American, Australian, Indian, Singaporean and so on. Depending on the kinds of questions we're asking, this may make sense. But in thinking about how to use language in a particular context, it only really makes sense to include specific varieties. For example, in Indian English, 'wallah' refers to a tradesperson or worker, usually of a particular kind that is specified in the first part of a compound noun phrase. Thus, 'taxiwallah' is a taxi driver. While in the abstract langue that encompasses all English 'wallah' would jostle for semantic space with 'tradesperson' and other similar terms, in other parts of the English-speaking world, it may not be relevant as a sign at all. It would simply be a sound, as there would be no conventional linking of this signifier ('wallah') to a signified. Thus when considering the relationship between various signs, we need to know which signs and relationships are relevant in the communicative context we're looking at.

We can talk about these changes over time with the following terms: **synchronic** and **diachronic**. The first, synchronic, refers to a particular point in time. That is, we can consider the state of a language at a particular point and describe it and the variation found in it. The second, diachronic, refers to considering a language over an extended period of time. A diachronic perspective means that we consider how language has changed from one point in time to another. In English, for example, around the 14th century, 'girl' was used to refer to a child of either sex (Oxford English Dictionary), but now it only refers to a female child. In Irish English, however, 'girl' still refers to a child of either sex.

We need to appreciate both diachronic and synchronic aspects to understand language, as language 'always implies both an established system and an evolution; at every moment it is an existing institution and a product of the past' (Saussure, 1966: 8). We'll see in later chapters that changes over time (diachronic) and comparing variation in language at a particular time (synchronic) are crucial if we're to understand how people are using language and what the significance of any use may be.

Find an etymological dictionary (like the *Oxford English Dictionary*), and trace the history of the meanings of 'troll', 'thug' or 'hysteria'.[1]

Activity 2.1

2.3 LINGUISTIC DIVERSITY

Linguistic diversity recognises that languages differ in their building codes (Chapter 1) and the lexemes they contain. Thinking about the differences between lexemes is a good place to start. Linguistic diversity is very easy to see at the level of the word (or sign). These differences are a source of interest to linguists and the general public alike. For example, recently in the UK and in the US (Gonzalez, 2017), there has been a great deal of discussion about the Danish verb 'hygge' and the related adjective 'hyggeligt'. The claim is that this word is both untranslatable to English and a key part of Danish culture. Levison (2013) glosses hygge as 'pleasant togetherness' and provides a detailed semantic explication of the word. It is hardly surprising that different languages have different ways of describing the world. The level of popular and commercial interest in the concept (Higgins, 2016) is interesting, but the important questions for linguists are how significant are these differences and what do they mean? An example that may be more familiar is the myth that 'Eskimos' have hundreds of words for snow. This myth is based on a misrepresentation of the linguistic evidence and a misunderstanding of the concept of linguistic diversity (Pullum, 1991). Because the proliferation of lexemes in a particular semantic field continues to attract much interest among the general public, it is all the more important that we understand what linguistic diversity is.

It was recently reported that the Scots language has 421 words for snow (*Scotsman*, 2015).

You can compare English words for snow and Scots words for snow by consulting an online historical thesaurus.

http://historicalthesaurus.arts.gla.ac.uk/

Do all the terms refer only to snow? Are they all in current use?

Image 2.1 'Eskimo'

2.3.1 Semantics

Linguistic diversity is very often discussed in terms of lexical items (like words for snow). Indeed, this is a very useful way of understanding the differences between languages and how languages can develop. Here we consider the semantic field of 'friendship' in order to see some of this diversity in more detail and to understand what it means more broadly.

We begin with new words developing in Swedish to describe the kinds of relationships that people have (Baer, 2016).

a   sambo: someone with whom you are in a long-term romantic relationship and live with
b   särbo: a long-term partner with whom you don't live
c   kombo: a friend you live with
d   mambo: parents you live with

In some varieties of English, the choices available for (a) would be 'girlfriend', 'boyfriend' or 'partner'. But none of these indicate a shared living space. Nor are they necessarily very helpful in conveying the kind of relationship the couple have.

Having different terms for friendship and other relationships is not unusual. In Russian, as Wierzbicka (1997: 57–71) outlines, there are a number of terms for 'friend'.

Drug: a very close friend

Podruga: a close friend, but less close than 'drug'

Prijatel' (Fem, prijatel'nica): a more distant friend, perhaps the closest to the English 'friend'

Znakomyj (Fem. znakomaja): an even more distant friend but closer than 'acquaintance'

Wierzbicka provides detailed explications of these concepts. But for our purposes, what is important to note is that the Russian terms and the Swedish terms do not match exactly the English terms for these concepts.

2.3.2 Syntax

Just as languages encode semantic differences in various ways, grammatical systems also vary. In English, word order is important for meaning. 'Alex greeted Chris' means something different to 'Chris greeted Alex'. English has what is called an SVO order (Subject, Verb, Object). But not all languages follow this order and not all languages rely on word order for meaning.

In 1982, Romero-Figueroa gathered linguistic data from the Warao language (spoken in parts of Venezuela). He argues that in Warao, it is usual to have the following word order: O(object) S(subject) V(verb). The default word order is OSV. He provides the following example.

Example 2.1

a   erike   hube   abun-ae
     Enrique   snake   bite PAST
     'A snake bit Henry (Enqrique)'.

b   ma hanoko   atamo   ine   nao -ya
     my house   OBL.   I   come PRES.
     'I come from my home'.

(Romero-Figueroa, 1985: 120)

We can see in the second line of in Example 2.1 that the verb comes last and that the object ('Henry' and 'my home') come before the subject ('A snake' and 'I').

An example of a language that does not always rely on word order is Greek. While SVO structure is common, it is not required.[2]

Example 2.2

a   I papia   pige   sti limni
     The duck   went.3sg   to-the pond
     'The duck went to the pond'.

b   sti limni   pige   i papia
     to-the pond   went.3sg   the duck
     'It is to the pond the duck went'.

Greek can have these different word orders for two reasons. First, verb forms in Greek contain information about the subject of the verb. So, when a Greek speaker hears/sees 'pige', they know there is a third person singular subject. Including this information in verbs means it is not always necessary to specify a subject because this information is encoded in the verb. Secondly, the nouns (the subject and object) also contain information to indicate which noun is the subject and which is the object.

How does a Greek speaker know which word order to use? The choice of what to put first depends on what is already known in the conversation. If people in a conversation had been talking about the duck and wanted to say something new about it, they would use example (a). The noun 'duck' comes first because it is **given information** – it is already known about as a topic of discussion. The pond, however, and the fact that the duck went there is **new information**. If the pond was the current topic of conversation, then speakers might choose example (b), as the pond is given information while the duck is new. This means that in answer to the question 'Where did the duck go?' we would respond (a) in Greek. While if someone was asked, 'What happened at the pond?' they would choose (b).

Linguistic diversity is interesting and valuable for a number of reasons. First, it makes clear that languages differ in their structure and content. Second, looking at the range of diversity in structure and content tells us something about language more generally. It was long thought, for example, that no languages followed an OSV or OVS structure. However, in the latter parts of the 20th century, such languages were documented. Had they died out before they had been documented, linguists would have come to incorrect conclusions about what is possible in language (see Palosaari and Campbell, 2011).

2.4 THE SAPIR-WHORF HYPOTHESIS

It is worth saying at the outset that although the Sapir-Whorf hypothesis (SWH) is generally referred to as a 'hypothesis', it is not, strictly speaking, a hypothesis, as that would suggest the SWH could be testable through a scientific investigation. Further, some aspects of the SWH (called the strong version of the SWH) do not have much standing among linguists. However, there are still important insights to be gained from it. Specifically, it can help us understand how ideology and language interact.

2.4.1 Linguistic relativism and determinism

The Sapir-Whorf hypothesis relies on linguistic diversity, as it considers what meanings we can attribute to this variation. The argument is that because of some aspects of linguistic diversity, different languages represent the world differently and that has consequences for how people see reality and think about the world. Sapir writes, 'The worlds in which different societies live are

distinct worlds, not merely the same world with different labels attached . . .'
(1958 [1929]: 69). Sapir was an anthropological linguist and, as such,
encountered the different ways languages represent the world. The SWH
suggests that the language that people speak has an influence on the way
they see the world (reality) and also how they think. That is, linguistic diversity is not just about differences among languages; the claim is that these
differences have consequences.

In its simplest form, the SWH claims that the language we speak has
an influence on the way we think. This is controversial in a number of ways.
The first thing to consider is how much of an influence language might have
on thought. The 'strong' interpretation of the SWH is often called **linguistic
determinism**, meaning that the language you speak determines the way
you think.[3] This suggests that if there is concept that your language does
not have a word for, it is impossible for you to imagine it. This is the concept that underlies the language called 'Newspeak' that is a feature of the
world described in George Orwell's novel *1984*. In this fictional world, the
government provides inhabitants with Newspeak, a very specific stock of
words that are supposed to be used in very specific ways. The government
believes that by forcing the citizens to use Newspeak, the citizens will think
and behave in the way that the government wishes them to.

But, as we've seen in Chapter 1, language allows us to create new
meanings, whether these are words for new objects, concepts or items of
specialist language. These days, the idea that a language completely determines thought is strongly questioned. It is easy to see why. If linguistic determinism were true, it would be very difficult to create new words (how could
the need for them be identified?). It would also be impossible to understand
concepts in other languages (like 'hygge').

The question then becomes, does language influence thought and
behaviour in any way at all? Benjamin Whorf, who was an amateur linguist
and fire inspector, argued that there was some connection between them.
In his work, he noticed that people behave according to the way things
are labelled rather than in terms of what they really are. The best-known
example from his work as a fire inspector is the way individuals threw ciga-
rette butts into oil drums labelled 'empty'. Even though 'empty' may signal
a benign absence, in the case of oil and other flammable materials, even a
small amount of residual material in the functionally 'empty' container can be
anything but benign. As Whorf puts it, 'the "empty" drums are perhaps the
more dangerous, since they contain explosive vapour' (1954: 198). Despite
the very real danger, the 'empty' sign appeared to encourage risky behaviour.

Linguistic relativism, the version of the Sapir-Whorf hypothesis that
does seem plausible, is much less confining than linguistic determinism. It
suggests that language, as in the case of 'empty' in Whorf's example, does
influence the way we think. However, if the connection between language
and thought is not absolute (as determinism would have it), then how far
does it go? It might help to think of linguistic relativism as relating to how
language *influences* the way we normally think; rather than language *determining* thought. The linguist John Lucy uses the phrase 'habitual cognition'

(Lucy, 2005: 303) to demonstrate that linguistic determinism is not the way to explain the connection between language and thought. That is,

> the broader view taken here is not that languages completely or permanently blind speakers to other aspects of reality. Rather they provide speakers with a systematic default bias in their habitual response tendencies.
>
> (Lucy, 2005: 307)

Lucy argues that the signs and structure of language influence thought. This is a much more modest argument than that of linguistic determinism. It is also incredibly useful, not just in comparing different languages and how they represent the world, but also in paying attention to more localised and specialised language use within a language. For example, some groups of English speakers will also have a routine way of describing something that others don't.

Habitual modes of thinking can be very important. Obviously habits can be changed, but to do so takes effort and will. Moreover, generally, we're not aware of our habits of thought. Have you ever considered it unusual that we describe space in terms of 'left' and 'right', 'ahead' and 'behind', that is, in relation to a forward-facing body? You probably haven't, since this seems normal; it is habitual. In some languages, space and location are described in relation to compass points, that is, whether something is 'north' or 'south'. This is certainly a habit that we all could learn, but it would take time before it was habitual. Until then, we would probably think in terms of 'left' and 'right' and then (with the aid of a mental compass) 'translate' into the new system.

2.4.2 Numbers and things

John Lucy argues that the language we speak influences our habits of thought. Lucy has spent a great deal of time researching Yucatec, a language spoken in Mexico. Comparing the language with English, it is possible to find a number of differences. One of these is the way that numbers are used. In English, in order to indicate a different number of items, we simply modify the noun, for example: 'one cup', 'two cups' and so on. In Yucatec, when a numeral is used, it 'must be accompanied by a special form, usually referred to as a numeral classifier which typically provides crucial information about the shape or material properties of the referent of the noun' (Lucy, 1996: 50).

> **Example 2.3**
> un- **tz'iit** kib = one **long thin** candle
>
> (Lucy, 1996: 50)

We see in Example 2.3 that specifying 'one' candle is not enough. A speaker also has to specify something about the object being counted. Lucy argues that these numeral classifiers suggest that '*all lexical nouns in Yucatec are semantically unspecified as to essential quantifications unit*, 'almost as if [the nouns] referred to unformed substances' (1996: 50). He therefore suggests that for Example 2.3, it is possible to understand 'kib' not as 'candle' but as 'wax' so that the gloss would be 'one long thing wax' (1996: 50). As Lucy points out, we do a similar kind of thing with some mass nouns. If we want to talk about a lot of flour, we don't say 'two flours' but rather, 'two cups of flour' or something like that. For those of us not literate in Yucatec or its culture, it might be difficult to assess Lucy's argument. But Lucy designed a nice experiment that may assist.

When Yucatec speakers are asked to classify different objects, they seem to have a preference for focussing on the material of the object. Thus, if asked to pick the 'odd one out' from a wooden comb, a plastic comb and a wooden bowl, the Yucatec speaker is more likely to identify the plastic comb. An English speaker, in contrast, is more likely to focus on the shape of the objects (and thus identify the bowl as the odd one out). That is, because Yucatec speakers are forced to pay attention to the material features of an object in order to give an appropriate numeral classifier, it makes sense that this aspect of objects might be important. As Lera Boroditsky puts it, 'Languages force us to attend to certain aspects of our experience by making them grammatically obligatory. Therefore, speakers of different languages may be biased to attend to and encode different aspects of their experience while speaking' (2001: 2).

Of course, these habits can be changed. English speakers can also pay attention to the material of an object. But all things being equal, this is not what the categories of English ask us to do. So while we can do it, we don't do it as a habit.

On Twitter, you can find a hashtag called #MoreAccurateNameFor. Do be aware that some of the terms are rather explicit. But the following are some examples of 'more accurate names for' things that Twitter users have suggested. Do they make sense to you? If you used them all the time, would it change the way you think about the thing?

Water	snowman's blood
Liar	not a reliable source of information
Gloves	finger pants
Shoes	foot bags
Toddler	drawer emptier
Hashtag	agenda shoehorn
Grass	earth carpet

Activity 2.3

2.5 ONE LANGUAGE, MANY WORLDS

Even in a single language like English, there are many ways of representing the world. These representations are often the result of particular habitual ways of thinking, or world views. For example, the way a botanist thinks and talks about plants depends on the botanical language available to them. Obviously if a new plant is discovered, that will have to be named. But when deciding how to classify this plant, the botanist will look at the kinds of features considered important in their discipline. The features that matter to botanists are directly connected to the aims of this science: to categorise and understand plants, trees and other flora. The features that the discipline gives importance to can be understood as being structured by the botanist's (world) view of plants. For a botanist, colour may not be important, but how the plant reproduces probably will be. We can say, then, that a particular set of values underlie this structure because some things are important and some are less important. Finally, we can call this world view the ideology of botany, that is, the values, ideas and features that define botany as a discipline, the things that are taken for granted in order to conduct the work of a botanist.

We tend to associate 'ideology' with beliefs that are somehow negative, subjective or simply other. But as we saw in Chapter 1, an ideology is a set of beliefs. The reason we tend only to identify the beliefs of other people is because we consider our own (individual and group) beliefs to be normal, natural and obvious. Fairclough calls this 'naturalisation', which he defines as giving 'to particular ideological representations the status of common sense, and thereby mak[ing] them opaque, i.e. no longer visible as ideologies' (1995: 42, see also Bourdieu, 1991).

Simpson writes:

> An ideology therefore derives from the taken-for-granted assumptions, beliefs and value systems which are shared collectively by social groups. And when an ideology is the ideology of a particularly powerful social group, it is said to be dominant.
>
> (1993: 5)

Here again, we see how ideology links to power. We all have beliefs. Such beliefs become significant with respect to other people when the belief holders are in a position to enable their point of view to be accepted as the norm.

We can see evidence of particular ideologies at work in language. As mentioned in the previous chapter, ideologies work like filters, changing the way things are represented according to the values of the ideology. For example, in many countries, there has been a change in the way recipients of government services are described when compared with a few decades ago (Mautner, 2010). Rather than being referred to as 'people' or 'citizens', we are now 'customers', 'service users' and 'clients'. This signals an ideological shift towards government services framing (and speaking to and behaving towards) the public in the way a business or corporation would. The power of government means that it's very difficult to question or change this way of referring to members of the public. Further, particular ways of using language may encourage certain kinds of behaviour.

Imagine what it would be like if you considered the relationships you have with friends as a 'customer/company' relationship. How would you talk about your friendships? What would you expect from your friends? How might this change the way you behave as a friend?

Activity 2.4

Thinking about friendships in the terms of Activity 2.4 would probably change both your behaviour and expectations. You might think about the time and money you have 'invested' in the friendship and whether you were getting 'good value' for this. You might expect your calls to be returned in a prompt manner, you would expect good 'service' from your friend and so on.

The idea that language influences the way we behave is perhaps most obvious in the case of certain metaphors. Lakoff and Johnson (1980) argue that our thought processes are structured along metaphorical lines. For example, when we describe a verbal argument, we are likely to use words such as 'attack', 'defend', 'won', 'lost' and so on. From evidence of the language we use to talk about arguments, Lakoff and Johnson suggest the existence of the metaphor ARGUMENT IS WAR. We use the language of war to describe arguments. They go further than this and argue that this metaphor (ARGUMENT IS WAR) actually structures how we think about arguments. For Lakoff and Johnson (1980), the words we use are thus evidence of the way we think.

This way of speaking (and thinking) about arguments is probably so familiar that it doesn't seem particularly interesting. The familiarity of these expressions may hinder our attempts to explore any effect they may have. Imagine someone is being fired. Their boss has a number of choices to convey this.

Example 2.4
a   You've been fired.
b   I'm making you redundant.
c   Your job has been outsourced.
d   All roles in your section have been demised.
e   We're providing you with new opportunities.

Firing someone can be represented and communicated in various ways. Everyone understands what 'being fired' or being 'made redundant' means. These days, the concept of outsourcing is probably also very familiar. But to 'demise' jobs is fairly opaque (*Guardian*, 2013). Perhaps the stress of having to decode the message somehow displaces the disappointment of being fired or makes it easier for the manager to fire them.

2.6 A MODEL FOR ANALYSING LANGUAGE

The discussion of Lakoff and Johnson's metaphor theory demonstrates that ideologies are recoverable from language use. In order to identify the underlying ideology of a speaker or a text, we must try to identify the beliefs on which it relies. This requires a particular analytic lens. When we're trying to identify the ideologies and habits of thinking in our own culture, we need special tools to uncover what is often very difficult to see. In order to do this kind of analysis, it's important to understand that even though we may not be conscious of it (or even intend to) we make linguistic 'choices' when we use language. These choices are significant. Saussure provides us with a model for seeing what these choices are.

Figure 2.1 is a visual representation of Saussure's model of the different relationships between the elements of an utterance. There are two axes we refer to in order to discuss the choices that are made when an utterance is created. The **syntagmatic** axis describes the order in which words are placed; the **paradigmatic** axis is used to refer to all the other words that could have been chosen for a particular slot. We can think of the syntagmatic axis as being horizontal and the paradigmatic as vertical, as shown in Figure 2.2.

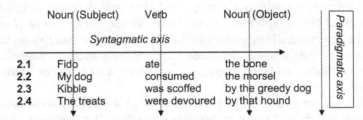

Figure 2.2 Syntagmatic and paradigmatic axes

If we consider simple sentences such as those in Figure 2.2, there are a number of choices available. As we can see from the form of the verb, the first two examples are in the **active** voice (ate, consumed) and the second two in the **passive** (was scoffed, were devoured). The active sentences **foreground**, that is, draw attention to, the dog who ate the food. The passive sentences, in contrast, foreground the food. We saw a similar kind of foregrounding in relation to Greek word order. Thus, choosing between the active and the passive has an effect on what the reader's attention is drawn to. What the choice of the active means can only be understood in relation to all the other choices that could have been made, in relation to the passive, for example (Montgomery, 2008).

The paradigmatic axis has been represented as running vertically. In each position, a choice has to be made. Do we describe the dog's action as 'eating', 'consuming', 'scoffing' or 'devouring'? 'Eat' looks like the neutral choice, but it is still a choice. If 'scoffed' had been chosen, a negative attitude is immediately signalled. 'Scoffed' only has meaning because of the relationship it has to all other linguistic signs and, most important, in relation to the other signs (verbs) that could have been chosen in its place (see Section 2.2.2).

When these choices are made, we're making a decision not only about language and signs but also about how we represent the world. By paying attention in our analyses to the choices made along these two axes, we can begin to reconstruct the values and beliefs that constitute a particular ideology. It's important to note that whether or not the choices are conscious, in a kind of premeditated way, they are still meaningful as choices. As we described in Chapter 1, one key insight about the relationship between language and ideology is that what may not seem like a choice to an individual speaker can nevertheless be said to be chosen by their own ideological position rather than consciously.

2.6.1 Transitivity

To analyse these choices in more detail, we need a way of talking about different linguistic choices. There are a variety of theories that make this possible. The following is a scaled-down version of Simpson's transitivity analysis (Simpson, 1993). Transitivity usually relates to whether a verb needs to take a direct object; 'hit' requires a direct object (something being hit), while 'sit' does not. 'Hit' is a **transitive** verb; 'sit' is an **intransitive** verb. Thus, **transitivity analysis** is concerned with who does what to whom/what. The difference between this model and others is that it has a slightly different terminology. This is because rather than describing the rules for a well-formed sentence (which is what some kinds of syntactic models do), this model includes information about the meaning of the clause.

Example 2.5 is a phrase that has two nouns and one verb. If we change the active form of the verb to the passive form, we have to change things around a bit to end up with a well-formed sentence. We have to change the form of the verb (from 'ate' to 'was eaten'), and we have to include a preposition ('by') before Fido.

Example 2.5
a   Fido   ate   the bone
b   The bone   was eaten   by Fido

As discussed earlier, example 2.5b starts with, and so focuses on, the bone. If we described these sentences in terms of nouns and verbs or subjects and objects, they would look the same, that is, both are structured noun, verb, noun, or subject, verb, object. We need the terminology provided by transitivity analysis that tells us which noun is doing the action to what. The doer is the actor, and that which something is done to is the goal. Verbs are always called process.

Example 2.6
ACTOR PROCESS GOAL
Fido   ate   the bone

You shouldn't think of the term 'goal' in the sense of something being aimed for. Dogs, broccoli and people can all occupy the goal position. The goal 'represents the person or entity affected by the process' (Simpson, 1993: 89). Usually, sentences will have more than an actor, process and goal. The detail that is often given can be labelled 'circumstances'.

In more comprehensive versions of this transitivity model, there is specific terminology for different kinds of verbs. 'Thinking', for example, is a 'mental process', while 'saying' is a 'verbal process'. In a similar way, the other roles have different terms in relation to these processes; for verbal processes, the 'actor' becomes the 'sayer' and the 'goal' the 'verbiage'.

The important thing is that even the stripped-down terminology of actor, process, goal and circumstances allows us to describe the relevant difference between our two examples.

Example 2.7

	ACTOR	PROCESS	GOAL	CIRCUMSTANCES
a.)	Fido	ate	the bone	in the doghouse

	GOAL	PROCESS	CIRCUMSTANCES	ACTOR
b.)	The bone	was eaten	in the doghouse	by Fido

You probably know that in the passive form, the actor is not required for a well-formed sentence. If we take away the actor, we are left with

Example 2.8

GOAL	PROCESS
The treats	were devoured

Because the actor has been deleted, we call this choice 'actor deletion' or 'agent deletion'. Note that the 'circumstances' can be deleted too, but their removal is not quite the same as the deletion of the actor, as circumstances provide additional information. When we are told that treats were devoured, we know that someone must have devoured them; they can't have been eaten without some actor intervention. Thus, the deletion of the actor serves to foreground the goal and background the person responsible. Sometimes such deletion may be because of lack of information; we know that the treats were eaten, but we don't know who did it. In other cases, it can be to deflect blame from the actor. Consider the following headlines:

Sikh man shot dead in Afghanistan

(Times of India, 2 October 2016)

Sikh man shot dead by suspected militants in Afghanistan

(Deccan Chronicle, 2 October 2016)

These headlines are similar, in that both foreground the 'goal', the 'Sikh man' who was killed.

Example 2.9

	GOAL	PROCESS	CIRCUMSTANCE
	GOAL	PROCESS	CIRCUMSTANCE
a	Sikh man	shot dead	in Afghanistan

	GOAL	PROCESS	ACTOR	CIRCUMSTANCE
b	Sikh man	shot dead	by suspected militants	in Afghanistan

In the first headline, we see an example of agent deletion. Despite the surface similarities here, the transitivity analysis reveals an important difference. In the second headline, the reader finds out who did the shooting. In the first, the actor has been deleted.

Compare the following headlines about the same event using the transitivity model and the syntagmatic and paradigmatic axes. By looking at the choices made in each headline, can you say something about what the writer wants to emphasise. That is, what is being foregrounded in each case?

1   Eight men deported from Singapore released after Indonesian police found no ties to ISIS

(Chan, 2017)

2   Indonesia releases eight IS suspects deported from Singapore

(*Star*, 2017)

3   Indonesian police free eight men deported from Singapore over IS images

(Vatvani, 2017)

Activity 2.5

Choices about whether to use active or passive verbs, whether to delete actors, and which lexemes to use to describe activities and people are all important for telling a story. What readers are told and how they are told it are influenced by linguistic choices. By looking in detail at these choices (and others like them), it is possible to reconstruct the underlying ideology of the point of view. In order to do this, we need to look at more than one sentence. But generally, over a longer text, a pattern will emerge.

The paradigmatic and syntagmatic axes were presented in Figure 2.2 using fully formed sentences in order to demonstrate what these terms mean. However, it is very helpful to bear in mind that all kinds of texts, representations and images can be analysed by considering these two axes. Every text has a structure in terms of what comes first, what comes next and so on. Even an image will have certain parts that can be considered in this way (the top, the bottom, the right and the left). It's possible to use the syntagmatic axis to analyse samples of language larger than a sentence. In a story, for example, some information will be given first, some will follow and so on. This order is crucial to how we interpret the story. In a similar way, it is possible to apply the paradigmatic axis to any kind of text. For any particular element (large or small) it is possible to ask: What other form could this element have taken? The colour of a sign, the typeface of a heading, the person presented as a major character are all elements that are the result of a choice. The choice that the author made is only meaningful in relation to all the other choices that could have been made.

2.7 SUMMARY

In this chapter, we've seen that the way people represent the world matters. Thinking about language with the tools that Saussure and transitivity analysis provide allows us to be precise about the choices people make in language and their consequences. Every language choice, whether consciously intended or not, demonstrates an ideology. While we often consider ideology to be a bad thing, it's important to remember that we all have habitual ways of thinking about the world, and this is reflected in the habitual choices we make in language. Because it's habitual, we don't think about the values expressed by the choices. To be able to think about these issues of representation, we need tools like transitivity analysis to describe the choices.

FURTHER READING

Fowler, R. (1991) *Language in the News: Discourse and Ideology in the Press*. London: Routledge.

Lakoff, G. and Johnson, M. (1980) *Metaphors We Live By*. Chicago: University of Chicago Press.

Lomas, T. (2016) Towards a positive cross-cultural lexicography: Enriching our emotional landscape through 216 'untranslatable' words pertaining to well-being, *The Journal of Positive Psychology*, 11(5): 546–558.

Lucy, J. (2005) Through the window of language: Assessing the influence of language diversity on thought, *Theoria*, 54: 299–309.

Majid, A., Bowerman, M., Kita, S., Haun, D. B. M., and Levinson, S. C. (2004) Can language restructure cognition? The case for space. *TRENDS in Cognitive Sciences*, 8(3): 108–114.

Martin, L. (1986) 'Eskimo words for snow': A case study in the Genesis and Decay of an anthropological example, *American Anthropologist*, 88: 418–423.

Orwell, G. (1988 [1946]) Politics and the English language, in *Inside the Whale and Other Essays*. Harmondsworth: Penguin.

Pullum, G. (1991) The great Eskimo vocabulary hoax, in *The Great Eskimo Vocabulary Hoax and Other Irreverent Essays on the Study of Language*. Chicago: University of Chicago Press.

Whorf, B. L. (1954) The relation of Habitual thought and behaviour to language, in Hayakawa, S. I. (ed.) *Language, Meaning and Maturity: Selections from Etc., a Review of General Semantics, 1943–1953*. New York: Harper: 197–215.

NOTES

1 Thank you to Professors Rebecca Shapiro and Jean Hillstrom for suggesting these.
2 Thank you to Dr Evi Sifaki, a native Greek speaker and syntax expert, for these examples and explanation.
3 Linguistic determinism is often called 'the prison house view of language', that is, that the limits of language are the limits of the world. The phrase 'prison house' is attributable to the philosopher Friedrich Nietzsche. The philosopher Ludwig Wittgenstein is also associated with the idea. Though he phrases it differently, *'The limits of my language* mean the limits of my world' (proposition 5.6, 1963, emphasis in original).

CHAPTER 3

Language and politics

3.1 INTRODUCTION

In this chapter, we consider the connection between language and politics. We begin by defining politics, making clear its connection to both ideology and persuasion as discussed in Chapter 2. We then explore linguistic features that are deployed in order to persuade audiences. These techniques are common across all kinds of persuasive texts, but they are generally easy to find in arguments that are clearly political. The linguistic tools of repetition and parallelism, presupposition and metaphor are introduced by taking examples from writing that argues both for and against what is commonly known as 'fracking'. These tools will help us see how we can be persuaded to accept particular ideologies and points of view. To further understand how these tools work, we then consider the language of war using the concepts of euphemism and dysphemism. This allows us to consider the consequences of representational choices. We also consider children's toys to show how the ideologies are communicated.

We then move on to the politics of education, specifically, the way the language of commercial transactions is increasingly used in the field of higher education. Here, we return to the link between ideology and metaphor discussed in Chapter 2. Because of powerful interests involved in education, it seems very difficult to challenge this ideology. However, we also consider a kind of politics, 'silly citizenship', that is more amenable to individual action.

3.2 WHAT IS 'POLITICS'?

In 2004, the Electoral Commission in the UK created and broadcast an advertising campaign to encourage people to vote and engage in politics. It was an animation, focussing on two male friends. When one friend, Tom, tries to discuss the European Parliament, his friend Mike says, 'I don't do politics'. The animation then follows the friends through a normal city on a normal day. Whenever Mike complains about something, whether it's graffiti or the cost of a drink, Tom waves his finger and remarks, 'But you don't do politics'. The advertisement finishes with 'Politics affects almost everything, so if you don't do politics there's not much you do do' (cited in Walker, 2014).

When people think of 'politics', they probably think of political parties, government and the way that nations and communities are governed. This kind of politics is obviously important and certainly linked with both language and power. Politics of the 'normal' kind, with governments, opposition parties and the debating and passing of policy and legislation, involves persuasion. In this chapter, politics is considered a little more broadly. We consider how language is used to persuade people in a variety of contexts. We will draw on some research that is closely connected to the politics of government and law-making, but it is important to see that these activities have consequences for how we view the world.

3.3 POLITICS AND IDEOLOGY

In the previous chapters, we described ideology as a way of thinking and examined how ideology has an effect on both thought and behaviour. When it comes to politics, ideologies are generally connected with beliefs about the proper organisation of society and how to achieve and maintain the goals that this entails. What is striking about this is that these beliefs are found to pattern among people in predictable ways. For example, Jost, Federico and Napier (1999: 310) explain that political positions we call 'conservative / right wing' and 'liberal / left wing' each have their own demonstrable and predictable belief systems:

> This formulation of the left-right distinction and many others contain two interrelated aspects, namely (a) advocating versus resisting social change (as opposed to tradition), and (b) rejecting versus accepting inequality.
>
> (Jost et al., 2009: 310)

Even a simple description like this, with only two factors, allows people to both explain and justify their political position. A person who thinks society is unequal and that inequality is not desirable would advocate for social change. If a person believes that inequality is justified or simply the natural order of society, they'll be more likely to want to keep things as they are.

Activity 3. 1

Regardless of your own opinion, write down the arguments you could use in support of

a   retaining the social system you have
b   changing the social system in a particular way

Note down the feature of society each would involve (this may relate to employment, education, family life, leisure time, the environment and gender roles), as well as arguments for the system generally.
    Is this difficult?

When putting together arguments for social change or maintenance of the current system, the points in your argument generally have to be consistent. For example, if you want a system that promotes financial equality, this will have consequences for your ideas about wages and employment and gender roles. You probably found it quite hard to come up with arguments for the side you personally don't support. Our beliefs, our sense of what the 'right' social order is, has a profound effect on the arguments we find convincing.

Language also has an important role in this kind of discussion. Few people would advocate 'inequality' in simple terms. 'Inequality' has a negative value attached to it; we generally support what is 'equal' rather than 'unequal'. This is considered 'fair'. Notice, however, what happens when we talk about 'fairness' rather than 'equality'. This is a good example of a linguistic tool called lexical choice (see Section 2.6 on the paradigmatic axis). 'Equality' suggests a straightforward equivalence – that everyone be treated in exactly the same way. 'Fairness', however, potentially allows for other factors to come into the equation. Fairness enables us to consider things like individual qualities and abilities, whether people have worked hard, whether people 'deserve' something. If you want to argue for maintenance of an apparently unequal system, you're likely to explain this in terms of 'fairness' rather than 'inequality'. Notice that changing one word can change the whole structure of an argument and the points that are needed to defend it (see also Danet, 1980). Moreover, it has been found that negatively framed arguments attract more attention from an audience than those phrased in more positive terms. That is, 'people pay more immediate attention to speeches if they hear negative messages, or if they are exposed to rhetorical schemes. Positively framed speeches without rhetorical schemes attract the least immediate attention' (Lagerwerf, Boeynaems, van Egmond-Brussee and Burgers, 2015: 294).

There are other linguistic tools that can be used to persuade people. In the following, we'll look at some extracts of arguments in favour of and against 'fracking'. It's important to state at the outset that the linguistic features we'll see in the examples are common across all kinds of persuasive text. They are not of themselves problematic or manipulative; rather, they are typical of persuasive texts.

3.4 THREE PERSUASIVE STRATEGIES

According to Aristotle (1991), persuasion can take place in at least three ways. He makes a distinction between arguments that rely on **logos**, the words or the argument itself; **pathos**, the emotion conveyed or the emotional connection to an idea or issue; and finally, **ethos**, arguments from personality, that is, we trust the argument or ideas because we trust the speaker.

Identify some texts (of any modality) that use logos, pathos and ethos to argue for different positions. Are there patterns in the types of arguments that rely on certain strategies?

Activity 3.2

Political persuasion, like all forms of persuasion, relies on all three tactics. Employing these tactics is not of itself deceptive or unusual. Nor are these tactics mutually exclusive. For example, a cosmetics advertisement might use all three. It might point out the science behind the efficacy of the cosmetic (logos), it might employ a celebrity to deliver the message (ethos: a trustworthy speaker) and the advertisement may generally appeal to the desire to look 'better' (pathos).

3.5 FRACKING: INTRODUCING LINGUISTIC TOOLS

Fracking refers to hydraulic fracturing, which is a process to extract natural gas from the earth. Because of arguments that natural gas is a better alternative than other fossil fuels in terms of its environmental impact, new ways of extracting it are very valuable.[1] For hydraulic fracturing to take place, first, a well has to be drilled into the earth. Hydraulic fracturing refers to the injection of highly pressurised fluids in order to release the natural gas.[2] Fracturing is a controversial topic because of debate about the environmental impact of the process. Objections stem from concerns about the large amount of water required for the process, allegations of the fluids contaminating ground water and the process causing earth tremors. Finally, some argue that it continues a reliance on fossil fuels instead of finding alternative fuel sources (BBC, 2015).

All the following examples are taken from texts relating to hydraulic fracturing in South Africa. While some are authored by politicians, others are not. A diversity of sources has been used for two reasons. First, all discussion, deliberation and action involved in daily life is political. Second, a range of texts are persuasive. In short, it is not the case that political persuasion is only concerned with what politicians do and say. As the discussion of Twitter (Section 3.8) will show, we all have at least some political agency.

3.5.1 Contrasts

In its simplest terms, a contrast involves comparing two things. The first example comes from a magazine article about fracking. At the end of the article, a geologist, Wlady Altermann, is quoted (Example 3.1).

> **Example 3.1**
> You don't need people with shovels and hammers. It's high technology stuff, skilled people will be flown in.
>
> (*Forbes*, 2016)

The contrast in Example 3.1 is between people 'with shovels and hammers' and high technology work. By highlighting the difference between manual work (with shovels and hammers) and high technology work, the speaker sets up a clear contrast. This contrast also presents an argument. The argument could be phrased as follows: don't think that fracking will bring jobs because the kinds of jobs created are those that the local labour force can't fill. Notice that the argument is not made explicitly, but it is easily inferred from the contrast. This argument also sets up a distinction between the local labour force (us) and other skilled workers who need to be flown in (them). The us/them distinction is perhaps one of the most pervasive in persuasive language (van Dijk, 2006).

3.5.2 Three-part lists and parallelism

Three-part lists (or triple structure) are very common in persuasive texts. They have a pleasing rhythm and as such are easy to remember. They are easy to identify, as they have the structure 'a, b and c' (Hutchby and Woffit, 2008: 183ff).

> **Example 3.2**
> However the Gas Utilisation Master Plan seeks to anticipate the infra-structure necessary to open up the gas market for the residential, com-mercial and industrial sectors.
>
> (Joemat-Pettersson, 2014)

Example 3.2 is from a 2014 Policy Budget Speech delivered by the Minister of Energy in South Africa, Ms Tina Joemat-Pettersson, MP. It may not be a particularly rousing topic, but the three-part list 'residential, commercial and industrial sectors' towards the end does important work. In this three-part list, the noun, 'sectors', which is modified by all three **adjectives**, comes last. This serves to draw all the sectors together – they are all *sectors*, and so they all have something in common. Thus, the speaker suggests that three groups of different stakeholders are unified and will benefit from the universal application of the Gas Utilisation Master Plan.

Example 3.3
South Africa is currently beset by a number of socio-economic challenges such as a lack of infrastructure, high levels of unemployment and a looming energy deficit.

(Ash, 2013)

In Example 3.3, we find another three-part list. Notice that the structure of **noun phrases** is syntactically similar. The use of similar syntactic structure in this way is called **parallelism**. The parallel syntactic structure encourages a reader to consider the entities in the same place in the same way.

Example 3.4
In a nutshell the Bill, which includes an expropriation clause, is designed to speed up strategic infrastructure delivery by extending state powers for the expropriation of land and shortening the approval time for projects by government authorities.

(Ash, 2013)

There is clear parallelism in the second part of the sentence. The parallel syntactic positions are

- speed up strategic infrastructure delivery *by* extending state power for the expropriation of land
- shortening the approval time for projects *by* government authorities

Notice that 'speed up' and 'shortening' are synonyms in this context and positive words. The structure and the lexical choices encourage the reader to view these changes positively regardless of the listener's position on the issue of expropriation (taking away) of land.

Find a recent speech from a public figure. See if you can identify parallelism and three-part lists in their talk. What is the effect of these choices? What arguments do they help encode and communicate?

Activity 3.3

The most straightforward form of parallelism is **repetition**. We know from our own use of language that if we want to emphasise something we repeat it. The same holds true in political texts. Repetition across a long text or speech can also help structure it. Just like repetition in a song or poem, this provides a focal point for the reader and allows them to see the structure of the text. Repetition used in this way works as kind of punctuation and is most common in spoken language. Example 3.5 is from the president of the Clean Water America Alliance, Ben Grumbles.

> **Example 3.5**
> Hydraulic fracturing can be 'safe' when done in the right place, on the right scale, with the right safeguards.
>
> (Yale Environment 360, 2011)

The repetition of 'right' in Example 3.5 draws our attention to, or **foregrounds**, the three-part list and the many variables that need to be considered for fracking to be safe. This repetition may also draw attention *away* from the use of 'can' as the main verb. To say that fracking 'can' be safe also suggests that it might not be. The use of such **modal verbs** in persuasive language are very important.

Activity 3.4

Considering the paradigmatic axis (Section 2.6), what other words could have been used in place of 'can' in Example 3.5. What would be the effect of these different choices?

Foregrounding is a useful analytic tool. It simply means that something is prominent in some way. Foregrounding may occur through any of the following:

- putting a word or phrase first
- repetition
- parallelism
- unusual word order (especially in binomials)

When something is foregrounded, usually other information will be de-emphasised or even omitted. We can see this in the following two examples (Examples 3.6 and 3.7).

Example 3.6
'Fracking' – or hydraulic fracturing – is the process in which oil and gas companies drill into the ground to extract natural gas from the shale rock that lays thousands of feet under the ground.

(Shale Stuff, 2014)

Example 3.7
'Fracking' – or hydraulic fracturing – is the process of drilling into the ground to extract natural gas from the shale rock that lays thousands of foot under the ground.

(rewritten version of Example 3.5)

If we compare Examples 3.6 and 3.7, we can see that the difference is one of omission. In Example 3.7, the activities of the 'oil and gas companies' are simply presented as happening without a real agent. This is done by using a **passive** structure. As we saw in Chapter 2, the passive voice allows for agent deletion, and that is exactly what has been done here. The focus is on the actions rather than the actors. By omitting the actor, an audience might think that the drilling is done by the government, for example, rather than by a company. For some texts, it can be a persuasive advantage to omit the actors in certain places.

3.5.3 Pronouns

Pronouns are very important when it comes to persuasive writing. If an argument is being made on the basis of ethos (see Section 3.4), for example, the author is likely to use lots of first person pronouns ('I' and 'me'), as this will remind the audience of who is making the argument. Other pronouns can be useful in setting up a contrast. Third person pronouns ('she', 'he' and 'they') can be used to immediately construct another who is neither 'I' nor 'you'. When arguments rely on creating an us/them contrast, third person pronouns are invaluable.

Perhaps the most commonly analysed pronouns in persuasive speech, however, are the plural pronouns in the first person ('we') and the second person ('you' plural) respectively. In English, 'we' does not specify who 'we' are in that it may include the audience (inclusive we) or exclude the audience (exclusive we). 'You' is also useful, because in English, 'you' does not distinguish between the singular and plural second person. Both pronouns allow the author to use these pronouns strategically. Possessive pronouns (for example 'our') perform a similar function.

Example 3.8
These developments herald a new era in the exploitation of this resource for our country, and the private sector is well advised to prepare for their contribution in this regard.

(Joemat-Pettersson, 2014)

In this sentence, 'our country' suggests that all citizens in South Africa have a stake in this issue. Whether or not they agree with the developments and the exploitation of a new energy source, they are brought into the terms of the argument simply through the use of 'our'. However, just because one instance of 'our' or 'we' appears to include the audience, it doesn't follow that all uses of the pronoun will include the audience. For example, shortly after the line in Example 3.8 we find the following:

Example 3.9
We will soon release the outcomes of a Gas feasibility study that is being completed with collaboration by Transnet, PetroSA, Eskom and government.

Clearly here 'we' cannot include the audience unless they too are involved in preparing the study. Nevertheless, the use of 'we' provides a stronger position than other alternatives (for example 'I').

3.5.4 Presupposition

There is another feature in Example 3.9 here that is useful to consider. Even if the audience doesn't know what a 'Gas feasibility study' is, they know that it exists and that it has 'outcomes'. Notice that the sentence doesn't specifically tell the reader that these things exist before discussing them, it simply discusses them. **New information** in a text can be presented as though it is **given information**. New information is something that has not been mentioned in the text before. In the case of nouns, this means they usually take the indefinite article. 'A kettle' signals that this is new information. 'The kettle', because of the use of the definite article, tells the audience it is given information. Therefore, the **semantic presupposition** in the example is that there are outcomes from a feasibility study. A semantic presupposition is information embedded in the sentence that is taken for granted in the composition and meaning of the text. Notice how 'the' is used for 'outcomes' and that this precedes 'a Gas feasibility study'.

In order to find presuppositions, there are number of linguistic structures you can look for, such as possessive pronouns, subordinate clauses, question structures and adjectives (especially comparative adjectives). The easiest way to test for a semantic presupposition is to negate the sentence and then identify what claims are still true.

Example 3.10
We will NOT soon release the outcomes of a Gas feasibility study that is being completed with collaboration by Transnet, PetroSA, Eskom and government.

Notice how in Example 3.10 (a negation of Example 3.9), it is still true that a Gas feasibility study with outcomes exists. One result of the strategy of presupposition, and one of the reasons they can be so effective in persuasive texts, is that when information is treated as given, we tend not to pay much attention to it.

The sentence below is affirmative. Try to negate it. What are the semantic presuppositions here?

The debates around fracking, its merits and dangers have filled hundreds of column inches.

(de Vos, 2014)

Activity 3.5

In the negated version, 'the debates around fracking, its merits and dangers have NOT filled hundreds of column inches . . .', the existence of 'its merits and dangers' is retained. This property allows us to distinguish semantic presuppositions from other information that may only be implied. For example, if someone says 'John found a veterinarian for his cat' this presupposes that someone called John exists and that he has a cat. It *implies* that the cat is somehow ill, but there is nothing in the sentence itself that says anything about the cat's health. You might assume that the cat is ill and that this is why the speaker is discussing John's search for a veterinarian, but this relies on your actual experience of the world, what you know about cats and veterinarians. It is background knowledge. It is not a property of the statement itself. This type of knowledge can be referred to as **pragmatic presupposition**. In this book, we use the term presupposition for *semantic presupposition* while referring to *pragmatic presupposition* as something implied by the text (see Simon-Vandenbergen, White and Aijmer, 1999).

Because of the way semantic presuppositions function, they can be used to efficiently incorporate a 'truth' into a text. This can have powerful persuasive effects. As Simon-Vandenbergen et al. remark, 'The reason why presuppositions are exploitable is that they are harder to challenge' exactly because they are embedded in the text (1999: 49). Semantic and pragmatic presupposition, however, are a natural feature of language and aren't always used to exploit or persuade.

3.5.5 Metaphor and intertextuality

Metaphors create and assert an equivalence between two things. Metaphors state that 'x *is* y'; by contrast, a **simile** simply draws a comparison, saying that x is *like* y. Because they assert and create an equivalence, metaphors don't need a verb; a **noun phrase** can express the metaphor all by itself.

Example 3.11

South Africa is in the midst of a heated energy debate.

(Schellhase, 2012)

The **metaphor** in Example 3.11 is contained in the noun phrase 'heated energy debate'. This idea of a 'heated debate' is a familiar one, a routine metaphor to describe a debate in which there is a great deal of conflict. In this example, however, we are more likely to interpret 'heat' as something that is actually hot precisely because of the use of 'energy'. Therefore, the author has taken a conventional metaphor ('heated debate') and given it additional vigour and a new twist by inserting 'energy' into the noun phrase. The use of 'energy' in this phrase is particularly astute.

There is one more textual feature worth commenting on.

Example 3.12

In May, Energy Minister Dipuo Peters, according to local media reports, called the gas beneath the Karoo a 'blessing that God gives us', adding, 'and we need to exploit it for the benefit of the people'.

(Schellhase, 2012)

The statement from the minister can be understood as exploiting a number of persuasive techniques. He focuses on the benefit to people of the gas and also refers to these natural deposits as a 'blessing' from God. He therefore alludes to religion and a particular view of the natural world. Such allusions can be described in terms of **intertextuality**. In referring to God, the minister is invoking another text: religious texts. One might even argue that he is alluding to a specific part of a specific religious text. In the book of Genesis, God gives man dominion over the earth. For people who know the Bible, the minister's words might well be understood as referencing these verses.

Intertextuality is not always obvious, and sometimes it is too obvious to seem relevant. That is, in this example, we could also discuss the reference to God and blessings as using a religious argument as authority. Nevertheless, intertextuality refers to the strategy of drawing on historical and cultural knowledge, without necessarily spelling out the full meaning and significance of that reference. To fully appreciate the choice made here, readers need to know something about this history. Intertextuality also reminds us that texts, and language, have a relation to previous texts and utterances.

Activity 3.6

Try to identify other examples of the features described here (parallelism, presupposition, intertextuality, metaphor) in an article about fracking or an environmental issue in your locality. What other features do you notice? Looking for repetition of particular words, phrases or syntax is a good place to start. What is the text trying to persuade the audience of?

3.6 WORDS AND WEAPONS: THE POLITICS OF WAR

War is a domain where we see the political and ideological effects of language. In the following, we explore some examples of how word choices can both reflect ideology and have persuasive effects. We consider the language used to refer to nuclear weapons drawing on our discussion in Chapter 2 about the connections between language and thought. 'Nuke-speak', or the language used to talk about nuclear weapons, has long been of interest to linguists (Chilton, 1982; Cohn, 1987; Woods, 2007). One of the reasons for this is that nuclear weapons and the production of nuclear power are fields where **euphemisms** are common. A euphemism is a word used to make something which might otherwise be unpleasant or disagreeable more benign. Euphemisms are also common in the domains of war. 'Collateral damage', for example, is a convenient way of backgrounding large numbers of civilian deaths, especially during times of war. We tend to use euphemisms in taboo fields, especially in relation to biological processes that we'd rather not think about. Dysphemism, by contrast, makes something more disagreeable or unpleasant than it might otherwise be. If you call a 'hamburger' a 'cowburger', you might find yourself less hungry than you thought you were.

Carol Cohn (1987) studied the language of nuclear weapons, spending a year with defence professionals in the US in 1984. Seeking to understand how defence policy is formulated, she argues that at least part of it is driven by the way these professionals talk about nuclear weapons. Further, having been exposed to this language for such a long period, she found her own thinking starting to change. Cohn notes that defence policy is a field full of 'abstraction and euphemism, which allows infinite talk about nuclear holocaust without ever forcing the speaker or enabling the listened to touch the reality behind those words' (Cohn, 1987: 17). Table 3.1 provides examples of some of these abstractions and euphemisms.

Table 3.1 Examples of euphemisms in defence policy making (Cohn, 1987: 17)

Euphemism	Gloss
clean bombs	'weapons which are largely fusion rather than fission and which therefore release a higher quantity of energy not as radiation but as blast' (Cohn, 1987: 17)
countervalue attacks	'incinerating cities' (Cohn, 1987: 17)
Christmas tree farm	'where missiles are lined up in their silos ready for launching' (Cohn, 1987: 20)
footprint	'the pattern in which bombs fall' (Cohn, 1987: 20)
cookie cutter	'a particular model of nuclear attack' (Cohn, 1987: 20)

Cohn also describes her acquisition of this new language related to nuclear weapons and warfare. She reported that knowing how to speak this language gave her a sense of power, in terms of not being so afraid of nuclear war, but also when speaking to those working in the industry. She also discovered that if she did not use this new language, the experts would consider her 'ignorant or simpleminded, or both' (1987: 22).

The use of euphemism is not just about making a single object seem more agreeable or about making a single action more acceptable. As with the choice of 'equality' and 'fair', it can structure a whole set of arguments such that some topics are to be spoken about in great detail. The choice of a word has consequences.

Woods (2007) explores another way language and nuclear weapons are discussed. He points out the normalisation of the **discourse** of nuclear weapons but also that there is a competing, strongly anti-nuclear discourse. This alternative discourse emphasises the notion of 'proliferation', the idea that 'the spread of nuclear arms is inevitable, unstoppable and dangerous' (Woods, 2007: 94). The word 'proliferation' manages to convey an entire argument and an ongoing process which can't be stopped. Paradoxically, perhaps, Woods suggests that this discourse of 'proliferation' has actually stopped the spread of nuclear weapons because of the form of the word itself.

Discourse in this context means two things. First, discourse refers to texts or language longer than a sentence or utterance. In this sense, nuclear discourse is extended talk or a text about nuclear weapons. Second, discourse describes the ideology underlying and structuring this talk. In the case Woods describes, 'proliferation' and the arguments that this term refers to can be described as a particular discourse about nuclear weapons. That is, the proliferation discourse relies on a set of beliefs and values that are ideological. More broadly, discourse used in relation to ideology is common across a number of fields and topics as we will see in later chapters.

The morphology of 'proliferation' tells us that this is a noun. While it is derived from the verb 'proliferate', if we use it in a sentence, we can see it is clearly a noun. The change of non-noun word to a noun is known as **nominalisation**. The reason is it so powerful is related to how we think about nouns. In simple terms, a noun is a naming word; it names a thing. Things have a physical reality, they tend to be stable and to have some kind of concrete existence. This is not to claim that all nouns refer to concrete things. Rather, the idea is that when we encounter a noun, we tend to orient to the idea that it is a thing. This means that when a verb (or something else) is turned into a noun, we are more likely to think of it as something solid, with a real concrete existence in the world. Once people start talking about 'proliferation', we are in a world of things rather than processes.

Woods argues that we need to understand the discursive formation of 'proliferation' and understand its effects in the contemporary world. He argues that it has serious and far-reaching consequences and is a 'cause of global inequality and double-standards' (2007: 116). It can have these effects because it is such a commonsense idea; the belief that 'proliferation' of nuclear weapons is a bad thing is completely normalised in many places around the world. It is part of a dominant ideology in the context of international affairs.

Activity 3.7

Nuclear power and nuclear weapons are the topic of much discussion. See if you can find examples of euphemism, dysphemism and nominalisation in articles about the events in Fukushima, Japan, or the tension between North Korea and the US.

3.6.1 Toys and politics

The language of warfare and nuclear weapons is linked to the normalisation of particular ideologies. As we saw, identifying who 'we' refers to is important in understanding persuasive texts. Who 'we' are can also depend very much on who 'they' are. When it comes to war and violence, who is 'us' and who is 'them' is a matter of life and death.

It's worth considering where these ideas come from; how do you find out who 'we' are? As this is a central question for any society, it's hardly surprising that who 'we' are is captured by dominant ideologies. What is a bit surprising is where these ideologies can be found. Linguistic features are not the only evidence of ideology. As we claimed at the start of the chapter, politics is everywhere. A place where you might not expect to find political ideologies is in children's toys. We take this example to show that language is not distinct from other forms of social practice.

David Machin and Theo van Leeuwen observe that toys related to war, such as toy soldiers, guns and other 'play' weapons have 'prepared children for specific kinds of warfare, fought in particular ways fused with specific political ideologies about the meaning of war and society itself . . .' (Machin and van Leeuwen, 2009: 52). If we look closely at toys and how they are used, we can find out something about who 'we' are.

Playing with toys may well involve language, but it also requires physical activity. Ideology is not just expressed in language; it is found in every aspect of our lives, including the way children interact with toys. Many plastic toy guns have lights and sounds, including voices shouting at the 'enemy'. The inclusion of 'technology' and the use of sounds makes the toys not only representative of contemporary war but also interactive and so 'allow the child to become physically, actively, involved in the representation' (Machin and van Leeuwen, 2009: 57). Machin and van Leeuwen found that the way children hold guns demonstrates a familiarity with the physical handling of weaponry. Moreover, the children can explain what the guns are for, who the soldiers are and what they do. The children in their study demonstrated fully developed discourses of war, such as saying that the special forces soldiers are the 'cleverest and best trained' and engage in the 'daring missions'. By interacting in this way with these toys, children learn to identify with these soldiers and their weapons, seeing them as representations of their own nation and society. This helps to build a picture for them of the difference between 'us' and 'them'. Who, in particular, 'them', or the 'enemy', represent in this play is left rather undefined (Machin and van Leeuwen, 2009: 58, 59). The children identify an 'enemy' but only refer to the enemy in a generic way, e.g., 'bad people' (2009: 59). For the perpetuation of ideology, this is convenient, as it allows for any number of actors, groups or nations to be inserted into this role.

Machin and van Leeuwen argue that particular views of war become part of the children's 'mental furniture' (2009: 59). The 'mental furniture' they refer to is akin to the concept of habits of thinking and ideology that we discussed in Section 2.4. That children might have particular views of war has consequences over and above the identification of us and them. For example, the toys emphasise the cultural importance of a particular kind of masculinity, the concept of the daring hero expert soldier and the practice of war as a way of resolving conflict (2009: 59).

Activity 3.8

Think of examples of toys made for and marketed to young girls. What do they communicate? (see also Boyle, 2013)

3.7 LANGUAGE, IDEOLOGY AND METAPHOR

In Section 3.5.5, we saw that metaphor can be used to create an image in the mind by comparing one thing with something else. This can be done overtly as in 'love is a battlefield' but metaphors are often implicit. As such they can form the base of an ideology.

Activity 3.9

Consider the following examples of people talking about time:

> He wasted so much time yesterday.
> I've invested a lot of time in you.
> She can't spare you any time.
> This technique will save you so much time.

How is time being described here? What else is described in these terms?

These phrases suggest that time can be wasted, saved and spent. In order for the phrases in Activity 3.9 to be meaningful, we need to believe (at some level) that time is valuable. In fact, the metaphor 'time is money' expresses that overtly.

As an ideology is a set of beliefs, the question to ask is 'what beliefs need to be in place for a particular statement to be true?' That is, what kinds of things do we need to believe, or accept as true, for particular pieces of language to make sense. If we believe that time is valuable this will have consequences for the way we behave in the world. For example, we may expect to be compensated when our time is wasted. This might take the form of money (for example of refund or discount) or a favour or gift to recognise that the person has taken something from you – your time. Thus, our beliefs have an effect on our thinking about people, events and actions in the world. They also have an effect on the language that we use and therefore on persuasion. Once we have identified the beliefs (ideologies) from which language draws, we can examine different ideologies to see what their consequences might be.

Metaphors rely on beliefs which in turn are composed of sets of beliefs that form a world view. Horner remarks, 'Metaphors evoke scenarios; scenarios suggest causal relationships and invite evaluation' (2011: 33). We've already seen that linguistic choices people make, the language that is used, can have consequences for how the world is understood. 'Metaphors link ideology with political discourse by providing models for making sense of [the world]' (Horner, 2011: 32). In this section, we consider the consequences of metaphors that are related to money, finance and the market (see also Portero, 2011).

It is common to use metaphors when there is a gap in the language. The creation of new metaphors is also common when complex political or financial news is being communicated to the public (Horner, 2011).

Consider the following terms and decide which action people would be more likely to accept. Why? In answering this question, think about how you might use these words in a sentence.

    rescue plan
    bailout
    intervention

Activity 3.10

While 'intervention' seems reasonably neutral, it still suggests an undesirable situation. We know this because of how the word is used. People talk about 'interventions' in the context of disputes and problems. You don't 'intervene' in a friendly conversation; you 'intervene' in an argument. A 'rescue plan' is clearly a positive thing, as it involves saving someone or something from a negative event. Of course, the presence of the negative event makes the term double edged. Finally, what you understand by 'bailout' may well be influenced by the way it was used in the wake of the 2008 financial crisis. In the US, government action, the 'Emergency Stabilisation Act', to support the financial markets and banks was referred to using these terms. Most widely, it was referred to as a 'bailout'. As Horner notes, this 'evokes images of disaster: sailors bailing water of sinking boats, pilots ejecting from crashing planes' (Horner, 2011: 30). Far from having some of the positive associations of 'rescue plan', Horner argues that some saw the bailout plan 'as a means of rescuing the guilty from the consequences of their actions' (2011: 31).

Underlying the language used to describe the financial crisis and subsequent intervention, Horner uncovered a series of metaphors that informed thought, language and action. The economy was conceived as a 'system' frequently described with plumbing metaphors. For example, the economic system was 'clogged' and needed to be cleared. The image of clogging was also found in relation to another metaphor: the economy is a human body. 'The circulatory system appeared in several instances of bailout talk to project the danger of a larger system failure should the symptoms remain untreated' (Horner, 2011: 35).

Once the economy is portrayed as a human body, a whole range of other metaphors become available. A body has arteries, which, if clogged, may lead to a heart attack. If the economy is a body, it also has a heart, which has to be protected (Horner, 2011: 35). When people understand that they are part of this body, views of the economy become more personal and more corporeal. No one wants to be sick – literally or metaphorically. Portraying the economy as a body, and by implication a person, is part of a broader set of discourses and representations. Choosing to represent the economy as a body makes discussion of the financial crisis both comprehensible and somewhat personal. As we all have bodies, we all understand how they work. As we are all part of the national body, we are necessarily part of this economic body too. Constructing the economy as a body also means it may be imagined as a person. The economy, then, can be said to have undergone **personification**.

Mautner has argued that the market, another name for the economy, has been personified. 'There is ample linguistic evidence that, in general usage, "the market" is reified (i.e., made into a "thing") and at the same time anthropomorphised (i.e., treated as it if it were a human being)' (Mautner, 2010: 14). The market has a 'will of its own'; it has moods that can be altered by some kind of external action; it can be 'encouraged', 'surprised' and 'misled' (Mautner, 2010: 14–15). Once the market is personified, important consequences arise from this. Just as a person in danger should be rescued and a person who is ill should be cured so too with the market and the economy. Moreover, as Mautner shows (2010) the market has become the most important person in the world. This is not simply a discourse; it is an idea that has outcomes for real people, for their employment, housing and every aspect of their lives. The construction of the market as a person is a political act.

Even personified, however, 'the market' is rather abstract. Unless a person works directly in financial industries, it might be difficult to see the consequences of this metaphorical personification. Mautner's argument that the market is the most important person, however, can be seen in a domain which may be more familiar: universities.

3.7.1 Student as customer

While in some parts of the world, it has long been the norm for university students to pay for their education, this practice has now spread to countries where for many years higher education did not cost a great deal of money. In Australia, for example, higher education required no fees between 1974 and 1989, and they were unknown in the UK until 1998. Having to pay fees to the university is only one of the costs associated with higher education and only one of the many things that should be considered when thinking about access to university. Perhaps deciding to levy fees changes the way we think, behave and talk about higher education. Here we explore some discourses of higher education where fees have been introduced.

One discourse involves students being described as 'customers'. Journalist Sean Coughlan writes, 'The market economy in higher education will mean students have to be treated as valued customers. Because, after all, they're paying the bill' (2011). Note the semantic presupposition here, 'the market economy in higher education'. Higher education is now fully integrated into a 'market economy'.

When money changes hands, a set of ideas about the relationships between parties comes into focus (see Section 2.4). Consider a normal consumer transaction, for example, buying something like a computer. If you pay a small amount of money for it, does this change your expectations? In the case of something tangible and functional like a computer, expectations and responsibilities are reasonably clear. Especially if you pay a lot of money for something, you expect it to work, you expect it to do what the seller told you it would do and you expect that if something goes wrong with the computer that you would be able to get this fixed. This seems reasonable and fair. We buy things all the time, and we have a great deal of experience in doing this. While it makes sense to draw on knowledge we already have about consumer transactions, is paying tuition fees for a university education the same as buying a computer? Does the student as customer metaphor fully describe the relationship between universities and students?

To answer these questions, we need to carefully examine the propositions that are connected to the 'student as customer' metaphor. This allows us to evaluate these points individually. Only after we have considered all the ideas connected to this metaphor can we assess the ideologies associated with the arguments and, hence, the metaphor itself. Specifically, the student as customer metaphor entails a number of beliefs.

© Russell Hugo

Image 3.1 Degree Mart

Example 3.13
a the relationship between student and university is transactional
b the customer is always 'right'
c the customer should get good value for money (good return on investment)
d services provided should be dictated by market demand
e only services demanded by customers are valuable

> Consider the statements in Example 3.13. Do you think they apply in a university context? Can you think of other propositions connected to the metaphor?

Consider Example 3.13. a.), the idea that the relationship between the student and university is transactional. A commercial transaction consists of giving money in exchange for goods or services. The student as customer metaphor might suggest that a student exchanges money for a degree. In fact, degrees are only granted when the student has successfully completed certain requirements. So, if we were to try to compare the university 'transaction' to a commercial transaction, it is more like buying gym membership than buying a computer. People join gyms to get fit and lose weight. The act of purchasing the gym membership itself does not guarantee any of these outcomes. Joining a gym is purchasing an opportunity to engage in beneficial behaviour, but the customer has to undertake these activities. A university education is similarly interactional. A student must undertake the activities provided by and, in fact, required by the university in order to receive the degree as evidence of their activity.

The example of 'student as customer' shows how metaphors can work in extended and powerful ways. While it may seem completely inconsequential to describe university students as university customers, this model is linked to a range of political and administrative decisions as well as to the economic features of the society we live in. The metaphor is connected to propositions that are ideological and difficult to challenge. That is not to say that there aren't other metaphors for the relationship between students and universities or that these models pass uncontested.

3.8 TWITTER AND POLITICAL AGENCY

In Chapters 4, 5 and 8, we will discuss social media and online communication. But in the context of politics, and especially in relation to some of the tools discussed earlier, we provide some discussion of Twitter,[3] as this platform shows that we all potentially have some form of political agency. Twitter allows users to communicate with a potentially global audience. As such, it is a powerful tool for politicians and anyone who wants to persuade us of something. Because Twitter users read, respond to and share other Twitter users' (like holders of political office) messages in real time, it is possible to generate, contribute to and follow political debates. In addition, users can highlight a specific topic in their tweet by adding a hash sign (#) to a word or phrase (the word/phrase and its hash sign are called a 'hashtag'). For example, '#Brexit' signals that the topic of the tweet is related to the UK vote to leave the European Union in 2016 called 'Brexit'. Using a phrase with a hashtag can serve as commentary about particular issues such as '#StopBrexitNow'. Davis (2013) describes the changes that Twitter has made to politics and uses the term 'Hashtag politics'. He draws particular attention to the **intertextuality** and polyphony (the presence of many voices) that Twitter allows. Because hashtags link to other discussions, users and internet material, Twitter is highly intertextual. That is, it is similar to the type of intertextuality that we described earlier in that it can allude to and reference other texts, but it also is a clickable link that directs users to similar hashtags.

The ability for people to comment on and retweet tweets also has the potential to change the political conversation. Discussions that may have been had in private before, or among friends, can now be had in front a worldwide audience, thus allowing for campaigning of all kinds and enabling rapid circulation of what many people think about current events and topics. This is an important form of political **agency**. Agency refers to an individual's ability to act, advocate or speak for themselves.

Activity 3.12

Find a hashtag for a political campaign. This might be for an upcoming election or for an issue that people have strong views about (like fracking). How do people use language in their tweets? Is there a unity or diversity of opinion around the hashtag?

In order to explore the different kinds of politics that can be found on Twitter, we now provide a few examples. The first links to environmental debates, while the second is linked to university policies.

Each year, the World Wildlife Fund (WWF) runs a global campaign concerned with environmental protection. It encourages people around the world to turn off all electronic appliances for one hour, calling it 'Earth Hour', in order to draw our attention to our reliance on electricity and to make us think about the resources required to use it. The hashtag #EarthHour is used year-round to refer to the event and create conversation among the public about the effect of natural resources on the environment. In August 2017, the WWF initiated another 'conversation' with Twitter users by inviting them to tweet 'five words to describe #climate change' in order to ascertain what Twitter users' concerns are and to inform new environmental campaigns. Users thus have at least some political agency in that they have been invited to contribute to the next campaign.

Social activism campaigns can also be more local. In South Africa in 2015, the hashtag #FeesMustFall was used to highlight rising fees and decreasing government investment in higher education. The campaign was student led, starting at Wits University with protests and other action in October 2015. The #FeesMustFall hashtag helped them to mobilise the campaign at a national level. The Twitter activity also helped students to challenge representations in the mainstream media of the protests. For example, 'On Twitter, participants sought to debunk various news reports that reported that the protests had turned violent, reckless and dangerous' (Peterson, Radebe and Mohanty, 2016: 7). As such, Twitter was a valuable tool for exercising political agency.

3.9 SILLY CITIZENSHIP

Discussions of ideology and war, nuclear weapons and the cost of education may suggest that we are politically powerless. The dominance of particular ideologies and the productive power of the language and metaphors connected to them can make us feel powerless. But as the example of Twitter shows, it is possible to have political agency even in a world full of many voices. In this final section of the chapter, we consider another kind of talk and action which is clearly political but that offers more scope for individual action, for change and for enjoyment.

In Chapter 4 we consider Twitter and YouTube and the way they are changing our consumption of media. Here, we will examine how they are also changing the political landscape. Social media and people's access to technology allows them to communicate in new media and new forms. One popular genre is 'news satire'. However, the tradition of critiquing power through humour is not new. Hartley points out that this practice can be found everywhere – 'from Aristophanes to Shakespeare'. He continues, 'Comedy is the go-to source for civic understanding' (Hartley, 2010: 241).

Hartley has coined the phrase 'silly citizenship' to describe certain kinds of 'media citizenship', that is, the playful and humorous ways people produce, consume and engage with the media. Hartley discusses a number of examples, such as spoof election ads in Australia and spoofs on political debates in the US (Hartley, 2010: 241). 'This kind of silly citizenship has become part of the mediated political landscape, with both professional and amateur creativity expended in the cause of political agency' (Hartley, 2010: 241). And while this may seem to have little to do with 'real' politics, it is important to remember that persuasive discourse takes a variety of forms.

3.9.1 'Terrorism alert desk'

Our example of silly citizenship comes from a daily television show which is broadcast in the US and available on YouTube. *Last Week Tonight*, by John Oliver, is a programme that comments on current events and their coverage in the media. Oliver has covered news stories about vaccines, televange-lism and, in the example we consider here, media ownership. The segment described here, appearing early in 2017, deals with the Sinclair Broadcast group, a media corporation that owns a number of media outlets and was poised to buy even more. The segment discusses how the Sinclair group requires that the television stations they own run selected video segments. Known as 'must runs' these segments include editorial comment on current events. One 'must run' segment that Oliver also discusses includes a daily 'terrorism alert'. Example 3.14 provides a transcript of part of the segment (italics indicates emphasis, bold signals strong emphasis, full stops mean a falling intonation and commas indicate a short pause).

Example 3.14
[13:56]

John Oliver (JO): ... but perhaps the most troubling thing of all is that Sinclair has a **daily** *must run segment* called the *terrorism alert desk* that is right, they report on terrorism *every single day* whether there is something major to report on or not which means that sometimes, the updates contain things like this.

[Video Tape 1: Terrorism Daily Alert on screen, presenter standing to the right mid shot] The company in charge of security for the Wimbledon *tenn*is tournament says the *ring* leader of the London Bridge attack *did* apply for a job. Now he was not *interviewed* and *no* interview was *scheduled* he just filled out an online application.

[Video Tape 2: footage of a flag in the distance – zooming in] an Isis flag was found *hanging* in a neighbourhood in New *Hamp*shire, it was taken *down* and police are looking into who put it there. [Terrorism Daily Alert on screen, presenter standing to the right mid shot] From the terrorism alert desk, in Washington, I'm Lindsey Mastis.

JO: In other alerts my grandma heard a loud noise, a man with a beard asked me when the next bus is coming, and Iran still exists [audience laughter]. From the terrorism alert desk in Washington *I* am just about *done* with this shit [audience laughter]. And look, look, there is no doubt that the terror alert desk has also featured some truly *terrifying* stories

[Video Tape 3: Terrorism Daily Alert on screen, presenter standing to the right mid shot] Isis has carried out a *gruesome* public execution in Iraq. They sliced *nine teens* in half with a chainsaw.

JO: Now *that* caught our attention, because it *feels* like the sort of thing we'd have seen reported elsewhere. So we tried to track down that story, and it originated with an anonymously sourced report, on something called *Iraqi News*. We weren't able to find *any outlet* that independently verified it and even when it was picked up by Brit-ish tabloids and Breitbart, they were careful to distance themselves with language like 'it has been claimed' and 'reportedly' and *I did not know* it was *possible* to dip *beneath* the journalistic standards of *Breitbart* [audience laughter] That's like being too bad a chef to work at a *carnival food cart* [audience laughter] [image of food truck left of screen showing a man shouting at a woman] 'Look your fried ham is unimaginative and bland and we cannot have that. We're Uncle Stickys Discount Ham Wagon' [image pans out to show food truck with name] [audience laughter] But but they *reported* it like it was a *fact* and what was perhaps even *weirder* about that chainsaw segment, was the story that closed it out

[VT4; footage of Isis flag then cuts to images of women in burkinis at a beach] And mayors in 22 French towns are ig*noring* a high court's ruling that says banning *burkinis*, is illegal. More than 30 towns initially outlawed the swim- swimwear worn mostly by Muslim women. From the terrorism alert desk, I'm Michelle Marsh.

JO: **what the f***!** [audience laughter] That is *not* about terrorism it's *just about Muslims*. [audience laughter] By that definition, terrorism is *anything* a Muslim does! 'Tonight, Mahershala Ali[4] on the cover of GQ, Kareem Abdul-Jabbar[5] sneezed in an airport, and happy birthday to Fareed Zakaria.[6] This has been your *terrorism alert desk*'. [audience laughter and applause] [16:34]

What point is Oliver trying to make in this segment? What linguistic tools is Oliver using to make his argument?

Activity 3.13

Oliver juxtaposes the story in the Terrorism Alert with his own comical exaggeration of their claims using both commentary and images. But the humorous constructions, which rely on the real content (**intertextuality**), also make powerful arguments about what we should expect from news outlets, public discussion of terrorism and the representation of Muslims. Silly citizenship can be very entertaining, but it can also be extremely serious. As Hartley puts it, 'the stage for citizenship is literally that. It is as much dramatic and performative as it is deliberative' (Hartley, 2010: 241). This genre of entertainment has become an important resource for consumers to engage with politics and encourage political agency. We will return to its place as an important part of the media landscape in Chapter 4.

3.10 SUMMARY

As the Electoral Commission advertisement we discussed in the introduction points out, politics is everywhere: political movements, higher education, toys, financial systems and humorous talk shows. If we pay attention to language used in these domains, we can uncover the ideologies that underpin the persuasive arguments made. Whether we're looking at repetition and contrasts or presuppositions and metaphor, examining the linguistic choices made gives us a way of understanding the arguments being made and how they are constructed. It then becomes possible to assess these arguments one by one to explore how we can be persuaded by ideologies that aren't consistent with our beliefs.

FURTHER READING

Beard, A. (2000) *The Language of Politics*. London: Routledge.

Bignell, J. (2016) Representing violence, playing control: Warring constructions of masculinity in Action Man toys, in Wesseling, E. (ed.) *The Child Savage, 1890–2010: From Comics to Games: Ashgate Studies in Childhood, 1700 to the Present*. London: Routledge: 189–202.

Boussofara-Omar, N. (2006) Learning the 'linguistic habitus' of a politician: A presidential authoritative voice in the making, *Journal of Language and Politics*, 5(3): 325–328.

Chilton, P. (1982) Nukespeak: Nuclear language, culture and propaganda, in Aubrey, C. (ed.) *Nukespeak: The Media and the Bomb*. London: Comedia Publishing Group: 94–112.

Evans, A. (2016) Stance and identity in Twitter hashtags, *Language@Internet*, 13, Article 1. (urn:nbn:de:0009–7–43402).

Nunberg, G. (2002) Media: Label whores, *The American Prospect*, 13(8), http://prospect.org/article/media-label-whores [accessed 23rd March 2018].

Simon-Vandenbergen, A.-M., White, P. R. R., and Aijmer, K. (1999) Presupposition and 'taking-for-granted' in mass communicated political argument: An illustration from British, Flemish and Swedish political colloquy, in Fetzer, A. and Lauerbach, G. (eds.) *Political Discourse in the Media: Cross-Cultural Perspectives*, Pragmatics and Beyond New Series. Amsterdam: John Benjamins: 31–74.

NOTES

1   It is not clear whether this is always true (see Zhang et al. (2014).
2   While fracking is often used to refer to the drilling and the use of fluids, in fact, only the injection of fluid is hydraulic fracturing (BBC, 2015).
3   For those not familiar with Twitter, it is a micro-blogging application, allowing individuals to author and disseminate messages of 140 characters called 'tweets' via a smartphone or computer.
4   US actor and rapper.
5   Retired American basketball player.
6   American journalist.

CHAPTER 4

Language and the media

4.1 INTRODUCTION

In this chapter, we consider language used in the media. If we consider 'mass media' to be information communicated 'from one sender to a large audience' (Jucker, 2003: 132), it is a very broad field. We will touch on aspects of social media and news media, as these resources have become a vital source of input for many members of society. Exploration of these areas provides us with a range of linguistic data as well as opportunities to use a variety of methods to analyse them. Consideration of these media sources also allows us to think about how particular ideologies are communicated and maintained, the linguistic choices that help do this and what counts as news, as well as changes over time in mass media news reporting. An important issue to consider when reading this chapter is how we interpret the information we find in the media. We refer to the skills audiences need to read and fully understand the texts they find in the mass media as media **'literacy'**. Our typical media consumption practices may not include noticing news values, ideological filters and the tools that platforms use to attract our attention. However, reading media texts critically and understanding how the mass media delivers content to us, including what they present and how, is a form of new literacy practices. Importantly, these skills, or literacy practices, are a form of power.

We will examine characteristics of the media that project and perpetuate ideologies before moving on to consider what counts as newsworthy and how news is represented. However, recent changes in technology have altered the ways in which news is produced and consumed. Microblogging sites like Twitter and the increased consumption of news online are key issues here.

4.2 MASS MEDIA

By definition, the mass media has a large audience. Further, there is often a significant degree of trust in the author of news (see ethos Section 3.4). People would be unlikely to watch, listen to or follow a news site that they didn't think was trustworthy. We expect our news to be true. However, because of this trust and the 'mass' aspect of mass media, these entities can have a significant effect on how a large number of people interpret events. Recently, however, 'fake news' has become both a fact and a topic of great public debate. We explore this here. In order to understand the contemporary news media landscape, it's very helpful to contrast the way things are now to how they were in the past. For example, traditionally, in the time before the World Wide Web and social media, there was an 'asymmetry' between producer and consumer. As Figure 4.1 shows, most people obtained the news through newspapers, radio and television before 2004. Before that point in time, the mass media could 'largely be described as one way communication'

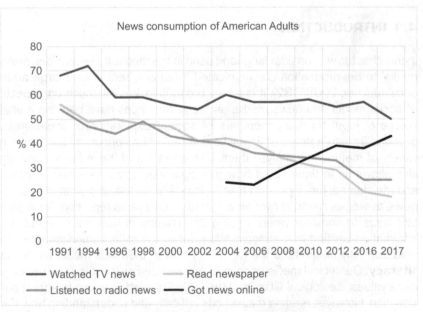

Figure 4.1 Where American adults get their news

Source: adapted from Gottfried and Shearer (2017); Pew Research

(Jucker, 2003: 132). And while this has now changed in complex and interesting ways, this historical asymmetry of producer and consumer of news is our starting point for considering language and the power of the media.

4.3 MANUFACTURE OF CONSENT

As we discussed in Chapter 1, ideologies can be built up, sustained and re-iterated over a long period of time. News is now broadcast 24 hours a day on a range of different media, including newspapers, radio, television and online in a variety of contexts. Looking at the language of news can provide important information about how power is created and exercised. While language is not the only consideration when thinking about power, it is extremely important. Fairclough writes:

> It is important to emphasise that I am not suggesting that power is *just* a matter of language . . . Power exists in various modalities, including the concrete and unmistakable modality of physical force . . . It is perhaps helpful to make a broad distinction between the exercise of power through *coercion* of various sorts including physical violence, and the exercise of power through the manufacture of *consent* to or at least acquiescence towards it. Power relations depend on both, though in varying proportions. Ideology is the prime means of manufacturing consent.
>
> (2001: 3)

The 'manufacture of consent' that Fairclough refers to is a concept that originates in the work of Noam Chomsky. While Chomsky is well known as a theoretical linguist, he also examines media and political representations of events. In their book *Manufacturing Consent: The Political Economy of the Mass Media*, Chomsky and Herman describe how the mass media functions, in both economic and ideological terms (1988).

Focussing on the mass media, they point to a number of factors that influence what stories we read and hear and in what form we receive them. Chomsky and Herman identify five 'filters' that influence the representations finally produced. Because of the way information is altered by these filters, the public's agreement with both the information and the ideologies that structure it is not a 'real' agreement; rather, it is 'manufactured consent'. Chomsky and Herman argue that the news media functions like propaganda, that is information designed to promote a particular argument or point of view, often one that is beneficial to those in power. The filters are

a   *media ownership*
b   *advertising income*
c   *the source of news stories*
d   *how groups and individuals respond to stories*
e   *communism must be avoided at all costs*

The concept of the 'manufacture of consent' is a way of understanding the cumulative effect of these five filters. The filters can be understood as structuring language and content at an ideological level. Though audiences are unaware of these filters when reading or watching the mass media, they are nevertheless important. These filters mean that events are presented in particular ways. Some events may not be covered at all; others may be given a great deal of importance. The way that stories are told, for example who is to blame or what the key issues are, is also influenced by these filters. Because we are only exposed to the filtered representations, over time, audiences find the values of the mass media are normalised; they become part of our collective 'common sense' and, as such, are part of the dominant ideology. Chomsky and Herman argue that such 'common sense' is constructed by the sustained representations of the mass media and that these representations are a product of the five filters they identify. Once we know that these filters exist, we can read texts in different ways. We can practice different kinds of literacies. Throughout this chapter, we'll consider examples which demonstrate these filters.

4.3.1 Filtering the facts

We can see how the filters work in the case of Edward Snowden, mentioned in Chapter 1, who revealed classified US information in 2013, because the way he was described in the mass media showed a polarised view of the situation. While filters were certainly in operation, the five filters have a different effect depending on the news outlets.

Activity 4.1

Examine the following news headlines. What ideological positions does the language suggest? What kinds of arguments do you think will be made in the articles that follow each headline? What other linguistic choices will be made in the articles?

a   NSA whistleblower Edward Snowden says US 'treats dissent as defection'

(The Guardian, McCarthy, 2013)

b   Edward Snowden leaks could help paedophiles escape police, says government

(Telegraph, Barrett, 2013)

c   Edward Snowden, Russian agent?

(Huffington Post, Thomson, 2014)

d   Edward Snowden, the insufferable whistleblower

(Washington Post, Marcus, 2014)

When discussing ideological representations in the mass media, the classic example given is that one person's 'terrorist' is another person's 'freedom fighter'. The issues raised in relation to Edward Snowden's actions remind us that this example is still relevant. Research conducted by Jens Branum and Jonathan Charteris-Black (2015) demonstrates that even in a single country, the UK, there was a difference among three newspapers and how they reported on Snowden. Analysing a large corpus of newspaper reports, they found that the two most common themes (also called 'news values' – see Section 4.4) in *The Guardian* newspaper related to 'criticism of surveillance' of the general public and 'justification of reporting' on the material that Snowden released (2015: 205). In the *Daily Mail*, however, the dominant themes related to 'lifestyle and personalisation' of Snowdon himself (2015: 210). Finally, the *Sun* focussed on 'defence of surveillance rights' in the national interest (2015: 213). Their analysis reveals that 'the same original story from the same initial source has been retold and presented in substantially different ways' (2015: 216). They continue, 'A reader with no prior knowledge of the events could get a very different perspective on the story depending on which newspaper they followed' (2015: 216). The 'reporting strategies' that the newspapers use are connected to their ideological views and those of the audience they are targeting. *The Guardian* takes a more liberal stance, arguing against surveillance of citizens, while *The Sun* and *The Daily Mail* seek to defend surveillance through an appeal to the security of the nation or through focussing on other aspects of the events and people involved. In short, the mass media exerts its ideological power by framing situations and people in a particular way.

It is worth considering where these ideologies and the particular representations of people come from. It is possible to argue that some choices can be connected to the ownership of the mass media (filter (a) in Section 4.2). Whether through explicit direction or something less overt, if the individual who owns a newspaper or media outlet has particular political and social views, it is not impossible that these may influence the content and perspective of the coverage in these outlets. That is, thinking about ownership of newspapers and television channels and the significance of advertising revenue to their success, it is tempting to conclude that this 'manufacturing' is consciously planned by powerful people behind the scenes. Recall John Oliver's commentary on Sinclair Broadcast Group in Chapter 3 (Section 3.9.1). However, the choice of the term 'filters' in Chomsky and Herman's model points to the automatic processes that occur without conscious intervention being necessary on the part of the producers. Newspaper editors do not need to be told to print or to withhold particular stories that may make large advertisers unhappy. In terms of running the newspaper, it's common sense to keep advertisers (filter (b)) and owners content. This is how ideology works; the ideology acts like a filter, to remove ideas that contradict the properties of the ideology. Nor is this filtering necessarily conscious. To suppose that it is would be to underestimate and misunderstand ideological processes. As we've already noted, when a way of seeing the world is ideological, it appears to be common sense.

In 2010, tuition fees for university students were raised considerably in the UK. In response to this, students and academics protested on the streets of London. Do the following newspaper accounts of this event tell the same story? Identify the different lexical choices and describe what they suggest about these events.

Example 4.1

Dozens of computers were destroyed, furniture was broken and fire hoses were turned on when around 200 protesters stormed the Tory HQ after smashing down the large plate glass windows on ground level.

... a death was narrowly avoided when one protester dropped a fire extinguisher from the eighth floor ...

Police admitted they were unprepared for the scale of the violence ...

(Bloxam, 2010)

Example 4.2

It was supposed to be a day of peaceful protest, with students exercising their democratic right to demonstrate against soaring university fees.

But anarchists hijacked the event, setting off the most violent scenes of student unrest seen in Britain for decades. Militants from far-Left groups whipped up a mix of middle-class students and younger college and school pupils into a frenzy.

(Gill, 2010)

It is impossible to know whether these are an accurate depiction of the events of that day. These extracts suggest that the protest was like a war zone, with uncontrolled violent behaviour; however, this is only one perspective. As it happens, the first author was present at the protest. From her perspective and experience that day, the discussion would look more like the following.

Example 4.3

A relatively peaceful protest against rising university tuition fees took place in London today. For most of the march nothing particularly remarkable happened. A number of groups were represented, including academics, unions and other members of the public. There was a small amount of property damage by a small number of people. According to Lewis, Vasagar, Williams and Taylor (2010), there were an estimated 50,000 people on the march.

You can see that the accounts from eye-witnesses can be very different. Our claim is not that the news is wrong; rather, the point is that it can only ever be a partial representation of what actually happened. Indeed, the extracts in Activity 4.2 are also only part of the stories by the journalists Bloxam and Gill and, as such, may not represent exactly the **narrative** they intended.

The next example (4.4) shows that the manipulation of even one word can change people's understanding of an issue. Lexical choices can bring with them a whole set of propositions, arguments, views and 'facts'. A monthly US magazine, *The Atlantic*, reports that while some Americans support 'the Affordable Care Act', they are opposed to 'Obamacare' in spite of the fact that both terms refer to the exact same legislation about health care (Hamblin, 2013). They open their story with a short interview from an evening television talk show, Jimmy Kimmel Live, in which a member of the public was interviewed about these policies and asked whether they preferred the Affordable Care Act or Obamacare. In the following excerpt are the follow-up questions and answers with an interviewee who says he prefers the Affordable Care Act.

Example 4.4
'So you disagree with Obamacare?'

'Yes, I do'.

'Do you think insurance companies should be able to exclude people with preexisting conditions?'

'No'.

'Do you agree that young people should be able to stay on their parents' plans until they're 26?'

'They should be able to, yes'.

'Do you agree that companies with 50 or more employees should provide healthcare?'

'I do'.

'And so, by that logic, you would be for the Affordable Care Act?'

'Yes'.

(Hamblin, 2013)

How can the person being interviewed support the Affordable Care Act and not Obamacare?

Activity 4.3

This is a very clear example of the real confusion that can occur because of different naming choices. The person interviewed had no trouble accepting that the Affordable Care Act and Obamacare were different things (even though they are not) when they were asked which they preferred. While in one sense this is a leading question, as it suggests a difference between the two things, the people shown in the video were able to offer reasons for preferring one over the other. The way a question is asked can have a significant effect on how people respond (see Loftus, 1975).

The naming of this piece of legislation is certainly political. The title 'Obamacare' has been created and maintained by the Republican Party, presumably to discredit and create negativity about the Affordable Care Act precisely because they oppose it. As shown in Example 4.4, the term has served to, at the very least, confuse citizens about the policy. Democrats initially objected to the term 'Obamacare'. Republicans defended it. One Republican politician argued that the term was now part of the language, referring to hits on Google and arguing that it was probably already in the dictionary (Parkinson and Jaffe, 2011). This, again, demonstrates the authority dictionaries are thought to have (see Chapter 1). The politician continues:

'It's in the vernacular. In fact', he quipped, 'it's in my spell check'.

(Parkinson and Jaffe, 2011)

Eventually, President Obama and Democrats accepted the term. This is an example of reclaiming, what was previously a negative word being used for positive purposes (see 'reclaiming', Section 7.4.2). President Obama acknowledged the Republican strategy of trying to discredit the policy by calling it 'Obamacare'. At a press conference, he said, 'Once it's working really well, I guarantee you, they will not call it "Obamacare"'(Richinick, 2013). Nevertheless, a poll conducted in 2017 showed that 35% of the respondents still did not know that Obamacare and the Affordable Care Act referred to the same policy. This demonstrates the strength of lexical choices (NPR, 2017).

4.4 NEWS VALUES

Allan Bell, a linguist and journalist, has outlined 'news values' (or 'newsworthiness') of news producers in his book *The Language of News Media* (1991). It is important to note the term 'news values' is used in specific fields to explain what is significant and 'newsworthy' for the people producing the news. It covers actors and events, what is esteemed in the news process and what is relevant for news text. This can be understood as complementing two of Chomsky and Herman's filters: (c) where our stories come from and (d) how we respond to them. While Chomsky and Herman are concerned with the macro level of news production and consumption, from who owns media outlets to audience responses, Bell focuses in more detail on the production of news at the level of what journalists choose to cover. His lists help explain, in a different way from Chomsky and Herman, why some stories are covered and why some aren't. And even though these values have been around for some time, research shows that news organisations still orient to them, even in new media contexts like Twitter (Al-Rawi, 2017).

4.4.1 Actors and events

In terms of actors (subjects of the news) and events, the news values that Bell outlines explain what stories are considered newsworthy and why. Bell, drawing on previous research, identifies the news values (1991: 156–158).

a   NEGATIVITY: negative events are more likely to be newsworthy than positive ones
b   RECENCY: the event should be recent
c   PROXIMITY: the event should be close by
d   CONSONANCE: events which can be made to cohere with ideas and understandings that people already have are likely to have high news value
e   UNAMBIGUITY: the events should be clear; if there is a dispute or a question, there should be some resolution
f   UNEXPECTEDNESS: that which is not routine is more newsworthy than that which is
g   SUPERLATIVENESS: the worst or best of something is more likely to be covered.
h   RELEVANCE: the audience should be able to see some relevance to their own life in the event
i   PERSONALISATION: if something can be reported in a personal rather than an abstract way, it will be more newsworthy
j   ELITENESS: this relates to the actors in the news; a story about powerful people is more newsworthy than the same kind of story about an 'ordinary' person
k   ATTRIBUTION: whether the facts or the story can be attributed to someone important or trustworthy
l   FACTICITY: figures, dates, locations and statistics are important for hard news (Bell, 1991: 156–158).

> Get today's newspaper online or in paper form. Looking at the first few pages or the homepage, see if you can relate these characteristics to the headlines and coverage you see.
>
> Activity 4.4

These features help us to understand why we get the news we do, how stories are chosen and which people become the focus of these stories. To really understand which news actors and events will be most important to a story, we need to know what kind of story it is. There are two distinctions that are often made about news stories. They may be hard or soft news, and they may be fast or slow news.

The first is the distinction between hard and soft news (or stories/features). Bell explains that the distinction between hard news and soft news is 'basic' for those working in the news (1991: 14). 'Hard news is their staple product: reports of accidents, conflicts, crimes, announcements, discoveries and other events which have occurred or come to light since the previous issue of their paper or programme' (1991: 14). Hard news stories might draw on the news values of RECENCY, NEGATIVITY, PROXIMITY, UNEXPECTEDNESS, RELEVANCE and FACTICITY. In contrast, soft news might draw on the values of PERSONALISATION, ELITENESS, CONSONANCE, SUPERLATIVENESS and ATTRIBUTION. As readers, we also know this. For example, if a national media outlet were to present on their front page a story about a local ice cream competition, readers would assume that some very important or very bad event occurred in conjunction with it. Because of our literacies in mass news media, we know that national media outlets don't normally put soft news stories on their front pages.

We can also distinguish between fast and slow news. Fast news refers to news that needs to be reported quickly but which will probably also be out of date just as quickly. A good, though specialised, example of fast news would be the state of the stock market or the price of particular stocks and shares. Those who buy and sell shares for a living need sound, up-to-date information about the prices of shares in order to conduct business. Slow news, in contrast, is not so time sensitive and refers to events that develop over a longer period of time. The two are not mutually exclusive, however. The voting results in the election of a new head of state will certainly be fast news; audiences will want to know who has been elected as soon as they possibly can. However, the consequences and implications of a change in government or head of state cannot be covered in short sound-bites. Careful analysis needs to take place, opinion leaders need to be interviewed and consulted and economists and social policy experts will be asked for their expert input. While the election result is fast news, the news that flows from this will be slower and will last for the full term of office and even beyond.

These news values might look rather static and deterministic. It is tempting to think that an event is either recent or not, superlative or not and that these attributes cannot be changed. But this is not the case. How news values are realised in a media representation depends on a number of factors. What counts as 'recent', for example, will change depending on the media outlet. What is 'recent' in a daily newspaper may well be old news on Twitter. Likewise, stories can be framed in particular ways in order to construct a particular news value (Bednarek and Caple, 2014). A story about a teenager winning a spelling bee may not seem to be particularly newsworthy. But the teenager could be presented as 'the best' or as 'local' in order to frame this story as both superlative and proximate. Bednarek and Caple (2014) show that word choices can construct events in line with relevant news values.

For example, making explicit a person's professional qualifications can construct FACTICITY or ELITENESS and choice of temporal markers can contribute to readers understanding an event as recent. As the example with Snowden showed, the same events can be represented in different ways. These differences can be connected to ideological points of view, but they can also be constructed so as to be in line with various news values.

Even with changes in how we consume the news, news values continue to have explanatory power. For example, Bednarek (2016a) finds that we can understand sharing behaviour on Facebook with reference to these news values. That is, these news values are all attested in stories from mainstream media that users go on to 'share' on Facebook. She finds that 'Eliteness, Superlativeness, Unexpectedness, Negativity and Timeliness [recency] seem especially important in shared news' (2016a: 252). Bednarek also found that NEGATIVITY seems to be more important than positivity for Facebook users and that unexpected news tends to be commonly shared (2016a: 253).

The World Wide Web has changed the way fast news is reported. How do you keep up to date with fast-moving stories and events?

Activity 4.5

4.5 EXPERTS AND THE NEWS

When we examine the news media very carefully, in addition to how it *represents* events/people, we can also see that the media can play a role in *creating* what is true (facticity). In this section, we examine the representation and construction of expertise in the news mass media. Boyce's (2006) work on the media reporting of the alleged link between the MMR (measles, mumps and rubella) vaccination and autism helps us explore the issues and challenges the media encounters when it has to report on a specialised subject. We will see how AMBIGUOUS information that is nevertheless both RELEVANT and PERSONAL is considered newsworthy. The MMR debate also shows us the changing profile of who is considered an expert.

In the UK, as in many other countries, children are given a series of vaccinations in the interests of their own health and public health more generally. In 1998, a scientific paper that argued for a link between autism and a 'rare bowel syndrome' was published in a reputable scientific journal, the *Lancet* (Boyce, 2006: 892). As Boyce reports, 'The paper in The Lancet did not present evidence linking the MMR vaccine to bowel syndrome and/or autism but at a press conference publicising the research Dr Wakefield [a research scientist] discussed this possible link' (2006: 892). Because of the apparent risk to children, this became a big news story. It was NEGATIVE, RECENT and very PERSONAL to anyone with children.

In the press conference Professor Wakefield presented the (untested) hypothesis that giving children the vaccines in three separate doses would be safer. However, this suggestion was not supported by the majority of his co-authors nor by any scientific evidence in the published research (or subsequent research, although Wakefield disputes this) (Boyce, 2006: 892).

The link between MMR and autism was reported in the media as true, even though it was only suggested by one expert (Dr Wakefield) at a press conference. Debate about the causal link ensued as other scientists, in fact, disputed Dr Wakefield's claim, pointing to the journal paper itself, which did not explicitly state a link between the MMR vaccine and autism. In the media, evidence was portrayed as ambiguous when in fact there was no empirical support for the link between MMR and autism. The facts were unambiguous (FACTICITY), but this is not how they were represented in the media. But because the story was so emotionally charged, it took on a life of its own.

Nevertheless, because this news story involved children, it had significant effects both in the news media and in the world. First, coverage of MMR in the news increased dramatically (Boyce, 2006: 892). More significantly, take up of the vaccine fell. Boyce examined the production, reception and content of stories about MMR in the years following these events. One might think that because this is a story about medicine, illness and vaccines, that audiences would be presented with a number of scientific experts. This is not what Boyce found (2006: 896).

The MMR debate is an example of the changing nature of 'expertise' in the media. Particularly in relation to health and medicine, accurate information is crucial. One of the problems in establishing information as factual is, as Boyce argues, 'there has been a real decline in trust of "experts"' (2006: 890). News producers rely on experts to satisfy the news value of ATTRIBUTION and FACTICITY. But in this case, what expertise means is itself contested. If scientists aren't trusted, are parents the experts? What about government bodies? In the absence of (or in spite of) compelling scientific evidence, all these people and institutions can become experts. From a news point of view, especially producers targeting particular audiences, which 'experts' are chosen will depend on the facts that producers want to be foregrounded and conveyed. It will depend on the ideology that the news producer wants to promote and the kind of story they want to construct (see also Example 3.14). This distrust of expertise in this case is so dramatic that discourses about the connection between autism and the MMR vaccine continue to have an impact even nearly twenty years later. The efforts to re-educate the public about the safety of the MMR vaccine have been contested by a range of groups. So much so that in 2015 the state of California passed legislation to remove the 'personal belief exemptions' to the state requirement for child vaccination. In 2017, the director of the University of Washington Autism Centre, wrote an editorial for the local newspaper reminding people that

'Vaccines save lives, and there is no evidence they cause autism' (Estes, 2017).

The issue here is not simply about who is spoken to, interviewed or reported; it is how they are positioned in respect of one another. While it is important to hear the views of parents, their expertise is different from that of a scientist who has conducted direct and relevant research. Boyce shows that sometimes these very different kinds of 'experts' were treated as comparable contributors to the debate.

Example 4.5
The following text is an extract from a UK ITV evening news story profiling the MMR debate.

Dr Robert Aston (*Wigan and Bolton Health Authority*): It makes me deeply sad as a doctor and as a grandfather that a sustained amount of anti-vaccine lobbying, amongst them organisations which claim to be not anti-vaccine, and by sections of the media to keep the controversy going has resulted in the undermine of public confidence in what is probably the safest and most effective of our vaccines. [The MMR vaccine] has done untold good and it prevents diseases, serious diseases and premature death in children …

Stephanie Sherratt (*parent*): You should be able to have your children vaccinated singly at your own doctors. I object strongly to being told what and when to inject into my children.

Dr Pat Troop (*Deputy Chief Medical Officer*): We have no concerns about our current vaccine. I think it will send a very strong signal that parents will say, hang on, we think maybe there is a problem around this vaccine why else would you offer us a single vaccine? And confidence would go.

Journalist: Eleven-year-old Nick Williams has autism. His parents believe it dates from the time he had his MMR inoculation at the age of 4.

Parents of Nick Williams: In the November of that year he had his MR booster and by the following Christmas his behaviour was totally different. He was a different child. He wasn't interested in Christmas presents (ITC, 4 February 2002).

(Boyce, 2006: 898, 900)

Look at the transcript in Example 4.5. How do the speakers position themselves as experts? What arguments do they make?

Activity 4.6

The speakers in these lines have different kinds of expertise. Notice, however, that they are treated as though they are competing voices, with the same kind of expertise. This is set up by the choice of the first speaker, who refers to himself as both a scientist and a grandfather. Indeed, Boyce's research shows that news consumers were interested in the *personal* views of scientists and other official kinds of experts. In particular, these experts are asked whether they would have their children vaccinated rather than being asked about scientific evidence. The importance of the personal value of this story is clear, as Boyce observed that if the experts had no children, their opinion was sometimes represented as less important (Boyce, 2006: 898). The story was framed as being about children and parents rather than about science.

The problem was that construction and presentation of the story led people to believe that there was in fact a dispute about the facts. Moreover, as Boyce's research shows, people overestimated both the amount of research on both sides and the number of subjects involved (2006). Given the amount and kind of coverage, this is hardly surprising. This story had a serious impact, as it resulted in people refusing to have their children vaccinated (Boyce, 2006: 892). In terms of media reporting and experts, it also shows that 'expertise' is not something a person simply has, whether by virtue of their experience or their position. Rather, 'expertise' is at least in part constructed by the very process of news production. The mass media can make an expert out of someone who wouldn't otherwise be considered to have expertise on a topic. Moreover, this is a process in which the created expert also has a role. As Thornborrow (2001) shows, 'lay' speakers will provide 'a salient comment on some aspect of their own personal status and identity, before going on to state their opinion, ask their question, or say whatever it is they have to say as a contribution to the talk' (2001: 465). This is not just about identifying themselves; it is about establishing that this is relevant to the comment, that they are somehow an expert on what they are about to say.

The decline of trust in experts that Boyce describes has a number of consequences. It makes it harder for important information to be conveyed, as now there seems to be a discourse of distrust, especially around health issues. This means that new stories related to health can be framed as consonant with these discourses of distrust. Moreover, because there is so much information available online, sorting the truth from the fiction has become even harder. This online environment is also challenging for news producers. They have to produce their content in a new way, in a new context for a new kind of audience.

4.6 NEWS ONLINE

So far, many of the examples we've been working with come from online versions of newspapers. Most newspapers, and other mass media news outlets, now have webpages. In fact, some news outlets only have an online presence and don't produce a printed version of their 'publication' (e.g., *Huffington Post, Slate*). The changes to news production and consumption that the internet has facilitated have been profound (see Figure 4.1). As a 2016 Pew Research poll shows, 38% of Americans often obtain news online and among younger people aged 18–29, 50% often obtain their news online (Mitchell, Gottfried, Barthel and Shearer, 2016). Still, TV continues to be the most widely used news platform; '57% of US adults often get TV-based news, either from local TV (46%), cable (31%), network (30%) or some combination of the three' (Mitchell et al., 2016; see also Newman, 2017). These numbers reveal how important it is to understand online news media. We first look at the changes that online news media has brought, think about how to analyse this material and then outline the different places where media can be found online.

Jucker identifies six ways in which the move toward new forms of mass media (internet-based) can be understood in contrast to previous forms of mass media (television, radio and newspapers). First, the internet allows for hypermedia, 'the integration of different channels of communication, such as written texts, still pictures, motion pictures and sound' (Jucker, 2003: 130). It is also becoming more personal, targeted at particular audiences. This is possible because of the relatively small amount of labour now needed to produce different version of the same text. Some of this work is done automatically. Third, levels of interaction have been increased dramatically. While it has been possible to write to newspapers or call in to radio stations in the past, the forms of communication between producers and consumers have changed dramatically. This will also have consequences for who counts as an expert. Moreover, even reading material online is a form of interaction, as producers can track exactly what is getting hits, what is being shared, retweeted and so on (Jucker, 2003: 139). Fourth, the 'traditional lifespan of information' is changing (Jucker, 2003: 130). People expect up-to-the-minute updates about news and events. Fifth is the change from communication between **synchronous** (at the same time) and asynchronous. An example of synchronous communication is talking on the phone; **asynchronous communication**, however, would be reading an email that was sent some time ago. Moreover, the forms of synchronous communication have been expanding. Twitter, text messaging, online chat and Skype have radically changed this aspect of communication. The more synchronous communication is, the more it may draw on conventions from spoken language. Snapchat, for example, in which images and short videos are designed to become inaccessible after a short period of time, can be seen in relation to spoken language rather than written (Soffer, 2016, see also Charteris, Gregory and Masters, 2018). Finally,

> the availability of media products is no longer subject to the same physical restrictions as traditional media, and the products, in particular media texts, are losing their fixity because their electronic publication format makes them susceptible to immediate modifications and changes wherever they are received.
>
> (Jucker, 2003: 131)

Kautsky and Widholm describe the distinction between printed news and online news as 'mono-linear, from writing, via editing to printing of a final version' versus online news, where various different versions of the same article may be found (2008: 82). Kautsky and Widholm pay attention to what this fast pace of online news production and consumption means for those interested in analysing these texts. We're going to draw on their work not so much to describe how to do the analysis but to highlight the changing profile of the news in this context. The production of news texts online makes information immediate but also subject to change. The story that was online yesterday may well be gone tomorrow and difficult to recover. Further, sites are updated all the time. The news is now very fast indeed. But how are these choices made? Why is the story that was a headline in the morning harder to find in the afternoon?

One way of understanding this is to look at the way Kautsky and Widholm distinguish between print media and online news.

Table 4.1 Media characteristics

	Print media	Online news
Distribution	Periodic	Parallel flow(s)
Presentation form	Yesterday's news	Extended 'now'

Source: Kautsky and Widholm, 2008: 88

As shown in Table 4.1, there are clear distinctions between the kind of news found in print and online. Printed newspapers are periodic, they come out every day (or sometimes every week, for local papers). The printed page doesn't change. Once the newspaper goes to press, the content and format is fixed. For online news, however, sites are designed so that they can be constantly produced; they are always being updated and changed. The text is not stable.

Activity 4.7

Over a few days, follow a topic or story on one newspaper website. Does the story remain the same? Are new items added? Are they linked together? Draw a map of the various (versions of) stories and how they link together.

You probably found, like Kautsky and Widholm, that there are differences in how a story is told even over a short period of time. While the same resources may be used (quotes, pictures, sources and facts), they will be presented differently and communicate different messages as the story 'evolves' and as the producers decide to emphasise different aspects of the story. Continuity has to be balanced with novelty. Moreover, different producers will update their sites according to a different time line. For what was traditionally a daily newspaper, the site may be updated several times a day. For publications that were traditionally published once a month, the updates won't be as frequent or probably as dramatic (until the next month comes).

When looking at the resources used to construct news online, many are those found in the traditional print media. Both print and online news media have content, a structure and a layout. But the move to an online environment provides new constraints and affordances for those producing the news. Bateman, Delin and Henschel identify five areas that we could consider when examining online news (2006: 155).

1   Content structure: what information is included and in what order?
2   Rhetorical structure: what is the relationship between the content elements, and what argument does it produce?
3   Layout structure – where are the different parts of the story (the text, the pictures and so on)?
4   Navigation structure – how should the reader move between parts of the story?
5   Linguistic structure – what is the detail of the language used?

Clearly these factors will interact. One would expect the headline to be at the top (layout) to be easy to find (navigation) and to entice the reader through its composition (linguistic structure).

We also need to remember that news online isn't always found on the home pages or social media accounts of mainstream media. Online journalism is broader than this. Deuze identified four types of news online:

1   mainstream news sites (e.g., newspapers and news shows)
2   index and category sites (e.g., search engines and news aggregators)
3   meta- and comments sites (e.g., sites about the media itself)
4   share and discussion sites (e.g., sites where individuals can connect and share information)

Figure 4.2 shows how these different types of online news vary in terms of how much they let members of the public contribute and whether their focus is editorial content or enabling public discussion. In the next section, we will look at how a story in the mainstream news varies depending on where it is found.

As we have already discussed, sometimes the mainstream media is constrained in what it can report because of ideological filters. It can also be constrained by political power being exerted by state governments. For example, laws may be passed limiting what can and cannot be covered (see Chapter 1). A government may take control of or exert a great deal of pressure on mainstream news providers, limiting what they can tell the public about a specific event without fear of punishment. In cases where the mainstream media has been restricted, share and discussion sites become

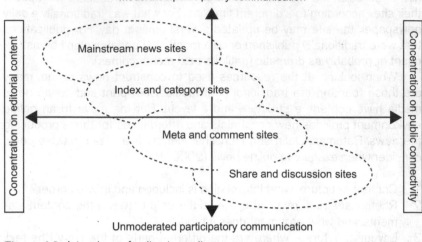

Figure 4.2 A typology of online journalisms
Source: Deuze, 2003: 205

incredibly important for people to know what is happening and to articulate their own opinions. Dashti (2009) studied two political events in Kuwait (the death of the head of state and changes to the electoral system) in order to compare how the local mainstream news sites and share and discussion sites reported those events. The mainstream media are very conservative and do not tend to criticise the rulers. But as Dashti reports, those writing on share and discussion sites were able to voice other, less positive points of view about what was happening. 'The enhanced level of freedom brought about by online journalism encouraged more Kuwaiti users to express their personal and individual views without fear of government retribution' (2009: 107). Share and discussion sites can be a powerful tool for exercising agency (see Section 3.8), voicing opinion and engaging in political discussion.

4.6.1 Presentation of news on the internet

In this section, we examine one story from Australia to examine the constraints and affordances of different online news media. We take as an example a story about two supermarkets (Woolworths and Coles) and their plan to implement a charge for plastic bags that customers use to take their purchases from the store. This practice is common in many parts of the world, but not everyone agrees that it is a reasonable thing to do.

We begin with an Australian newspaper, the *Sydney Morning Herald*. The *Sydney Morning Herald* (SMH) is distributed as a print edition (published daily) and also presents stories online on Facebook and Twitter.[1] Table 4.2 presents information about the plastic bag story in each of the SMH online platforms. People familiar with these platforms will of course not be surprised by some of the features that differ, but it is important to bear these differences in mind when analysing text. Further, comparing different types of media dissemination (rather than just looking at one) is a good way to find out which features or variables may be relevant to an analysis.

An interesting difference to keep in mind about Twitter and Facebook is that both of these platforms serve as navigation tools to the main website; a way of encouraging readers to visit the newspaper's homepage (see Al-Rawi, 2017: 707). Both the Twitter feed and the Facebook headline posts provide links directly to the article on the newspaper webpage (see Figure 4.3). This, in turn, encourages a particular kind of reading behaviour. That is, these platforms allow users to follow up on the things they're interested in (on the main site) without having to skim through a whole newspaper (either printed or online). At the same time, it's important to remember that a news story like this won't be the only item on a person's Twitter feed or Facebook page. News stories from mainstream publications, like the *Sydney Morning Herald*, will be interspersed with other kinds of news (what your friend ate for breakfast, a funny video about cats or a call to sign an online petition). As Jones remarks, 'The real currency of the information age is not information, but attention' (2005: 152). News stories are vying for attention with other 'news'. It makes sense, then that the tweet and the Facebook post are dominated by an image (signalling the supermarket involved) and a short headline and framing information for the reader. These act as 'hooks' to deliver the reader to the full story on the newspaper webpage.

```
┌─────────────────────────────────────────┐
│ Tweet text here                           │
│  ┌─────────────────────────────────────┐ │
│  │ Image here                           │ │
│  │                                      │ │
│  │                                      │ │
│  │                                      │ │
│  └─────────────────────────────────────┘ │
│ Headline here                             │
│ Lead here                                 │
└─────────────────────────────────────────┘
```

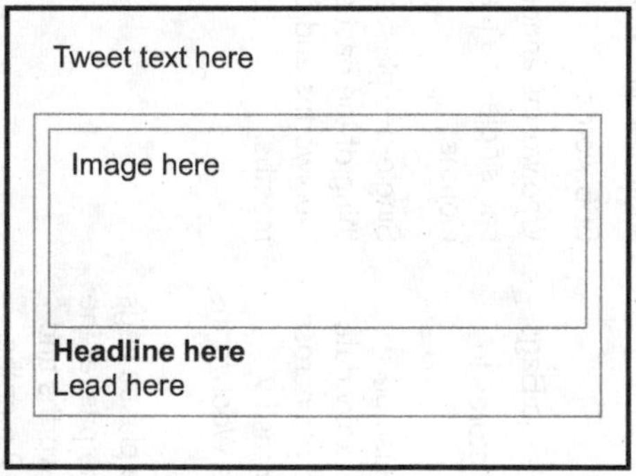

Figure 4.3 Anatomy of a tweet with embedded link

The news story we analyse is about Woolworths decision to no longer give out single-use plastic bags to their customers (Cormack and Singhal, 2017). Woolworths made this announcement on Friday, July 14, 2017. SMH subsequently reported this news online and on social media. Later the same day, Coles announced that they would also be charging for plastic bags. The SMH print edition came out on Saturday, July 15, and included news about both supermarkets. Table 4.2 compares the SMH news story as it appears on different platforms. It highlights the differences in the syntagmatic structure (see Section 2.6) of the news reports on different platforms. All of them

Table 4.2 Comparison of media

	SMH print	SMH online	SMH Twitter	SMH Facebook
Time line	Available 15 July 2017, Australian time	Dated 14 July. First comment, 13:54 Australian time, 14 July 2017. Seems to have been updated sometime late Friday afternoon	Ca. 16:45 Australian time, 14 July 2017	Ca. 14:30 Australian time, 14 July 2017
Word count	662 words	666 words	35 words	75 words
Headline	*Front Page:* R.I.P. Plastic Bags *Story (page 2):* Big stores to ban plastic bags	Woolworths announces all stores will ban single-use plastic bags within 12 months	Woolworths to ban single-use plastic bags at all stores	Woolworths to ban single-use plastic bags at all stores
Leader (first sentence after the headline)	*Front page:* Single-use plastic bags now have an expiry date – they will be phased out across Australia in 12 months by supermarket giants Woolworths and Coles. *Page 2:* Single-use plastic bags will be a thing of the past at the checkouts of Woolworths and Coles in the next 12 months.	Single-use plastic bags will be a thing of the past at the checkouts of Woolworths and Coles in the next 12 months.	Supermarket giant Woolworths has announced that it will phase out single-use plastic bags over the next 12 months.	The move will extend to Big W and BWS stores, which are owned by the Woolworths group, and is expected to be in place by July 2018.

Frame	N/A	Coles follow suit after Woolworths' plastic bag ban.	Update: less than two hours after Woolworths announced that it will stop giving out single-use plastic bags in the next 12 months, Coles announced that it, too, would be phasing out single-use plastic bags over the next 12 months.
Other content	To the right of two images, some figures are given, including '4 billion' – the number of plastic bags used in Australia annually and '3%' the number of which are recycled	There is an embedded video that is a television news story from an Australian broadcaster (Channel Ten Eyewitness News) recounting the content of the article (1 minute and 46 seconds)	
Images	On front page, image of non-branded plastic bags; Inside (p. 2): two images, one representing Woolworths, one representing Coles	Four. Two representing Woolworths, one representing Coles and one of plastic bag in the wind	Photo depicting Woolworths branding; Photo depicting Woolworths branding
Interaction	Comments section below the story; Share to email, Twitter, Facebook and so on at the top; it is also possible to share the individual images in this way	Twitter facility to retweet, reply, direct message or like	Facebook facility to like, share and comment

have a headline and a leader (the first sentence after the headline), but Twitter and Facebook must present these differently. On Twitter and Facebook, the headline and a leader are presented inside a frame with a photo above them, which serves as the direct link to the story on the SMH homepage (see Figure 4.3). The tweet accompanying the link repeats a salient detail about the story (that another store will ban plastic bags) while the Facebook post provides more text about the same salient detail of the story. The tweet and post also foreground temporality, or 'breaking news'. The tweet and the Facebook post, which include an image, headline, leader and comment, work in a similar way to the front page of the printed paper. The front page of the print edition has very little text. It invites the reader to turn to page 2 to read more. The Facebook post and the tweet invite the reader to click on the link that will take them to the full story on the newspaper website.

The story about Woolworths on the SMH website was updated to reflect the breaking news about Cole's. This update, however, was not made clear to readers. The final print copy differed in small ways from the online version. Despite their differences, the stories do of course report on the same event. The headlines and leaders are similar, and if one takes the headline, leader and frames altogether, the reader is given a key summary of the story. It is interesting, however, that in this case, the constraints of Twitter (previously restricted to 140 characters in the tweet but expanded to 280) seem to have been replicated in the Facebook domain. Facebook does not have the same limits on how many characters can be put in a status update. But this similarity indicates that newspapers think (or know) that readers consume news on social media in a similar way to Twitter.

4.6.2 The inverted pyramid

In order to explore the presentation of news, let's look more closely at the structure of news stories and home pages for news outlets. Typically, a news story follows a structure known as the 'inverted pyramid'. Herbert describes it as follows:

> Traditionally the inverted pyramid story begins with all the main facts and relegates the less important details to the apex of the pyramid, and can therefore be cut from the bottom.
>
> (2000: 105)

Because printed newspapers have limited space, the stories have to be amenable to deleting sections to make them fit the page. Online articles are not (in theory) subject to the same kinds of limitations. Nevertheless, as with the carryover of conventions from Twitter to Facebook, some conventions of the print journalism genre have carried over to the online environment. The inverted pyramid structure also makes sense in relation to reading habits and how people consume information, that is, we tend to read headlines and leads first.

The structure of an online story is related to the layout and the naviga-tion tools available to the news producers. Online newspapers have to deal with a range of layout constraints. Part of this will be determined by the kinds of advertising the publication uses and where this needs to be placed. They will also have to think about their audience and the kinds of devices they may use to read the news. What looks good on a computer screen is very difficult to navigate on a smartphone screen. Thus, even between different devices, it's possible to see changes in the way online newspapers present their information.

Because of the online environment, news producers have to provide navigation tools (Bateman, Delin and Henschel, 2006: 168). The homep-age is instructive in this respect. The navigation tools on a homepage include headings for different sections, search functions, 'most read' boxes and short snippets of articles that enable readers to click through to the full story. Knox explains that the homepage, more than a collection of navigation tools, 'is a complex sign, consisting of a range of visual and visual-verbal signs which function as coherent structural elements' (Knox, 2007: 23). Kautsky and Widholm point out that newspapers online are 'not simply digital versions of newspapers, but a fusion of radio, television and traditional print media' (2008: 84). This means that the organisa-tion and analysis of online news has to take account of the **multimodal** nature of the internet. Once the elements have been identified, it is pos-sible to analyse them by using the syntagmatic and paradigmatic axes (see Section 2.6).

4.6.3 Commenting on the news

Changes in technology allow for new modes of communication and new forms of interaction between 'producers' and 'consumers' such that these very categories become blurred. It has long been possible to comment on newspaper stories (e.g., through letters to the editor), but the presence of news media online has expanded the range and speed of such interac-tion. The ability to comment on stories online often leads to conversations between readers, with very little input from the original writer or producer of the story that led to the comments.

Find an online newspaper that allows commenting on stories. Look at a range of stories, from national and local news to features. Do they all allow comments? What kinds of things do people write? Are they engag-ing with the story or with other commenters?

Activity 4.8

As shown in Table 4.2, all the SMH stories about the plastic bag ban allowed for some kind of reader contribution. While not present in relation to the plastic bag ban, readers might post violent, sexist or obscene commentary, which is usually (but not always) removed by the publisher (Hlavach and Freivogel, 2011). Nevertheless, the reader comments are helpful for understanding how the event or issue is understood and provide readers with a variety of opinions on the story that may be different from their own. For example, while the SMH story seemed to frame the plastic bag ban as positive, many commenters were not so keen on the news. We looked at the first 35 comments and replies to comments on the homepage. While some commenters applauded the move as a benefit for the environment, others expressed dislike for the policy because they would be required to pay for shopping bags (and even reported that they would no longer be shopping at Woolworths). Some comments diverged to related issues, for example, what to use as garbage bags or whether Woolworths is a well-run company. The comments also provide evidence that the publishers updated the story after its first publication without alerting readers to the update.

The comments on the Woolworths story on the SMH Facebook page were similar in content to those on the website. Some people were very pleased about the ban; others complained that they would have nothing to use as garbage bags and that they would shop only at Coles in the future. The level of interaction between commenters, however, was much greater than on the website. While this did take place on the website story, some Facebook comments resulted in as many as 29 replies. As we noted earlier, it is typical for the publisher itself to not respond to reader comments, and this is true in this story as well. The interaction is taking place among readers rather than between the news producers and their audience. Al-Rawi reports, though, that not all news organisations have this policy about reader comments. Some news organisations are more proactive in this domain (2017: 706). For example, a Canadian company, the CBC, respond 'in a timely manner' to 'questions, comments & complaints' (Al-Rawi, 2017: 706). It is important to remember that a publisher's proactive engagement with the reader comments serves the goals of the publisher in that it keeps readers engaged and enables them to deliver them more content and deliver readers to its advertisers.

4.7 TWEETING NEWS

Twitter was founded in 2006 and has been taken up by a range of people and institutions for a variety of reasons. Twitter is a micro-blogging application, allowing individuals to author and disseminate messages called 'tweets' using 140 characters (although this was recently expanded to 280). You will probably be familiar with the platform, with many users accessing it on their mobile phones. As well as the character limit, tweets have other features. To access Twitter, you need a user name, and this may allow people to tweet directly to you, by including your Twitter handle (which is signified by @). In addition, as we described in Section 3.8, hashtags (#) are an important part of Twitter. These work to identify the subjects or orientations of tweets. It is also possible to include images and links to webpages in tweets (as seen in Figure 4.3). The Twitter interface allows users to see what subjects are being hashtagged and circulating widely (called 'trending') as well as allowing users to follow a subject regardless of who is tweeting. Events and television programmes often publish their hashtag so that people can follow and contribute to a running commentary. As Twitter is a platform that relies on **user-generated content**, users are free choose how they wish to interact with and use Twitter. A user might read the tweets of other users (or 'follow' another user), post their own messages to their followers, respond to other users, post photos and so on. Because there are so many ways to communicate via Twitter, the conventions for using it that have developed have been generated by its users (boyd, Golder and Lotan, 2010).

In Section 3.8, we saw how students exercised agency using Twitter to protest university fees. This is a use of Twitter that is akin to **citizen journalism**. Citizen journalism refers to non-professional journalists producing news content. In fact, Twitter has changed what citizen journalism means in that it allows anyone with a smartphone access to the public sphere. Traditional news bodies monitor Twitter because it can provide an important cue to trending topics and current events. Bruno calls this 'the Twitter effect' because Twitter 'allows you to provide live coverage without any reporters on the ground, by simply newsgathering user generated content available online' (2011: 8 cited in Hermida, 2012: 663). Hermida points out that sourcing news from Twitter makes verification of stories very important for journalists but also very challenging given the fast pace of contemporary news reporting (2012: 661). 'The process of determining the facts', Hermida writes, 'traditionally took place in newsrooms' (2012: 665). However, 'Arguably, some of the process of journalism is taking place in public on platforms such as Twitter' (Hermida, 2012: 665). Twitter can be used for sharing other news and need not be seen as 'journalism'. That is, Twitter (like other digital technologies) can be used to bring people together in a digital communicative context. The circulation of trending topics on Twitter also means that those who do not use Twitter become aware of what Twitter users are discussing. But there is still, even in the developed world, a 'digital divide'. The 'digital divide' describes the fact that not everyone has access to these technologies. It's worth considering what it means to be a participant in this kind of media or be excluded from it.

Next time you're watching television in 'real time' rather than pre-recorded or through an online platform, see if there is a hashtag for it on Twitter. Follow the hashtag on Twitter. Are you surprised by the kinds of comments made?

Activity 4.9

As well as its other functions, Twitter has become valuable in times of crisis. Starbird and Palen (2010) examine its use in emergency situations. While mainstream media is a significant presence in that context, they also found that the 'most popular retweets among locals [affected by the emergency] were tweets containing much more locally relevant information' (2010: 7). This included information of a timely and local nature, advising people of where help could be secured, what was happening to protect them and so on. They remark, 'Generalisations about the triviality of Twitter communications at the broad level therefore will not necessarily hold for tweets sent, received and retweeted during an emergency event' (2010: 9). Twitter has also been used to track illness and thus plan for demand on local health services. In the UK, the Food Standards Agency has used information from Twitter in order to map the spread of the norovirus (a contagious virus causing vomiting). This helps in tracking the spread of the virus and managing the resources necessary to cope with outbreaks (Rutter, 2013). Researchers tracked hashtags such as #winterbug and #barf in order to see whether an increase in use of these correlated with lab reports about levels of norovirus from the same periods and places. Finding that this was the case, they are now able to track the spread of the virus before lab work confirms it.

4.8 FAKE NEWS

Because news and information circulate in different ways and can be easily divorced from their point of origin, they are susceptible to misinterpretation. It's not surprising that sometimes news that isn't true is reported as though it is. Understanding the different types of 'fake news' and their purposes can help us to read and understand this material more critically. It is an increasingly important kind of media literacy.

As we have seen in this chapter (and in Chapters 2 and 3), we make choices all the time about how to represent people, events and the world and also news stories are based on a particular point of view. Because of these representational choices, it's difficult to draw a simple distinction between what is true and what is not (see Section 4.2). Recently the notion of 'fake news' has become a much more widely discussed topic. When it comes to 'fake news', we must draw out a number of differences. Firstly, what do we mean by 'fake news'? It is a very complex subject, but briefly, we can summarise 'fake news' as referring to a few slightly different but related concepts (Zimmer et al., 2017):

1   a term used to delegitimise news reports
2   a term used to refer to fabricated news reports that are
   2a   intended to be untrue and whose goal is to misinform, or
   2b   intended to be untrue and whose goal is to entertain

It is important to remember that fake news is not new. Early usages of this term can be found around the turn of the 20th century (Zimmer et al., 2017).

However, the discourse about 'fake news' has changed and public aware-ness of the issue has increased recently. The accessibility of social media and other forms of new digital technology do make it easier to produce, dis-tribute and consume 'fake news' (for further interrogation of the concept of 'fake news', see e.g., Starbird, 2017; Allcott and Gentzkow, 2017).

4.8.1 'Fake news' as delegitimising accusation

A newer meaning of 'fake news', labelling news as 'fake' in order to dele-gitimise it, can be found in Donald Trump's use of the term. Since he was elected president of the United States, Trump has often suggested that the media does not represent him accurately, in spite of the unequivocal accuracy of stories, in order to discredit the stories (see also Leonhardt and Thompson, 2017). In his Twitter posts before the election, Trump referred to 'failing' news organisations and the 'phoney' media (Osborne and Roberts, 2017: 194, 196). After winning the election, the phrase 'fake news' began appearing in his tweets (December 10, 2016: Osborne and Roberts, 2017: 237). In a press conference in 2017, Trump accused an entire news net-work, CNN, of being 'fake news'. This seems to be an allegation that news organisations have particular agendas and that these agendas shape (and distort) their coverage of Trump. By doing this, Trump can call into question the validity of a story about him and exploit distrust of news sources (see Section 4.6).

4.8.2 Fabricated news reports to misinform

Another kind of 'fake news' that dominated discussion in the 2016 US presidential election was reporting or coverage of events that didn't actually happen. Here, the use of 'fake news' involves purposeful misinformation to gain an advantage over a political rival. For example, one story that circu-lated widely via the internet involved accusations that Hillary Clinton (Trump's opponent) and her team were running a child traffic ring. This accusation was completely debunked (Aisch, Huang and Kang, 2016). This practice is not limited to the US. Misinformation campaigns have also been docu-mented in France (Ferrara, 2017) and Poland (Gorwa, 2017). In June 2017, an image of the UK prime minister, Theresa May, accompanied by a quote that seemed to be attributed to her, circulated on Facebook and Twitter. The quotation was represented as originating from May when she was a councillor in an area of London called Merton. The text quoted her as saying, 'Curbing the promotion of lesbianism in Merton's schools starts with girls having male role models in their lives'. There is, however, no evidence that she ever said this (Waterson, 2017). Nevertheless, this meme was circulated very widely. Because May had historically been inconsistent in her support of LGBT rights, people may have been more inclined to assume the attribu-tion of the quotation was accurate (see CONSONANCE Section 4.5). For people who did believe it, this representation was consistent with what they already believed about May. Establishing the veracity of news was traditionally the role of mainstream media organisations. As discussed in Section 4.2, we could trust the news because we trusted the author. But these days, people get their news from a variety of sources, and we don't always know the origins of what we are reading. The increasing occurrence of fake news suggests that before accepting something as true, we should verify stories ourselves. Unfortunately, research by the Stanford History Education Group suggests that some high school and college students don't have the skills necessary to evaluate claims made on social media or to distinguish between actual news and content that someone else has paid for (Wineburg, McGrew, Breakstone and Ortega, 2016). In recognition of the lack of such skills among college students, faculty members at the University of Washington developed a class called 'Calling Bullshit' to provide students an opportunity to learn how to evaluate the news critically (University of Washington School of Information, 2017)

Social media outlets and internet search engines have also made efforts to try to curb the circulation of fake news on their sites (Waddell, 2016). Twitter has raised the possibility of including a 'fake news' button on Tweets so that users can report suspect items (Sulleyman, 2017b), while Facebook has issued a guide on how to establish whether something is fake news or not (Sulleyman, 2017a).

There is a further problem with this kind of fake news. Gorwa (2017) suggests that fake news on Facebook and Twitter 'can have an amplifying effect on content and help game [as in influence] trending algorithms'; however, scholars don't know how much 'they really effect the experience of the average user, especially if they [the user] are simply engaging with content created within their potentially insular groups of friends and followers' (2017: 26). However, Vosoughi, Roy and Ara (2018), in their study about the spread of news stories on Twitter, found that false stories 'diffused significantly farther, faster, deeper and more broadly than the truth in all categories of information' (1146). As the possibilities for misinformation afforded by digital media continue to be exploited and developed, online news media must be carefully scrutinised.

4.8.3 Fabricated news reports to entertain

There is also fake news that is intended to be untrue and whose goal is to entertain. The *Onion*, *Faking News* and the *Betoota Advocate* are all examples of platforms that circulate this kind of fake news. Although their 'fake news' is inspired by actual events, the spoof nature of the stories on these sites may be easier to detect simply because the examples they provide are so outrageous. For example, the *Betoota Advocate* published a story about drug dealers moving to recyclable and environmentally friendly baggies for distributing drugs (Overell, n.d.). Notice that the *Betoota Advocate* story references and relies on the actual news story about Woolworths banning plastic bags (discussed in Section 4.7). They begin by reminding readers that large supermarkets are set to ban plastic bags. They continue:

> However, it isn't just big business that has stuck their neck out for the environment, with the nation's small businesses and criminal networks also declaring a move towards more sustainable options (Overell, n.d.).

Nevertheless, like truly fake news, there are cases of spoof fake news being published in mainstream media outlets as factual news. Sometimes traditional news outlets mistake fake news stories for real ones and circulate them (e.g., Chang, Lefferman, Pedersen and Martz, 2016; Leber and Schulman, 2017; MacFarquhar and Rossback, 2017).

Wardle (2017) points out that in order to understand fake news, we need to understand (1) 'the different types of content that are being created and shared', (2) '[t]he motivations of those who create this content' and (3) 'the ways this content is being disseminated' (Wardle, 2017). Look at the *New York Times* account of the fake news story about Hillary Clinton in Section 4.11.2 (also referred to as #Pizzagate – Aisch et al., 2016). Look for Wardle's three elements in the story about Pizzagate to see if they help make sense of what occurred.

Activity 4.10

4.8.4 Comedy news shows

We should also consider comedy news media that engage with genuine current events for the purpose of informing and entertaining. These shows have often been referred to as 'fake news' even though the content was real (Zimmer et al., 2017). *The Daily Show* and *Full Frontal* in the US and *The Daily Mash* and *Have I Got News for You* in the UK are examples of parody news television programming (see also Section 3.9). 'The starting premise of the [comedy style] fake news routine often begins with real journalism' (Borden and Tew, 2007: 306). Therefore 'Fake in the sense of "counterfeit" does not apply to these programmes' (2007: 306). Borden and Tew explain that these programmes 'parody the news while simultaneously presenting and criticising it' (2007: 306), as we saw in the example from Section 3.9.1 from *Last Week Tonight*. This genre of programme can even be found in countries where presenting this kind of news programme is risky because of the critiques they present (e.g., *Parazit* in Iran, *Al Bernameg* in Egypt, *ChistoNEWS* in Ukraine).

4.9 SUMMARY

In this chapter, our concern has been with the role that the mass media plays in society and the power it exercises. We have described how the mass media constructs and exercises its power by paying attention to the way information is filtered and represented, how ideology is recoverable through analysis of lexical and syntactic choices and how news stories are structured in order to present a particular point of view. Individual choices (at the level of lexis and syntax) interact with each other and build to a single interpretation of the facts. What counts as an expert in the mass media was also considered. This demonstrates that experts are constructed by the media, and that expertise is not something a person has, but something they are given. This construction of expertise can also be seen when considering Twitter and the citizen journalist. We have also explored the way the traditional media producers choose what to cover. The concept of 'news values' explains why news producers consider some events to be newsworthy while others are not. The move of mass media from print-based publications to the World Wide Web has changed some aspects of news production and consumption. However, it is important to remember that even though information is presented through a different technology, the linguistic and ideological choices made are still relevant. Indeed, given the fast pace of news online, the power that such media exerts is even stronger. The more we understand about how mass media works, the better we can adjust our literacy practices and therefore our understanding of the texts we consume.

FURTHER READING

Bednarek, M. (2016b) Voices and values in the news: News media talk, news values and attribution. *Discourse, Context & Media*, 11: 27–37.

Briant, E., Watson, N., and Philo, G. (2013) Reporting disability in the age of austerity: The changing face of media representation of disability and disabled people in the United Kingdom and the creation of new 'folk devils', *Disability & Society*, 28(6): 874–889.

Chouliaraki, L. (2006) Towards an analytics of mediation, *Critical Discourse Studies*, 3(2): 153–178.

Irwin, A. (2008) Race and ethnicity in the media, in Blain, N. and Hutchison, D. (eds.) *The Media in Scotland*. Edinburgh: Edinburgh University Press: 199–212.

Miller, L. (2004) Those naughty teenage girls: Japanese Kogals, Slang, and media assessments, *Journal of Linguistic Anthropology*, 14(2): 225–247.

Philo, G., Briant, E., and Donald, P. (2013) *Bad News for Refugees*. London: Pluto.

Thornborrow, J. (2001) Authenticating talk: Building public identities in audience participation broadcasting, *Discourse Studies*, 3(4): 459–479.

NOTE

1   Thank you to Karla Pandelus, who sourced the original print edition of the *Sydney Morning Herald*.

CHAPTER 5

Linguistic landscapes

5.1 INTRODUCTION

In Chapter 1, we considered the question 'What is language?' In this chapter, we are concerned with the question 'Where is language?' Language is all around us. When we speak, we use language; when we write and read, we're also using language. Recently, linguists have become particularly interested in the use of language in the everyday semiotic landscape, in what might normally be considered banal or mundane contexts. We begin by explaining what the linguistic landscape is, and in contrast to the abstract signs we investigated in Chapter 2, we explore types of concrete signs and their authors. We consider multilingual linguistic landscapes, the ideologies and power hierarchies that signs communicate and the different meanings of graffiti. The importance of the virtual landscape is then examined to show how signs communicate in this context as well as how the division between online and offline linguistic landscapes is collapsing.

5.2 DEFINING THE LINGUISTIC LANDSCAPE

In cities and towns around the world, there is an abundance of linguistic and other **semiotic** material. Alongside official signage indicating street names, traffic regulations and building numbers, there is a wealth of material that people may or may not pay attention to. Advertising billboards, posters and handwritten notices are placed all around us; they are all part of the linguistic landscape.

Scholars working in the field of linguistic landscapes (LL) and semiotic landscapes (SL) have directed their attention to the use of language and other meaningful objects in the construction of space. It's worth taking a moment to think about what 'construction of space' means.

Imagine you're blindfolded and taken to a public space somewhere. When the blindfold is removed, how would you know where you are?

In the scenario in Activity 5.1, you would probably quite quickly figure out what kind of place you were in. You might look for street signs, the names of roads and directions to other places. From this, you may be able to orient yourself. If you happened to be placed in another country, you would be able to deduce this simply from the way the signs were composed, from their typeface, colour and size. You might look for shop signs, to try to find something familiar. If you found yourself inside a building, the surroundings may also indicate where you are. You would probably be able to tell if you were in a government office, for example, or a bus station. Language and other semiotic features help us understand what kind of space we're in.

Research in LL studies the way 'linguistic objects . . . mark the public space' (Ben-Rafael, Shohamy, Mara and Trumper-Hecht, 2006: 7) and the '*symbolic construction of the public space*' (Ben-Rafael et al., 2006: 10, emphasis in original). In the introduction to the first issue of the journal *Linguistic Landscapes*, Shohamy and Ben-Rafael write:

> The main goal of LL studies is to describe and identify systematic patterns of the presence and absence of languages in public spaces and to understand the motives, pressures, ideologies, reactions and decision making of people regarding the creation of LL in its varied forms.
>
> (2015: 1)

For example, researchers might consider signage, the languages in which they are written, who produced them and to whom they are directed. It is useful when looking at the linguistic landscape to draw a distinction between official and non-official signs. Official signs are usually produced by the government, local councils or the owner of a building or site. The messages that they convey can be described as 'top-down' discourses (Ben-Rafael et al., 2006: 10). In contrast, signs produced by individuals or small groups can usually be identified on the basis of the message and the form of the sign. These can be described as 'bottom-up' discourses. Image 5.1 is an example of a top-down message because it is posted by the government. In Wales, all official signage is bilingual so the text is in English and Welsh. Note that this use of 'bottom-up' and 'top-down' does not relate to the placement of English and Welsh on the sign itself.

The difference between 'top-down' and 'bottom-up' discourses can be seen in Image 5.2 and Image 5.3.

Image 5.1 Bilingual Welsh sign

Image 5.2 Official no smoking sign

Image 5.3 Hand-drawn no smoking sign

Immediately, one can see that Image 5.2 is an official sign. The standard typeface, the normal no smoking icon and the reference to 'this station and its platforms' immediately communicates that it is official and a top-down discourse. It has been professionally produced, and the use of the passive, 'have been designated', points to the authority authoring the sign. In addition to asking people not to smoke, it demonstrates its authority to make such a request. Note, however, that there is actor deletion. We have to infer who the authority is.

In contrast, the picture in Image 5.3 is a hand-drawn sign on a single piece of A4 paper. It is immediately identifiable as a bottom-up discourse. This sign was posted outside a university building, next to an official no smoking sign. It would be reasonable to hypothesise that this sign has been created by an individual wanting to add their voice to the official signage on the same wall. It is then possible to interpret it as a personal plea not to smoke in this space.

Kress and van Leeuwen argue that we can apply strategies to further interpret visual material. Specifically, we can treat it in a similar way to reading written texts and think about it in terms of given and new information. We discussed this in relation to Greek word order in Section 2.3.3. Given and new is about the **syntagmatic** structure of language. In writing, we expect a writer to start with what is already known or 'given' before moving to new information. We can transfer this understanding to visual signs. Thus, the left-hand side of an image or a page can be understood as 'given' and that on the right as 'new' (1996). Kress and van Leeuwen argue that we can understand content at the top as 'ideal' and content at the bottom as 'real'. This works particularly well for large billboards or full page advertisements in magazines. The claims for the product will often be at the top (ideal) while information about how to contact the vendor will be at the bottom (real). These strategies do vary across cultures, however, because of different reading practices; not all languages are written left to right. As Scollon and Scollon caution, 'there is always a danger of overgeneralising from closely situated semiotics to broader social, cultural, or universal categories' (2003: 159–160).

In analysing the linguistic landscape, we also have to consider the paradigmatic access of language and transitivity analysis (see Section 2.6.1). That is, in order to determine what the sign means, we need to think about the other choices that have been made (in terms of words, images, colour and so on). Further, if there are people represented, you can also ask 'who is doing what to whom' and apply a kind of transitivity analysis to the image.

Image 5.4 Harrogate sign

In Image 5.4, the public are told
RESTRICTIONS ON DRINKING ALCOHOL APPLY IN THIS AREA

> Analyse the words in Image 5.4 using transitivity analysis. What does this suggest about the author of the sign and its purpose?

Activity 5.2

We can see that this sentence is quite hard to deal with, as there are no people in it. Someone must have authorised the restrictions, but we have to go outside the main message to see that it was authorised by Harrogate Borough Council (Harrogate is a town in England). The line at the top 'Criminal Justice and Police Act 2001' is also part of this authorisation. Councils have to invoke a particular kind of legal authority in order to impose restrictions like these. In this case, the council draws its authority from a law: the Criminal Justice and Police Act.

If we isolate the verb, 'apply', we can see that 'restrictions on drinking alcohol' is in the position we normally find an *agent* (a person doing something). But it's not really an agent. The *circumstances* are straightforward, 'in this area'. If we were to have an agent, the sentence would have to be something like 'Someone has applied restrictions on drinking alcohol in this area'. But we have to reconstruct the agent, Harrogate Borough Council, from outside the sentence.

Visual signs, and legal signs in particular, have their own structure. As members of a community, we usually have the necessary literacy (see Section 4.1) to figure out whether a sign is official or not.

5.2.1 Space and meaning

The signs in Images 5.2 and 5.3 both tell us something about the space in which they are located and about the sign maker. Paying attention to the features of these signs enables you to attend to the 'symbolic functions of language [which] help to shape geographical spaces into social spaces' (Leeman and Modan, 2009: 336). The very presence of the signs alters the space where they are found. The meaning the sign conveys also depends on where it is placed. This is why Scollon and Scollon emphasise the 'material placement' of signs as a key concern when analysing them. They call this mode of analysis geosemiotics.

> **Geosemiotics**: the study of the social meaning of the material placement of signs in the world. By 'signs' we mean to include any semiotic system including language and discourse.
>
> (Scollon and Scollon, 2003: 110)

Where a sign is placed tells us something about its meaning and the intentions of the sign maker. It is also worth noting the importance of where signs are placed in two other respects. First, signs need to be well-placed in relation to the information they convey. We have all had the experience of looking at a sign with an arrow and not being sure where it is pointing. The **deictic** nature of these signs means they need to be carefully placed in order to fulfil their informative function (see Denis and Pontille, 2010); *'the sign only has meaning because of where it is placed in the world'* (Scollon and Scollon, 2003: 29 emphasis in original). A stop sign in the middle of a field, even though it has all the features of an official traffic sign, has a very different meaning to one at a street corner.

All of the signs and symbols take a major part of their meaning from how and where they are placed – at that street corner, at that time in the history of the world. Each of them indexes a larger discourse whether of public transport regulation or underground drug trafficking.

(Scollon and Scollon, 2003: 2)

This is particularly clear in terms of regulatory and top-down signs. As we saw in Image 5.4, official signs index, that is, they point to, the authority able to create and place these signs. Moreover, the placing of signs can define a boundary.

Mautner argues that physical signs can function as 'boundary markers ... playing an important part in carving up space into public and private areas, and into zones where it is permissible to enact some social roles (e.g., cyclist or angler), but not others (e.g., busker or dog-walker)' (2012: 190). The drawing of these boundaries depends on the deictic function of signs. We can see this boundary drawing in Image 5.4. It is rather vague 'in this area'. But this phrase nevertheless marks out a space. Sometimes, we have to infer the space being referred to.

Image 5.5 No ladders

Image 5.5 is a photo of a sign on a lamppost. The sign can't possibly be a prohibition on the use of ladders in general, and so we infer that it is telling us not to use ladders on this lamppost.

As well as creating boundaries and defining space, signs index other meanings, discourses and messages. As we noted earlier, Scollon and Scollon suggest that signs index a 'larger discourse' (Scollon and Scollon, 2003: 2). For example, the no-smoking signs (Images 5.2 and 5.3) point to at least two other discourses. The first is the rather widespread ban on smoking in public spaces. In many countries, it is now illegal to smoke in workplaces, public buildings and even on public streets. The presence of a conventional, official no smoking sign indexes the laws that brought these bans into effect. The second discourse is the stigmatisation of smoking. Since widespread smoking bans have taken effect, smoking is now a more stigmatised practice than it was. This may explain the hand-drawn image in Image 5.3. In any case, the illegality of smoking in many places has perhaps made it more acceptable to ban it in other spaces.

In public spaces, people are often urged to behave in a particular way. Whether this relates to putting rubbish in bins, covering your mouth when coughing or safely crossing the road, many of these interventions are useful in spaces with multiple users. Traffic signs, to take the most obvious example, allow road users to co-exist in a reasonably safe manner. While traffic signs play an important regulatory function, they also provide motorists and pedestrians with a clear understanding of what is appropriate and what is not. The line between law and good behaviour in this domain is not always clear. A pedestrian can cross a road without a designated crossing in many countries without breaking the law. They may nevertheless be breaking the rules of what counts as good behaviour from a pedestrian. In other transport domains, particularly public transport, signs may urge passengers to behave in appropriate ways. In order to have maximum effect, these signs may be organised into a wider campaign.

All signs, but particularly top-down official signs, structure space through boundary marking and by indexing other discourses. Such structuring of space is an exercise of power and is ultimately ideological. This does not mean, however, that it might not have positive intentions or effects.

5.2.2 Different kinds of signs

To understand the range of signs we encounter in the linguistic landscape, considering the distinction between top-down and bottom-up, even with attention to materiality is not enough. Scollon and Scollon (2003: 217) provide four categories of discourses that signs invoke:

- ■ Regulatory discourses – traffic signs or other signs indicating official/ legal prohibitions
- ■ Infrastructural discourses – directed to those who maintain the infrastructure (water, power etc) or to label things for the public (e.g. street names)
- ■ Commercial discourses – advertising and related signage
- ■ Transgressive discourses – 'a sign which violates (intentionally or accidentally) the conventional semiotics at that place such as a discarded snack food wrapper or graffiti; any sign in the "wrong space"'

(Scollon and Scollon, 2003: 217)

Note that these categories may overlap. The hand-drawn no smoking sign in Image 5.3 does seem to be regulatory. But as it's not top-down, it can also be considered transgressive. If we consider these categories together with the other characteristics we have considered, it is possible to be quite specific about the kinds of signs we find.

Activity 5.3

The next time you leave your house, try to document the signs you encounter on the way. This can be done on even a very short journey – and this is preferable, as some spaces have a great proliferation of signs. Note the signs you see and mark on a map where you found them. How many are official top-down signs? How many are bottom-up and of what kind? It may help to use Scollon and Scollon's four categories. What does this tell you about the space you're in? What kind of people are in the space? What kinds of activities take place there?

5.2.3 Top-down and bottom-up as a continuum

It is not always easy to know where to draw the line between top-down and bottom-up. Ben-Rafael et al. (2006), for example, suggest the signs on individual shops are 'bottom-up', as these allow for personal choice in their composition and display (2006). However, within the context of the shop itself, they could be regarded as top-down. Leeman and Modan (2009) argue that the

> distinction between top-down and bottom-up signage practices is untenable in an era in which public-private partnerships are the main vehicle of urban revitalisation initiatives in urban centres in many parts of the world and when government policies constrain private sector signage practices.
>
> (2009: 334)

Nevertheless, if the distinction is thought of as a continuum whose orientation points may shift in different contexts, it is still helpful in understanding how signs are constructed and consumed.

The distinction between top-down and bottom-up can also be supplemented by other factors in order to figure out how to read the sign. For example, the materiality of a sign may give some clues to its status and legitimacy. This is the case with the sign in Image 5.3 (the hand-drawn smoking sign). However, sometimes official signs, authored by the government or a local government body, depart from semiotic choices we may associate with top-down discourses, as in Image 5.6. The text on this sign, found in a nature reserve, appears to be informational. But the semiotic choices are playful and child-like. The background is black, and the words are in different pastel colours (suggesting chalk on a chalkboard). We know it is an official sign, however, as it has 'rspb' in the bottom left-hand corner – the acronym of the UK's Royal Society for the Protection of Birds.

Image 5.6 Nettles

The next sign, Image 5.7, is also an example of an official and top-down sign.

Image 5.7 Littering

Rather than tell people what the penalties might be, this sign seeks to shame them into not littering. The list of choices given for why one might litter are hardly flattering, and we are not given an 'Other' choice. The humour here may well draw people's attention and result in their compliance. This style of persuasion is not expected from an official sign.

It is also likely that we attend to signs with specific features more than we might otherwise. The sign in Image 5.8 was found in a women's bath-room in a theatre in Vancouver, British Columbia. The fact that it is metal and screwed to the wall tells the audience it is permanent and therefore, perhaps, important. The use of a standard serif typeface and the use of the symbol conventionally used to prohibit something (a red circle with a line through it) all suggest that authority stands behind what is ultimately a request to consider the experience of others.

Image 5.8 Ladies' bathroom sign

Image 5.8, the sign in the women's bathroom urges women to be considerate of other patrons. This kind of signage doesn't specifically prohibit something; rather, it asks the audience to behave in a particular way. Public transport spaces also contain many such signs. See if you can find examples on buses, trains or trams or in transport hubs (bus and train stations, bus stops and so on).

Sometimes, the top-down and bottom-up are found on the same sign. This is clear when an official sign (top-down) is altered in some way by the public (bottom-up). These alterations may pass judgement on the authors of the sign and their actions or on a social issue of wider significance (see Image 5.9).

Additions to signs such as the one in Image 5.9 and Image 5.10 bear some resemblance to graffiti. Whether or not you think such alteration is acceptable depends very much on your attitude to the original sign and to the intervention of individuals in public sign space. We consider this in the following.

Image 5.9 Stop sign

Image 5.10 was taken in Barcelona.[1] Maps provided by the city in the street (presumably to help tourists navigate the city) have had large stickers added to them. These stickers have a skull and crossbones and the words 'Tourism kills'. The choice of English for this message suggests that the intended audience are not the local people but rather tourists themselves (given the state of English as a global lingua franca, see Chapter 10).

Image 5.9 and 5.11 exploit the conventions of top-down signs to creatively intervene in the everyday space of signs. What is particularly striking about examples like this is that the audience may not immediately notice that there has been an intervention. Because traffic signs are part of our everyday semiotic landscape, we expect to see signs telling us to stop or give way or indicating the speed limit. Therefore, we don't read them in detail because we don't need to. The artists' interventions capitalise on the conventional

Image 5.10 Tourism kills

Image 5.11 High fives: Ryan Laughlin

nature of traffic signs in order disrupt the everyday LL. This may well be entertaining and invite passers-by to look at their environment in a new way and may also critique the top-down control of the built environment.

5.3 SIGNS AND MULTILINGUALISM AND POWER

Scholars studying LL are often concerned with questions of multilingualism and uncovering the everyday communicative strategies of the people who actually use a particular space. It is important to consider a whole range of signs and semiotics in relation to each other, across a landscape. This is particularly valuable when considering power. Considering multilingualism in LL can also tell us about the languages used by inhabitants of those spaces and whether this 'matches' up with the 'official language'. While multilingualism is a rich field of research in LL, we can explore it only briefly here.

In Image 5.1, we saw a sign from a nation that is officially bilingual. The inclusion of both Welsh and English on this official, top-down sign shows that there are now two official languages in Wales (May, 2011). Official recognition of a language is an important marker of power and acknowledgement by those in authority. In places where the official language is contested, the languages included on this kind of top-down signage is a subject of intense debate (Heller, 2006). Official language policies represent all aspects of the linguistic landscape (Ben-Rafael et al., 2006). Nevertheless, regardless of what those in power claim about the linguistic profile of their community, the linguistic landscape is a testament to the languages actually being used in a place. That is, it may not be the case that the only languages used in a community are the 'official' languages and close examination of the linguistic landscape can reveal languages that would otherwise be invisible.

5.3.1 Invisible language

Some research on linguistic landscapes focuses on the range of different languages with specific attention to their presence and the ways they are used. This can provide insight into linguistic diversity not captured by official top-down discourses or even by official audits (e.g., a census). Blommaert (2013) describes the linguistic landscape of his local community in a part of Antwerp, Belgium. This area, Berchem, is 'predominantly Turkish and Belgian ... both groups being the most visible (and audible) ones there' (2013: 46). While he notes that there has been some Chinese migration to the area, 'it is not Chinatown' (2013: 46). When conducting his ethnography, however, he documents a handwritten sign in Chinese script found in the window of an empty shop. It advertises a flat to rent. Because it is written in Chinese, it is clearly addressed to a Chinese audience. But careful examination shows that its meaning is not straightforward.

The Chinese sign is written 'in a mixture of traditional Mandarin script (used in, e.g. Taiwan, Hong Kong and most of the traditional Chinese diaspora), and simplified script (used in the People's Republic)' (Blommaert, 2013: 45). Blommaert points out that this may suggest that the author is not fully competent in either form or is trying to accommodate to a likely audience. Because this sign is placed on the inside of a window, it communicates more than simply a flat for rent. It adds to the semiotic landscape and claims ownership of the space in which it is placed (even if only a very small space) (Blommaert, 2013: 46), suggesting an emergent, or otherwise invisible, Chinese network.

Multilingualism in a community may have several sources. We show how this might happen by considering the language and sign choices in Image 5.12.

Image 5.12 Mondo Macho

Image 5.12 was taken in Arles, France. From the sign directing people to hotels, we can already deduce something about this place. The names of the hotels are in French; we know we are in a French-speaking area (though this need not be France). That there are directions to six hotels suggests that this is a tourist area. The design of these signs suggests they are not made by each individual hotel; they are not just advertising signs, or commercial signs in Scollon and Scollon's terms. They are more like official street signs, directing people to the relevant local tourist infrastructure – hotels. They have an 'informing' function (Blommaert, 2013: 54).

The shop front in the background, however, is a form of advertising, with a 'recruitment' function (Blommaert, 2013: 54). This shop sign, like many others, announces '(a) the kind of transactions performed in that place, (b) the kinds of audiences targeted for such transactions' (Blommaert, 2013: 54). Shop signs take many different forms.

Have a closer look at the signs for hotels and the shop front in Image 5.12. Did you notice the other texts? How would you classify them?

There is also some regulatory text on a barrier behind the hotel sign. Whether this barrier is out of place (waiting to be moved to and thus regulate another space) or whether it belongs there is not clear from the photo. Finally, there is more text on the shop window. Unlike the signs painted on the glass, one is written 'femme' (woman) directly on the glass by hand and the other has been written on a piece of paper and then fixed to the inside of the window. This sign is in French, 'Boutique a vendre', communicating that the shop is for sale. As this is written in French, it seems to be addressed to the local, rather than tourist, population.

5.4 SIGNS AND IDEOLOGY

So far we have considered single instances of signs. But signs can also be part of a broader multimodal communicative strategy or movement. The following example features the Umbrella Movement to show how the linguistic landscape influences and is influenced by public participation. The Umbrella Movement refers to a grassroots pro-democracy protest that took place in Hong Kong over four months (September to December) in 2014. The protest involved hundreds of thousands of protesters occupying several sections of Hong Kong for 79 days as a reaction against changes to voting eligibility that had been made in Hong Kong. The movement is an example of a bottom-up organisation that has no formal leadership or structure but that nevertheless was able to mobilise thousands of people and attract global attention.

While other 'Occupy' movements have described themselves in terms of the places they occupied (e.g., Occupy Wall Street), the name 'Umbrella Movement' was picked up early in the events because protestors used umbrellas to protect themselves from tear gas and pepper spray used by police (Lou and Jaworski, 2016: 611). This long and heated protest had an impact on linguistic landscapes in Hong Kong. Lou and Jaworski report:

> [T]he Umbrella movement was marked by an intense production and display of signs, posters, banners, flyers, stencils, graffiti, stickers, cartoons, comics, scrolls, road signs, petitions, photographs, postcards, personal messages, post-it notes, prayers, artworks (including sculptures

and installations, children's art, chalk drawings etc.), t-shirts, board games, newspaper pages, maps, flags, toys (e.g. toy umbrellas), jewelry (e.g. necklaces with beads and yellow ribbons), balloons, and wide range of other ephemera.

(Lou and Jaworski, 2016: 612)

The wide and varied placement of these items in addition to a range of temporary structures constructed by the protesters in the occupied neighbourhoods changed the nature of the space that was being occupied.

Many of the protest signs were written in Cantonese. This is the most frequently used language in the city despite its status as 'merely a "dialect" when spoken and a "non-standard" variety when written' (Lou and Jaworski, 2016: 614). Using Cantonese for the signs is therefore a significant choice (ibid). In addition, some signs were written in English, perhaps suggesting that protesters were addressing English speakers in Hong Kong or even global audiences. Not only was the protest covered by international news media, it was live-streamed and people shared images and thoughts on social media and blogs and YouTube films (ibid).

Another common sign in the UM read 'I want true universal suffrage' (我要真普選; Lou and Jaworski, 2016: 637). The sign included a simple umbrella shape at the top with #umbreallamovement at the bottom. It was originally in the form of a very large banner and was hung at Lion Rock (October 23, 2015).

> The location of the banner's first appearance is highly charged for Hong Kongers as it evokes 'Lion Rock Spirit' which used to represent the resilience and unity of grassroots Hong Kong society in the face of hardship during the 1970s and 1980s while Hong Kong was still a British colony.
> (Lou and Jaworski, 2016: 637)

The significance of this initial placement is thus imbued in the meaning of the sign. The 'Lion Rock' sign was widely reproduced and used in various places. These uses were in turn documented and shared on social media. Together with the umbrella, it became the 'default slogan' of the movement.

The umbrella was interpreted in a very different way by the police, who saw it as a weapon. This argument, however, fuelled parody through the sharing of clips from martial arts films in which an umbrella is used as a weapon (ibid). As Lou and Jaworski note, the umbrella became an icon; it was turned 'from a mundane object and a tool of self-defence to a symbol of the movement' (2016: 634–635). It can be considered a 'brand' for the movement (Lou and Jaworski, 2016: 635) in that it was widely taken up, easy to produce, reproduce and recognise. As mentioned, it was also turned into a commodity that could be purchased in acts of positive affiliation. Lou and Jaworski explain that the symbols of the movement were co-constructed. That is, while people shared documentation of the actual protest online, material originally produced online also made its way into the physical protest space.

The re-interpretation of the umbrella image was so consistent and so widespread that what this image means has fundamentally changed so that, in addition to referring to an object that protects one from the rain, in Hong Kong (and those spaces that are connected with the UM, whether in the 'real' world or online), the umbrella now has an additional meaning.

5.5 TRANSGRESSIVE SIGNS: GRAFFITI

We defined a transgressive sign 'as a sign which violates (intentionally or accidentally) the conventional semiotics at that place, such as a discarded snack food wrapper or graffiti; any sign in the "wrong space"' (Scollon and Scollon, 2003: 217). Here, we focus on one kind of transgressive sign, graffiti, in order to demonstrate some of the different meanings it can have. We're especially interested in transgressive signs because they provide marginalised people a voice in public space. Transgressive signs thus provide a measure of agency for people without conventionally recognised power.

Carrington (2009) notes that graffiti is 'an unsanctioned urban text', one that 'sits in direct competition with the sanctioned texts displayed in the production of commercial advertising, shop front signs, street signs and noticeboards' (2009: 410). The fact that graffiti is present at all may suggest that the space is contested in some way (see Image 5.9). And while Carrington describes graffiti as 'vernacular', we can also understand it in relation to the bottom-up scheme described earlier. As these signs are not top-down, they allow the viewer to see the contributions of other people to the built environment. Graffiti points to the existence of people engaged with their environment in an active way.

A sign may contain both 'commercial graffiti' and 'non-commercial graffiti' (Lee, 2000 cited in Carrington, 2009: 411–412). The former is 'about authority and control of public spaces and buildings in a consumer culture and can be found on most city surfaces' while 'non-commercial graffiti' is 'an alternative system of public communication' (Lee cited in Carrington, 2009: 411–412). Both mark out space and ownership of space. Both comment either on that space or the world more generally. But while we generally know how to read commercial graffiti and generally agree on how it should be understood, not everyone reads non-commercial graffiti in the same way. One of the key differences between them is that commercial graffiti is paid for; the textual space is purchased in some way and is therefore considered to be legitimate.

Carrington argues that the 'imperative for these ways of writing on the city revolves around voice, identity and space' (2009: 417). Graffiti seeks to claim back space that has been colonised by commercial signage for ordinary people to mark and comment on the spaces they inhabit.

It is loud: it screams from the walls 'I am here and I want you to know'. It screams 'I don't respect your boundaries – textual or spatial'. It is hypervisible – large, messy, prominent, strategically transgressive, dismissive of private ownership and corporate power – and therefore directly reminds us of the inter-medial nature of text. Our eyes see its visual qualities as well as convert it to meaning chunks.

(Carrington, 2009: 418)

Graffiti is a way for disempowered people to make a visible mark, to disrupt the landscape that is increasingly occupied by the more and more powerful. Carrington argues that it creates a **narrative** and is a form of 'participatory culture'. The people who live in the space provide evidence of their experiences, views and actions. In this sense, it is a form of citizenship, not unlike the silly citizenship described in Chapter 3. It allows for the visibility of a hidden community and allows this community to see itself in its environment.

5.6 ONLINE LANDSCAPES

The division between 'online landscape' and 'physical landscape' is becoming harder to distinguish. This means that the linguistic landscape isn't confined to the physical landscape. The blurring of the distinction between the physical world and the online world can be seen in the Pokemon Go phenomenon that occurred in July 2016. Pokemon Go is a game that uses a mobile phone to find and 'capture, fight and train' different Pokemon creatures. Participants can view the virtual creatures placed in the physical world by looking at the screen of their mobile phone, which produces a virtual visual overlay of the Pokemon creatures onto the users' current physical world. The creature therefore appears to be present in the same physical world of the user at that moment. Other examples that blur the line of physical landscapes can be found in museums where exhibits are enhanced by allowing visitors to integrate exhibit material with physical reality (see, for example, http://startrekblackpool.co.uk/).

In Section 5.2–5.5, we considered how, as you walk through the street, you are exposed to an abundance of linguistic and other semiotic material which we call a linguistic landscape. In the same way, when you engage in online searches, online shopping, social media, computer-mediated communication and so on, you are 'walking through' a virtual landscape where you are exposed to linguistic and other semiotic material. Seeing the online environment as a landscape allows us to pay full attention to the semiotic choices made by the actors within that space as well as the new spaces created in these environments. In addition, this virtual landscape is further embedded in the 'real' linguistic landscape as we juxtapose our electronic communication devices with the material world. For example, people tend to take their mobile devices with them and check them often when they are at work, with friends or walking down the street. It seems, therefore, important to consider the online environment as part of the 'public space' we move through as a linguistic landscape.

In Section 5.2, we noted some of the key features that we look for in linguistic landscapes, such as patterns of language and signs in public spaces, top-down and bottom-up discourses, emplacement and ideology. We can find online parallels to several of the features in the linguistic landscapes of the material world.

The online landscape and the signs found there, however, may require some different analytic tools to those used before. For example, the platforms used to deliver information have a variety of effects on how the virtual linguistic landscape is constructed and interpreted. To understand the ideologies, power hierarchies and potential for agency found in the online linguistic landscape, we need to understand the different kinds of virtual spaces, how they are constructed and what users can do with them. We'll see that there is much more scope for bottom-up discourses and the creation of personal narratives because social hierarchies are somewhat 'flattened' online. In addition, the large number of 'observers' and the global reach of online landscapes complicates the design and consumption of signs online.

5.6.1 Twitter

Having discussed Twitter in Chapter 4, we can think here about how this platform as a virtual landscape has changed our linguistic landscape. The types of 'signs' one finds in this virtual landscape depend on the platform but also on the choices the user makes. An individual's experience of Twitter, for example, will depend on who they are following, which hashtags they are interested in and so on (see Section 4.7). Moreover, the way people use Twitter can vary widely. It may be used for keeping up with developments in your work and career, making sure your train is running on time, following your favourite singer or interacting with friends. Twitter, and other online platforms, provides opportunities (though always with some limitations) and resources for making choices in how we create a personalised linguistic and semiotic landscape. Gillen and Merchant refer to these choices in terms of constructing a 'point of view' (2013: 51).

The different ways people use language (e.g., T. Jones, 2015) or what people think about language is sometimes visible on Twitter. Vessey (2016) discovered a range of language ideologies (see Section 2.5) when she researched Tweets made about a controversy in Montreal (2016). The controversy involved the owner of an Italian restaurant, Massimo Lecas, and the fact that he had included the English word 'pasta' in his menu. Because the official language in Montreal is French, he received a letter from the Office Quebecois de la Langue Française (OQLF) objecting to his use of English and other 'linguistic offences' in the menu. Lecas shared a photo of the letter on Twitter and Instagram. A local journalist raised interest in the story by retweeting and reporting on the story on his radio blog, resulting in it becoming an international story referred to as 'pastagate'.

Vessey's analysis of the Tweets about pastagate found that the OQLF policies were mocked, and many expressed profound disagreement with the actions of the OQLF. This was, of course, not universal. Some questioned the behaviour of restaurant owners, but others expressed the idea that French needed to be protected from English (see Chapter 10). Vessey argues that this suggests 'evidence of ideologies of language endangerment, which presume that some languages require protection (and, indeed, that it is possible to protect them) because of ecological factors that threaten their existence' (2016: 20). Vessey also found a form of standard language ideology (see Section 1.4) in that 'a small number of French Tweets suggested that attention should be paid to the quality of French in Quebec . . .' (2016: 20).

The pastagate story had serious effects. The head of the OQLF resigned, and policy changes subsequently took place. Moreover, as Vessey writes, 'more than a year later the term [pastagate] is still frequently used to index anglocentric perspectives on Quebec news and events . . .' Vessey continues:

> What began as a story about one menu in one restaurant turned into a way of opposing language policy more generally, and Quebec politics too.
>
> (2016: 20)

As it is public, however, 'Like many social network sites, Twitter flattens multiple audiences into one – a phenomenon known as "context collapse"' (Marwick and boyd, 2011: 122). A tweet you compose with a friend in mind may nevertheless be read by your boss. This means that communicating on Twitter is quite different from engaging in a conversation with visible participants. The Montreal restaurant owner likely didn't consider that his tweet might be shared and be read by a larger audience than his own followers. Some users are more aware of this context collapse. Marwick and boyd explore how people with large followings on Twitter 'manage' their audience and construct their own identity and found that while some tweeters report that they do not have an imagined audience in mind, others carefully design what they tweet in order to construct a particular identity in this context. And while the Twitter users that Marwick and boyd interviewed placed value on 'authenticity', they also engaged in self-censorship (not tweeting about some very personal things) and balancing personal information with more strategic posts (e.g., for building a brand or professional identity).

5.6.2 Instagram

Instagram has attracted much attention from scholars who view it as a good candidate for the kind of semiotic analysis that we use in relation to visual signs. Instagram is a digital platform for sharing visual material. As such, it is an interesting example of a virtual landscape. Instagram users post photos and short videos accompanied by hashtags (see Section 4.7).

Like on Twitter, Instagram users can follow and respond to other users. The most commonly shared images in Instagram include self-portraits, friends, activities, captioned photos, food and gadgets (Hu, Manikonda and

Kambhampati, 2014). Sheldon and Bryant (2016) suggest four main purposes for using Instagram:

■ 'Surveillance/Knowledge about others' – to find out what was going on and who was doing what and to interact with people
■ 'Documentation' of users' own lives
■ 'Coolness' – to construct a particular kind of identity
■ 'Creativity': 'showing off one's skills and finding people who have similar interests'

(2016: 93)

Sheldon and Bryant find that surveillance is the main purpose people use Instagram. As a means of information seeking and as a means of social interaction, it is an important part of the online linguistic (and visual) landscape. 'Documentation', 'Coolness', and 'Creativity' seem to suggest that users who create content on Instagram are motivated by the ability to present their own point of view (Gillen and Merchant, 2013: 51) about themselves and other topics in public space. The more flattened nature of hierarchies online allows people to do this in a way that is different from how it is done in the material world.

The point of view is certainly partly constructed by the image posted. The ability to tag posts with hashtags also helps to communicate a point of view. Instagram posts are tagged with hashtags (as in Twitter), but the convention in Instagram is to have more hashtags attached to a post than in a tweet. This makes it possible to convey both information and a personal view on that information. For example, Matley (2018) shows how users are able to post positive news about themselves without seeming to indulge in too much self-aggrandisement by including the hashtags #brag and #humblebrag. This allows the poster to signal that they are bragging, but because they are conscious of this bragging, the less attractive elements of this activity are reduced.

Multiple hashtags also allow users to tell a story. While the purpose of the (multiple) hashtags is to increase the number of people who see and pay attention to the post (as it is possible to follow and search for hashtags), they can also be put to other uses. Here, as with other forms of digital media, it is possible to apply the 'small stories' framework. While a narrative (a 'story' for our purposes) usually has a beginning, a middle and an end and takes some time to tell, a small story is rather more compact. Georgakopoulou describes the small story as follows:

under-represented and 'a-typical' narrative activities, such as tellings of ongoing events, future or hypothetical events, shared (known) events, but also allusions to tellings, deferrals of tellings, and refusals to tell.

(Georgakopoulou, 2006: 130)

That is, small stories may be fragments of what we might normally think of as narratives. Given the **multimodal** nature of Instagram, it is possible to tell a (small) story simply with an image and some hashtags. For example, you might post an image of a sunny sandy beach and attach the hashtags #holiday, #familytime, #livingthedream, #Barbados. The hashtags and the image allow your readers to know that you are on holiday in Barbados, relaxing on a lovely beach with your family and having a wonderful time. While the post may not look like a **narrative**, it provides enough in the way of information that a reader can reconstruct a story.

Like the Tweet from the restauranteur in Montreal (Section 5.6.2), sometimes the identities and narratives on Instagram are contested. In 2017, the wife of a US government official posted on Instagram a photo of her husband and herself getting off a US government aeroplane and included the following hashtags:

#daytrip, #Kentucky!, #nicest, #people, #beautiful, #countryside, #rolandmouret pants, #tomford sunnies, #hermesscarf, #valentinorockstudheels, #valentino, #usa

Presumably, the woman's purpose was what Sheldon and Bryant (2016) call 'Coolness' or identity construction. However, the post was harshly criticised for the hashtags describing her very expensive designer clothing. These hashtags were perceived by some viewers as an inappropriate flaunting of wealth by the wife of a government employee. The controversy was fuelled by further commentary as it spread via other forms of digital media. Thus the linkage of online platforms allows broader access to each of the platforms (e.g., those without an Instagram account nevertheless hear about those stories). This example also demonstrates the importance of 'material placement' (geosemiotics) in online linguistic landscapes. Imagine the reaction of an audience if the photo and hashtags had been posted on a blog for *Vogue* fashion magazine. The space in which the message is posted dramatically affects its meaning.

5.6.3 Emoji

Emojis are a good example of signs in the online landscape, as they can be seen as signs in terms of linguistic landscapes and in Saussure's terms (see Chapter 2). Emojis can be understood as the next generation of emoticons because they emerged from the use of emoticons. Emoticons draw on symbols available on a standard keyboard that are combined such that it is read as an image. For example, :) communicates a happy face. As technology allowed users to incorporate more sophisticated images in texts, emojis became widely used in digital communication and therefore a common feature of virtual landscapes. While these signs communicate emotion (e.g., through facial expressions), emojis may also appear to reference things (e.g., bunnies, telephones or food). However, what specific emojis communicate may well vary from person to person. Friends, for example, may have a 'secret language' of emoji that they use only among themselves. Indeed, in contrast to the assumption that the face emojis are the carriers of affect and emotion, Riordan (2017) found that even non-face emojis communicate emotion. She reports that it seems that even though such non-face emojis can't change a message from negative to positive, they nevertheless 'show many of the same effects as face emojis' (2017: 562). Emojis are now so much a part of our culture that there is a World Emoji Day (17 July). And far from indicating a decline in linguistic ability, Evans (2017) argues that emojis make people more effective communicators.

An important role that emojis have is to take the place of paralinguistic information. What might be conveyed with tone of voice, facial expressions or body language in a face-to-face setting may be conveyed through emoji. Thurlow calls this 'paralinguistic restitution' (see Chapter 8). Though emojis can perform paralinguistic restitution, Riordan (2017) reports that they are not always easy for a reader to translate and understand. Riordan (2017: 5) also points out that emojis can be 'seen as deliberate emotion expressions' and thus may not be understood as authentic. She explains:

> [T]he inclusion of a smiling emoticon at the end of a message is a deliberate act, which is understood more as an expression of feeling that may or may not be actual feeling. In that way, the emoticon is akin to the oft-used 'LOL' in which it is understood that the person who wrote it is not actually 'laughing out loud'; the cue serves as a polite response, an expression of intimacy by informality, a method of self-presentation, sarcasm, or other nonaffective relational purposes.
>
> (Riordan, 2017: 5)

5.6.4 Memes

The quick circulation of 'memes' (see Section 4.8.2) on the World Wide Web makes them another common feature of the virtual landscape.

> Memes are contagious patterns of 'cultural information' that get passed from mind to mind and directly generate and shape the mindsets and significant forms of behavior and actions of a social group. Memes include such things as popular tunes, catchphrases, clothing fashions, architectural styles, ways of doing things, icons, jingles and the like.
>
> (Knobel and Lankshear, 2007: 199)

As Deumert notes, the spread of material 'via personal networks is not new', but 'what is new is the speed and scale with which this happens' (2014: 87). Memes are a good example of this. In the online context, '"meme" is a popular term for describing the rapid uptake and spread of a particular idea presented as a written text, image, language "move", or some other unit of cultural "stuff"' (Knobel and Lankshear, 2007: 202). Memes are a striking example of extensive, bottom-up activity that changes the linguistic landscape.

Memes are a new kind of text production and consumption: they point to another kind of '**literacy**' (see Section 4 .1) that is needed to both produce and understand memes (Knobel and Lankshear, 2007: 203). What these skills are can be examined by looking at the 'doge' meme. The meme consists of a picture of a shiba inu dog accompanied by a series of words and short phrases. The words are in Comic Sans font and in bright, fluorescent colours. Anyone producing a doge meme would follow these formatting conventions. The construction of the phrases in the meme follows the pattern intensifier +adjective/noun. Intensifiers are usually words like 'so', 'very', 'much' and 'many'. This pattern is found in various examples of the meme and for those who are literate in the conventions of this meme, the phrases are immediately recognisable as doge phrases (McCulloch, 2014).

What makes doge phrases distinctive is that they don't obey the normal conventions of combination (McCulloch, 2014). Intensifiers normally used with nouns are used with adjectives and vice versa; thus we find 'much happy' and 'very word'. While the doge meme is clearly an internet phenomenon, it has not stayed within these virtual walls. Image 5.13 is a photo taken in a university library.

Image 5.13 Doge graffiti

Image 5.13 includes a doge phrase, 'much surprise' and a picture of a dog. Written beside it, 'You thought Doge would not appear?' makes clear the move from appearing in virtual space to a table in a library. While we certainly don't want to condone drawing on library furniture, this transgressive use of language suggests that the conventions of doge are not only well established but also well-travelled.

Knobel and Lankshear argue that 'replicability' is important to consider for online memes (2007: 208). This means they should be easy to copy. They should also have the feature of 'fecundity', which refers to the 'rate at which an idea or pattern is copied and spread' (2007: 202). Research on successful memes, that is, those which are picked up and reported on by mainstream media, suggests that memes should be humorous (though they may contain an element of satire or social commentary), be richly **intertextual** (referring to other texts, cultural products or practices see Section 3.5.5) and contain some kind of 'anomalous juxtaposition', that is, the placement of two mismatching or incongruous elements together (Knobel and Lankshear, 2007).

Memes can be used for other purposes too. Varis and Blommaert (2015) argue that while memes may not appear to communicate a 'real' message, they have an important function. They are a form of **phatic** communication. Phatic communication draws attention to the act of communicating for its own sake. Engaging in ritual greetings, small talk and discussion of the weather are all examples of phatic communication. The creation and sharing of memes is also a way to construct and communicate identity. We share memes with people we like and who we think will like and appreciate the meme. This does send a message. It communicates something like 'I like you, and we are like each other'. The creation, sharing and liking of memes is, as Varis and Blommaert argue, an important way of being social.

What is striking about memes is the linguistic and semiotic creativity involved in their creation and consumption. Their success, indeed their existence as memes, depends on a number of people consuming, circulating and building on the meme. They are indicative of a kind of semiotic democracy because the conventions they rely on are generated from the bottom-up and shared by a large number of people. Memes rely on a particular kind of literacy, a fluency in the **codes** and rules that inform the meme (see Section 4.1). Because of the online nature of these memes, they also require some facility with software, the manipulation of text, image and sound. Consuming the memes helps one to learn these rules and thus replicate and reproduce the meme by following the rules established by a collective.

5.7 SUMMARY

Understanding the linguistic landscape is important for understanding the spaces in which we live. While many of the signs we encounter on a typical day seem normal and inconsequential, they nevertheless communicate messages and convey ideological information that we tacitly consume. While some signs are clearly the preserve of the powerful, there are spaces in the linguistic landscape where other voices can be seen. These spaces may be understood as contested, but they show that space and place are more varied than we normally think. Examining signs, both in the 'real world' linguistic landscape and the virtual landscapes of the World Wide Web, shows us how people make meaning and understand the contributions of others. The increasing access to technology has made individual agency more visible. But we find these voices only if we know how to look. The tools described in previous chapters, together with those introduced here, allow us to examine the world in which we live in new ways.

FURTHER READING

Gawne, L. and Vaughan, J. (2011) I can haz language play: The construction of language and identity in LOLspeak, in Ponsonnet, M., Dao, L., and Bowler, M. (eds.) *Proceedings of the 42nd Australian Linguistic Society Conference*: 97–122; ANU Research Repository, http://hdl.handle.net/1885/9398

Jaworski, A. (2011) Linguistic landscapes on postcards: Tourist mediation and the sociolinguistics communities of contact, *Sociolinguistics Studies*, 4(3): 569–594.

Lazar, M. (2003) Semiosis, social change and governance: A critical semiotic analysis of a national campaign, *Social Semiotics*, 13(2): 201–221.

Lorenzo-Dus, N. and Di Cristofaro, M. (2016) #Living/minimum wage: Influential citizen talk in twitter, *Discourse, Context & Media*, 13: 40–50.

Lou, J. J. (2016) *The Linguistics Landscape of Chinatown: A Sociolinguistic Ethnography*. Bristol, UK: Multilingual Matters.

McElhinny, B. (2006) Written in Sand: Language and landscape in an environmental dispute in Southern Ontario, *Critical Discourse Studies*, 3(2): 123–152.

Trinch, S. and Snajdr, E. (2017) What the signs say: Gentrification and the disappearance of capitalism without distinction in Brooklyn, *Journal of Sociolinguistics*, 21(1): 64–89.

NOTE

1   Thank you to Dr Sarah Pasfield-Neofitou for providing us with all this material.

CHAPTER 6

Language and gender

6.1 INTRODUCTION

In this chapter, we examine language and gender. We begin by considering the meaning of 'gender' by contrasting it with 'sex'. We then turn to issues of hierarchies of gender groups in language. We explore the use of the generic 'he' and other lexical items that represent women less favourably than men as an example of inequality. We then look at different kinds of talk, including the form of communication known as gossip, in order to evaluate whether and how men and women use language differently. To examine the language of more deeply entrenched ideologies associated with gender, we then consider whether women talk more than men. Finally, we investigate how gender identity is performed through language and the connection between gender and sexuality.

6.2 WHAT IS GENDER?

There is a strong relationship between language and gender. In order to explore these relationships, there are a few key things to remember as you read this chapter. Firstly, we must establish what we mean by 'sex' and 'gender'. 'Sex' is generally defined as someone's biological state, that is, whether they are male or female. In the past, many linguists used the term 'sex' rather than 'gender' in research about language. In the first wave of linguistic studies of variation, academics were usually interested in broad patterns, across a large population. In this context, it makes sense to divide people according to their sex. However, other models developed to explain the linguistic differences found between individuals and this culminated in a recognition that sex is not always the best category of analysis. That is, sex is biological and gender is socially constructed. It is possible to be biologically female but talk 'like a man'. People can demonstrate their identities in various ways. It is not the case that all genders share the same fundamental qualities (whether in relation to language or anything else) simply because they are of the same biological sex. Instead of assuming biological categories (sex), referring to *socially constructed gender* allows us to make different distinctions and to talk about people as being more or less 'masculine' or 'feminine'. However, even this preserves a distinction that is not always helpful (as we tend to associate 'masculine' with male and 'feminine' with female). It is perhaps better to simply talk about how people construct their gender (Eckert, 2014).

Analysing behaviour as connected to socially constructed gender rather than sex is crucial in understanding the different ways people perform their identity as well as how they are judged. Sex is not the same as gender. Sex, as a biological category, may have little influence on how gender is constructed. Gender, then, is not something a person has or is born with; it is something they accomplish through their behaviour, clothing, habits and speech. Scholars often characterise this as 'performing' gender. Talking about gender in this way allows an understanding of people's behaviours in nuanced and detailed ways. And while it is true that a wide range of genders and gender performances are available, this does not mean they are all understood as equal. The current inequality of sexes (discussed in the following) is evident in the performance and interpretation of gender identity. We will see that there are certain expectations of people according to biological sex. Very often, however, in reality, people don't always conform to those expectations. The gender norms in a society generate conventions that people are judged against. There are dominant ideologies of gender that we all orient to, whether we agree with them or not. It is, of course, possible not to conform to these gender expectations, but there are often consequences for the individuals who do this.

We will see through our exploration of gender and language that inequality is an important factor underlying the linguistic patterns we find. Although most countries have legally recognised the equality of men and women, there are still pervasive examples of everyday **sexism**, and they can be easily found in language and society. For example, the Australian website *Women's Agenda* lists a number of 'awards' for the 'best' examples of sexism in 2016 (*Women's Agenda*, 2016). One of the 'winners' was the New South Wales Department of Education, 'For proposing that experienced School teachers who take 5 years off to have children be downgraded to beginner teacher salary when they return to work'. In 2017, in the UK, after revelations about gender pay differences at the BBC, Sir Philip Hampton commented that it probably happened 'because they [women] weren't doing much about it' (Urwin, Cecil and Dex, 2017: 1).

Activity 6.1

Find out how many of your political leaders are men and how many are women. What does this mean for the leadership of your city/province/country? Are all citizens equally represented?

It is very important to understand that despite the advances in equality of gender groups, complete equality has not yet been achieved.

6.3 INEQUALITY AT THE LEXICAL LEVEL

6.3.1 Marked terms

Activity 6.2

Consider the meaning of the following words:

master/madam
waiter/waitress
host/hostess
Bachelor/bachelorette/spinster

What do these words refer to? Now consider what they mean? Are men and women treated equally here?

There are a few differences between the terms referring to men and the 'equivalent' terms for women. If we consider the difference between 'bachelor' and 'spinster', while both refer to an 'unmarried adult', these terms represent different types of unmarried adults. If we consider how these terms are used, it becomes apparent that 'bachelor' has a positive meaning, while 'spinster' has a negative one. For example, common **collocations** for bachelor are 'eligible bachelor' or 'bachelor pad'. These collocations reflect a positive view of single life for men; their lifestyle is desirable, and they too are desirable. 'Spinster', in contrast, is more likely to be collocated with 'lonely' or 'old' and suggests an image of an older, unattractive woman. The two different terms for unmarried adult ('bachelor' and 'spinster') suggest more generally that being unmarried is a positive characteristic for a man but a negative one for a woman. The difference between 'bachelor' and 'spinster' and terms like this can be discussed in terms of lexical **asymmetry** because terms that are meant to be referring to equivalent positions for women and men are not actually used in the same way. These patterns of asymmetry generally go in one direction; the negative judgements are related to the female role (Schulz, 1975) but not the male one.

While 'bachelorette' is used in some varieties of English, it does not always have positive **connotations**. Moreover, it is also a **marked** term. A term is marked when it has a relationship with a seemingly 'neutral' and generic counterpart ('bachelor' versus 'bachelor*ette*'). For example, 'actor' is referred to as an 'unmarked' term because it refers to a male and actors in general. 'Actress', however, refers only to a female 'actor'. By having a different form to indicate only a female 'actor', it is 'marked'. In the context of gender, we find that terms referring to men are generally unmarked and considered neutral, while those referring to women are marked for sex. Similar examples are prince/princess, waiter/waitress, host/hostess and so on.

This marking would not be problematic if it were not for the asymmetry. Female occupation terms often have negative connotations. This can be seen in the 'master' and 'mistress' pair. While 'master' is a position of authority, 'mistress' has undertones of loose sexuality.

Asymmetry is found in other domains too. Consider the titles available to men and women in Example 6.1.

Example 6.1

Female	Male
Miss	Mr
Mrs	
Ms	

One might think that in the modern world, with high levels of divorce and the recognition of alternative lifestyles with respect to relationships, the use of titles would be less important. But many organisations still require you to indicate your title on a subscription form, order form, over the phone and so on. While women's titles indicate their marital status, the only title available to men is 'Mr', which provides no information about their relationship status at all. Occasionally, 'Master' will be available for males, although this tends to be restricted to young boys. The difference between Miss and Mrs is straightforward; Miss means an unmarried woman, and Mrs signals that the woman is married to a man. The meaning of 'Ms', interestingly, is rather more contested. It was initially proposed as a replacement for both 'Miss' and 'Mrs', so that women, like men, would only have one title that didn't refer to marital status. As often happens with words, Ms has taken on a range of other meanings according to the way it is used and how people understand it. It is often thought to indicate that a woman is divorced, a feminist, a lesbian or unmarried (Schwarz, 2003; see also Lawton, Blakemore and Vartanian, 2003). The result is that whatever choice of title a woman makes, information about her will be revealed. If she chooses 'Miss', it will be assumed that she is unmarried. The fact that men don't have to make this choice shows again the importance society places on marriage for women (as shown in the discussion of bachelor and spinster). If a woman chooses 'Ms', she may have very little control over what people think this means, exactly because of the range of meanings that Schwarz has identified. Again, this is not a choice men have to make. There is asymmetry in having to make a choice as well as what these choices may communicate.

In relation to the representation of women, however, Baker's research on Ms and other titles suggests that they are being used less than in the past (2010). Moreover, other sex and gender-neutral titles have also been proposed and are seeing some uptake. The most successful of these is Mx. Mallinson reports that Mx ('mix') dates from 1977, 'since then, in the 1980s and particularly in the 2000s, the LGBT community has advocated for *Mx.* as a term of **address** for transgender or non-gender-identifying individuals' (2017: 429). It seems to be more widely offered as an option in the UK than in the US (Rosman, 2015).

6.3.2 'Generic' he

In relation to some terms, especially occupation terms (e.g., host/hostess, manager/manageress), it is often argued that the male term is not really sexed but rather is generic and refers to both sexes. This, however, raises the question of why female marked terms are required at all. Some of the problems with supposed generic terms become clear when considering **pronouns**.

Activity 6.3

1 Every student should bring his books to class.
2 Every student should bring their books to class.
3 Everyone should cast his vote on polling day.
4 Everyone should cast their vote on polling day.
   Do the sentences in Activity 6.3 include women?

Prescriptivists might argue that (1) and (3) are the only acceptable forms. The suggestion that one could use 'their', as in (2) and (4) in these contexts, is met with the objection that such use would result in disagreement in terms of number (i.e., 'every' and 'everyone' suggest the singular form). This is despite the fact that singular 'they' and 'their' has a long history of use in this way. Prescriptivists have argued that number agreement is more important than representing both sexes (Bodine, 1975). Nevertheless, Baranowski investigated the use of generic pronouns in the British and American press and found that 'he is no longer the preferred singular epicene pronoun in English' (2002: 395) and 'they' is the most common and encouraged by guides on writing styles (e.g., Linguistic Society of America (LSA), 1996; The National Council of Teachers of English (NCTE), 2002).

It is important to note that numerous attempts have been made to encourage the use of existing generic pronouns (e.g., they) or to invent new pronouns (e.g., 'ze') (see Baron, 1981) which are not marked for sex. New pronouns have not been particularly successful. While new words are taken up in language very easily, closed linguistic groups, like pronouns and other grammatical particles, are much more resistant to change (see Section 2.6).

6.3.3 Sexism in word order

The recent acceptability of 'they' as generic does not mean that sexism in language has been eradicated. Even the order of words can demonstrate gender inequality. Heidi Motschenbacher (2013) examined the patterns of ordering when both a male and a female are mentioned in a noun phrase. While one often hears 'ladies and gentlemen' when an audience or other large gathering is addressed, this ordering is unusual. It is far more common for the male noun to be placed first, as in 'man and wife' (See Table 6.1).

Table 6.1 Gendered order preference in personal binomials

	Order f-m	Order m-f
General Nouns		
woman/man	285	2,375
girl/boy	125	425
female/male	7	233
Address terms		
lady/gentleman	161	5
madam/sir	0	10
Mrs/Mr	0	546
Nobility titles		
queen/king	1	126
princess/prince	0	154
duchess/duke	0	65
lady/lord	1	49
countess/earl	0	15
Heterosexual roles		
wife/husband	66	551
widow/widower	16	1
bride/(bride) groom	115	3

(Continued)

Table 6.1 (Continued)

Kinship terms		
mother/father	278	170
mum (or mom)/dad	349	7
mummy/daddy	35	7
aunt/uncle	55	44
niece/nephew	14	22
sister/brother	31	505
daughter/son	41	288
Occupations/functions		
actress/actor	0	42
hostess/host	0	19
policewoman/-man	0	108
other woman/man compounds	0	136
Pronouns		
she/he	60	554
her/him	17	411
herself/himself	3	81
her/himself versus him/herself	7	41
hers/his	8	14

Source: adapted from Motschenbacher, 2013: 223

Activity 6.4

Table 6.1 describes the results of Motschenbacher's (2013) research. What does her research show about which sex most commonly occurs first in personal binomials? What does this order suggest about our cultural norms for women and men?

In the majority of cases of personal binomials, Motschenbacher (2013) found that the male form comes before the female. The instances where this does not occur are domains which are considered feminine, specifically, parenting and children. This tells us that there are some fields which 'belong' to women. Marked terms (Section 6.3.1) also demonstrate cultural conventions of this kind. The collocation 'lady doctor' or 'female doctor' is reasonably common as is 'male nurse'. These terms suggest that that the 'default' sex for a doctor is male and the 'default' sex for a nurse is female.

The ordering of **binomials** is so deeply ingrained that women included in a binomial may not be given priority even in a text where women are the focus. For example, in the Convention on the Elimination of All Forms of Discrimination against Women (CEDAW, UN, 1979), the noun phrase 'men and women' occurs 28 times while 'women and men' occurs only once. It may be that these orderings are simply conventional, such as 'fish and chips' or 'salt and pepper'. Nevertheless, Motschenbacher demonstrates the ordering of other noun phrases where power is clearly at issue. The data from her research in Table 6.2 suggests that the more powerful subject will come first.

Table 6.2 Order of personal cojuncts in relation to power

Cojuncts	More power/less power e.g. 'master and servant'	Less power-more power e.g., 'servant and master'
Master/servant	22	2
Employer/employee	59	19
Mother/child	156	17
Father/child	22	0
Parent/child	306	81
Teacher/pupil	146	73
Doctor/nurse	146	23

Source: adapted from Motschenbacher, 2013: 216

Motschenbacher's research suggests that the ordering of words is linked to power. The conventional ordering, with men first and women second, may be an indication of women's less powerful position in the social hierarchy. We now consider the way words associated with women often become less positive over time.

6.3.4 Semantic derogation

Further examples of sexism, and especially gender inequality, can be seen in cases of semantic derogation. **Semantic derogation** refers to the process by which a word comes to have negative meanings over time. Some of the terms we've already examined have been subject to this. Around the year 1362 (Oxford English Dictionary), 'spinster' (Section 6.3.1) referred to a person who spins yarn. While this term could be used about men, it was most often used to refer to women, probably because this work was typically done by women.

'Slut' too has been subject to derogation. In 1402, it meant '[a] woman of dirty, slovenly, or untidy habits or appearance; a foul slattern' (Oxford English Dictionary). Only later did it become linked to loose sexual morality. Although this word has always been used to judge women in relation to an expected standard, whether this is related to keeping house, maintaining appearances or being chaste, 'slut' has recently been reclaimed (see Section 7.4.2). Women have begun to use the word to refer to themselves to resist the sexist usage of the term (Attwood, 2007). It is also noteworthy that there is no term that refers to males in exactly the same way. While a 'stud' is a sexually promiscuous male, this is not negatively evaluated in the way 'slut' is.

Further examples of semantic derogation relating to women can be found in the domain of animals. Schulz (1975) shows that animal terms acquire negative connotations (e.g., pig, dog, cow) once associated with women. Even the term 'woman' is problematic. As Bebout's (1995) research shows, 'woman' (as opposed to 'lady' or 'female') is associated with sexuality while 'lady' seems to **denote** a more respectable form of femininity.

Derogation and sexism toward women through language is not always obvious. Hines's (1999) research on associations of women with food shows how difficult it can be to notice and appreciate the ways women are objectified in language. Hines documents the 'WOMAN AS DESSERT' metaphor, drawing attention to the way women are conceptualised as something sweet to be eaten and shared. She provides a list of desserts that are also used to refer to women (see Example 6.2).

Example 6.2
cheesecake
cherry pie
poundcake
cookie
crumpet
cupcake

(Hines, 1999: 152)

There are many semantic fields in which this kind of derogation occurs. As Schulz remarks:

Again and again in the history of the language, one finds that a perfectly innocent term designating a girl or woman may begin with totally neutral or even positive connotations, but that gradually it acquires negative implications . . . after a period of time becoming abusive and ending as a sexual slur.

(Schulz, 1975: 65)

This is true not only in English but in other languages too (Fernández Fontecha and Jiménez Catalán, 2003). Although gender inequalities have been addressed in significant ways since Schulz's research in 1975, the different treatment of men and women at the lexical level continues today (Hastie and Cosh, 2013; Mills, 2008; Parks and Roberton, 2004).

6.4 DIFFERENCES IN LANGUAGE USE: DOING BEING A WOMAN OR A MAN

In 1975, Robin Lakoff published *Language and Women's Place*. While this book has been criticised for its introspective nature (e.g., Dubois and Crouch, 1975), the questions it raised and the features of 'women's language' that Lakoff identified led to a great deal of research on women's language. Lakoff argues that 'women's language' is characterised by a number of features, including the avoidance of swear words, the use of hedges or fillers ('you know', 'sort of'), the use of **tag questions**, empty adjectives, intensifiers, specific colour terms, more standard syntax, rising intonation on declaratives and high levels of politeness (Lakoff, 1975). Subsequent research on what women actually do linguistically doesn't always match up with Lakoff's claims. However, nearly 40 years later, if we understand Lakoff's features as typifying a kind of 'ideal' woman against which real women are measured, the list continues to work well. Indeed, this seems to be the argument that Lakoff was making. In this way, Lakoff's features provide us with an account of what people *expect* from women in their language use. An important feature of the concept 'women's language', and Lakoff's account of it, is not that there actually is a way that men and women use language differently but that society expects them to do so without questioning this expectation. The belief that women speak one way and men another is strongly entrenched.

Lakoff's list of the features of 'women's language' has had other benefits. It provided linguists with a clear research agenda. Academics proceeded to gather data from women to find out whether they really did use more tag questions, colour terms and so on. Here we consider the research on one feature: tag questions. Tag questions are an ideal feature to examine because they are associated with uncertainty, lack of power and women (Lakoff, 1975). They also demonstrate that assumptions about the function of linguistic features can be wrong. Research on tag questions allows us to see the key issues in language and gender – first, that we have ideologies about how men and women use language and, second, the complexity of linguistic features requires careful examination before we come to any conclusions about how people use language.

6.4.1 Tag questions

A tag question turns a declarative sentence into a question by 'tagging' or adding something onto the end.

Example 6.3
a   She's a good-looking girl, *isn't she*?
b   That's not right, *is it*?

In Example 6.3, 'isn't she?' and 'is it?' turn the declaratives into tag questions. Some tag questions may express uncertainty about the declarative that it follows, as (b) above seems to (an **epistemic** function). 'That's not right, is it?' might be used by someone who really isn't sure whether it's right or not. But there are other functions tags can have. Consider example (b) in a different context. Imagine a teacher saying this to a school student. Is the teacher expressing uncertainty? In such a scenario, the teacher would be inviting the child to reconsider their position and to respond in some way.

Lakoff identified tag questions as part of 'women's language' (1975). Women's alleged use of tag questions was interpreted as expressing uncertainty and a lack of confidence. Linguists started researching tag questions in order to establish whether women use them more than men. In the process of doing this work, however, they also discovered that tag questions have more than one function. As Example 6.3 shows, tag questions don't just indicate uncertainty. Tag questions can have a modal or **affective** meaning. Modal in this context refers to the amount of certainty the speaker is expressing while affective tags signal the speaker's attitude to the addressee or even the topic being discussed. People do use tag questions to express uncertainty. But they also use them to invite another person to speak and to signal that what is being discussed or said is sensitive.

Research shows that while women do use more tag questions, they are more likely to be affective tags, which facilitate conversation (Holmes, 1984). In Holmes's research, more than half of women's tag questions were of this type. In contrast, the majority of tag questions used by men were modal, that is, they expressed uncertainty. In fact, tag questions can have even more functions if considered in conversational context. Consider (a). Depending on the context, this might be a way of inviting a shared appreciation of an attractive woman or a way of expressing displeasure at the wandering eye of a boyfriend. The analysis of tag questions shows that while a linguistic form may have a conventional function; it may have other functions too. Therefore, we must be very careful about making claims about what use of a tag question means (Holmes, 1986, 1987).

A troubling aspect of the tag question hypothesis is that, for some observers, the claim that 'women use more tag questions because both are associated with uncertainty' seemed to be self-evident. All cultures have ideas about how different groups of people should use language. People take as given the difference between men and women; one of the consequences of this is that we have no trouble accepting the idea that women and men use language differently. What we see in the detail of these assumptions is that women are thought to use less powerful language as a reflection of their lower position in the social hierarchy. Even though it is not true that women use 'less powerful' language (Conley, O'Barr and Lind, 1978), the ideology remains. Taken together with the lexical asymmetries and **semantic derogation** described earlier, these linguistic features are a reflection of the lower rank women hold in the social hierarchy. The same ideologies about the difference between men and women's speech in addition to the negative value attached to women's speech can also be seen in the case of gossip.

6.5 GOSSIP

Gossip usually refers to talk about other people. It is often considered to be meaningless unreliable information and sometimes even malicious. In popular discourse, gossip is particularly associated with talk that women engage in with other women.

Deborah Jones defines gossip as 'a way of talking between women in their roles as women, intimate in style, personal and domestic in topic and setting' (1980: 194). According to Jones, 'Gossip' is something that women do with close friends, often in their homes or other private settings. While Coates argues that Jones's claim that gossip revolves around women's roles as wives, girlfriends and mothers is too strong (2014: 97), this kind of talk does allow women to explore and negotiate what it means to be a woman in a variety of contexts. Coates found a wide range of topics covered in the women's talk she collected. She observes, '[I]t seems to be typical of all-women groups that they discuss people and feelings, while men are more likely to discuss things' (2014: 97). This characterisation seems rather different to the popular conceptions of gossip. Far from being scathing and malicious, women's talk among themselves deals with their relationships with other people and their feelings and opinions about events in the world. Linguists have taken up gossip as a legitimate object of study and found that, firstly, gossip is a very complex form of communication and, secondly, both men and women equally engage in this form of communication.

Several key linguistic discourse strategies typical of talk involving groups of women can be seen in Example 6.4.

In the following example, Coates has used stave transcription. All the spoken lines in each numbered group should be read simultaneously. So in stave 1, C and B are talking at the same time. The % means the words are spoken more quietly and/indicates the end of a tone unit or chunk of talk.

Example 6.4

1   C: I didn't go over for my father/ I asked my mother
     B: it's so odd that you should

---

2   C: if she wanted me/I mean . I – I immediately said

---

3   C: 'Do you want me to comer over!' – and she said

---

4   C: 'Well no I can't really see the point/he's dead'

---

5   C: 'isn't he?'/<LAUGHS> . and .   and she
     A: mhm/
     B: well that's right/ that's

---

6   C: said no/I mean   {{xxx}}   no point in
     B: what John was saying/ that they-
     E: you've got

---

7   C: coming/   so
     A: yeah
     E: terribly forward-looking parents you see/ it

```
 8  E:   depends on the attitude of- . mean is- is his
 ────────────────────────────────────────────────────────────
 9  C:                                                  I don't
    B:                              %I don't know%
    E:   father still alive?                            because
 ────────────────────────────────────────────────────────────
10  C:   think – I don't think they had a funeral either/
    E:   that would have a very big bearing on it/
 ────────────────────────────────────────────────────────────
11  D:   if they were religious I mean/ yes/ it would all
    E:                                         yeah
 ────────────────────────────────────────────────────────────
12  C:   yeah I don't think they had a funeral/
    D:   depend/              if there were life
    E:           yeah/ . I mean if there was – if there
 ────────────────────────────────────────────────────────────
13  C:   they had a memorial service/
    D:   after death/             then they'd KNOW
    E:          was-               if they- if-
 ────────────────────────────────────────────────────────────
14  D:   that you hadn't come/
    E:                    that's right/
```

(Coates, 2014: 101–102).

Normally in a conversation, we expect that only one speaker will talk at a time (Sacks, Schegloff and Jefferson, 1974). Speakers are expected to take **turns**. This is not what we see in Example 6.4. Firstly, more than one person is speaking at once without any members of the conversation expressing an objection to that. This is called a **shared floor** (rather than a one-at-a-time floor) (see Edelsky, 1981; Talbot, 1992). Secondly, the use of **minimal responses** (stave 5, 7 and 11) signals that participants are paying attention to the speaker. This is also known as **backchannelling**. They do this by providing small utterances, like 'mhm', 'yeah', without disrupting or interrupting the current speaker. Thirdly, speakers use expressions like 'I mean' (stave 2 and 6), that can be understood as signalling that the speaker knows this is a sensitive topic and is trying to express respect for other speakers' points of view. This strategy is called **hedging**. These strategies are typical of women's conversations with each other (Coates, 1996). Women tend to be co-operative in this context; they construct a shared floor, provide support for the speaker, and carefully manage any points of conflict or disagreement (Coates, 1996). The preference of men for a one-at-a-time floor and of women for a shared floor has also been found in sign languages (Coates and Sutton-Spence, 2001).

The structure outlined here facilitates a particular type of discussion. In the case of Example 6.4, Coates points out that 'At one level, individual speakers are dealing with their own feelings about the topic under discussion' (Coates, 2014: 102), but they do this in order to explore more general ideas: Who is a funeral for? Do other people's expectations matter? Is distance a good reason not to attend a funeral? The discussion of these more general ideas can be seen as part of the process through which the women discover and articulate their own values.

This type of engagement with personal attitudes to broader social norms and conventions are often part of conversations that are considered 'gossip' in the popular sense. For example, discussing a friend's decision to leave her husband or someone's dating habits might seem like pointless speculating. Further, such talk can seem intrusive because it may require a great deal of very personal contextual information (did the husband do something and so on). But among friends, such talk can also be a way of reflecting on social norms and conventions and one's own attitude towards them. These conversations are very often part of sustaining relationships (establishing if there is agreement on these matters) and figuring out one's own position on social rules. Coates argues that the function of gossip is 'the maintenance of good social relationships' (2014: 98). Talk is an important way of building and sustaining relationships between people; gossip is more than simply **phatic talk**, the relational function of phatic talk is clear in this genre (see Section 5.6.3).

6.5.1 Gossip and men

In the preceding section, we considered women's talk, or 'gossip'. This is not usually a form of communication associated with men, but that doesn't mean they don't engage in it. Cameron (2011 [1997]) examined the speech of an all-male group of college students. While their talk can be discussed in terms of the 'typical' features of male talk, we can also examine it in terms of the functions of 'gossip' that we discussed. Example 6.5, from Cameron's research, is a transcript of the talk of five young white middle-class men while watching sports. 'Sports talk' is considered to be a masculine activity, but as a number of scholars have noted, it bears many similarities to women's talk (Johnson and Finlay, 1997; Kuiper, 1991). Moreover, Cameron's data shows a male discussion that contains more than simply 'sports talk'. The men discuss their day, decide who will go grocery shopping, they discuss wine and exchange stories about women. They also engage in

> discussion of several persons not present but known to the participants, with a strong focus on critically examining these individuals' appearance, dress, social behaviour and sexual mores. Like the conversationalists themselves, the individuals under discussion are all men.

> (Cameron, 2011: 181–182)

Example 6.5

BRYAN: uh you know that really gay guy in our Age of Revolution class who sits in front of us? he wore shorts again, by the way, it's like 42 degrees out he wore shorts again [laughter] [Ed: That guy] it's like a speedo, he wears a speedo to class (.) he's got incredibly skinny legs [Ed: it's worse] you know=

ED: =you know like those shorts women volleyball players wear? it's like those (.) it's l[ike

---

BRYAN: [you know what's even more ridicu[lous? when

ED: [French cut spandex]

BRYAN: you wear those shorts and like a parka on ...
(5 lines omitted)

BRYAN: he's either got some condition that he's got to like have his legs exposed at all times or else he's got really good legs=

ED: =he's probably he'[s like

CARL: [he really likes

BRYAN: =he

ED: =he's like at home combing his leg hairs=

CARL: his legs=

BRYAN: he doesn't have any leg hair though=   [*yes* and oh

ED: =he *real*[*ly* likes

ED: his legs=

AL: =very long very white and very skinny

BRYAN: those ridiculous Reeboks that are always (indeciph) and goofy white socks always striped=   [tube socks

ED: =that's   [right

ED: he's the antithesis of man

(Cameron, 2011: 183–4)

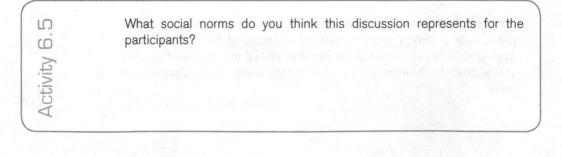

Activity 6.5

What social norms do you think this discussion represents for the participants?

The young men's discussion presents two key characteristics of gossip discussed earlier: discussion of non-present people in some detail and discussion of a topic of importance to the speakers. The men are discussing a classmate whom they are apparently not friends with. At one level, they are discussing this person's clothing and his personal appearance in a detailed and negative way. In addition, they assert that the women this student is attracted to are not attractive enough to merit attention. But at another level, just as in Example 6.5, the men are dealing with their own ideas and feelings about social norms – in this case, social norms of what it means to be a man. For the men participating in the discussion, the man they criticise is not performing his masculinity appropriately; he is 'the antithesis of man'. In this talk, we can see the participants identifying characteristics of the social norms young heterosexual men are expected to follow.

6.5.2 Features of men's talk

We saw in Example 6.4 that the women had a shared floor, used hedging strategies and provided support to speakers with minimal responses. Research shows that men's talk tends to have different features (Coates, 2002). Cameron describes male talk as:

> competitive, hierarchically organised, centres on 'impersonal' topics and the exchange of information, and foregrounds speech genres such as joking, trading insults and sports statistics.
>
> (Cameron, 2011: 179)

Saying that men are competitive is linked to the observation that men seem to prefer a one-at-a-time floor. Holding the floor is esteemed; this is why there might be competition for it. Men are also said to signal that they are listening by remaining silent. For women, silence may signal a breakdown of communication; for men, it appears to be acceptable (Pilkington, 1998). While competition and silence can be found in men's talk, there are two things we need to bear in mind. First, as the conversation in Example 6.5 shows, these features are not always present. Second, the way some of these features are characterised may not reflect how conversational participants understand them. For example, it has been shown that men seem to prefer topics like cars, technology and sport (Coates, 2002). These topics are described as 'impersonal' topics. But it may be that these topics are intensely personal for the men who talk about them. Certainly, they are not 'personal' in the way that emotions are (a topic found in women's talk and not so often found in men's talk). But characterising them as 'impersonal' may misrepresent what they mean to the participants and to the conversation in which they occur. Moreover, other research finds that the distinction between how men and women use language is not clear and that both sexes employ both co-operative and competitive features depending on the context (Mullany, 2007; Schleef, 2008; Woods, 1989).

Activity 6.6

See if you can find, in Example 6.5, examples of the conversation features described in the preceding section. Do people talk at the same time (shared floor) or not? Are there silences? Does this look like competitive talk?

It is possible to find evidence of competition in the talk in Example 6.5. The young men all contribute observations about their fellow student in a critical or humorous way. There is some simultaneous talk, which might be seen as interruptive, but there is no evidence that the speakers object to this. The simultaneous talk might better be referred to as **overlaps** rather than **interruptions**. There are no silences or breaks in the conversation. They also support each other in their conversational contributions. For example, Bryan suggests that the student may have really good legs. Ed furthers this by commenting that he must spend time combing his leg hairs. This topic is then taken up by Bryan.

6.6 GENDER AND POWER

From the discussion of gossip, we see that while the structure of this type of talk may be different among gendered groups, it serves the same purpose for each. Gossip is way of exploring, negotiating and contesting social norms for many speakers. We have to wonder, then, why is gossip only associated with women although everyone engages in it? Additionally, why is gossip negatively evaluated? The answers can be found in the androcentric rule (Coates, 2004: 10). This rule states that anything women do linguistically will be negatively judged and everything men do with language will be seen as normal. In essence, the androcentric rule means that men's language is unmarked and women's language is marked.

The androcentric rule is a gender-specific statement of the more general process of linguistic subordination (Lippi-Green, 2011). Wolfram and Schilling-Estes describe this as a principle whereby:

> the speech of socially subordinate groups will be interpreted as linguistically inadequate by comparison with that of socially dominant groups.
> (Wolfram and Schilling-Estes, 1998: 6)

This 'principle' operates widely and will inform our understanding of language, society and power in several other chapters of this book. Next, we explore another feature of so-called women's language. We'll see, again, how inequality is present in understanding linguistic behaviour.

6.6.1 Do women talk more than men?

Example 6.6

Women's tongues are like lambs tails – they are never still. *English*

The North Sea will sooner be found wanting water than a woman at a
   loss for words. *Jutlandic*

Where there are woman and geese there's noise. *Japanese*

Nothing is so unnatural as a talkative man and a quiet woman. *Scottish*

(Holmes, 1998: 41)

Consider the proverbs in Example 6.6. What do they say about women and their linguistic behaviour? What do they imply about men and their linguistic behaviour?

Activity 6.7

You might have heard that women use 20,000 words a day while men only use 7,000. This claim has been circulating in the media for some time. In fact, recently, in a free London newspaper, the *Evening Standard*, a headline read 'Women speak 12,000 words a day. Men speak 4,000' (Saatchi, 2017). Like the 'Eskimo words for snow' myth (see Chapter 2 and Pullum, 1991), it is reported frequently in the media and is generally accepted as true. Linguist Mark Liberman (2006) attempted to find the source of these numbers of word use by men and women. His exhaustive research found no study to support these figures. In fact, he found that these numbers are often used without reference to any source or supporting evidence at all (see also Cameron, 2007).

In Chapter 4, we discussed media and expertise. What parallels do you see between the claim that women use 20,000 words a day and the issues we discussed in Section 4.6?

Activity 6.8

The belief that women talk more than men is a pervasive one. As the proverbs suggest, many cultures pass judgement on how much women talk. As with tag questions, exploring actual linguistic behaviour and the possible reasons for that behaviour will help us understand some of the issues behind language, society and power.

A very important point when considering the issue of 'who talks more' is knowing there are different types of talk (Coates, 2004). Giving a full account of different types of talk isn't possible here, so we'll simply say that *where* the talk takes place is a key feature of this issue. That is, we must consider whether the talk takes place in the public or private domain because these domains have different qualities. Public talk has the purpose of informing or persuading and is often associated with higher status/power (e.g., one generally has to be 'invited' to participate in public talk in some way). Private talk serves interpersonal functions, such as making social connections, developing relationships, and so on.

Activity 6.9

Which type of talk (public or private) do you think is more valued by society?

Not all kinds of talk are the same. Some talk is highly valued. Examples of highly valued talk include talking in public, such as at a formal meeting, giving a presentation or in the mass media. In these public contexts, research suggests that men talk more than women (Woods, 1989). Talk in the public sphere is undertaken by powerful people; it is one of the ways they express, claim and perform their power. This kind of language tends to involve expressing facts or information, persuading an audience or making some kind of change in the wider world. In the private domain, however, research suggests that women talk more than men (DeFrancisco, 1991; Fishman, 1980).

Private talk, such as talking to family members, consoling children or talking with friends, involves looking after people, building relationships. Talk in the private sphere, in domestic or other private settings, is not as highly valued as public talk. For example, consoling a child is not as esteemed as giving a speech.

If research has established it isn't the case that women talk more than men (in the public sphere at least), then why is the belief that they do talk more so pervasive?

6.6.2 Gender or power?

Spender (1980) suggests that the belief that women talk too much is explained by the fact that any talk from a woman is considered 'too much'. That is to say, women do not need to speak very much in order to be perceived as speaking too much. Spender argues, 'The talkativeness of women has been gauged not in comparison with men but with silence. Women have not been judged on the grounds of whether they talk more than men, but of whether they talk more than *silent* women' (Spender, 1980: 41; italics in original). That is, it is not the case that women talk more than men, but they are *perceived as doing so*. Part of this has to do with different purposes and types of talk. It is also related to the cultural norm that public talk belongs to men, that is, women do not have equal rights to the floor in the public domain (Coates, 1996).

The belief that women should be silent, or that they talk too much, may not be about gender at all. As O'Barr and Atkins (1980) found in their study of men and women in the legal system, it is not the case that only women use features of 'women's language'. What is more important is power. This is demonstrated by Herring's research (2010) on an online discussion list (see also Herring, Johnson and DiBenedetto, 1992). Herring uses the concept of floor (see Section 6.5) in order to determine whether it is a useful concept for computer-mediated communication (CMC, see Chapter 5) and whether there are differences between how women and men communicate online. As she observes, 'having the floor' in an online discussion is not quite the same as in a face-to-face conversation. She argues, 'Thus an analysis of "floor" in CMC should take into account not only individual messages, but patterns of participation and response across messages' (2010: 2). Herring studied participants' contributions to three academic discussion lists. She looked at extended discussions on one topic (called a 'thread') in order to find out what kinds of conversational floor were being constructed by the users.

Despite the difference between face-to-face communication and online communication, Herring found types of floor online that are parallel to those in face-to-face conversation. She found that one-at-a-time floor CMC discussions 'are of long duration and contain longer messages; are interactionally "sparse" have a single thematic focus; tend to be contentious; and are hierarchically dominated by a minority of individuals who participate and are responded to disproportionately more often than others' (2010: 10). Discussions with a shared floor 'are of shorter duration and contain shorter messages; are interactionally "dense" have multiple thematic foci; tend to be supportive and collaborative; and are egalitarian in that participation and responses are distributed more evenly across participants' (2010: 10).

As seen in Section 6.5, men tend to prefer a one-at-a-time floor. Herring found evidence of this in her CMC data too. The male-predominant threads were structured as a one-at-a-time floor. In the female-predominant threads, Herring found evidence of both floors. That is, in the female-predominant threads, rather than everyone constructing a shared floor, the men still orient to a one-at-a-time floor. Herring argues that this suggests the way contributors behave is not so much about floor but rather about 'preferred gender styles of conversational interaction' (2010: 17). This would mean that women and men should behave in the same way across all threads. The men do, preferring a one-at-a-time floor. The women, however, do not show the same kind of consistency. In some female-predominant threads, she did find evidence for a shared floor, but she also found some women 'dominating' the floor in female-predominant threads. She writes that this 'suggests that power conditions some behaviours. Power can be exercised by both women and men' (2010: 19) just as O'Barr and Atkins found.

In terms of getting the floor, Herring did find that men's posts were more likely to be taken up than women's. There are two strategies Herring found for 'highly successful floor holders': posting a lot of messages or posting 'impactful messages' (2010: 21). Posting a number of messages results in similar response rates, whether the poster was male or female. However, posting impactful messages did show a difference. This strategy includes posting jokes or messages that are 'provocative (including offensive) or controversial' (2010: 21). These messages tended to get a high number of responses. They also tended to be posted by men. 'Highly successful floor holders – that is, individuals who succeed in gaining multiple responses – fall into two categories: those who post numerous messages, and those who post few but impactful messages' (2010: 21). However, some messages posted by men received a lot of attention without conforming to either of these strategies, while that was not the case for the women posters' messages.

6.7 GENDERED TALK: PERFORMING IDENTITY

6.7.1 'Dude'

In this section, we focus on the way individuals perform their gender identity. This may be done in a range of ways, through choices about clothes, hairstyles, how one walks and sits or any number of physical activities. Language is also an important way people perform their gender. And while the gender a person performs can be understood as the sum total of all these choices, here we focus on what the use of one word tells us about how to do being a (heterosexual) man.

Kiesling (2004) describes how young men in a North American fraternity use the word 'dude'. 'Dude' is a very useful form of address. It can be used at the start or end of an utterance (Examples 6.7 a. and b.) and has a range of meanings depending on the intonation the speaker uses (Kiesling, 2004: 291).

Example 6.7
a   dude it was like boys in the hood man ai: n't no: lie:
                                                    (Kiesling, 2004: 294)

b   Everybody plays that damn game, dude.
                                                    (Kiesling, 2004: 295)

> Do the men (or women) you know use the term 'dude' to address their male (or female) friends? Do they use a different term? List the different ways the term can be used and how it is said. What do these different uses do?

While 'dude' may serve many purposes, such as help speakers follow the structure of conversation, express positive or negative evaluation or even signal agreement, it is the relationship between speakers that 'dude' invokes that is of interest here. Also note that not all English speakers use 'dude'. As we'll see, in some varieties, other similar terms can be found.

When talking or using language, we express feelings about our relationship with that person by the language we use. Terms of address (or **address terms**) are an important way of doing this. For example, we express respect by using 'Sir' or 'Madam' or express affection by using 'honey' or 'darling'. Kiesling argues that for his speakers, 'dude' projects a stance of solidarity and camaraderie 'but crucially in a nonchalant, not too enthusiastic manner' (2004: 282). That is, 'dude' can be used to express friendship without being too affectionate by projecting a 'stance of cool solidarity' (2004: 282). Societal expectations for heterosexual men are such that they shouldn't express too much closeness in their friendships, especially with other men. According to societal expectations, if a man were to express his positive regard for a male friend, he risks being perceived as homosexual. Expressing solidarity among friends, therefore, is potentially in conflict with those societal expectations. Kiesling suggests 'Dude allows men to create a stance within this narrow range, one of closeness with other men (satisfying masculine solidarity) that also maintains a casual stance that keeps some distance (thus satisfying heterosexism)' (2004: 283).

6.7.2 Mate

While 'dude' is commonly associated with English in the US, there is a term used in Australia which may express similar attitudes. 'Mate' has long been considered a term of **address** used by and to Australian men. It is, together with an ideology of 'mateship', an important discourse of national identity (see Wierzbicka, 1997). It has generally been understood to signal the solidarity of ordinary working men. Recent research, however, suggests that the male associations of 'mate' may be shifting.

Joanna Rendle-Short (2009) asked Australians how they use the word 'mate' as a term of address (like 'dude'). She surveyed people in Canberra

Table 6.3 Self-reported use of 'mate' by men and women

	Men	Women
Use 'mate'	88.4%	60.4%
Don't use 'mate'	11.6%	39.6%

Table 6.4 Self-reported use of 'mate' by women

Age	18–29	30–49	50 and over
Use 'mate'	75.9%	63.4%	36.6%
Don't use 'mate'	24.1%	36.6%	63.4%

Table 6.5 Self-reported use of 'mate' by men

Age	18–29	30–49	50 and over
Use 'mate'	93.8%	87.6%	82.6%
Don't use 'mate'	6.2%	12.4%	17.4%

(the capital of Australia) about whether they used 'mate' as a **vocative** and whether they liked it.

As Table 6.3 shows, overall, men still report using 'mate' more than women. But looking at the age profile (in Tables 6.4 and 6.5), we can see that younger women are more likely to report using 'mate' than older women. Her data also shows that younger women who use mate are more likely than older women to use 'mate' to address both women and men. Rendle-Short also found that younger men who use mate are also more likely to address both men and women that way than older men. But they are still more likely to use 'mate' to address men only than both women and men.

When looking at the meanings that speakers associate with 'mate', Rendle-Short found that men and women understand it differently. For men, it seems to be associated with equality, while for young women, it is used to express intimacy and fun. 'By re-defining *mate* as a term of endearment, young women are able to express both intimacy, friendliness and fun, while at the same time appropriating what has been characterised as a traditionally masculine term' (Rendle-Short, 2009: 264). What 'mate' means to women and men is not quite the same. It should also be noted that both 'dude' and 'mate' can express different meanings according to both context and intonation (see Kiesling, 2004).

The examples of 'dude' and 'mate' show us two important things. First, they demonstrate that even a single lexical choice can have a range of functions, including the performance of gender. Second, they show that gender performances depend on social expectations (ideologies) about what appropriate performances of being a man or a woman look like. Further, these ideologies rely on the position that heterosexuality is unmarked (see Example 6.4) and that homosexuality is marked.

6.7.3 Variation

In the case of 'dude' and 'mate', we see the different ways that people can perform a gendered identity with language. It is important to remember that even with the changes in attitudes towards gender, we still orient to hegemonic norms about what is expected for particular genders. Hazenberg (2016) shows clearly that while it is indeed possible to construct an identity that does not fit into traditional concepts of 'man' and 'woman' these categories remain relevant. And as seen in the preceding sections, they exist in a hierarchical relation.

Hazenberg gathered data in Ottawa, Canada, by conducting sociolinguistic interviews with young adults. From a larger set of data, he selected interviews from individuals who identify 'either as transsexual or cissexual, and as straight, gay, or lesbian' (2016: 274). Trans is 'an umbrella term to refer to anyone whose internal sense of gendered identity is not congruent with the sex assigned at birth' (2016: 290). Thus, trans men were assigned the female sex at birth but identify as men. Trans women were 'born' male but identify as women. A cissexual person is someone who is not trans. The data are thus divided in relation to gender and sexuality. He recorded speech from

straight men
straight women
queer men
queer women
trans men
trans women

Straight men and women are heterosexual, and their sex is congruent with their gender. Queer women and men self-identify in this way, as they do not consider themselves to be 'heterosexual' or 'heteronormative' (that is, 'oriented to the traditional heterosexual sets of values and expectations' (Hazenberg, 2016: 276)). Hazenberg writes that '*queer* is a label that many youth-oriented organisations embrace because its underspecificity allows for more fluid identities' (2016: 272). Vincent, one of Hazenberg's self-identifying queer informants says:

> Where I think is interesting is in the more progressive, the more *now* queer community, which is where I identify myself, because I'm not macho. I'm not a straight-acting guy. I'm probably more straight than gay, and yet I'm still more gay-acting, right? Which is kind of fun. But I certainly don't do it on purpose, I'm not flexing my flamingness or queerness intentionally. I just say and do what I want to say, and it comes out pretty flaming a lot of the time (Vincent, queer man, age 31).
>
> (Hazenberg, 2016: 276)

Drawing on existing research on intensifiers in Canadian English (e.g. Tagliamonte, 2008), Hazenberg explored the use of intensifiers in this group

Table 6.6 Rates of use of intensifier (as a percentage)

	Very	Really	Pretty	So
Straight women	21.8	25.7	4.0	20.3
Straight men	10.3	25.0	14.7	6.0
Queer women	19.0	28.1	5.1	14.6
Queer men	25.4	15.2	3.7	20.1
Trans women (Male to female)	25.6	24.6	5.5	5.5
Trans men (Female to male)	15.7	33.3	6.3	8.5

Source: adapted from Hazenberg, 2016: 280

in order to determine whether the different gender groups use them in the same way (Hazenberg also examined phonetic variables, but here we concentrate on the results for intensifiers). Intensifiers are expressions that increase or modify the force of an adjective or adverb (e.g., 'so' or 'pretty').

Table 6.6 shows that the most common intensifier in this group is 'really'. Nevertheless, it is not the most used intensifier by all groups. We can also see that the straight men use 'pretty' the most and much more than other groups. Hazenberg writes: 'Pretty does not signal masculinity in general, but only a particular style and kind of masculinity' (2016: 281). Straight women, however, use more 'so' than other groups. On the basis of intensifier use, Hazenberg suggests three groups of speakers.

1   'high users of *pretty*' straight men
2   'low users of both' ('so' and 'pretty') trans women, trans men
3   'high users of *so*' straight women, queer women, queer men

(2016: 282)

What is striking is the difference of the straight men group. No other group resembles them. We saw that generally women are positioned lower on the social hierarchy than men. Hazenberg makes a similar point: 'one does not have to search particularly far or wide to see that women are positioned as weaker and less powerful than men' (2016: 286–287). Hazenberg suggests that straight men need to hold on to their powerful position, and this is reflected in the variables they use. In contrast, because of women's position on the social hierarchy, straight women and queer women do not have this option. Queer men also have little reason to try to draw on the linguistic capital of 'straight man' talk as 'they have already confronted the potential loss of privilege associated with their non-heteronormative identity' (2016: 287).

Trans men and women, however, require more consideration. Hazenberg offers a number of reasons why trans women/men don't use more of the variables associated with their straight counterparts. One of the reasons he suggests is related to avoidance of variables. He suggests that for these trans speakers, it may well be that avoiding speech features associated with a gender that is not theirs may be more important than performing the ones that are in line with their gender: 'it is more important for them to *not* be seen doing the wrong thing than it is for them to be seen doing the *right* thing'

(2016: 288). Thus, trans women will avoid features associated with men and trans men will avoid features associated with women. 'Thus a woman may or may not use the intensifier so without having her femininity called into question, while a man's use of the same variant will automatically cast a shadow over his (heteronormative) masculine identity' (2016: 288). This is a small sample of speakers, and it isn't possible to come to definitive conclusions about what all speakers do. Hazenberg's argument is important, however, because it takes into account both the performance of gender and the prevailing social hierarchies among people.

6.8 SUMMARY

In this chapter, we have considered a range of issues in the field of language and gender. This has shown that inequality between women and men is still an important concern in contemporary society and that women continue to have less status than men. This status difference is reflected in other examples we have considered, including beliefs about quantity of talk and who has rights to the floor in different contexts. While claims are made about the differences between the way men and women use language, men and women also do very similar things with it, as seen in the example of gossip. Moreover, differences in language use are best explained by the way people are expected to perform their gender, rather than because of any innate difference between men and women. The performance of identity, including gender identity, is complex and important. We continue to examine this performance in the following chapters.

FURTHER READING

Baker, P. (2010) Will Ms ever be as frequent as Mr? A corpus-based comparison of gendered terms across four diachronic corpora of British English, *Gender & Language*, 4(1): 125–149.

Cameron, D. and Kulick, D. (2003) *Language and Sexuality*, Cambridge: Cambridge University Press.

Coates, J. (2013) *Women, Men and Everyday Talk*. Basingstoke: Palgrave Macmillan.

Frable, D. (1989) Sex typing and gender ideology: Two facets of the individual's gender psychology that go together, *Journal of Personality and Social Psychology*, 56(1): 95–108.

Khosroshahi, F. (1989) Penguins don't care, but women do: A social identity analysis of a Whorfian problem, *Language and Society*, 18(4): 505–525.

Pauwels, A. (2001) Non-sexist language reform and generic pronouns in Australian English, *English Worldwide*, 22(1): 105–119.

Pauwels, A. (2003) Linguistic sexism and feminist linguistic activism, in Holmes, J. and Meyerhoff, M. (eds.) *The Handbook of Language and Gender*. Oxford: Blackwell: 550–570.

Pichler, P. (2009) *Talking Young Femininities*. Basingstoke: Palgrave Macmillan.

Talbot, M. (1992) 'I wish you'd stop interrupting me!' Interruptions and asymmetries in speaker-rights in 'equal encounters', *Journal of Pragmatics*, 18: 451–466.

CHAPTER 7

Language and ethnicity

7.1 INTRODUCTION

Holmes notes that people may 'signal their ethnicity by the language they choose to use' (2008: 183). In this chapter, we examine the various ways ethnicity may be expressed and communicated through language. We'll consider how the position of ethnic groups in the social hierarchy is reflected by language use. As with other variables, such as gender, class and age, a person's ethnicity has at times been treated as a simple part of their essential nature – stable, determined and unchanging. It is true that some research shows a correlation between particular **linguistic variables** and ethnicity. However, we will see that it's not always quite so straightforward. How individuals articulate their ethnicity and how it is understood may vary because of the communicative context they're in, the people they're interacting with. Ethnicity may also interact with other aspects of identity, such as gender, age, sex and so on.

7.2 WHAT DO WE MEAN BY 'ETHNICITY'?

It's useful to have a sense of what the term 'ethnicity' includes. Allan Bell notes that ethnicity 'is one of the most slippery social dimensions' (2014: 173). He continues:

> [Ethnicity] has to do with a group sharing sociocultural characteristics – a sense of place, ancestry, a common history, religion, cultural practices, ways of communicating, and often a language. When sociolinguists question their informants about ethnicity, they are nowadays most likely to ask what ethnic group a person identifies with, indicating the socially constructed nature of ethnicity.
>
> (2014: 173–174)

How do you define your ethnicity? How do you distinguish between your ethnicity and that of other people? Compare the features that define your ethnicity to the ones Bell mentions.

Activity 7.1

If you are part of the ethnic majority, you probably don't even consider that you have an ethnicity. But as with accents, we all have an ethnicity. Again, if you are part of the ethnic majority, the only time you think about ethnicity might be when filling in forms that specifically ask you for your background. The categories that are chosen and the way they are labelled can reveal a great deal about the makeup of a particular nation and the characteristics it sees as relevant. They can present a challenge though, as they often treat 'race' as synonymous with ethnicity. While 'race' is connected to biology and physical characteristics, ethnicity is far more appropriate in understanding how people align with sociocultural groups, how they construct their identity and how they use language to do this.

Ethnicity is not a straightforward concept. Just as women don't all speak in the same way simply because they are women, people who by some definition belong to the same ethnicity don't necessarily speak in the same way. Carmen Fought writes 'ethnicity is not about what one *is*, but rather about what one *does*' (2002: 444; original emphasis).

It is important to highlight the distinction between race and ethnicity. The relationship between these two categories is analogous to that between sex and gender. Ethnicity, like gender, is socially and culturally constructed. In addition, as Harris and Rampton (2003) have argued, the roots of linguistic difference related to social categories are very similar regardless of the social category. For example, linguistic subordination (see Chapter 6) is a factor in some way in most social categories.

Earlier, we used the phrase 'the ethnic majority'. While this will vary from place to place, the ethnic majority is generally **unmarked**, that is, it is perceived as the norm. Indeed, the majority doesn't need to be a numerical majority; it just needs to be the unmarked ethnicity. What the unmarked ethnicity is depends on a variety of political, social and historical factors. Whether an ethnicity is labelled as such also depends on the conception of the 'nation', the idea that people have about who they are and their cultural backgrounds. 'Ethnic' tends to be reserved for groups that are at some level thought of as marked or 'other'. What happens as a result is that the terms 'ethnic' and 'ethnicity' typically only refer to minority groups. In short, groups we describe in terms of 'ethnicity' are very often 'the other', invoking an oppositional relationship of a 'them' to an 'us'.

A good example of the 'unmarkedness' of an ethnic majority is found in the Canadian blog 'Stuff White People Like'. Because white is the unmarked ethnic identity in Canada, this blog creates an 'alternative public forum where privileged Whites may have the unfamiliar experience of being confronted with "non-White" perspectives and stereotypes on their class/race habitus' (Walton and Jaffe, 2011: 287). This blog is a humorous take on white identity and therefore presents a less threatening confrontation of social class and privilege. The author of the blog is white; however, he presents the view as a non-white outsider. For example, one post explains that white people like 'picking their own fruit':

> When white people harvests [sic] a crop it's known as 'berry picking' or 'pick your own fruit'. Under these conditions, white people are expected to work leisurely with no real expectations and then they pay for the privilege to do so.
>
> (Stuff White People Like, 2010)

By drawing attention to this practice, the author makes clear that white people also have an ethnic identity.

Activity 7.2

Go to the *Stuff White People* like website, https://stuffwhitepeoplelike. com/, and have a look at the activities, television programmes and items that Lander identifies as 'stuff white people like'. Are these familiar to you? Why do you think Lander has identified these as being connected to white people?

7.3 ETHNICITY, THE NATION STATE AND MULTILINGUALISM

One of the most important 'boundaries' in the modern world is that of the nation state. We don't deal with multilingualism and language policy here in detail; however, the relationship between nation, language and ethnicity is an important one. While the three are often thought to exist in a stable relationship, such situations are far more complex.

There is a persistent idea that nations should be ethnically and linguistically homogenous (Irvine and Gal, 2000). But this is very rarely the case. Nevertheless, we can see this ideology at work in calls for migrants to learn the majority language and for the designation of an official language and in calls for cultural assimilation of minorities more generally. In the UK, the idea that immigrants should learn English as soon as possible is seen as 'common sense'. One politician remarked, 'A community of broken English is no community at all' (Pickles, 2013). The idea that learning English is 'common sense' signals that this is part of the dominant ideology. The underlying argument is that a community should be linguistically homogenous, that it can't be a community otherwise.

Although some people think that nation states *should* be this way, it is not usually the case. Thus, when people propose language legislation or complain about the 'deterioration' of or need for an official language, this may be a covert way of expressing negative views of 'the other'.

Canagarajah observes, 'In social practice . . . language has always been a hybrid and fluid repertoire of semiotic resources that people can employ strategically for their diverse interests, needs, and objectives' (2012: 252). This view sees language as a resource for meaning and identity-making and prompts us to examine the full range of what people can do and what they actually do to perform these identities and create meaning in specific contexts. 'We can agree that ethnic identities are socially and linguistically constructed, and yet affirm the importance of these identities' (Canagarajah, 2012: 255). Language policies that effectively demand the eradication of a person's first language prevent people from freely expressing their identity.

The use of a variety of languages by one speaker is so widespread that recent research in linguistics suggests that the noun 'language' does not capture all the things that people do with their language. Instead, they suggest we refer to 'languaging' (e.g., Makoni and Pennycook, 2005). By referring to 'languaging', what people actually do with the various linguistic resources they have in their repertoire is emphasised.

Find out what the language requirements are for immigration or citizenship in your country. Is competence in a particular language required? Which language(s)? How is this assessed? What does this signal about the identity of the nation?

Activity 7.3

7.4 RACISM AND REPRESENTATIONS OF ETHNICITY

In this section, we consider how different ethnicities are represented. Because minority ethnicities are not generally afforded positions of power in the social hierarchy, it is not surprising that representations of these groups are not positive. Racism can be seen as 'the everyday, mundane, negative opinion, attitudes and ideologies and the seemingly subtle acts and conditions of discrimination' (van Dijk, 1993: 5). When a group is singled out, it draws boundaries and allocates people to membership in categories they might not themselves have chosen.

Teun van Dijk has worked extensively on racist discourse and defines it as follows: 'Racist discourse is a form of discriminatory social practice that manifests itself in text, talk and communication' (2004: 351). Framing this discourse as a 'social practice' reminds us that speaking (and writing) is action, that in using racist discourses we are *doing* something. Van Dijk argues that there are two forms of racist discourse: '(1) racist discourse *directed at* ethnically different Others; (2) racist discourse *about* ethnically different Others' (2004: 351). One of the most obvious ways that racist discourse manifests is in pejorative words.

Van Dijk (2004: 352–353) identifies three ways that people construct racist discourse about the 'other':

a   *difference* – the 'other' is not like 'us'
b   *deviance* – the 'other' behaves in a way that 'we' feel is amoral
c   *threat* – the 'other' is dangerous

In addition, examples of more implicit racism can be framed as *difference*. The way different kinds of migrants are described is a good example. Mawuna Remarque Koutonin points out that white people who are migrants are referred to as 'expats', while other people are described as 'immigrants' (2015). Why would the term 'expat', one of the many terms used for people who are living outside their home nation (like 'immigrants', 'asylum seekers' and 'refugees') seem to be reserved for white people?

The association of *deviance* and *threat* with ethnicity is also very common and has a long history. An Australian member of Parliament expressed her view on Islam, which is represented in Example 7.1.

Example 7.1
Islam is a disease, we need to be vaccinated against it.

(cited in Remeikis, 2017)

A disease is both deviant and threatening. Here we also see the dehumanisation of a group of people. Muslims as represented in Example 7.1 are no longer people but are represented as vectors of disease. These strategies of depersonalisation are also commonly found in representations of migrants and asylum seekers.

In addition to using overtly racist words, the backgrounding of anything explicitly racist is another common tactic in discourse that is, in fact, racist. Van Dijk (1993) observes that people go to great lengths to deny that they are racist by presenting themselves positively. A common way of doing this is through an explicit denial, 'I'm not a racist, but...', followed by a statement about an ethnic group in negative terms (Bonilla-Silva and Forman, 2000).

Racist discourse can often be found in media representations. Arguments may be phrased in 'positive' terms, but the representation of the other is worthy of attention. One of the topics in which racist discourse often emerges is in relation to migrants. This is found around the world, but here we look at research conducted by Nguyen and McCallum (2016) in Australia in relation to 'maritime asylum seekers' (MAS). MAS are people who come to Australia by boat. It is worth remembering that an asylum seeker is a particular kind of migrant. While they are sometimes represented as 'economic migrants' (that is, people migrating in order to improve their life), an asylum seeker is someone who is applying to a new country to be recognised as a 'refugee' – that is, someone who is claiming a 'well-founded fear of persecution' (United Nations High Commissioner for Refugees, 1951) in their country of origin. Asylum seekers have rights under international law because they are seeking refuge from harm in their own country while economic or other kinds of migrants are not given such protection.

Nguyen and McCallum (2016) examined media representations of MAS using Lakoff and Johnson's metaphor theory (see Section 2.5). Considering previous research and representations, they state, 'Metaphors generally construct MAS as dangerous, ungrateful, unworthy, aggressive, economically draining and polluting to the Australian society and economy' (2016: 163). In their own data, the most common metaphors referring to MAS were types of flowing water, such as 'influx' or 'flows', as in Examples 7.2 and 7.3.

Example 7.2
Torres Strait Island Regional Council mayor Fred Gala has demanded a major funding boost to help island communities *cope with an expected influx* of asylum seekers trying to escape from PNG [Papua New Guinea].
(Scott, Taylor and Scarr, *Daily Telegraph*, 26 July 2013, cited in Nguyen and McCallum, 2016: 166)

Example 7.3
There should be a debate to ensure countries are not shirking their obligations . . . Indonesia talks of a regional solution to *asylum seeker flows* and a good start for it would be to sign on and help share the rules.
(Deeds, not mere words, *The Age*, 19 July 2013, cited in Nguyen and McCallum, 2016: 166)

The representation of migrants as a 'flood' is not unusual. It is such a common representation that it is sometimes difficult to see the metaphor at work here. As Nguyen and McCallum note, it is a particularly productive metaphor in so far as such movement is unidirectional and comes with a great deal of force. It also suggests that the destination of the 'flood' is a container of limited capacity.

Their data also showed that the territorial concept of 'home' was an important theme in that MAS were represented as not belonging in Australia; the MAS have other 'homes', and they should remain there.

Example 7.4

Asylum seekers trying to get to Australia could be *stopped at the door* and permanently resettled in developing countries . . .

(Benson, *Daily Telegraph*, 19 July 2013, cited in
Nguyen and McCallum, 2016: 168)

In Example 7.4, the country, Australia, is represented as a house. In Western culture, a house is private. It is something from which 'owners' have the right to exclude outsiders. Thus, representing the country as a house or home is extremely effective in terms of persuasion, as it resonates with a number of cultural values. It also clearly demarcates, in geographical terms, an 'us' from a 'them' (see Chapter 3).

7.4.1 Ethnicity online

Racism is also readily found online. For example, some of the reactions to the #Black Lives Matter campaign (BLM) in the US can be explained as racist. While the campaign was seeking to draw attention to the violence that black people suffer, some people understood the campaign to be **implying** that other lives don't matter. This belief was so strong that a campaign called #AllLivesMatter was initiated. Critics of #AllLivesMatter suggested that the misinterpretation of the BLM campaign is a result of racism because it overlooks the intention of BLM. As Barack Obama explained in a town hall meeting in 2016, 'What they [BLM] were suggesting was, there is a specific problem that is happening in the African-American community that's not happening in other communities. And that is a legitimate issue that we've got to address' (cited in Townes, 2015).

Because people can provide comments to all sorts of online media (see Section 4.9), language that may previously have only been found in the private sphere is now (at least potentially) visible to other people. As Hughey and Daniels remark, '[T]he internet provides no escape route from either race or racism' (2013: 333). And while the worst examples of racist, sexist and other violent and discriminatory language may be moderated out by mainstream news media, this itself is problematic, as it hides the extent of these practices.

The language that people use to convey racist ideas online should be examined carefully. Hughey and Daniels note that language can be 'coded' 'to convey subtle, yet potent, racial meanings in ways that appear well reasoned and focused on the common good' (2013: 337). This means that it is necessary to look beyond overtly racist words or phrases. However, clearly identifying what is racist is not always easy, as the BLM example shows.

Brown notes that there are some features of online communication which may be important when thinking about the similarities and differences between racist language online and offline (2018): anonymity, invisibility, community and speed of communication. First, it is easier to be anonymous online, thus an author might not be directly accountable for views put forward. Invisibility online is also not difficult: the author does not see and is not seen by their readers. Community and speed of communication may be even more important online. While someone may not interact with racists in their everyday life, it would be easy enough to find those individuals online. In relation to speed, creating anonymous printed text involves writing, publishing and distributing a newsletter, for example. This requires more elaborate activity than posting social media does. A tweet can be composed and sent out to a (potentially) very large audience with very little intervention of others.

7.4.2 Reclaiming terms

Sometimes, whether discourse can be racist depends on context, including who is speaking. For example, a term may be racist when a person from the out-group uses it but a positive identity marker when used by the group itself. In other words, terms that were originally used to demean a group are sometimes reclaimed for use by the in-group as a positive marker of identity. Although reclamation of negative terms may be a relatively unconscious action by a group, it can be considered a form of agency (see Section 6.3). One example of this is the word 'nigger', an extremely derogatory word used to refer to African Americans in the US. The term is so inflammatory that US speakers typically use the euphemism 'the N-word' in public discourse about the term (Rahman, 2012). When used by African Americans to each other, the term 'nigger' can mean a variety of things, however, that are not always pejorative (Kennedy, 1999; Croom, 2015). Thus, this marginalised group takes charge of the use and meaning of a word that had been used by out-group members to demean them. This process allows a marginalised group to reject the majority group's portrayal of them.

A similar case of reclamation exists in Australia where 'wog' is a term used to refer to migrants (and their children) from Italy, Greece and the Mediterranean generally, including Lebanon and the Middle East. While it was once a derogatory term, it has since been reclaimed and 'used to claim a common migration experience and background' (Kiesling, 2005: 4). As a marker of identity, 'wog' began to be used to positively (by in-group members) to affiliate with a particular ethnic identity. This was so much the case that the group even parodied their own language, their ethnolect, and other cultural behaviours, in productions for television and theatre, such as *Wogs out of Work*.[1]

Can you think of other previously pejorative terms that have been reclaimed? You might know some that aren't connected to ethnic identities but to some other aspect of identity. Do your colleagues agree that they have been reclaimed? Can everyone use these terms, or are they restricted for the use of certain people?

Activity 7.4

7.5 ETHNICITY AND LANGUAGE VARIATION

Hoffman and Walker (2010: 42) describe an 'ethnolect' as a language variety that can 'serve to differentiate speakers who wish to convey membership in a particular ethnic group'. While an 'ethnolect' might be thought to be used only by members of an immigrant community, this is not always the case. In fact, the linguistic features that distinguish an ethnolect may have no connection to a heritage language at all (Labov, 2008).

A person might claim membership in an ethnic group based on where their parents were born. But whether this will be accepted or acknowledged by other members of this group may depend on what kind of evidence of membership is provided. Identities based on ethnicity sometimes have to be ratified by other members of the group. Some of this evidence might be constituted by linguistic variables, for example, a certain proficiency in a language may be enough to have an ethnic identity accepted. However, there might be other identity markers that need to be addressed in different ways, or even shown with different signs, by wearing certain clothes, having bodily markings and so on.

Crucially, groups don't always assign value to the same things; thus, ideological differences may result in the positive evaluation of a language variety in one community but not in another. Labov's concept of 'covert prestige' makes this clearer (1972a). The notion of 'covert prestige' acknowledges that some speech communities, usually ones that don't have a great deal of power in relation to other dominant groups, value different kinds of speaking, often involving non-standard varieties (such as **AAE**). For those communities, these non-standard varieties are 'covertly' prestigious, or valued within the community but not outside it. '**Overt prestige**' is awarded to varieties that are valued according to **hegemonic** norms. Thus, speaking the standard variety of a language confers prestige in wider society but may not within particular communities. These features relate directly to the 'linguistic push-pull' that Rahman (2008) refers to (see Section 7.3.2).

7.5.1 'Wogspeak' HRT

Like age, class and gender, it is possible to find some correlations between ethnicity and specific **linguistic variables** while being careful about how we define ethnicity and how we interpret these correlations. Scott Kiesling's (2005) research on 'wogspeak' demonstrates the importance of considering the interaction of a number of features that occur when language is used to indicate identity.

Migration to Australia has occurred in various waves from various places since colonisation by the British in the 18th century. In the mid-20th century, significant numbers of Italian and Greek workers arrived in Australia with further waves of migration since. The children and grandchildren of migrants from the Mediterranean may now call themselves 'wogs'. Kiesling (2005) studied the ethnolect of this group, which he calls New Australian English

(NAusE). Kiesling's data come from interviews with four ethnic groups conducted by a Greek Australian student in Sydney. Kiesling examined a number of linguistic variables, notably vowels and high rising terminal phrases (HRT). HRT is used to describe the way a speaker's intonation will go up (rise) at the end of a word or utterance. It is similar to the intonation pattern for questions but used in a declarative statement. Specifically, he examined the vowel sound ('ah') in Australian English, like at the end of 'better', to ascertain whether it was pronounced differently by Anglo and ethnic groups. Kiesling's data did, in fact, show a difference in the pronunciation of 'ah' in HRT. The data showed a difference in two aspects of voice quality ('openness' and 'length'). However, there is also variation in use in individuals as the Figures 7.1 and 7.2 show.

In spite of the variation among individuals, we can make some generalisations if we cluster the individual results into groups. Kiesling summarises as follows:

1   Greek-Australian speakers, when using HRT on (er), exhibit a dramatically longer average length [of the vowel] than all other groups.
2   Lebanese-Australian speakers are also significantly different from Anglos but exhibit much more variability than Greek-Australians.

(Kiesling, 2005: 20)

The first conclusion means that when high rising terminals occur with the sound (ah), the length of this sound is longest for Greek Australian speakers. Kiesling emphasises that the features shouldn't be examined

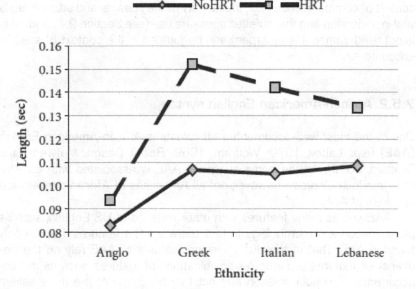

Figure 7.1 Length by ethnicity and HRT
Source: Kiesling, 2005

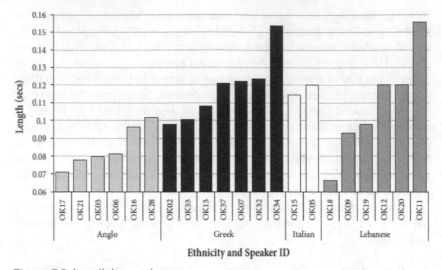

Figure 7.2 Length by speaker
Source: Kiesling, 2005

in isolation. Rather, together, vowel length *and* openness with regard to HRT create the **style** identified by speakers in Australia as 'wogspeak' (Kiesling, 2005: 20).

Kiesling also points out that the ethnicity of the interviewer who gathered this data has to be taken into account when analysing the data. Interviewees might take various stances towards the interviewer based on whether their experiences as migrants are similar to hers or not. Taking into account the context of communication (e.g., the identity of the speaker and addressee) is vital in understanding the varieties speakers use (see Section 9.4.2). Identity is not fixed; rather, it is emergent and negotiated in the context of specific encounters.

7.5.2 African-American English syntax

One of the most well-documented ethnolects is African-American English (**AAE**) (e.g., Labov, 1970; Wolfram, 1969; Bailey, Baugh, Mufwene and Rickford, 2013). As the name suggests, AAE is associated with an African-American ethnicity; however, not all Americans of African descent are speakers of AAE.

AAE shares many features with other varieties of US English, such as pronunciation and morphology. In fact, there are few features that are only found in AAE. That is, the distinguishing features of AAE rely on the frequency of features or particular combinations of features, such as the co-occurrence of copula deletion and habitual be. Some of the more salient features to out-group members tend to be structural. Table 7.1 provides some examples of features of AAE (Wolfram, 2009: 330).

Table 7.1 Features of AAE

Linguistic feature	AAE	European-American English
Copula deletion: deleting the verb 'to be'	He late. They running.	He is late. They are running.
Habitual 'be': to indicate habitual or intermittent activity, usually in the 'be' +-ing form	Sarah don't usually be there. John be late.	Sarah isn't usually there. John is always late.
Absence of 'possessive s'	John hat Jack car	John's hat Jack's car

Source: adapted from Wolfram, 2009: 330

AAE is not homogenous across geographic regions; thus, AAE varies depending on where speakers acquire it, just like other varieties of US English (Wolfram, 2009).

Labov and many other scholars have also described the perception in society that AAE is somehow linguistically deficient, that it is a 'faulty' version of standard English (Labov, 1970). Although linguists have shown that AAE is a logically structured language just like any other language, AAE is strongly disfavoured. This negative attitude toward AAE is an example of the strong roots of language ideologies and linguistic subordination. In Chapter 2, we explored the structure and power of language ideologies. With regard to AAE, perceptions of AAE show that people think that it is not a language but simply a degenerated form of English (e.g., Smitherman, 1977; Lippi-Green, 2011; Wolfram, 1998).

> All linguists agree that nonstandard dialects are highly structured systems; they do not see these dialects as accumulations of errors caused by the failure of their speakers to master standard English. When linguists hear black children saying 'He crazy' or 'Her my friend' they do not hear a 'primitive language'.
>
> (Labov, 1972b)

The belief that AAE speakers are unintelligent or cognitively lacking in some way is an enduring misconception that extends to speakers of other nonstandard varieties. Rosa, in describing the interaction of ethnicity and language in the Latinx population in the US, explains it this way: '[W]hat might appear as perceptions of particular nonstandardised practices can in fact racialise populations by framing them as incapable of producing any legitimate language' (2016: 163). These kinds of misconceptions can have serious consequences in terms of education, access to employment and to how one is generally perceived. Research tells us that even a few features of AAE are enough to trigger an identification of a speaker as being of African-American ethnicity (Purnell et al., 1999). This suggests that in these speech communities, AAE is a salient variety.

At the same time, like many marginalised varieties, AAE also carries a great many positive connotations within its community of speakers. This puts speakers in a difficult position. Rahman (2008) studied the views that middle-class African Americans have of AAE and how they use it. She sets out the central concern:

> The dilemma for many African Americans is that language that serves as a symbol of ethnic identity may also serve as the focus for discrimination in mainstream society and language that can be useful for socioeconomic advancement may lead to suspicion in the African-American community.

(2008: 142)

She refers to this dilemma as a 'linguistic push-pull' (Rahman, 2008: 142), a problem that many speakers of marginalised sociolects face. As we'll discuss later, sociolects can be very important for speakers in performing their identity.

Activity 7.5

Jones (2016) uses data from social media to describe the use of an AAE quotative (see also Section 7.5.5) 'talmbout', an expression derived from 'talking about', as in the following examples (Jones, 2016: 91):

a   Everbody laughing nshit & here you come talmbout some 'I don't get it'.

(Twitter)

b   Man I cannot stand Jackie w that trench coat talmbout she was getting her Hepburn on.

(Twitter)

Go to Twitter and find examples of 'talmbout'. What are the different ways that 'talmbout' is used? What are the linguistic constraints on using 'talmbout'?

Quotatives are expressions that a speaker uses to indicate that they are reporting what someone else said. Jones explains that 'talmbout' is used to introduce both direct and reported speech and is similar to quotatives like 'be like', but it can also introduce unuttered thoughts and nonlexical sounds. As such, talmbout can express more than quotative 'be like' because it can signal social and pragmatic meanings that other quotatives cannot.

7.5.3 Lumbee English syntax/rhoticity

Schilling-Estes describes the performance of ethnicity in Robeson County in North Carolina in the US. Robeson County is located in the American South 'where a biracial classification system has long been firmly entrenched' (2004: 166). The two groups in this system are black and white. But in North Carolina, as in many other parts of the world, there are indigenous people too. In Robeson County, the Lumbee Indians have always been a significant part of the population and have 'struggled to assert themselves as a separate people who are neither White nor Black' (2004: 166). The Lumbee have also faced difficulties because of ideas about what it means to be an 'authentic' Indian tribe. The Lumbee have been variously described over the years in terms of ethnicity. Prior to 1885, 'they were referred to simply as "mixed", "free persons of colour", or, occasionally, "free White"' (Schilling-Estes, 2004: 167). The Lumbee, themselves, have resisted this biracial classification. For them, being identified as black was to be subject to all manner of discrimination, and identifying as white would be to erase their indigenous ethnic identity (Schilling-Estes, 2004: 167). Describing ethnicity sometimes involves disassociating from the groups and values one doesn't want to be identified with. This complex positioning of groups is well demonstrated in Schilling-Estes's research. She analyses conversations between two young men, one African American, Alex, and the other Lumbee, Lou. While both ethnolects share common features, there are differences in both the level and range of use. For example, both AAE and Lumbee English make use of uninflected 'habitual be', as in 'He be talking all the time' (Schilling-Estes, 2004: 168). But in Lumbee English, unlike AAE, 'be' can be inflected; 'He bes talking' and 'in certain non-habitual contexts', for example, 'I might be lost some inches' (Schilling-Estes, 2004: 169).

The conversation ranged over a number of different topics. The two men knew each other from university and so at times would be talking about people they both knew or past events they both participated in. But they also discussed politics, race relations and the American civil war. Another one of the linguistic features Schilling-Estes examined was **rhoticity** after vowels. Both AAE and some varieties of Southern English are non-rhotic in some contexts. The Lumbee, however, show a slightly lower percentage of non-rhoticity when compared with both whites and African Americans (Schilling-Estes, 2004: 171). Figure 7.3 shows the percentage of non-rhoticity in the speech of Lou and Alex according to topic of conversation.

Figure 7.3 charts the percentage of non-rhoticity for each speaker when discussing different topics. What do you notice about the patterns of usage? Consider the upper and lower values of each speaker. When are the two levels of use closest? What explanation might there be for this?

Activity 7.6

As Schilling-Estes notes, Alex generally uses a higher percentage of non-rhoticity than Lou. But for this variable (Schilling-Estes also looked at others),

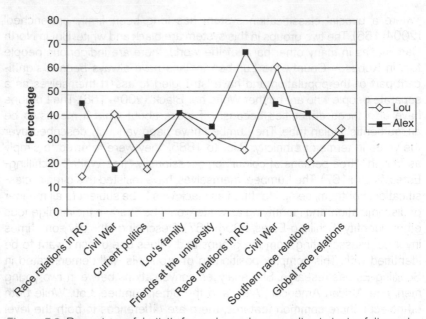

Figure 7.3 Percentage of rhoticity for each speaker according to topic of discussion
Source: Schilling-Estes, 2004: 173

Alex and Lou are closest in their level of usage when discussing family and friends. If language is connected to ethnicity, how are we to make sense of this? It's not the case that Alex's and Lou's ethnicity changes over the course of the interview. Schilling-Estes writes,

> One explanation for the linguistic distance in the sections on race relations is that considerations of ethnic group membership may be more salient when the two are talking directly about the subject than when taking about family and friends, at which point considerations of personal friendship are uppermost.
>
> (2004: 177)

The change in language use can indicate a distance from the other person but can also be used to indicate closeness.

7.5.4 Gang identity creaky voice

Mendoza-Denton's (1996) research on Latina gangs in Northern California describes the use of language and other practices to construct an identity which is linked to a particular type of ethnicity and femininity. Mendoza-Denton undertook an **ethnographic** study of Latina gangs in California, spending a lot of time with and around the gangs in order to understand the way they construct their identities. In her field site, there were two gangs.

The first group, Sureñas/os (Southerners) are generally recent migrants from Mexico. In contrast, the Norteñas/os (Northerners) tend to be American born. These groups orient to the world in different ways; 'they are in deep conflict over the politics of identity in their community, and this conflict is reflected in their language attitudes, discourse patterns, and eventual success (or lack thereof) in the American educational system' (1996: 52). Sureñas tend to orient to Mexico and Mexican culture, while Norteñas value the cultural products and practices associated with the US. The importance of these identities is seen very clearly in the social practices that the Sureñas and Norteñas use to display these identities. Here we consider a range of semiotic resources, including language, these women use to perform a specific local identity.

Mendoza-Denton describes one of the gang members' use of a linguistic feature called 'creaky voice' 'in narratives for the construction of a hardcore persona' (2011: 266). Creaky voice describes a type of vibration (a type of phonation) of the vocal cords (vocal folds) while talking. Creaky voice is also known as 'vocal fry'. In other English-speaking communities, it has been associated with a variety of social characteristics (Mendoza-Denton, 2011: 265). Mendoza-Denton's research documents the speech of one young Norteña, 'Babygirl'. Babygirl uses creaky voice to perform a tough, female persona but not all the time, as the following shows (creaky voice indicated in bold).

Example 7.5
Transcript: Babygirl at home (0:56) Mendoza-Denton (2011: 267).

```
1    All my homeboys respect me a lot//
     they never/you know //
     they always look up to me/and they're always like/ you know //
     tell me what's up/you know //
5    and they always protect me/you know //
     it seems like //
     I'm like the only female there //
     but they always seem to protect me //
     you know //
10   from other guys //
     you know //
     from other dudes //
     so it's like they're //
     it's like/we're like a whole big family //
15   you know //
     we could uhm //
     we could talk about uhm ... //
     we could talk about uhm ... //
     it's like a – we're –
20   we could talk about like//
     we could talk about like//
```

what happened/at home/you know //
how do you **feel about things** at home you know //
and we could talk **about** //
25   anything

Mendoza-Denton argues that creaky voice is found at points where emotion is being managed. 'In this young woman's narrative, creaky voice participates in a local economy of affect centred around being silent, being hard of heart (hardcore), and being toughened through experience' (2011: 269). Mendoza-Denton describes how creaky voice signals toughness among Norteñas when used in conjunction with other semiotic resources, such as makeup (Mendoza-Denton, 1996). Norteñas and Sureñas both use makeup and clothing to signal group membership (see Table 7.2). Norteñas, for example, use both solid and liquid eyeliner to create a strong, hard and long line, sometimes almost to the temples. It is understood as an expression and marker of power and toughness. The same is true of other practices as Babygirl suggests:

Example 7.6
We never wear earrings
just in case we get in a fight
It's not our style to wear earrings/me entiendes/ (you know?)
Don't even smile
That's the weak spot
Don't ever smile

(Mendoza-Denton, 1996: 56)

Mendoza-Denton argues that 'creaky voice assists these gang girls in the construction of a hardcore persona in the context of a locally defined economy of affect' (2011: 266). The performance of the hardcore identity exploits existing language resources in order to construct an identity which is locally relevant and which is appropriate to Babygirl's audience. This kind of creativity is not unusual among adolescents. As we will see in Chapter 8, this period of life is one of experimentation with social roles, ideas and personal presentation, thus, it is hardly surprising that the same kind of creativity should be found in language.

Table 7.2 Semiotic resources for indicating group membership in Norteñas and Sureñas

	Norteñas	*Sureñas*
Colour	Red burgundy	Blue navy
Hairdo	Feathered hair	Vertical ponytail
Eyeliner	Solid first, then liquid	Solid only
Lipstick	Deep red / burgundy	Brown

Source: adapted from Mendoza-Denton, 1996: 53

Table 7.3 Use of quotative verbs in New Zealand English

Quotative	Maori English	Pakeha English
be like	41.9%	58.5%
say	11.7%	14.9%
think	4.9%	5.0%
go	11.7%	11.6%
'zero' (i.e., no quotative used)	24.2%	7.9%
Other	5.7	2.1

Source: adapted from D'Arcy, 2010: 68

7.5.5 Ethnolect or repertoire?

In New Zealand, the two main ethnic groups are Europeans (Pakeha) and indigenous Maori (te tāngata whenua). English, however, is the dominant language for both groups in that it is the most commonly used. D'Arcy (2010) examined the use of 'be like' as quotatives in the speech of young men, both Maori and Pakeha. As noted, quotatives are words used to indicate that a person is quoting (or seeming to quote) someone else or one's own thoughts.

Table 7.3 shows the different quotatives that speakers used and the percentage of use of each quotative. It is clear that 'be like' is the most commonly used, and more used by Pakeha men than Maori men. For Maori men, not using a quotative at all ('zero' in Table 7.3) is much more frequent than for Pakeha men. Further statistical evaluation leads D'Arcy to conclude that 'be like' 'is favoured in Pakeha English and disfavored in Maori English' (2010: 69).

It's important to notice that Maori and Pakeha speakers use the same set of quotative expressions and that what distinguishes one group from the other is patterns of use. D'Arcy thus argues that it is more helpful to consider the *set of features* that speakers can draw on to construct their identity, or an 'ethnolinguistic repertoire' (Benor, 2010), than referring to 'ethnolects'.

> Selective use of the elements of an ethnolinguistic repertoire may or may not be conscious on the part of the speaker, and may or may not be perceived by interlocutors, but such elements nonetheless function as linguistic resources for ethnic distinction.
>
> (D'Arcy, 2010: 79)

7.6 ETHNICITY AND IDENTITY

As we have already seen, linguistic features can be used to signal ethnicity and other kinds of identity. In this section, we focus on other practices and discourses that can be used to construct identity in interaction.

7.6.1 Mexican ethnicity and code switching

In this section, we focus on research by Petra Scott Shenk which examines how individuals claim a Mexican ethnicity through their discourse. Shenk takes up a theme which is current in contemporary sociolinguistic research; that is, what is authenticity? She notes that authenticity, in this case claims of ethnicity, is not predetermined. Rather, individuals appeal to ideological constructs of that ethnicity in order to formulate defensible claims to authenticity. Shenk argues that 'positioning oneself as authentic often depends on positioning the other as inauthentic' (2007: 198). She also notes that power is crucial here, even if it is a local power structure, as 'the authentically positioned participant has the authority to delegitimise the authenticity of the other participant' (2007: 198).

Shenk's research examined Spanish-English code switching among a small group of **bilingual** Californian university students. We use the term **code switching** to refer to the use of two or more linguistic codes within a conversation or even within the same utterance. Shenk writes, 'In these data, Spanish linguistic proficiency, place of birth, and purity of bloodline are evoked as ideological tests for authenticity' (2007: 199). Not all of the informants were born in Mexico, and they don't all have Mexican born parents. Finally, none of them are fluent in Spanish. Shenk argues that all of these individuals are 'on the margin of the group' (2007: 199) that could claim Mexican ethnicity according to the three tests just mentioned. That they all know this means that claims to authentic ethnicity are important but also problematic. This kind of non-central membership is far from unusual. What it means, though, is that rather than ethnicity being a binary category (where you either belong or you don't; you're part of 'us' or 'them'), we find 'internal hierarchies of ideology and power that cannot be completely separated from the ideologies of the external dominant culture' (2007: 200). Thus, potential members of this group are positioned both by authentic/core members of the ethnic group as well as by values of the exterior majority.

The relationship of these in-group tests for membership to out-group norms is clearly demonstrated in the case of purity of bloodline. Even though colonial American institutions valued 'European blood' over anything else, mixed European and indigenous bloodlines meant impurity and a lower place on the hierarchy of power. Indeed, Spanish was seen as 'white' and Mexican as 'mixed'. While the informants here have a concept of 'pure' Mexican bloodlines (as opposed to the colonial view of their ethnicity as mixed and impure), there has nevertheless been an incorporation of the broader ideological position in relation to blood and its purity. We can see appeals to purity and birthplace in the following exchange from Shenk (2007: 206–207) [Lalo is a man and Bela a woman]:

Example 7.7

11	Bela: Este,	*Okay,*
12	Bela: mira mira,	*look look,*

{ 13	Bela:	[no empieces] {smiling voice}	don't you start {smiling voice}
{ 14	Lalo:	[hhh, {laughter}]	[hhh, laughter]
15	Bela:	T´u ni siquiera eres original	You're not original either.
16	Lalo:	M´as original quet u {smiling voice}	More original than you {smiling}
17	Lalo:	(.) Both of my	Both of my
{ 18	Lalo:	[parents are-]	[parents are-]
{ 19	Bela:	[Mas origi]nal?	[More origi]nal?
20	Lalo:	(.) are Aztec BLOOD	(.) are Aztec BLOOD
{ 21	Bela:	Ay cal[mate]{smiling} [Tu]?	Oh calm down. {smiling}.You?
{ 22	Lalo:	[hhh {laughter}] [{laughter}]	
23	Lalo:	{laughter}hhh.	
{ 24	Bela:	donde nacis[te] [En don-]	where were you born. Wher-
{ 25	Lalo:	[Soy][PURO]	I'm PURE
26	Lalo:	Yo soy PURO.	I am PURE
{ 27	Bela:	Cual [PURO:] {smiling voice}	What (are you talking about) PURE.
28	Lalo:	[Soy nacido]-	I was born-
29	Lalo:	Soy nacido aqu´i pero,	I was born here but,
30	Lalo:	soy PURO	I'm pure.
{ 31	Bela:	Ay [sí mira mira]{mocking}.	Oh yeah look look. {mocking}
{ 32	Lalo:	[Please man]	Please man
33	Bela:	Donde nacieron tus papas	Where were your folks born.
34	Lalo:	Z:acatecas Jalisco,	Z:acatecas Jalisco
35	Lalo:	that's like the HEART.	that's like the HEART
{ 36	Bela:	[Zaca]tecas Jali:sco .hhh	{laughter}{mocking}
{ 37	Lalo:	[Ye]-	
38	Lalo:	Yeah,	
39		my mom's from Zacatecas,	
40		my dad's from –	
41		(-) from Los Altos {smiling voice}	
42		(.)That's the HEART fool.	
43		That's where the REAL Mexicans come from.	
44	Bela:	Ay mira y tu? {smiling voice}	Oh look and you?
{ 45	Bela:	(.)De donde [saliste] {smiling voice}	Where are you from.
{ 46	Lalo:	[Psh that's-] Psh that's	
47	Lalo:	% that's my land fool %	
48		(-) I came from my mother's WOMB.	
49	Bela:	[laughter]	

Adapted from Shenk (2007: 206–207)

We can see that both acknowledge that they're not 'original', and so the dispute begins to establish who is 'more original' (line 16 ff). Lalo links this to his 'Aztec blood' as 'the Aztecs, as precolonial and hence pure-blooded Mexicans, ideologically represent the archetype of Mexicanness for many Mexican American people' (Shenk, 2007: 208). It is somewhat strange that when

Lalo provides evidence for his 'more original' position, he switches to English. It may be that he considers his lineage such strong evidence for his ethnicity that any performance in Spanish becomes redundant. Indeed, Shenk points out that the Spanish he does use here is not idiomatic. Thus, his switch to English may be to background his problematic position in relation to the requirement for Spanish fluency. Nevertheless, competence in a language is common as a discourse to claim ethnicity as well as a resource to display it.

7.6.2 African-American ethnicity and lexicon

Cutler (1999) studied a white middle-class teenager, Mike, who at times in his life adopted features of AAE in order to project a particular kind of identity. Cutler suggests that Mike uses AAE features to take advantage of the prestige associated with African-American youth culture (Cutler, 1999: 429). Mike seems to be demonstrating an alignment with hip-hop. It should be said that hip-hop is certainly not synonymous with African-American culture. Rather, hip-hop itself might be said to draw on the cultural value of features of AAE and its association with a cool toughness, especially for young men. As well as adopting phonetic features of AAE, Mike also uses some of the **lexical items** associated with this language.

Example 7.8

a   Mike (age 16; 1996): You ever hear of Frank Frazetta? Dis is some **phat** shit, yo. **Yo,** when the dude dies, dis book will probably worth like a thousand dollars. **Yo,** tell **that shit** is not **phat**!

(Cutler, 1999: 422)

b   Mike (age 16; 1996): Dis is gonna sound **mad** weird, yo. Don't worry, don't worry. I'll put **THE SHIT** OFF! Don't touch it. **Chill,** DON'T TOUCH IT! DON'T TOUCH IT! I got this over here!

(Cutler, 1999: 423)

For Mike, the use of linguistic features was coupled with other behaviours. He joined a gang, tagged his name in graffiti and generally tried to behave in ways inconsistent with normative expectations of what a middle-class white boy might do. While at one point in his life, he seemed to be trying to perform an African-American identity, over time, this changed. While he retained some AAE linguistic features, 'this was no longer an attempt to construct a black identity' (Cutler, 1999: 435). This makes sense when remembering that hip-hop draws on the linguistic features of AAE without requiring that these index some kind of 'objective' ethnicity or indeed be related to ethnicity at all. Thus Mike is able to draw on various semiotic resources associated with African-American identity as he develops his own identity.

7.6.3 Welsh turfing practice

Language proficiency can be a clear and expedient indicator of belonging and of having verifiable and demonstrable roots. At the same time, it takes considerable effort to acquire such competence for L2 speakers. Yet linguistic competence isn't the only way of claiming an ethnicity. There are other forms of cultural capital which can be developed and exploited. For example a study of Americans who claimed a Welsh identity found the higher informants' competence in Welsh, the more intense affiliations to Wales they reported (Coupland, Bishop, Evans and Garrett, 2006: 363).

Wray, Evans, Coupland and Bishop (2003) argue that it is possible to 'turf' an identity, that is, create connections even though there is no historical personal link to the ethnic community.

> Turfing entails the deliberate attempt to revitalise a historically 'rooted' community by encouraging outsiders to adopt aspects of its cultural identity. We use the metaphor of turfing because the outward manifestations of the culture are not, as with the original rooted community, an expression of a pre-existing identity. Rather, they are put into place before the affective identity arises, in the hope that 'roots will grow down', anchoring the new community members permanently into the adopted identity.
>
> (2003: 49)

The research subjects, American college students participating in a Welsh choir, are thus able to 'turf' an identity, in part by enacting salient practices: singing and specifically, singing in Welsh at their college in the US and also during trips to Wales. We can also understand how people seek to trace their family history, especially those from former colonies, as a way of establishing a claim to an ethnic identity. It should be noted that the creation and maintenance of such identities is labour intensive. Individuals generally perceive some kind of cultural capital resulting from this labour. However, not all the consequences of ethnolects are quite so valued.

7.6.4 Situated ethnicity

The term 'authenticity' suggests that there is one true identity that people can lay claim to. As we have seen, language skill can be used as a warrant for certain kinds of identity claims. But sometimes people are very pragmatic about the kinds of identity they lay claim to. This can already be seen in the Shenk example. Bela and Lalo draw on the resources they have (both linguistic and biographical) in order to situate themselves in relation to each other and in relation to ideas that they both seem to share about what is authentic.

When people are dealing with other communicative contexts, however, the identity claims may shift too. This is particularly clear in the case of migrants and those who belong to minority groups. Ndhlovu's (2013) research on the language practices of refugees shows how this works among African migrants in Australia. He demonstrates that the languages people speak are evidence of their migration journeys and the linguistic economies (see Section 10.10) of their places of origin. These linguistic economies don't always match up with the ideas that the destination country has about how language and place are connected.

He cites the example of a woman who can speak a range of languages, including 'English, French, Kibembe, Kiswahili, Lingala and Shona' (Ndhlovu, 2013: 432). When Ndhlovu asks what her 'ethnic language' is, she replies, 'It's Kibembe but I can't speak it anymore that's why I say I am going to Kiswahili' (cited in Ndhlovu, 2013: 432). Because, as Ndhlovu observes, Kiswahili is not usually associated with a particular ethnic group, but is rather considered a regional **lingua franca**, her choice of Kiswahili as her 'ethnic language' is connected to the bureaucratic structures in Australia that migrants have to interact with. He writes, 'Kiswahili is among the few African migrant languages that are officially recognised by service providers in Australia and for which interpretation and translation services are readily available' (2013: 432). The choice of language is not about being authentic as such but rather about choosing from the available linguistic resources an individual has in order to strategically relate to existing structures in the new place.

Banda and Peck's (2016) research in South Africa also shows the complexity of how language choice constructs identity. They looked at the language choices of students at the University of the Western Cape (UWC) in South Africa, a historically black only university. In South Africa, as in other places, designations of ethnicity, language and their social meanings can change according to context. Although English is a common lingua franca at UWC and the 'official language of education and business' (Banda and Peck, 2016: 580) some students who are fluent refuse to use it in informal interactions. However, some students maintain English rather than using another language in which they are fluent (e.g., Xhosa). A student who maintains English, while being fluent in Xhosa, says:

> I know how to say it in Xhosa, but I can't cheat myself out of who I am because I want to get accepted. I speak in English whether you understand it or not.
>
> (quoted in Banda and Peck, 2016: 581)

Here, the choice of language seems to be driven by the identity the speaker wants to construct. It is important to remember that this identity construction is influenced by the surrounding context and the values that language and ethnicity carry with them. This can be seen in another study from South Africa involving school children. Wilmot (2014) shows that young people are adopting English as a language of prestige and identity and, further, **accommodating** their English to the prestige variety. She studied students in two single-sex girls' schools. One was predominantly white (where students' L1 was generally English) and one predominantly black (where L1 was generally isiXhosa). She found the isiXhosa speakers embracing English not only because of its prestige in South Africa in general (and in educational contexts in particular) but also as a way of expressing identity. While these students were proud of their isiXhosa cultural and linguistic heritage, they also recognised the value that English has in the **linguistic market** (see Section 10.10).

The isiXhosa L1 speakers experienced social distance, however, from isiXhosa peers who were not being educated in or were not fluent in English. Various negative labels were applied to the black English speakers (including 'coconut' and 'oreo') by the non-English speaking isiXhosa peers. But as Wilmot explains, as the isiXhosa are bilingual, they did not consider these labels to apply to them. That is, 'identity is no longer seen to be limited to race or language group; rather, through language, the participants are able to take up multiple identity positions that best suit different circumstances and contexts' (Wilmot, 2014: 330).

7.7 CONSEQUENCES FOR ETHNOLECTS

There are a variety of negative consequences for speakers of ethnolects. These consequences could be as innocuous as minor misunderstandings or as serious as educational discrimination and incarceration. In the following, we describe examples of miscommunication to demonstrate the varying effects of cross-dialect interaction.

7.7.1 Caribbean English

The potential for misunderstanding always exists in cross-dialectal interactions. Nero (2006) describes the differences between Caribbean English (CE) and Standard American English (SAE) with a particular interest in educational contexts. In this case, the context was Caribbean migrants to North America. As she points out, documenting and exploring these differences has consequences not only for particular interactions and settings but also for what we mean by 'language' and 'ethnicity' (2006: 501). Caribbean English can be discussed in terms of global Englishes (see Chapter 10). CE speakers are found throughout the world and come from different parts of the Caribbean, including Jamaica and Guyana (2006: 503). As with many Creoles and global Englishes, there is more than one kind of CE. It is possible to distinguish between the basilect, 'an English based Creole', a mesolect, 'between English and Creole', and an acrolect 'regionally accented varieties of the standard language' (2006: 502). Nero includes other distinctions that can be made in the particular case of CE, but this three-way distinction serves us well here.

As it is closest to standard English, the acrolect may present fewer opportunities for misunderstanding. But this puts speakers in a difficult

Table 7.4 Lexical items in CE and SAE

Word	Meaning in CE	Meaning in SAE
Hand	Part of the body from the shoulder to the fingers	Part of the body from the wrist to the fingers
Foot	Part of the body from the thighs to the toes	Part of the body from the ankles to the toes
Tea	Any hot beverage	Specific beverage made from tea leaves

Source: adapted from Nero, 2006: 506, Table 1

position as 'the basilect and especially the mesolect are often used to assert 'true' Caribbean identity in informal and private domains' (2006: 503). Moreover, the basilect is also stigmatised, as it is associated with lack of education and a low socio-economic position (2006: 503).

Nero argues that one of the most common ways in which miscommunication occurs between CE speakers and SAE speakers is confusion about **lexical items**. While the words have the same form across languages, their meanings are very different (see Table 7.4).

Misunderstanding is also attributed to accent, although this can usually be resolved by listening carefully or through context (Nero, 2006: 506–507). In an educational setting, where a great deal may depend on pronouncing words 'correctly', however, accent can have negative consequences in terms of perceptions of ability and learning trajectories.

The lexical differences will have effects for writing, and the importance of writing in educational (and other contexts) is well known. While this may not result in severe misunderstanding, it may lead to misunderstanding intended politeness or simply be attributed to faulty use of the language. In an educational context, Nero argues that teachers responsible for the education of CE speakers should be trained in the specific features of CE, have a full understanding of Caribbean culture and be familiar with communicative norms. In terms of the latter, for example, Nero points out that 'direct eye contact with the teacher or an adult is considered rude in Caribbean schools' (2006: 508). Not knowing this may lead a teacher to attribute an attitude to a student which they don't actually mean to convey. One might summarise the many useful recommendations that Nero provides as 'don't assume'. She suggests that teachers should probe students' intended meaning, provide opportunities for the use of different varieties of English and be open to the different conventions of languages both when selecting teaching materials and activities and interacting with students (see also Labov, 1982). Language itself can then become a topic for discussion and learning rather than being an obstacle to understanding. This is a constructive strategy in any educational context, especially given that most varieties of English are not in fact 'standard' (see Chapter 10).

7.7.2 Australian Aboriginal English

Eades (2003) studied the way indigenous Australians are treated in the legal system. She found that the conventions of Aboriginal English (AE) put indigenous people at a serious disadvantage in a legal system that relies on and enforces Anglo conventions of communication. Eades points out some of the causes of misunderstanding are discourse strategies such as silence, gratuitous concurrence, syntactic form of questions and interruption. For example, silence is 'important and positively valued' (2003: 202) by speakers of AE. It signals, for example, the importance of the topic under discussion and as such can be understood as a sign of respect and attention. The rules of the courtroom, however, construe silence from a witness or suspect as evidence of deception or lack of co-operation.

Gratuitous concurrence describes how speakers of AE may answer 'yes' to **closed questions**, 'regardless of either their understanding of the question or their belief about the truth or falsity of the proposition being questioned' (Eades, 2003: 203). In any communication context, this convention may lead to miscommunication with non-AE speakers. In a legal context, this can be very damaging and lead to serious injustice. There are other aspects of questioning conventions that differ for speakers of AE. Eades notes that it is not unusual for a declarative with rising intonation to be understood as a question that invites more than simply a 'yes/no' response. It is treated as 'an invitation to explain' (2000: 172). Because speaking rights in the courtroom are restricted, any extended speech may also be construed negatively in the legal context. Because of the differing discourse strategies of AE and Anglo speakers, AE speakers are often interrupted and silenced in the court. Eades finds that such interruptions are often made by the judge. Example 7.9 is a transcript of an interaction between an AE witness and an Anglo judge. The judge's interruptions are linked to the witness trying to provide a detailed response to what is, for non-AE speakers, a closed question.

Example 7.9

```
31  J:  Have you spoken to them since?
32  W:  Oh [(xxxxx)
33  J:      [Since this event?=
34  W:  =at court I did yeah – last=
35  J:  =Have you indicated to them what you're telling me that you
        feel it was unwarranted and that you're sorry for it?
36  W:  Yeah – yeah it's=
37  J:  =You've said that to them?
38  W:  Yeah – yeah.
39  J:  You tell me that truly?
40  W:  Yeah (1.2) I said it when I got charged that that was – you
        know – my stupidness
```

(adapted from Eades, 2000: 174)

The question asked in line 31 could be answered with a simple 'yes', and given that the judge keeps asking the question, it is clear that this is what he wants. When the witness tries to provide more than this, the judge interrupts. Had the witness been allowed to speak at line 32, the judge may not have needed to ask so many questions. These misunderstandings occur because of different communicative conventions in what look like the same language. When obviously different languages are involved in the same communicative context, it is at least easier to anticipate misunderstandings.

Activity 7.7

Can you think of other contexts where cross-dialect miscommunication may occur? What are the consequences of this?

Misunderstandings occur all the time, even between speakers of the same variety. Sometimes this can be resolved with **metalinguistic** talk. In the case where varieties have significant differences, however, difficulties may be harder to resolve. As Eades's work shows, the common conventions of communication that would inform such metalinguistic talk may not be present. A misunderstanding when making a purchase in a store is benign; however, a misunderstanding when being arrested is dangerous. As we have already noted (Chapter 1), discrimination linked to cross-dialect communication has been found in the areas of education, housing, employment and the general accumulation of social capital.

7.8 CROSSING

Code switching (see section 7.7.1) demonstrates membership of a particular language community on the part of the speaker and acknowledges the hearer's membership of the same. There are a variety of reasons why a speaker may switch linguistic codes, whether consciously or unconsciously. It may be related to the topic, or it may occur if another person joins the conversation who can only speak a particular code or variety. A switch may, therefore, also indicate solidarity and inclusion or, conversely, distance and exclusion (see Milroy and Gordon, 2003: 209).

Crossing, 'language crossing' or 'code crossing', describes the practice of using language that is associated with, or belongs to, ethnic groups that the speaker doesn't belong to. As we have seen in Section 7.6, competence in a language, or the 'right' to use it to claim membership of a group, may have to be ratified. The sociolinguist Ben Rampton demonstrates how crossing involves 'borrowing' a variety and perhaps trespassing on language territory that one can't authentically claim. Rampton's preliminary definition is that crossing 'refers to the use of language which isn't generally thought to "belong" to the speaker' (1997: 2). Rampton thus differentiates crossing from code switching by stating that crossing involves a 'disjunction between speaker and code that cannot be readily accommodated as a normal part of ordinary social reality' (Rampton, 1995: 278). That is, according to the normal 'rules' of communication, the speaker should not be able to use the code. Therefore, the speaker can only use this code when the ordinary norms of 'social reality' and communication do not apply. As Rampton puts it, 'crossing either occasioned, or was occasioned by, moments and activities in which the constraints of ordinary social order were relaxed and normal social relations couldn't be taken for granted' (1997: 2).

Rampton's research study involved two years of **ethnographic** fieldwork with teenagers in a South Midlands town in England. He recorded conversations, interviewed participants and also asked them to comment on the data he'd recorded. He analysed instances of crossing into Panjabi, conversations involving stylised Asian English and those where Creole features were evident. He found that there were three different contexts where crossing occurred:

1   when the teenagers interacted with adults;
2   when they were with their peers;
3   and also events such as listening to bhangra[2] music which was very influential amongst the young people in the neighbourhood.

(1997)

Rampton concluded that crossing performed a variety of functions for the speakers. For example, it indicated resistance to adult norms, challenge of expectations about ethnicity, and indication of identities not related to ethnicity. Significantly, crossing appears to be connected to 'liminality' and the 'liminoid' (Rampton, 1997: 7). Liminal spaces exist in between recognised, ratified spaces. Liminal spaces are often defined by what they are not. For example the language of the participants in Rampton's study took place in the school playground. The playground is potentially a liminal space because while it is on school grounds, it is not subject to normal school rules of the classroom. Because it takes place in liminal spaces, 'crossing never actually claimed that the speaker was "really" black or Asian' in the way that code switching does, and it also suggests that in 'normal' spaces, 'the boundaries round ethnicity were relatively fixed' (1997: 7).

Shankar (2008) also found crossing among students in her study at a California high school. Example 7.10 is a transcript of three South Asian (Indian subcontinent) American students interacting at lunchtime.

Example 7.10
Setting: 'a lunchtime conversation [where] Kuldeep (M) uses Spanish in an exchange with Uday (M) and Simran (F)' who use Punjabi (Shankar,

2008: 274). Bolded words are South Asian Accented English, italicised words are Punjabi, underlined words are Spanish.

1   Uday: *Saleya eh* **garbage** *can vai*? [Is this a garbage can, stupid?]
2   Kuldeep: <u>No habla Inglés</u> [I (sic) don't speak English].
3   [*loud round of laughter*]
4   Kuldeep: **Don't know what you say . . .**
5   Simran: Throw that fuckin' shit out!
6   Kuldeep: *Oh balle! Hon boleya!* [Oh wow! At least you're talking to me now!].

In line 2, Kuldeep reacts to being scolded by Uday (line 1) (for not throwing his rubbish in a bin) by saying in Spanish that he does not speak English. Everyone laughs at Kuldeep's Spanish response in part because they often use Spanish when joking with each other and also because Uday's reprimand was in Punjabi and therefore did not rely on knowing English. Kuldeep then responds that he doesn't understand Uday, using South Asian American accented English. Simran reiterates the reprimand in English, and Kuldeep responds sarcastically in Punjabi. This use of Spanish in line 2 represents crossing; these students learn Spanish at school but do not use it in everyday life. Shankar explains:

> By occasionally speaking in Spanish in a school environment where they are routinely mistaken for Latinos, [these] boys use Spanish as a way to mock faculty who cannot easily differentiate between them and Latinos. Ridiculing this misrecognition is a continual source of humor for [these] teens.

(Shankar, 2008: 274)

In Example 7.10, we see a range of varieties used in a single interaction to do different kinds of things. The use of Punjabi can be understood as signalling their shared ethnicity, while the use of Spanish in this humorous way signals their shared understanding of what Spanish means in this context. As Shankar explains, it also indirectly comments on the way they are misidentified in the school context. The use of Spanish helps them manage their status as 'other' at the school. What looks like a simple conversation has a number of layers and meanings.

Although the research discussed here involves teenagers, crossing isn't just a feature of adolescent language. That is, even though there may be a perceived connection between such stylisation and a particular period of life, research suggests that older speakers also employ crossing (Rampton, 2011) different styles.

7.9 SUPERDIVERSITY

Because of increased migration and movement in a globalised world, nations and cities are much more diverse than they used to be; in fact, they're 'superdiverse'. Vertovec (2007) argues that this 'superdiversity' requires scholars to consider more carefully the ways that standard variables of analysis (e.g., ethnicity, class, gender) interact. These intersections are especially important in the creation of social policy. In terms of ethnicity, for example, Vertovec argues that making assumptions about an individual based on their country of origin overlooks a variety of important characteristics. Migrants will come from different social classes and different regions, have different languages, religions and different reasons for migrating in the first place. It makes little sense, for example, to treat all migrants from India in the same way; some will be students, some will be business people, some will be Hindu, others will be Christian, and they won't all share a first language.

Recently superdiversity has been taken up in sociolinguistic research. While it is true that research making generalisations across whole populations must take superdiversity into account in some way, recent focus on communities of practice (see Section 9.6) in sociolinguistic research has already drawn attention to the way identity is emergent and constructed through interaction with others in particular circumstances. As such, it may be that superdiversity overlaps in many respects with the ways that diversity has been addressed in the field in previous years (see also Pavlenko, 2017).

7.10 SUMMARY

Language can be used to demonstrate or claim an ethnicity. However, because the link between language and ethnicity is not straightforward, any claims to an ethnicity may be challenged. Such a challenge may be directly posed by an 'authentic' member of the group. The claim may also not be acknowledged because of lack of understanding of the linguistic features and semiotic resources used to signal ethnicity. Further, what looks like a claim to ethnicity may in fact be something else, as we saw in the case of crossing. How claims are made, how ethnicity is performed, depends on the local context, including the interactional situation, and the features available for exploitation. Moreover, it is important to consider the range of features a speaker relies on, as it may be the use of a specific combination of features that makes the claim to ethnicity and identity. Being able to use a linguistic variety brings with it cultural capital. In the case of ethnolects, this might be minimal because of linguistic subordination. In addition, linguistic subordination also means that ethnolects are disparaged and misunderstood and result in speakers being vulnerable to a variety of risks that can be more or less serious.

NOTES

1   This was a popular stage show that toured in Australia in the 1990s.
2   A kind of Panjabi music.

FURTHER READING

Albury, N. J. (2017) Mother tongues and languaging in Malaysia: Critical linguistics under critical examination, *Language in Society*, 46(4): 567–589.

Allport, G. (1954) *The Language of Prejudice, in The Nature of Prejudice*. Boston: Beacon Press.

Cheshire, J., Kerswill, P., Fox, S., and Torgensen, E. (2011) Contact, the feature pool and the speech community: The emergence of Multicultural London English, *Journal of Sociolinguistics*, 15(2): 151–196.

van Dijk, T. (2004) Racist discourse, in Cashmere, E. (ed.) *Routledge Encyclopaedia of Race and Ethnic Studies*. London: Routledge: 351–355.

Eades, D. (1996) Legal recognition in cultural differences in communication: The case of Robyn Kina, *Language & Communication*, 16(3): 215–227.

Gumperz, J. J. (2003) Cross cultural communication, in Harris, R. and Rampton, B. (eds.) *The Language, Ethnicity and Race Reader*. London: Routledge: 267–275.

Labov, W. (1972) Academic ignorance and Black intelligence, *The Atlantic*, 72, June: 59–67.

Rosa, J. D. (2016) Standardization, racialization, languagelessness: Raciolinguistic ideologies across communicative contexts, *Journal of Linguistic Anthropology*, 26(2): 162–183.

Walton, S. and Jaffe, A. (2011) 'Stuff white people like': Stance, class, race, and internet commentary', in Thurlow, C. and Mroczek, K (eds.) *Digital Discourse: Language in the New Media*. Oxford: Oxford University Press: 199–219.

Warren, J. (1999) Wogspeak: Transformations of Australian English, *Journal of Australian Studies*, 23(62): 85–94.

CHAPTER 8

Language and age

8.1 INTRODUCTION

In this chapter, we explore the way age plays a role in the **stratification** of society. We are particularly interested in how that stratification is represented in the *use* of language and how language is used *about* and *in communication with* different age groups. One way that different usage of language according to age group can be seen is in patterns of language change. Another pattern of language variation can be found in age groupings across the life span. These kinds of variation are reflective of an age group's place in the social hierarchy. In addition to examining how different age groups use language, it's also important to consider how language is used to communicate to people of different ages. For example, the terms used to refer to people of different ages tell us something about how we perceive age in our society. As we saw in Chapters 6 and 7, the way a person is described reveals a great deal about their position in the social hierarchy and thus how much power they have.

8.2 WHAT DO WE MEAN BY AGE?

When we talk about age and language, it's important to remember that although chronological age is relevant to some degree, what is even more important is the **life stage** that a person has reached. Eckert (1997: 151) explains, '[A]ge and ageing are experienced both individually and as part of a cohort of people who share a life stage, and/or an experience of history'. The life stage perspective considers the various culturally constructed age groupings a person passes through in their life, called 'life stages', such as childhood, adolescence and adulthood. Life stages do not make specific reference to chronological age since not all people experience these stages at exactly the same age. In addition, the life stage perspective allows us to consider the culturally constructed expectations about each life stage that may be unique to particular social groups. The transition from adolescence to adulthood can be marked at a variety of chronological ages depending on the social group. For example, this may be marked by entering the workforce or by finishing formal education. For some people, that may happen at age 18 when they finish secondary education, while for others, it may begin at age 23 when they get a university degree. In addition, the way people divide up age groups and the objective chronological age attached to these groups depends on the age group making the divisions. Younger people, for example, are more likely to set the threshold for 'elderly' lower than older people (Giles and Reid, 2005: 398). This is a reflection of the social construction of age. As we stated earlier, our chronological age may not be the same as our 'subjective' or 'contextual' age. In sociolinguistics the life stage perspective has been an approach taken by scholars such as Penny Eckert (1988) and Gillian Sankoff (2005), whose research demonstrated that considering life stages can often provide a better explanation of speakers' language behaviour than chronological age. However, sometimes examining age in chronological terms can be useful. Comparing the language use of speakers in different age groups at the same point in time (a **synchronic** study) can give insights into language change (**diachronic** change).

Look at the following table and discuss with your colleagues where you would place the chronological age of these groups. What does society expect of these groups of people in terms of behaviour, language and habits?

lifespan period	chronological age	cultural expectations
childhood		
Adolescents		
Adult		
Older adult		

Now think about people you know who fit into these age groups; do they match the cultural expectations you noted down? Does this change how you might categorise these individuals?

8.3 EARLY LIFE STAGE

The early life stage refers to the stage where a large amount of parental intervention is necessary for existence. This usually includes babies and young children. Children are not yet fully capable members of society, which affords them a special status in Western society. One of the expectations of this life stage is that because of their vulnerability, they need to be protected from certain kinds of ideas and representations (Sealey, 2000).

8.3.1 Language used to talk to children

It's not difficult to see that the way people speak to children differs from the way they speak to older people. In many languages, talking differently to children is routine. We call the language that adults use only with children **'child-directed language'** (CDL). Example 8.1 is a transcript of a mother talking to her baby.

> **Example 8.1**
>
> **Mother Ann**   **(3 months)**
>   (smile)
>
> Oh what a nice little smile!
> Yes, isn't that nice?
> There
> There's a nice little smile   {*burps*}
> What a nice wind as well
> Yes that's better isn't it?
> Yes
> Yes   {*vocalises*}
> Yes
> That's a nice noise
>
> (Snow, 1977: 12 in Ochs and Schieffelin, 1984: 475)

Peccei (1999: 56) describes some of the features of CDL, a few of which are evident in Example 8.1. She suggests CDL often includes the use of the child's name, directing attention to current tasks or the immediate environment and the use of full nouns rather than pronouns. Other features of CDL suggest that adults consider speaking to children as educational; they are teaching them to use the language.

The language used to speak to and about children is closely linked to the ideas that we have about children and their linguistic and social development. Sealey (2000) examined the portrayal of children in the public sphere, such as newspapers, radio and advertising. She suggests that children are frequently characterised as 'targets of harm', 'beneficiaries of care', and dichotomously as both 'angel and demon' (2000: 69). This is not universal, however, and Sealey reminds us that these characterisations are limited to the location and time in which they were observed. For example, Ochs and Schieffelin (1984) note that while the Kaluli of Papua New Guinea are very attentive to the needs of their babies, they do not speak to them in the way the mother in Example 8.1 does. The Kaluli cultural norms hold that interactions with babies are minimal. The child is greeted, but adults 'rarely address other utterances to them' (1984: 483). Nor do the Kaluli simplify their language with children. This is avoided, as it is thought to inhibit language development (1984: 495). The Kaluli example demonstrates, again, that societal expectations for certain groups are reflected in language use (see also Berman, 2014).

With respect to language use during this life stage, much research has been conducted about how children acquire language, and it is too complex for us to detail here (e.g., Fletcher and MacWhinney, 1996; Roberts, 2004; Peccei, 1999). In terms of social influences on their language, linguists have come to understand that children develop sociolinguistic competence from the earliest stages of speech (e.g., Romaine, 1978; Labov, 1989). In a child's early years, their caregiver is the most important model for language. When children begin to socialise independently of their caregivers, their most important models for language become their peers (Chambers, 1992; Payne, 1980; Stanford, 2008). This is especially important in the adolescent life stage.

8.4 ADOLESCENT LIFE STAGE

Adolescence is a relatively new age group, historically speaking. Eckert observes that adolescence is the 'product of industrial society, its history closely tied to the development of universal institutionalised secondary education' (2003: 112). Like most other social groups, it is not a homogenous group. What adolescents do share is a kind of **liminal** status; they are neither children nor adults. They are also generally delegitimised (Eckert, 2003: 114). While adolescents have some rights and even some economic power, these are not the same as those acquired in adulthood. Adolescents are required to stay in education and abide by specific rules of behaviour, dress and activity. Because of their marginalised status, their development of individual taste, through clothing and leisure choices, is often derided (Eckert, 2004).

Activity 8.2

Go to a search engine on the World Wide Web, and type in 'why are teenagers so' allowing the autofill function of the search engine to predict what word comes next in this question. What does it produce? What does this tell you about perceptions of teenagers?

8.4.1 What teenagers do?

Eckert (1997) suggests that the transition from childhood to adulthood is a key feature of this life stage. This transition brings with it a number of obstacles that must be overcome. Firstly, this is a time when young adults are often given certain levels of autonomy and freedom to develop their own identity. Secondly, adolescents are negotiating and navigating their marginalised status. Part of this development and negotiation may include a purposeful divergence from adult norms in order to assert an identity that is their own (Eckert, 2005). This divergence may take the form of words or phonological forms that are different from their parents' (e.g., Eckert, 1988). 'The development of adolescent social structure provides a major impetus for phonological change' (Eckert, 1988: 197).

Activity 8.3

What words or expressions have you noticed adolescents using? Do you understand what they mean? How do you think they are evaluated by other groups?

8.4.2 Multiple negation

Eisikovits' (2011) research in Sydney examined the speech of teenage boys and girls over two years to understand ways young men and women negotiate their marginalised status in different ways. Students (10 girls and 10 boys) from a working class area of inner city Sydney in year 8 (at about age 13) and in year 10 (at about age 15) were interviewed. One of the linguistic features of this group (among many others) is **multiple negation**. Multiple negation refers to the use of more than one negative morpheme or lexeme in an utterance. For example, instead of saying, 'I <u>didn't</u> do anything', multiple negation is used by including another negative word as in 'I <u>didn't</u> do <u>nothing</u>'. Multiple negation is a feature of non-standard English and often stigmatised by prescriptivists.

Table 8.1 shows Eisokovits' results for the use of 'multiple negation' by age and sex. The first numbers show the actual number of times multiple negation was used compared with the number of times it could have been used, and the second number is the resulting percentage.

We can see that for the younger students, levels of multiple negation are roughly the same. The older students, however, demonstrate a different pattern of use. Older girls use multiple negation less frequently than younger girls, while older boys and younger boys use multiple negation at roughly the same rate.

Table 8.1 Percentage of multiple negation, according to gender and age in Sydney

Younger girls	Older girls
56/115; 48.7%	42/192; 21.7 %
Younger boys	Older boys
54/107; 50.5%	56/127; 44.1%

Source: adapted from Eisikovitz, 2011: 41

In the case of other non-standard features Eisikovits examined, the older girls showed reduced use of other non-standard linguistic features, while the boys did not. The boys increased their use of some non-standard variables. Example 8.2 from Eisikovits' interview data suggests a reason why this pattern is found among these Sydney adolescents. In this example, a female and a male respondent both correct their own usage. Both correct themselves but in entirely different directions; the female repeats herself using a more prescriptively correct form, but the male does this using a more prescriptively incorrect form.

Example 8.2

a   female respondent: 'An me an Kerry – or should I say, Kerry and I – are the only ones who've done the project'

(Eisikovits, 2011: 45)

b   male respondent: 'I didn't know what I did – what I done'.

(Eisikovits, 2011: 46)

Eisokovits argues that these choices are related to perceptions of what it means to be an adult woman or man in their society. As we saw in Chapter 6, expectations about how women should speak relate to ideas about how women should behave (e.g., they should use 'correct' language). The same is of course true of men; it is simply that these expectations are rather different (e.g., they may use 'correct' language less frequently), resulting in a different use of language. Eckert (2009) also investigated multiple negation use among adolescents in Detroit, Michigan, US, and found similar results (see Chapter 9).

8.4.3 'Like' as a discourse marker

A common linguistic feature that people mention when they criticise young people's use of language is the discourse marker 'like' (D'Arcy, 2007). A discourse marker structures utterances and provides important cues about the attitude of the speaker with regard to what they are saying or responding to. With regard to the meaning of this discourse marker, Underhill (1988: 234) explains that 'this discourse marker is neither random nor mindless. Instead, it functions with great reliability as a marker of new information and focus' (see also D'Arcy, 2007; Laserna, Seih and Pennebaker, 2014). Sali Tagliamonte (2005) studied how young Canadians use this discourse marker as shown in Examples 8.3 a-c (2005: 1897).

Example 8.3
a   I'm just like so there, you know?
b   Like, that's what I like told you.
c   I just decided and just went.

Tagliamonte found that, among the Canadians she studied, the youngest and oldest speakers in the sample used 'like' the least. There was a concentration of more usage of 'like' among the 15- to 16-year-olds. Figure 8.1 shows this distribution of use.

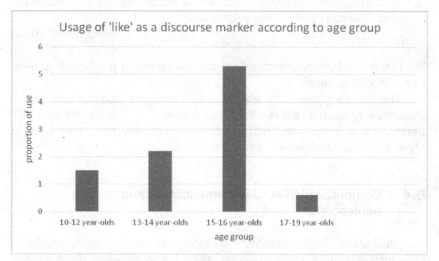

Figure 8.1 Usage of 'like' as a discourse marker among Canadian youth; numbers reflect proportion of total words

Source: adapted from Tagliamonte, 2005: 1903

What characteristics of life stages might account for the difference in usage among these age groups?

Activity 8.4

Tagliamonte suggests that the pattern of higher usage of 'like' among 15- to 16-year-olds reflects the innovative use of language often found among adolescents, as described by Eckert (1999) (see also Wagner, 2008). This is followed by a reduction in the 17- to 18-year-olds, reflecting 'linguistic change towards standard (mainstream) norms as adolescents enter young adulthood' (Tagliamonte, 2005: 1910). This sort of pattern of change across the life span can be referred to as age grading, that is, change in the use of language that correlates with life stages and does not reflect change of community norms.

As Tagliamonte and other linguists have shown (e.g., D'Arcy, 2007), 'like' used as a discourse marker is a strategic functional use of language. However, as we have already seen with regard to other non-standard features, this use is highly criticised.

> Many parents and teachers have become irritated to the point of distraction at the way the weed-style growth of 'like' has spread through the idiom of the young. And it's true that in some cases the term has become simultaneously a crutch and a tic, driving out the rest of the vocabulary as candy expels vegetables.
>
> (Hitchens, 2010)

Hitchens's (2010) comments reflect the marginalised position of adolescents described earlier.

The sociolinguistic competence that teenagers acquire and exploit depends very much on the environments in which they live and the identities they want to communicate. This development of identity is also connected to styles of dress, hairstyles and leisure activities.

8.4.4 Computer-mediated communication and adolescents

Crispin Thurlow (2006) examined the representation of computer-mediated communication (CMC) in the popular press. These representations are discussed in terms of computer-mediated discourse (CMD). CMD examines the public debates and discussion about the use of computer-mediated language. This research examines **metalanguage**, that is, the language used to talk about language. This type of study reveals the attitudes that people have towards this language as well as what they think it is (Preston, 1996). It also tells us what attitudes are held about the users of this language.

Thurlow examined newspaper representations of CMC and uncovered three major themes.

1 Computer-mediated language is a new form of language.
2 Statistical panic – this language is being used too much.
3 Moral panic – use of CMC has negative effects on society.

The idea that CMC is new was common. Evidence for this can be found in the terms used to describe it (e.g., 'netlingo', 'weblish' and 'netspeak') (Thurlow, 2006: 673). The claim that it is new is also made by comparing CMD with other language forms or by describing it in terms usually used for separate languages. For example, users of CMC are said to be 'fluent' and 'bilingual', and there is coverage of the inclusion of CMC items in dictionaries (2006: 673–674). Thurlow argues that the newness of CMC is promoted by those with an interest in the form being seen as new (2006: 674). Therefore, providers of technology are often quoted or referred to when claims about the newness of CMC are being made.

The second theme Thurlow identifies relates to levels of use of CMC. Thurlow notes that 'the use of numerous, superlative numerical citations' about its use were found in the data set (2006: 675). The third theme is the most relevant to our discussion about life stages, as it relates to the moral panic surrounding the use of CMC. This 'new' kind of language is represented as a threat to the language, one specifically associated with young people (2006: 677) and one that older people don't understand.

> While it would be untrue to suggest that there were no positive claims made for the effects of CMD . . ., for the most part the nexus of popular discourses about language, about technology, and about young people generates an overwhelmingly pessimistic picture.
>
> (Thurlow, 2006: 677)

Once CMC is established as a threat to the language, it can be represented as a threat to social order, to progress and to culture in general. This is one more example of the kinds of arguments used against language change (see Chapter 2) that have been common throughout history (Milroy and Milroy, 1999). A part of this argument is the claim that CMC is being used by young people in their written exams (Thurlow, 2006: 684). Such stories are used as evidence for the negative effect of CMC on literacy and language skills. Linguistic scholarship, however, does not support this claim (Thurlow, 2006: 679).

In addition, further research conducted by Thurlow and Brown (2003) shows that what people think teenagers are doing with CMC is not necessarily what they are actually doing. In an effort to examine SMS text communication among university students and describe how young people are using this media, Thurlow and Brown (2003) collected text messages from 135 students at Cardiff University. He examined message length, the typographic and linguistic content (emoticons, abbreviations and letter homophones) and the primary purpose of the text. The average message length (14 words and 65 characters) did seem to be rather short, especially given the former 140 (now 280) character limit of texts. The linguistic forms used were also surprising. While the use of 'x' was high (443 of all instances of emoticon – 509), emoticon use was generally rather low. Double exclamation marks '!!' occurred 35 times and J 17 times. These three are the most used, showing that other emoticons are only infrequently employed (only 6 times). Texters also used around 3 abbreviations in each message. There were some (73) homophones with letter/number play, for example 'u' for 'you' and 'b4' for 'before' and some use of onomatopoeia (e.g., 'haha').

When considering the function of the messages, Thurlow found that rather than conveying information, the young people use texting to build and maintain relationships, that is, to interact with their friends in much the same way as they might do face to face. Moreover, texting was also used to communicate when they were in the same location, in order to create a parallel communicative space.

Thurlow identifies three features of texting he examined:

1   brevity and speed
2   paralinguistic restitution
3   phonological approximation

The brevity relates to the short message length. Paralinguistic restitution is the use of available forms to communicate paralinguistic information, information that is usually conveyed in addition to the actual content of the speech, such as tone, volume or emotion. For example, the use of capitals (to indicate shouting) and employing emoticons or punctuation (e.g. '!!!') to convey affect are ways to communicate paralinguistic features. The third feature, phonological approximation, refers to the way texters exploit the conventions of written language to convey features of spoken language. For example, changes are made to conventional spelling (e.g., 'goin') to evoke spoken use. Thurlow concludes that the text messages of these students are on the one hand 'remarkable' in their use of creativity to project particular identities and 'unremarkable' on the other in that they conform to sociolinguistic and communicative conventions (Thurlow and Brown, 2003). We can see in Thurlow's examination of texting by young people that students are not, contrary to popular belief, losing the skills of either written or spoken communication.

Instant messaging (IM) has developed into an important means of CMC. Like texting, IM tends to be one-to-one communication, but unlike texting, it tends to be synchronous (although people may be doing other things while chatting on IM so it may not be quite as fast as 'synchronous' suggests (Tagliamonte and Denis, 2008: 8)). We tend to IM people we know and exchange information briefly and quickly and so may use some similar strategies to texting. That is, abbreviations, lack of punctuation and errors/stylistic variation will probably all occur (see Crystal, 2006). As we noted, CMC is perceived by some as a form of communication that has a negative impact on language. However, as Tagliamonte explains in *Teen Talk* (2016), lexical usage typical of IM (e.g., ttfn, lol, nvm – nevermind, nm – not much) (2016: 216–219) is not as prevalent as IM critics assume. Tagliamonte and Denis (2010) examined the use of acronyms and abbreviations in the Toronto Instant Messaging Corpus (TIMC). They found that only 2.44% of the corpus was composed of such forms (see Tagliamonte, 2016: 218). They further explore the most frequently used acronyms. These turned out to be expressions of emotion such as lol, hehe and haha. Table 8.2 shows the frequency counts and percentages of use of the most common forms used to express laughter.

As Table 8.2 shows, the feature used the most is 'haha'. Indeed, of all the forms examined in the corpus, this was by far the most common. But it was still less than 1.5% of the total corpus. Perhaps the most interesting finding from this data relates to age. Figure 8.2 shows the percentage of use of three laughter forms according to the age of the user.

Table 8.2 Most common forms used to express laughter

Form	Frequency	As percentage of total word in corpus
haha	16,183	1.47%
lol	4,506	0.41%
hehe	2,050	0.19%
lmao	63	0.01%

Source: adapted from Tagliamonte and Denis, 2008: 12

In Figure 8.2, we see that the use of 'lol' decreases as age increases while the use of 'haha' increases as age increases. This demonstrates that there are differences in language use even in environments (like IM) and age groupings (age 15–20) where one might expect there to be consistency among them. Tagliamonte reports that her daughter at age 16 said, 'I used to use *lol* when I was a kid'; thus giving 'anecdotal confirmation of lol's puerile association' (Tagliamonte and Denis, 2008: 13).

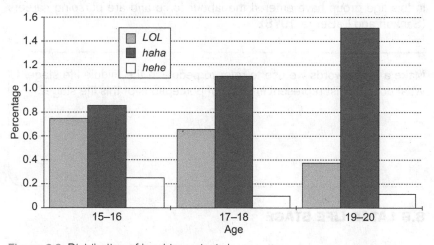

Figure 8.2 Distribution of laughter variants by age

Source: Tagliamonte and Denis, 2008: 13

Which CMC forms do you use? Does your peer group have forms that are not used and those that would not be understood by others? And how do you 'laugh' in CMC? Have emojis overtaken 'haha'?

Activity 8.5

8.5 MIDDLE LIFE STAGE

Much of the sociolinguistic research we have explored in many of the chapters in this book describes the language use of speakers in the middle life stage (e.g., Labov, 1972a; Trudgill, 1974). Research has focussed on this age group for a few reasons. Firstly, this age group is seen as the 'unmarked' age group. That is, childhood, adolescence and later life are frequently described in terms of how they are different from adulthood. Secondly, there is an assumption that the middle life stage is one where language use is stable and not expected to change, especially with regard to child language development (Roberts, 2004). In addition, in practical terms, as subjects of research, adults are easier to access because they can give consent to participate; neither do they tend to have age-related cognitive or physical attributes that interfere with language research.

Because this life stage has been the subject of a good deal of research, a few generalisations can be reliably made about their language use. In addition to the gendered, socio-economic and ethnicity-based variation previously discussed, people in this life stage are usually conservative in their language use. That means that they use standard language features more than the other age groups (Chambers, 2009). Scholars suggest this is due to the need for linguistic capital in the labour force because most people in this age group have entered the labour force and are pursuing careers (Sankoff and LaBerge, 1978).

Activity 8.6

Make a list of words we use to refer to people in the middle life stage. What does the list represent in terms of perceptions of this life stage?

8.6 LATER LIFE STAGE

As we noted, because middle age is the unmarked life stage, the language use of older adults has been the subject of linguistic research much less. Only recently have people in the later life stage been the focus of sociolinguistic research (e.g., Coupland, 1997; Giles and Reid, 2005; Ylänne-McEwan, 1999). Sociolinguistic research on language use and older people takes as its primary focus the representation and performance of identity of people in the later life stage. This research has shown that people in this life stage, like children and adolescents, are frequently depicted in a negative way, which reflects prominent age-stereotyping, or ageism, in society.

This ageism can be prominent in terms referring to people in this life stage. While children and babies may be spoken about as cute, playful, mischievous and annoying, the terms and stereotypes associated with the elderly are not as varied or attractive. Research shows that while there are some more positive portrayals of older people, such as 'as kind, supportive, and wise' (Zhang, Harwood, Williams, Ylänne-McEwen, Wadleigh and Thimm, 2007: 266), 'older people are perceived as incompetent, fragile, complaining, socially unskilled, overly self-disclosive, and dominating' (Zhang et al. 2007: 266). Gerlinde Mautner (2007) examined a large collection of language (a corpus) in order to explore the term 'elderly'. Charting the words that commonly occur together with (such word pairs are called **collocates**) 'elderly' makes the negative **connotations** of the term clear (as we saw with gendered terms in Chapter 6). Table 8.3 shows the most common **collocates** of 'elderly'.

Table 8.3 Lexical collocates of elderly with the highest joint frequencies among the top 50 collocates

Collocate	Joint frequency
People	255
Woman	75
disabled	55
man	51
Care	51
couple	41
Children	41
Lady	37
Woman	35
Sick	32

Source: adapted from Mautner, 2007: 57

Mautner's analysis shows that the elderly are associated with 'disability, illness, care and vulnerability to crime' (2007: 63). Also significant is that one does not find evidence of 'independence, initiative, and empowerment' or of 'education, jobs, experience' (2007: 63). These perceptions suggest that citizens in the later life stage don't so much *do* things but rather have things done for them.

The term 'elderly' has come to be associated with being infirm, disabled, handicapped and sick (Mautner, 2007). These results do not establish that elderly people are necessarily infirm or ill; rather, they demonstrate that these are the ideas that people associated with the word 'elderly'. As Mautner points out, 'elderly' is a 'social' rather than a 'chronological' label (2007: 60), a perspective that is reflected in a 'life span' approach and other approaches to social categories that we've discussed, such as gender (see chapter 6).

8.6.1 Representations of older people

The media we consume and are exposed to has an effect on our understanding of the world. Because media, including advertising, has to communicate with its audience, it draws on existing ideas about people. Even if an advertisement challenges the common conceptions of a product or a group of people, it nevertheless draws on these very conceptions. A good example of this is a campaign for a margarine made from olive oil (Zhang et al., 2007). The study of these printed advertisements shows that the ads began by providing information about the health benefits of olive oil but also linked these to portrayals of age. Specifically, older people are used in this context 'to symbolise longevity and healthy, active old age' (Zhang et al., 2007: 237). Using older people sends a message: consume this product, and you too will live for a long time. The campaign continued to develop this theme in several stages, by portraying older people in a family context and partaking in particularly active pursuits. This includes positive visual portrayals of older people as well as using words normally associated with younger people to describe them. For example, an older man is featured in an ad with the caption 'babe magnet, the new name for handsome fellow' (Zhang et al., 2007: 273). This campaign provides positive representations of older people in terms of longevity, life fulfilment and sexuality and perhaps even 'new ways of being old' (Zhang et al., 2007: 274). Further, '[t]hese images and messages might reflect changing attitudes and stereotypes of old age, in turn affected by changes in the ageing cohort group' (Zhang et al., 2007: 274).

8.6.2 Self-representation of older people

Considering Table 8.3, it's hardly surprising that older people would reject the term 'elderly' as a self-descriptor. At the same time, because we don't have complete control over our identity, the negative associations of 'elderly' are real and problematic. 'The labelling expressions, in turn, shape both people's identities and interpersonal relationships. In the process, both individuality and non age-related group identities are backgrounded or forfeited altogether' (Mautner, 2007: 53).

Activity 8.7

Complete a table based on the one below. Write down the terms associated with each of the partners in the relationship. For example, in the top right-hand box, write down the terms that might be used to describe a younger woman in a relationship with an older man and those use for the older man in a relationship with a younger woman. What kind of age difference would be required for the terms you identify? What do the terms say about society's views of these relationships and the people in them?

	Younger man	*Older man*
Younger woman	[unmarked]	Terms for a woman: Terms for a man:
Older woman	Terms for a woman: Terms for a man:	[unmarked]

8.6.3 Language used to talk to older people

Because of the negative associations of people in the later life stage and because age is a characteristic assumed by looking at someone, older people sometimes find themselves being spoken to in entirely inappropriate ways. One of these ways of speaking is called 'elderspeak' (Kemper, 1994: 18).

> [Elderspeak] refers to the use of a patronising speech style resembling speech addressed to children; this patronising speech style results from and reinforces (negative) stereotypes that older adults are cognitively impaired. Elderspeak also refers to the use of a simplified speech regis-ter which is assumed to enhance older adults' comprehension.
>
> (Kemper, 1994: 18)

This kind of speech is used by some people when interacting with older people and appears to be driven by stereotypes rather than its efficiency for communi-cation. The features of elderspeak are similar to those of child-directed language, e.g., the simplification of language, shorter utterances, **imperatives**, repetition, a high level of tag questions, interruptions, changes in pitch and particular forms of address (Sealey, 2000, see also Marsden and Holmes, 2014: 18–19). While speakers may use these features to communicate care and affection, they may also be heard as patronising or infantilising (Sealey, 2000; Giles and Reid, 2005).

Marsden and Holmes (2014) studied interactions between caregivers and older residents in a residential care home in New Zealand. While it is pos-sible to find some features of elderspeak, they show that the presence of at least some of these features can establish and maintain positive relationships between caregivers and residents. Moreover, they argue that these linguistic strategies can be useful for both participants in managing the difficult situa-tion of caring for / being cared for by another person. In Example 8.4, a carer (Keira) is helping a resident (Rosalie) to get ready for a shower.

Example 8.4

Context: Keira (K), the caregiver, assists the resident, Rosalie (R), with preparing for her shower.

Material in parenthesis ( ) is unclear speech. //indicates start and end of overlapping speech. Numbers indicate pause in seconds.

K: right **my love**
right you hold my hands I'll help you
very good //very\ good **lovey** (6)
R: {*groans*}
K: Would you like to use the toilet?
R: mm (5) (I think) (2)
K: the toilet?
R: (I think)
K: I be- I think you better too [laughs]
right **my love** I'm gonna help you one two three very\ good

R: /{*sighs*}\\ mm
K: yeah take your time
          right **love** (10) that okay? //
          I'm\ just gonna make your bed give you some privacy
R: /yes\\
          {*rattling of cups, rustling of bedclothes, as Keria makes bed*}
K: you over **lovey**

(Marsden and Holmes, 2014: 24)

The use of terms of endearment here ('love', 'lovey') is noticeable. They have been marked in bold only to draw attention to them. It would be possible to argue that Keira is using these terms in order to get Rosalie to do something, that is, to take her shower. Marsden and Holmes, however, demonstrate that the use of terms of endearment in this care home is reciprocal: the residents also address their caregivers in this way. The data also shows that terms of endearment are used when the caregiver is not trying to get the resident to do something. They argue that 'Reciprocal usage of endearments suggest an equal and friendly relationship' (2014: 25).

Marsden and Holmes also draw attention to the way humour is used. Humour can be used to make difficult situations less anxious but also may be employed unkindly. Marsden and Holmes show that in their data, humour is collaboratively constructed and positively used.

Example 8.5
Context: Taniela (T), the caregiver, is assisting Florence, the resident, to take a shower.

F: oh it's hot
T: hot it's a bit hot? (3)
F: {*laughs*}
T: yeah and next minute it will go freezing cold isn't it
F: {*laughs*}
T: that's the thing they can't make up their mind (2)
          oopsie still hot okay feel it now
F: that's not bad (2)
T: okay okay that flannel in your hand that's for your face eh
          oh it's cold?
F: {*laughs*} (2) I'm not a fan of cold showers [laughs]
T: {*laughs*}

(Marsden and Holmes, 2014: 28)

In Example 8.5, Taniela is helping Florence to take a shower. The transcript shows that both are laughing while Taniela tries to regulate the temperature of the water. Taniela also engages in general talk about the water system – that it is now too hot but may soon turn cold (lines 4 and 6). This suggests that rather than only being concerned about having Florence shower, Taniela is ensuring that Florence is physically and interactionally comfortable. As Marsden and Holmes note, 'Even when engaged in the most task-oriented talk, the importance of the relationship dimension was evident in the linguistic choices that caregivers made' (2014: 31).

Whether specific language features are appropriate can only be determined by examining interactions in more detail. As we saw in Example 8.4, the presence of endearments is not necessarily patronising. The linguistic features that are used are important in an interaction but the broader interactional context must also be considered.

8.6.4 Construction of age in a travel agency

Research on interactions in a travel agency by Virpi Ylänne-McEwen (1999) shows how representations of age are brought into a conversation in a commercial interaction. In addition, she examines how brochures of holidays aimed at older customers are used to explain and illustrate the kinds of product on offer. Ylänne-McEwen points out that these brochures construct and rehearse stereotypes about travel and ageing which may be received as patronising or reassuring.

Example 8.6 is a transcript of a conversation between customers and travel agents. Mrs and Mr Morgan are the customers, who have already disclosed they are in their 70s. The other participants are employees in the travel agency. Alun is 24, Emma is 25 and Mary is 40.

Example 8.6 Travel agency conversation

```
 1  Mrs Morgan:   well er (.) what we want we as I [said]
 2  Alun:                                          [mm]
 3  Mrs Morgan:   we'd like to go to Portugal we only want
 4                to go for seven days
 5  Mary:         yes
 6  Mrs Morgan:   we want to go with people (.) and [we
 7  Mary:                                           [do you
 8                want something like a Young at Heart
 9                type of holi[day?
10  Alun:                     [yes yes
11  Mary:         [something] like that
12  Mrs Morgan:   [well uh] {very hesitantly} (1.0)
13  Mary:         is do you wan do you want to be
14                categorised (.) as one of [(.) one of =
15  Mrs Morgan:                             [{laughs}
16  Mary:         = the over fifty fives [or
17  Mrs Morgan:                          [oh yeah
18  Mr Morgan:                           [yeah
19  Mrs Morgan:   we're over one definitely over the fifty
20                [fives {laughs}
21  Mr Morgan:    {laughs}
22  Mary:         [{laughs}cos that's what they're [they
23  Mrs Morgan:                                    [yeah
24                our own age group then [you know yes yeah
25  Emma:                                [yeah not eighteen
```

26		thir[ty
27	Mr Morgan:	[thirty two =
28	Mrs Morgan:	= oh no no no no [(laughs)
29	Emma:	[you're sure?
30	Mrs Morgan:	positive {*laughs*}

(Ylänne-McEwen, 1999: 424–425)

Age is clearly made relevant in this conversation. There is a great deal of discussion not just about age in general terms but about particular ages and the products (holidays) associated with them. Lines 13–14 are particularly interesting. Ylänne-McEwen points out that Mary's statement can be understood as a request for age disclosure, something which can be very **face threatening** (1999: 425). That is, in most contexts, it is thought to be rude to ask how old someone is. Mary's statement is an indirect request, however, which may reduce the face threat that the question poses (Ylänne-McEwen, 1999: 426). It also invites the client to participate in the identification of their age; 'they are given the choice to comment on or to self-construct their contextual age' (1999: 426). The exchange is rather humorous in nature, especially in the discussion of the 18–30 age group holidays (lines 24–30). Ylänne -McEwen argues that Mary's question is 'ironic'; as suggested by the fact that Mrs Morgan starts to laugh before the question is finished.

It is also possible to understand Mary's question in a slightly different way (without claiming that this is how Mary or the Morgans understood it). Mary's use of the word 'categorised' suggests a particular kind of treatment, a particular classification of people in terms of their age. Given the context of interaction, it may well be that Mary is trying to establish what kind of holiday the Morgans want. That is, do they want a holiday that has been created for the 'category' of older people? While it has already been established that the Morgans would like something 'like a Young at Heart type of holiday', Mary's question may be seeking further confirmation of this. As Ylänne-McEwen explains, these holidays are aimed at older people who want to travel with other people of a similar age, be looked after by 'hosts' and engage in particular kinds of activities, such as ballroom dancing, bingo, walking tours and so on. These holiday products are aimed at a particular kind of older person, a particular 'category'. This category may be seen as ageist (assuming older people only want to play bingo and so on) or positive as 'promoting an active lifestyle for older people' (Ylänne-McEwen, 1999: 437). It looks like the Morgans orient more to the second interpretation. There may be no way for a travel agent to be sure of this. This makes their job quite difficult. They need to ensure that clients know what kind of products are on offer without offending people by offering something that would be inappropriate. Offering a customer who appears to be older than 55 a holiday aimed at 'the over 55s' is risky because it reveals an assumption about the customer's age. However, one also can't assume that the customer would not be interested in these kinds of products, even if the products seem be ageist and patronising. As Ylänne-McEwen succinctly puts it, 'Moral issues . . . underlie the discourse strategies adopted by assistants who sell these holidays' (1999: 437).

In order to market products, certain assumptions are made about potential consumers in relation to their interests and self-perception. In the case of the travel agency conversation, age identity is prominent. Negotiation of personal identity takes place in all kinds of interactions whether they are commercial or personal and involve dealing with the expectations and assumptions of the **interlocutor** and society in general.

8.6.5 Learning to use the internet

As we have discussed, and as Ylänne-McEwen's work makes clear, age is not a fixed thing. Rather, we construct a social age depending on who we are interacting with and for what purposes. There is good evidence of this in Divita (2012), a study that examines the interactions between a younger male teacher and older students who are taking a class on how to use the internet. The class takes place in Paris, but the students and teacher interact in Spanish because the students are migrants. Because internet and computer-mediated communication are generally associated with young people and because the students are older people, age is a salient issue. Because this is a learning environment, age is relevant in another way. Typically (though of course not universally), teachers are older than their students. In this case, however, the teacher, Josep, at age 38, is much younger than his students.

All participants invoke and exploit these identities (i.e., young versus old; teacher versus student) as can be seen in the following excerpt.

Example 8.7

1	Josep:	a ver Carmen.
		let's see Carmen.
2	Carmen:	yes presente
		yes present
3	Josep:	Pilar (.) Marco.
4	Marco:	yo [estoy
		here [I am
5	Josep:	[Juana.
6	Pilar:	no está no [está
		she's not here she's [not here
7	Josep:	[María.
8	María:	ah eh eh no he oído mi nombre
		ah hey hey I didn't hear my name
9		sí lo has dicho, {laughs}
		if you said it,
10		es igual ya me ves
		it doesn't matter you can see me
11	Juana:	{laughs} y a mí también
		and me too
12	Josep:	{referring to computers} están encendido o no?
		are they turned on or not?
13		(5.1)

(Unintelligible commotion as students respond to Josep's query by explaining why their computers have not been turned on and rushing to do so. Macintosh computer chimes.)

14. Josep: {*sitting down and sighing*} uh jo´venes (.) uh
              um young people (.) um
15 Carmen: dí´game viejo
              tell me old man
16 Pilar: {*smiling voice*} jo´venes=
              young people=
17 Carmen: =viejo=
              =old man=
18 Pilar: =viejo   [viejo
              =old man [old man
19 Carmen: [que te has tomado la pastilla ya,=
                        [have you taken your pill yet,=
20 Pilar: =ya has tomado la pastilla, {*laughs*}
              =you've already taken your pill,
21 Carmen: {*referring to the Firefox browser icon*}
              como decí´a el zorro (xxxxxxxx)
              the fox like he was saying (xxxxxxxx)
22 Josep: cuantos dí´as llevamos – dos o tres?
              How many classes have we had – two or three?
                                      (Divita, 2012: 591–592)

In this example, we see at least two kinds of invocation of the concept of age. In lines 1–11, Josep is engaged in the common classroom practice of taking the register. While, at first, the students reply in the expected way ('yes, present'), in later lines, the students respond differently to this routine activity. They are not antagonistic to the process of 'taking the register', as Divita reminds us that they are laughing at this point. Rather, Maria and Juana point out that Josep can see them.

Age is also explicitly referenced in later lines. Josep addresses the students as 'young people' (line 14). Divita explains that this is a way to manage the difference in age and expertise in this context.

> Josep exploits the potential incongruity between their chronological age and age-related social categories; such a move enables him to play the institutional role required of him as instructor while simultaneously indexing its context-specific nature qua role and mitigating his imposition of authority on an older, more experienced population who, in other contexts, might exert authority in relation to him.
>   (2012: 592)

After this, when Josep sits with a sigh, the students playfully address him as 'old man' and ask whether he has taken his pills. While this last remark draws on stereotypes about older people being infirm, the students also demonstrate that they are comfortable with the altered roles and indeed with the playful talk.

Example 8.8

15 Josep: hay cientos de miles de chats en el mundo
there are hundreds of thousands of chats in the world

16 cientos y cientos y cientos de miles
hundreds and hundreds and hundreds of thousands

17 co´mo funciona un chat?
how does a chat work?

18 un chat funciona
a chat works

19 so´lo (.) tu´ te inscribes
all you have to do is register

20 normalmente de forma gratuita vale
normally it's free okay

21 y se habla de temas ...
and you talk about topics ...

22 si yo lo que busco es un chat de: cocina
if what I want is a chatroom about cooking

23 chat [cocina
chat [cooking

24 Enrique: [cocina ouais ouais ouais
[cooking yea yea yea

25 Josep: y Google me dara´ resultados de chats (.) de cocina
and Google will give me results of chat rooms (.) about cooking

26 me dara´ muchas cosas que no sirven para nada
it'll give me a lot of things that aren't useful

27 pero me dara´ algunos vale
but it'll give me some okay

28 la gran mayori´a de chats –
the vast majority of chats –

29 no os voy a mentir porque ya sois grandecitos vale
I'm not going to lie to you because you're all grown up now

30 no tene´is catorce años
you're not fourteen anymore

31 Juan: son los ligues no?
are dates right?

32 Josep: son – es del sexo.
They're – it's for sex.

33 Juan: los ligues
dates

34 Josep: sexo.
sex.

35 Carmen: la chatte {*laughs*}
            pussy
36 Josep: ma´s que el ligue – ma´s que ligue, sexo directamente
            more than dates – more than dates, sex directly

(Divita, 2012: 602–603).

In Example 8.8, Josep is explaining to the student what chat rooms are. In the lines just before, Josep has explained that 'chats are pages that let you speak live with other people' (2012: 601). In the lines here, we see age referenced again in line 29. In the same way a teacher might speak to young adults, Josep tells his class that he's not going to lie to them because they're 'all grown up'; they're 'not fourteen anymore'. Divita explains that 'grandecitos' is an 'affectionate diminutive' which can be glossed as 'little old people' (2012: 604). And while Juan seeks confirmation of his understanding, Carmen 'engages in a form of bawdy language play' (2012: 604) as 'chatte' is 'a vulgar term in French for female genitalia' (2012: 604) of the kind one might expect from a teenager. More generally, however, Divita observes that the teacher and students are interacting here like adult peers.

While both Josep and his students are obviously aware of the 'normal' roles and associations of teacher/student and younger/older person, these are not followed completely but rather exploited for humorous and friendly effect. The playful talk that they engage in can be seen as a way of managing the older student/younger teacher. But it is also indicative of how these students perform their social age in this particular context.

8.7 THE CREEP OF AGEISM

While most attention has focussed on the way older people are discriminated against, both in the way they are represented and the way they are spoken to, scholars make clear that ageism can affect many age groups. Ageism is not always explicit; that is, one may be discriminated against on the basis of something that is not age as such but rather related to expectations of age. Considering someone 'too young' as well as 'too old' could be a result of ageism depending on the context. For example, a 28-year-old may be 'too old' to be a member of a new boy band while a 50-year-old may be considered 'too young' to be appointed as a senior member of the judiciary. Or, instead of someone being told they are 'too young' for a particular post, they may be told they don't have enough experience. Societal expectations associated with age can be used as a kind of 'cover' for age discrimination.

Gendron et al. point out that 'Evidence of ageism can be found on a macro level (e.g., antiaging beauty campaigns), as well as on a microlevel (e.g., everyday language incorporating subtle expressions of contempt and derogatory remarks about ageing and older people)' (2016: 997). The words used to describe older people and the lack of appropriate words for some age groups (as we saw in Chapter 1) is emblematic of the acceptability of ageism. Ageism is perhaps not considered as 'bad' as sexism or racism.

Because of this, examples can be found even from speakers who would not consider themselves 'ageist'.

Gendron et al. worked with student doctors on a course for gerontology (medicine for older people). They paired up older people with some students so that the students would have a better understanding of what it is like to be older. As part of their assessment, students could tweet about what they had learnt from their older mentors. Gendron et al. analysed these tweets. Of the 354 tweets they analysed, 43 contained 'a form of bias through language based discrimination' (2016: 1001).

They found in the data evidence that the students believed (or used language that suggested they believe) that older people are different with unusual characteristics, such as having active lifestyles or that old is 'bad' and young is 'good'. Language that infantalises older people (see Section 8.6.3) was also found in the tweets. Table 8.4 presents some examples.

Table 8.4 Tweets from student doctors about older mentors

Generalisation	Tweet
Older people are different from other people	. . . made me realise the importance of treating the elderly with the same attitude and approach as treating younger patients.
	Treat elderly people as normal people, no different!
Older people aren't active	94 years old and still sharp as a tack! 'Honey, you take Plavix!'
	I wish when I grow old I can still be as fashionable and full of life as my mentor is!
	My mentor is a truly amazing woman. She maintains great health and keeps a daily activity that very few people at her age are able to accomplish.
Old is negative	My mentor, a 71-year-old grandma, proves that age is just a number!
	Just had an intriguing convo with a new friend, who just happens to be 80 years young.
	. . . the youngest senior I've ever met #fullofenergy #independent
	Orange is the new black, 90 is the new 17! #goodhumorneverages
Young is positive	It's all about attitude. Her infectiously positive outlook is what keeps her looking younger every day.
	Our mentor was 92 but didn't look a day over 70 and was still just a kid at heart.
	A seasoned troublemaker with a young heart of gold.
Infantalising	What a sweet woman! I especially love her little winks #herecomestrouble
	Best quote from our mentor . . . 'We got married because we could never finish an argument, and we still haven't' A truly adorable and inspiring couple!

Source: adapted from Gendron, Welleford, Inker and White, 2016: 1002

It is perhaps not surprising that the students use the language that they do. The dominant ideology about older people suggests that they are infirm, forgetful, unattractive and very different from younger people. Gendron et al. (and Activity 8.1) show that individuals of all ages draw on these discourses in order to construct their own identity and their audiences will do the same. Finding a way out of this requires finding a new ideology, a new set of beliefs, about what it means to be older. 'Acknowledgement of these pathways and the use of discriminatory language based on age represent the first step in a larger attempt to disrupt the social standard' (Gendron et al., 2016: 1004).

Activity 8.8

It is important to note that positive representations of older people do exist. Ari Seth Cohen's photography is a good example of this (www.advanced.style/). Cohen photographs older people (men, women and couples) to document their 'advanced style'. This kind of work challenges the assumptions that people have (because of ideology) about what it means to be older and what is 'appropriate' for older people to wear. But notice that the people are still (at least implicitly) marked as older.

Do you think that Cohen's project provides a platform for reframing representations and performances of age identities?

8.8 SUMMARY

Age plays an important role in social hierarchies. In this chapter, we have seen how each life stage has unique challenges. Societal expectations of what certain life stages involve creates specific pressures on people in that life stage. These pressures can manifest themselves in the particular usage of language, such as the avoidance of non-standard features or innovation of grammatical features. We have also seen that perceptions of life stages by society result in the use of certain forms of communication with people in a particular life stage (e.g., babytalk, elderspeak) and certain ways of referring to people associated with a particular life stage (e.g., 'elderly', 'tween', 'tearaway') that further limit and marginalise members of those groups.

FURTHER READING

Aldridge, M. (ed.) (1996) *Child Language*. Bristol, UK: Multilingual Matters.

Baron, N. S. (2010) Discourse structures in Instant Messaging: The case of utterance breaks, *Language@Internet*, 7. Article 4. (urn:nbn:de:0009–7–26514).

Berman, E. (2014) Negotiating age: Direct speech and the sociolinguistic production of childhood in the Marshall Islands, *Journal of Linguistic Anthropology*, 24(2): 109–132.

Eckert, P. (2004) Adolescent language, in Finegan, E. and Rickford, J. (eds.) *Language in the USA: Themes for the Twenty-First Century*. Cambridge: Cambridge University Press.

Evans, A. (2016) Stance and identity in Twitter hashtags, *Language@Internet*, 13. Article 1. (urn:nbn:de:0009-7-43402).

Makoni, S. and Grainger, K. (2002) Comparative gerontolinguistics: Characterizing discourses in caring institutions in South Africa and the United Kingdom, *Journal of Social Issues*, 58(4): 805–824.

Smith, J., Durham, M., and Richards, H. (2013) The social and linguistic in the acquisition of sociolinguistic norms: Caregivers, children and variation, *Linguistics*, 51(2): 285–324.

Ylänne, V. (ed.) (2012) *Representing Ageing: Images and Identities*. Basingstoke: Palgrave Macmillan.

CHAPTER 9

Language, class and symbolic capital

9.1 INTRODUCTION

In this chapter, we explore social class and **symbolic capital**. The reason for considering both together is twofold. First, social class is notoriously difficult to define. Second, in order to fully understand the effects of class and the power it may bring, it's important to engage with the notion of symbolic capital. Objective definitions of class don't always explain language variation. We begin by examining attitudes to class before considering research on the correlation between language and class. We then consider social networks and communities of practice in order to see that language use and symbolic capital may be rather more local than traditional definitions of class suggest. Finally, we examine a recent model of class that gives symbolic capital a central place.

9.2 WHAT IS SOCIAL CLASS?

Social class has long been associated with how much money a person has. That is, the amount of money a person possesses or can earn may place a person in a particular position in a social class hierarchy. However, this relationship has been complicated by the fact that the possession of money no longer relies on being born into a particular family or pursuing a particular profession. While personal wealth can still be considered one of the factors that contribute to the perception of 'class', other factors, such as education, where someone lives and, of course, the language a person speaks play an important role in the perception of social class.

Many people think that social class is no longer relevant. However, even in societies presented as lacking social class distinctions, it can still be found. In Denmark, like other Scandinavian countries, there is a strong ideology of egalitarianism. As Ladegård puts it, 'Denmark . . . is often presented as a country in which social class distinctions are virtually non-existent' (1998: 183). To investigate this, Ladegård recorded people using different regional varieties of Danish, as well as 'Standard Danish'. He then asked informants to listen to the voices and rate their intelligence, education, socio-economic status, reliability, friendliness, sense of humour and so on (1998: 187). Significant differences in evaluation emerged across all categories. Standard Danish scored well across all domains, as did a variety known as High Copenhagen. The difference in evaluation of these two varieties compared to all others, however, across all domains, was significant. Ladegård observes,

> [T]he Danish subjects do *not* perceive members from different social groups in their society as equal. They see, for example, the Northern suburban Copenhagener as intelligent, well-educated, rich and with great leadership potential, as opposed to the inner-city Copenhagener, who is perceived as relatively unintelligent, poorly educated, and with low socioeconomic status and poor leadership potential.
>
> (1998: 188)

Even in a country with low objective inequality, social class and attitudes about social class can still be found and linked to linguistic performance. As Kristiansen's (2010, 2017) research demonstrates, an association between language variation and social class continues to be present (although it is configured in new ways). While we may think we live in classless societies, the reality is rather different, as we see in the linguistic research we cover here.

As we have seen with other social categories, social class intersects with other aspects of identity, and it should not be considered separately from other variables. The way a working-class woman uses language, for example, may well differ from how a working-class man does, thus demonstrating the intersection of social class and gender identities. We will return to this notion of intersectionality in Section 9.5.

What other things might be associated with social class? Imagine a person from an upper-class, middle-class and lower-class background. Where to do they work, how do they spend their leisure time and how do they dress? Discuss this with your colleagues, and see if you can paint a full picture.

Activity 9.1

9.3 ATTITUDES TO CLASS

As we saw in Chapter 1, the idea that there is a 'correct' and 'standard' form of the language is widespread. This prescriptivist perspective has a number of components and consequences. First, any non-standard language variety will be viewed as somehow deficient in relation to the 'standard' (Milroy and Milroy, 1999). Even though prescriptivists argue that standard language is more 'logical', more 'beautiful' and more 'correct', these are subjective judge-ments (see Labov, 1970; Milroy and Milroy, 1999). The valuation of standard language over all other varieties is an arbitrary one. This view of the stan-dard language is not just held by a few people but rather forms the basis of a widely held and powerful ideology. That is, insisting that the standard variety is better than others is a way of expressing, claiming and maintain-ing power (Wolfram and Schilling-Estes, 1998: 164). The importance of the consequences of negative attitudes to language varieties is the link between access to power and language. Because of the principle of linguistic subor-dination (see Section 6.6), the language of a marginalised group will also be marginalised. For example, as we saw in Section 8.3, perceptions that the language use of adolescents is impoverished reflects the marginalised posi-tion of adolescents in the social order. Social class hierarchy is also reflected in complaints about language usage. The result is that those in marginalised groups may be denied access to power because of their language use. In terms of social class, there are degrees of marginalisation. The lower on the social hierarchy a person is, the more marginalised they are.

Comments on language use and change relate directly to social order. Foges (2015) acknowledges that in the case of Great Britain, 'one thing above all others stands in the way of true social mobility. We need to talk about talking: about voices, accents, pronunciation – and the way speech can hold some people back'. For example, in 2013, a school in Middlesbor-ough, England, sent a letter to the parents of its students advising them to correct their children's English usage. The letter provided eleven examples of grammar and pronunciation that the school deemed frequently incorrectly used. The school administrators claimed the corrections would enable the students to learn 'standard' English and prevent them from being 'disadvan-taged' in the world (Robson, 2013). Nevertheless, many of the features in the list are correlated with socio-economic status (e.g., 'I done it' rather than 'I did it' or 'I seen it' rather than 'I saw it'). Other features are regional ones. In the UK, regional linguistic features are very often also markers of class. This may explain comments made on social media to a Labour Party MP, Angela Raynor, who speaks a regional variety of British English. She received emails from constituents that critiqued her accent. One critic claimed she sounded 'as thick as mince' (which means 'very stupid') (Gill, 2016).

9.3.1 Social class as other

Very often, the 'hidden' ideologies we find in talk about social groups reveals the negative attitudes held about them. Just as we saw with other marginalised groups, social class creates a social hierarchy that marginalises and 'other' groups that are positioned lower in the hierarchy. The significance of social class in this respect is often overlooked because the terms used to refer to these groups are not obviously connected to social class. Nevertheless, close examination of the representation of social class demonstrates the negative attitudes held toward these groups by members of society. Because social class is salient everywhere, analogous terms that 'other' lower social classes exist in all English-speaking countries, such as 'bogan' in Australia, 'chav' in Great Britain (Hayward and Yar, 2006) and 'white trash' in the US (Hartigan, 1997). Note that these terms index social class and a set of characteristics, including clothing, behaviour and language. Scholars have described the very negative attitudes that society has toward these groups (Tyler, 2008; Hartigan, 1997; Gibson, 2013). The Australian term 'bogan' exemplifies how this 'othering' takes place.

> Bogans are stereotypically associated with crime, hard rock music, beer barns, customised old cars, and cheap clothing such as track suits, flannelette shirts, mullet haircuts, and the now iconic Australian sheepskin 'ugg' boots.
>
> (Gibson, 2013: 62)

While the term 'bogan' is generally associated with low income, there is more to the designation than this. They are also defined in terms of their consumption and leisure activities, both of which are perceived as unappealing by groups who are higher in the social hierarchy (Gibson, 2013; Pini and Previte, 2013). 'The use of bogan in some circles implies poor upbringing and bleak fortunes, a synonym for lack of wealth. But more deeply, bogan means an absence of cultivated aesthetics or tastes' (Gibson, 2013: 64). In the case that someone who is labelled bogan acquires a certain amount of wealth (a 'cashed up bogan'), they are not considered 'middle class' and continue to be labelled bogan (Gibson, 2013: 64). Gibson and others argue that this is part of a middle-class strategy to protect their power and hegemonic status. The clothing and habits attributed to bogans thus take on a greater significance for social class attribution than wealth or income.

9.3.2 'Chavspeak'

In the UK, the term 'chav' refers to:

> (originally the south of England) a young person of a type characterised by brash and loutish behaviour and the wearing of designer-style clothes (esp. sportswear); usually with connotations of a low social status (Oxford English Dictionary).

Joe Bennett (2012) has explored representations of how chavs use language by examining books with titles such as *Chav!* and the *Chav Guide to*

Life. These are meant to be humorous books and intended for a mass audience. Note that Bennett is not concerned with the actual language of chavs as described by linguists but rather with the ways 'chavspeak' is defined by non-specialists. This type of sociolinguistic study is called 'folk linguistics'. Bennett finds in these books detailed accounts of the stereotypes and ideologies held about working class Britons.

Bennett observes that the linguistic features attributed to chavs are features that are actually widely used and reflect stereotypes of several marginalised varieties of English. For example, in order to speak like a chav, the reader is instructed on pronunciation such as using 'f' instead of 'th' (Example 9.1 a), to drop h (Example 9.1 b), to include glottal stops (Example 9.1 c), and to avoid pronouncing 'ing' in the standard way (Example 9.1 d).

Example 9.1 'chavspeak'

a   muvaaa – mother
b   'ave – have
c   aun'ie – aunty
d   aahyagaahndaahntaahnlayhtaah? – Are you going down town later?
(Bennett, 2012: 10–11)

There is more than simply pronunciation to chavspeak, however. Bennett notes that chavspeak has a range of other conventions, including novel vocabulary items, specific topics of conversation and communicative **style**. Features attributed to chavs seem to be stereotypical linguistic features found in many other varieties borrowed from other sociolects, including Black Englishes, West Indian English, rap and hip-hop music. The books Bennett examined portray chavs' language as 'rude and incoherent: their language varies from a "mutated" form of English to "white noise"' (2012: 19). These books also show how 'language is available as a material on which to peg various social associations' (Bennett, 2012: 20 following Hudson, 1996: 211–216). That is to say, a range of negative characterisations about a group associated with a social class (or, other social groups) can be expressed simply by describing their language. Even wearing a particular piece of clothing may be enough to invoke these language ideologies and label a person as a 'chav'.

9.3.3 Representations of social class

'Poverty porn' refers to a type of reality television that focuses on people in receipt of social welfare payments, and while the kinds of representations of people vary, as a genre, it marks out people receiving welfare primarily in negative terms. Poverty porn is not an entirely new genre, but in the UK and other countries, there has been a sharp increase in the amount and visibility of it in recent years (see Biressi, 2011; Jensen, 2014; Paterson, Coffey-Glover and Peplow, 2016). It has also been characterised as 'the media portrayal of the feral and feckless poor as the source of social breakdown' (Squires and Lea, 2013: 12 cited in Paterson et al., 2016: 197). In order to understand this characterisation of poverty porn, it is necessary to consider the ideologies it communicates. In separating out a group and suggesting that they are unproblematically identifiable, poverty porn 'performs an ideological function; it generates a new "common sense" around an unquestionable need for welfare reform' (Jensen, 2014: 2.2). That is, the 'common sense' it generates is that poverty is self-inflicted and that only lazy people are poor.

The distinction between the 'deserving' and 'undeserving' poor is not a new one (Garthwaite, 2011; Lansley and Mack, 2015: 121ff; Shildrick and Mac-Donald, 2013). Rather, differences throughout history tend to be about who is identified as undeserving. Paterson, Coffey-Glover and Peplow have examined people's reactions to poverty porn, specifically, a UK programme called *Benefits Street* (2016, 2017). Audience reaction to the programme was generated from focus group data. Some focus group members found it depressing, others thought it exploited those represented and still others thought it was useful in drawing attention to social problems and issues (2016).

One of the features Paterson et al. consider are the verb choices that focus groups make (see 'transitivity' Section 2.6.1) when discussing the people in *Benefits Street* (2016). They write 'There is a tendency to represent the people on Benefits Street as talking rather than acting' (2016: 201). When they are described as doing something, 'benefit claimants are constructed as the recipient or goal of an action, as in "why should I work, let the state keep me" and the related comment that "because of the benefit culture, they are so used to people doing things for them, they tend not to do things for themselves"' (Paterson et al., 2016: 202). As the authors explain, the people featured on *Benefits Street* are understood 'as people who cannot take independent action' (Paterson et al., 2016: 202). They are, however, shown to be doing other things, 'such as smoking and complaining' (2016: 202). Finally, they are said to be 'taking' and 'getting' benefits rather than 'receiving' them (ibid). As one focus group participant says, '[T]hey are quite happy to take money off the State' (2016: 202).

Although not all focus group participants agreed, Paterson and colleagues show the groups did 'construct an overarchingly negative stereotype of those on benefits' (2016: 212). This of course provides insight on how individuals on benefits are seen by wider society and therefore has an effect on policy at the national level. As Paterson, Coffey-Glover and Peplow conclude, 'The programme, and others like it, invites negative evaluations of poor people and benefit recipients, and should, therefore, be subject to critical linguistic analysis' (2016: 202). It also demonstrates how critical linguistic awareness (see Chapter 1) has important and potentially wide-ranging effects.

9.3.4 Pittsburghese

It is important to note that the stereotyping of non-standard Englishes can have positive functions too. Johnstone, Bhasin and Wittofski (2002) describe features of US working-class English in Pittsburgh, Pennsylvania. In contrast to the negative perceptions of chavs, Johnstone notes that linguistic features in Pittsburgh seem to allow both positive and negative interpretations.

> In Pittsburgh, the same features that are in some situations, by some people, associated with uneducated, sloppy, or working-class speech can, in other situations and sometimes by other people, be associated with the city's identity, with local pride and authenticity.
>
> (Johnstone, 2009: 160)

Local pride is evident in artefacts such as T-shirts, mugs and dictionaries containing local terms that are common in many parts of the English-speaking world. Johnstone found that T-shirts from Pittsburgh display dialect words, local pronunciation and local values. These items are evidence of what people think of the English spoken there. One of the most salient features of Pittsburgh English is the word used for the second person plural pronoun. While standard English does not have such a pronoun, several English varieties do have one (e.g., 'y'all' in southern US English). In Pittsburgh, this pronoun is 'yinz'. Because 'yinz' is a non-standard feature, it is stigmatised. However, 'yinzer' has been positively embraced by locals (Johnstone, Andrus and Danielson, 2006: 97). The reproduction of words like 'yinz' on T-shirts raises the profile of the pronoun by turning local **linguistic variation** into a product that can be bought. This is a signal of both identification of and even pride in the local language. Such reclamation has been found in other communities, such as Corby, England, and Kingston, Jamaica (Wassink and Dyer, 2004).

Activity 9.2

The commodification of local language is found in many places. Have you noticed this in your region? Or, perhaps, a region you're familiar with? What does the linguistic variation that has been commodified represent? Where is it found? What does it mean?

9.4 LINGUISTIC VARIATION

9.4.1 New York City

Noticing that different department stores often cater to particular social classes, William Labov (1972a) investigated whether the use of a feature of New York City English (NYC) by store clerks varied according to the different store they worked in. In NYC, the pronunciation of 'r' has high prestige. Speakers who pronounce the 'r' in words like 'card' and 'bar' are said to be 'rhotic'. It is important to note that although **rhoticity** is a prestigious feature in US English, it is not in many varieties of British English. This demonstrates the arbitrariness of value attributed to a linguistic feature (see Section 9.3).

Labov conducted his study in three department stores: Saks, Macy's and S. Klein. He determined their relative prestige on the basis of the location of the stores, the price of goods they sold, where they advertised and the general layout and aesthetics of the store itself. Saks was the most prestigious, Macy's was less prestigious than Saks and S. Klein the least prestigious of the three. In order to elicit the linguistic feature of rhoticity, in each department store, he identified an item sold on the fourth floor and then asked clerks where he could find that item. Naturally, the person would respond 'fourth floor'. He would pretend not to have heard so that they would be required to repeat the answer. This provided up to four examples where rhoticity could be present. Figure 9.1 shows the results.

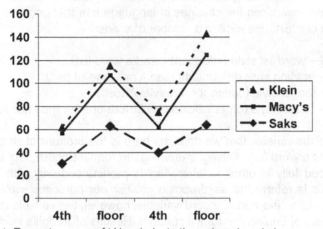

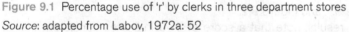

Figure 9.1 Percentage use of 'r' by clerks in three department stores
Source: adapted from Labov, 1972a: 52

These results suggest that rhoticity is socially stratified; that is, it is used more by people associated with higher social class. It also appears to be used more when in word-final position (in the word 'floor'), and there is some increase when the response is repeated. Of course, not everyone who works in a store necessarily shares the same social class. Labov argues that salespeople 'borrow' prestige from the store in which they work (1972a: 45). The results certainly suggest that this is the case. A replication of this study in 2009 showed the same 'general pattern of social and stylistic stratification of [r]', although there were some differences, especially in relation to ethnicity and age (Mather, 2011: 353; see also Becker, 2009).

9.4.2 Norwich

Another classic study that reveals patterns in linguistic usage associated with social class was conducted in the UK. Peter Trudgill (1972) examined a

number of pronunciations in the English spoken in Norwich. In order to allocate his informants to a social class, he considered their occupation, father's
occupation, income, education, where they lived and in what kind of house.
Each characteristic was given a score, and then these scores were taken
together in order to allocate people to a class. This resulted in 5 classes.

LWC – Lower Working Class
MWC – Middle Working Class
UWC – Upper Working Class
LMC – Lower Middle Class
UMC – Upper Middle Class

(Trudgill, 1972: 181)

In addition to examining the effect of social class on linguistic variables,
Trudgill also examined the changes in language use that occur in different
speaking contexts. He elicited a number of styles:

WLS – word list style (informants read a word list)
RS – reading style (informants read a passage of text)
FS – formal style (during the 'interview' itself)
CS – casual style (other talk, usually before or after the interview)

The linguistic variable that we consider here is the pronunciation of 'ing' at
the end of a word (e.g., fishing, swimming). In formal English, 'ing' is usually
pronounced fully. In other varieties, 'ing' is pronounced only with 'n'. In lay
terms, this is referred to as 'dropping gs'. For our purposes, we'll refer to
'dropping gs' as the 'non-standard' variable; however, this variable is used by
all speakers of English in informal contexts. Results of Trudgill's study can be
seen in Table 9.1 and Figure 9.2.

In these results, note that a score of 100 indicates consistent use of
the non-standard variable. There are two important features to notice in
the results. Firstly, each group uses the variable in varying amounts overall.
Notice that none of the lines in Figure 9.1 overlap, showing that each social

Table 9.1 Percentage use of non-standard (ng) by Norwich speakers according to
social class

Class	Word list	Reading passage	Formal speech	Casual speech
Middle middle class	0	0	3	28
Lower middle class	0	10	15	42
Upper working class	5	15	74	87
Middle working class	23	44	88	95
Lower working class	29	66	98	100

Source: adapted from Trudgill, 1972: 91

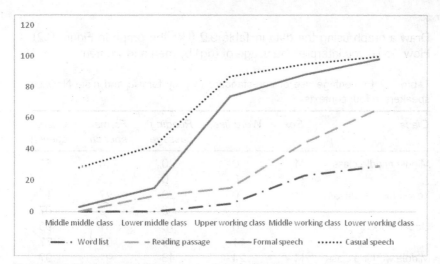

Figure 9.2 Percentage use of non-standard (ng) by Norwich speakers according to social class

Source: adapted from Trudgill, 1972: 91

class group uses the variable at a different proportion. The LWC uses the highest proportion of 'g dropping' of all the social groups, regardless of the speech context: they use it 100% of the time in the casual style and 29% in the most formal style.

Secondly, each group's percentage of use changes according to speech context. That is, all groups use the non-standard variable less in the most formal context and vice versa. This type of change according to speech context is called style shifting. Even more interesting, with regard to style shifting, is how the lines/numbers in Figure 9.2 diverge. The lines representing (ng) use by the LWC and MWC run more or less parallel to each other, as do the LMC and MMC. The percentage for (ng) among the UWC shifts abruptly from the reading passage style to formal style. Trudgill observes that UWC speakers appear to have a 'greater awareness' of 'the social significance of linguistic variables', which can be 'explained by the "borderline" nature of their social position' (1974: 91). Trudgill describes this in terms of Labov's concept of **'linguistic insecurity'** (1974). Linguistic insecurity refers to a speaker's perception that their own (variety of) language is inferior to others'. In the case of Norwich, this means that the LWC speakers believe their English isn't as 'good' as that of the MMC and UWC speakers.

While this pattern of usage of non-standard features in different contexts has been found in other groups, it's also important to remember the other variables we have considered in previous chapters that may interact with and influence language use. Trudgill's Norwich study provides a good example of this. Table 9.2 adds the variable of sex to Table 9.1 (Trudgill, 1972: 182).

Draw a graph using the data in Table 9.2 (like the graph in Figure 9.2). How would you interpret the usage of (ng) by men and women?

Table 9.2 Percentage use of non-standard (ng) by female and male Norwich speakers in four contexts

Class	Sex	Word list	Reading passage	Formal speech	Casual speech
Middle middle class	M	0	0	4	31
	F	0	0	0	0
Lower middle class	M	0	20	27	17
	F	0	0	3	67
Upper working class	M	0	18	81	95
	F	11	13	68	77
Middle working class	M	24	43	91	97
	F	20	46	81	88
Lower working class	M	60	100	100	100
	F	17	54	97	100

Source: adapted from Trudgill, 1972: 182

Drawing a graph of the data from Table 9.2 will show you that in each social class, men use more of the non-standard variant than women. There is one exception, the men in the LMC in the casual context use less than the women. Trudgill explains that the low score of men in this group, which would suggest they are using the prestige variant, is 'due to the fact that only a very small number of instances of this variable happened to be obtained for this group in CS' (1974: 93 n 1).

There are a number of explanations for this difference between women and men. Trudgill (1972: 182) suggested that women need to choose their linguistic variables carefully because of the lower social status they have in relation to men and because women are often evaluated not by their occupations but by how they behave. It is also possible to explain the difference by considering men's language. Trudgill argues that the men's linguistic behaviour may be explained by the 'covert prestige' associated with this variety. Working class speech has 'connotations of masculinity, since it is associated with the roughness and toughness supposedly characteristic of WC [Working Class] life, which are, to a certain extent, considered to be desirable masculine attributes' (1974: 94).

9.4.3 Glasgow

We saw that rhoticity is a prestige variable in New York. In the UK, however, it is associated with a variety of non-standard Englishes, including Scottish English. Because this is a non-standard accent, we might expect it to be stigmatised and thus not used by the middle classes. Research undertaken in Glasgow, however, shows that this is not the case.

Stuart-Smith, Timmins and Tweedie (2007) undertook research on teenagers from both the working class and middle class in neighbourhoods of Glasgow. Of particular interest here is the fact that the neighbourhoods border each other. Bearsden, the middle class neighbourhood, lies to the north of the working class neighbourhood, Maryhill. A number of linguistic variables were investigated. Here, we discuss two: rhoticity (see Section 9.4.1) and a sound called a voiceless velar fricative, represented as /x/. The /x/ sound is found in words like 'loch'. While a standard English speaker would pronounce 'loch' in the same way as 'lock', many Scottish speakers use a different sound. Rather than using a /k/, some use a sound more like 'kh' pronounced in the back of the throat, like the final sound in the name of the German composer 'Bach'.

The results of Stuart-Smith et al.'s research show that working-class teenagers in Maryhill do not use /x/, nor are they rhotic. That is, for these two features, working-class Maryhill teenagers use the same variants a speaker of Standard English does. The Bearsden teenagers, however, use the Scottish variants of rhoticity and /x/.

As we have shown, typically we find working-class speakers using more non-standard linguistic features than social classes above them. Among Glasgow teenagers, this is not what Stuart-Smith et al. found. In order to explain the use of these features, we need to consider what these features mean in the contemporary Glasgow context. Stuart Smith and colleagues suggest that if we consider 'the language ideologies which speakers construct to make sense of social and linguistic practices in Glasgow' we may be better placed to understand what these features mean for the speakers using them (Stuart-Smith et al., 2007: 248).

Stuart-Smith et al. argue that working-class teenagers are positioning themselves in opposition to the middle-class teenagers (2007: 243). What the working-class teenagers understand to be 'standard' is informed by the speech they hear middle-class peers using. Working-class teenagers 'are innovating and changing their form of Scots, as they polarise themselves linguistically and ideologically from middle class speakers' (Stuart-Smith et al., 2007: 254). Working-class teenagers abandon rhoticity and /x/ not because they want to align with 'Standard English' but because they want to disassociate from the middle-class teenagers. This shows that language and class can interact in various ways, with speakers' perceptions and attitudes having an effect on the meaning attributed to particular features. What seems to inform these changes is not social class as such, but rather 'class based language ideologies' (Stuart-Smith et al., 2007: 224). Example 9.2 is a transcript of an interaction between a researcher and Maryhill teenagers.

Example 9.2

CT:	(shows card with 'loch')
All:	loch [k]
CT:	You know how it's really meant to sound?

All:	loch [x]
CT:	And so why don't you say it that way?
All at once:	that's pure gay
	you need to be poofs
	cos we're not poofs
	pure Bearsden
	pure daft
	[and other similar comments for several seconds]

(Stuart-Smith et al., 2007: 253)

The Maryhill teenagers' comments suggest that there is nothing about the variant itself that they object to. Rather, they object to the people who they perceive to be using it: posh people. 'Being in opposition is the point' (Mac-Farlane and Stuart-Smith, 2012: 768).

9.4.4 London

Young people in London are also drawing on the associations of particular codes to express their identities and also their attitude to specific events. Rampton (2011) shows that his subjects at Central High in London clearly understand the difference between 'posh' and Cockney English and use linguistic features to express different stances to topics and to other speakers. Example 9.3 is a transcript of speech from one student that took place in a drama class as students were about to make presentations.

Example 9.3

1	Ninnette:	{calling out to the teacher, loudly:}
2		MISS
3		(.)
4		MISS
5		WE AINT EVEN DONE NU-IN
6		(.)
7		{even louder: } MISS WE AIN'T DONE NOTHING
8		(2)
9		{not so loud, as if Miss is in closer range: }
10		miss we aven't done anything.

(Rampton, 2011: 1240–1241)

In Example 9.3, look at the different ways Ninnette says the same thing in lines 5, 7 and 10. What differences are there? How might you explain it?

As line 7 shows, Ninnette clearly 'knows' the Standard English form – 'haven't done anything'. Even though 'have' is produced as 'ave', there is a progressive difference between her utterances in lines 5, 7 and 10. Ninnette appears to know both the 'posh' and the Cockney variants and uses them in her normal speech (Rampton, 2011: 1241). It is possible to argue that she uses the non-standard form to attract attention (line 5), but once the attention of the teacher is secured, she shifts to a more 'correct' variant (line 10). Ninnette seems to be aware of the prestige of Standard English and the working-class associations of Cockney. In this school, Cockney 'evoked solidarity, vigour, passion and bodily laxity, while posh conjured social distance, superiority, constraint, physical weakness and sexual inhibition' (Rampton, 2011: 1239). Ninnette understands that the world in which she lives in contains these social class ideologies and that these are associated with particular values and codes.

The examples of research in this section demonstrate that there is an association between language features and social class. Linguistic features can be used to index social class, attitudes to topics and other speakers or perform different kinds of action. How the associations between language and social class are exploited depends on the context.

9.5 INTERSECTION OF SOCIAL CLASS AND OTHER VARIABLES

It is very important to recognise that linguistic variation is the result of an intersection (or interaction) of several factors. Some of those factors are linguistic, and some are extralinguistic (e.g., gender, age, ethnicity). Young and Bayley (1996: 254) call this the 'Principle of Multiple Causes'. What this means is that it is rarely the case that a speaker's language use is influenced by one single contextual factor. An older white woman in London will not use language in the same way as a younger black woman in New York. The fact of being a woman is not enough to explain how these people are using language. We also have to consider age, ethnicity and local context. Social class is a good example of how a single extralinguistic factor does not work on its own to influence linguistic variation. Milroy (1987) and Eckert (1989a, 1989b, 1999) provide foundational examples of this principle that is now a key assumption in research on language and society.

9.6 SOCIAL NETWORKS

Because of the complex relationship between language features and social class, models that don't rely on income or occupation to define social class have also been developed. One way to do this is to represent and quantify the relationships among people in a community. These relationships are called **social networks**. In this context, social network does not refer to online communities of people. Rather, it describes the type and frequency of interactions people have with one another. A social networks model allows us to focus on an individual while taking account of their relationship with other people.

Research undertaken in Belfast, Northern Ireland, by Milroy (1987) examined the social networks of the individuals in three neighbourhoods. They developed a network strength score (NSS) in order to quantify the strength of ties of individuals to the local area. Informants received 'points' for the following:

a   'membership of a high-density, territorially based cluster'
b   kinship ties with other households in the neighbourhood
c   works in the same place as at least two other people from the neighbourhood
d   works at the same place as at least two other people of the same-sex
e   voluntarily associates with workmates outside of work

(Milroy, 1987: 141)

A person with stronger ties with the local area would result in a high NSS while a person who is less connected to their neighbourhood would result in a lower NSS. These social networks can be described in terms of **density** and **plexity**. Density accounts for the *number of other people* they interact with. Plexity accounts for the different *kinds of ties* people have with others. For example, if a woman both works and socialises with her sister, this would be a multiplex (rather than uniplex) relationship. Dense, multiplex social networks are more common in traditional working-class neighbourhoods (Milroy, 1987: 137). Milroy also found that dense, multiplex social networks compel conformity to local linguistic norms (1987).

Activity 9.5

Using Milroy and Milroy's network strength score, calculate your own network strength score. What do you think your score says about your social network?

While some linguistic variables showed the same patterns found by Labov and Trudgill, that is, women used more of the prestige variant than their male counterparts, not all of the women followed this pattern. For one linguistic variable (the pronunciation of /a/), young women in the neighbourhood called the Clonard used more of the non-standard variant than their male counterparts and more than women in the other two neighbourhoods. The NSS provides a way to interpret this result. In the Clonard, women had to find employment outside the neighbourhood, changing the nature of their social network. They had a high NSS as they were part of dense, multiplex social networks. What explains the difference between young men and young women in the Clonard is not their sex but their social networks. The fact that these women are working outside their local neighbourhood is also important, as this provides access to new linguistic variables. The Belfast study shows that the 'traditional' working-class neighbourhood was already changing.

9.7 COMMUNITIES OF PRACTICE

Penelope Eckert's Belten High study (1989a, 1999) provides a different way of thinking about the intersection of social class and gender. Eckert did not classify informants according to where they lived or their parents' occupations. Instead, she spent time at the high school observing the behaviour, interaction and social practice of the students. It became apparent that there were two main groups in this high school; the 'jocks' and the 'burnouts'. Jocks were very much focussed on academic achievement and success in school-sanctioned activity (note that in spite of its name, membership in the jock group does not require being on a school sports team). Burnouts were less interested in school and oriented to urban culture. The two different orientations of these groups with regard to school seem to reflect social class based cultural norms, yet Eckert found that social class groupings did not account for the linguistic variation she observed. Eckert notes that these two groups define the extreme poles of social positions available in the school and that the majority of students belong to neither group and refer to themselves as 'in-betweens'.

Eckert argues that the jocks and burnouts should be thought about in terms of 'communities of practice' rather than representations of social class groups. A **community of practice** (CoP) is a group of people who have a shared common goal or activity. Because of the nature of the interaction in a CoP, they may develop their own linguistic norms. The individual CoP's norms are not predetermined, rather, they evolve and are developed collaboratively by members of the group.

One of the linguistic variables Eckert investigated was **multiple negation**. This linguistic feature involves using more than one negation in a sentence such as in 'I didn't do nothing'. Multiple negation is considered non-standard in English and is often stigmatised. Figure 9.3 shows the use of this feature by jocks and burnouts.

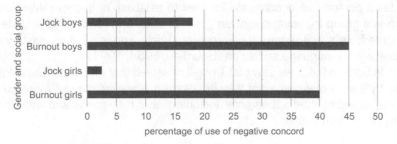

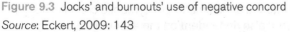

Figure 9.3 Jocks' and burnouts' use of negative concord
Source: Eckert, 2009: 143

Figure 9.3 displays some striking contrasts. While the jock girls hardly use multiple negation, the burnout girls use it a great deal. In addition, the jock group overall uses multiple negation less than the burnouts. Figure 9.3 does seem to bear out the predictions one would make, based on other research we have examined so far. However, if we examine the groups more closely and abandon the notion that jocks and burnouts are homogenous CoPs, we find that within the groups, there are some finer distinctions. Some of the women in the burnout group distinguish themselves with more or less extreme burnout behaviour. Females who engage in the most extreme burnout behaviour are labelled 'burned-out burnouts'. Figure 9.4, shows the usage of multiple negation by subgroups of each CoP.

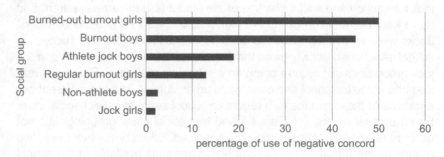

Figure 9.4 Percentage use of negative concord by six subcategories of jocks and burnouts

Source: Eckert, 2009: 146

Figure 9.4 shows that the burned-out burnout girls used more multiple negation than any other group and that jock girls used it the least. Thus young women at Belten High were found at both extremes for usage of this variable. Neither social class nor communities of practice alone fully explain the results in Figure 9.4. To understand this, we need some new perspectives.

9.8 SYMBOLIC CAPITAL

According to Eckert (1989b), **symbolic capital** refers to intangible attributes a person can 'accumulate' in order to establish or improve their position in a group including society in general. Such attributes might include a degree from a well-regarded university, an uncle who is a judge, mastery of a prestigious language and so on (Bourdieu, 1984, 1991).

In Section 9.4.2, we saw that Trudgill observed that men are often identified by their profession, what they do. Women, however, may be more likely to be judged by their appearance, including what they speak and what they wear. As Eckert states,

> women are thrown into the accumulation of symbolic capital. This is not to say that men are not also dependent on the accumulation of symbolic

capital, but that symbolic capital is the *only* kind that women can accumulate with impunity.

(1989b: 256 italics in original)

Thus, the male jocks and burnouts can establish their jock or burnout status through their activities (e.g. sports, fights) while the female jocks and burnouts have to develop their jock or burnout image through symbolic means, such as demeanour, clothes and language (1989b: 259). Eckert explains, 'Status is not only defined hierarchically: an individual's status is his or her place, however defined, in the group or society. It is this broader status that women must assert by symbolic means' (1989b: 256). The adolescents orient not to the 'standards' of broader society, but to their own local symbolic markets.

With regard to language, conforming to standard language practices is a key feature for being identified as a jock because jock activities are directed towards mainstream definitions of success: good grades in school, being an athlete and so on. What has symbolic capital for a jock (doing well in school) has very little value for a burnout. Non-standard language is valued in the burnout group; it has **covert prestige** (see Section 9.4.2). Members of both communities of practice want to accumulate prestige in their groups; precisely how to do this depends on what is valued by the particular community of practice. Figure 9.4, then, reflects the value that multiple negation has as symbolic capital for the burned-out burnout girls. For the burnout girls to display and perform their chosen identity, within their community of practice, the choice of the otherwise stigmatised multiple negation is logical. The same processes operate in other contexts and communities. Eckert's research demonstrates the importance of symbolic capital in understanding the performance of identity, especially for adolescents and women.

9.9 REVISING THE BRITISH SOCIAL CLASS MODEL

In the preceding examples, we considered some models of identifying social class that focused on income and occupation and noted that these models are sometimes unsatisfactory for accounting for linguistic patterns we find. Savage et al. observe, '[T]his occupationally based class schema does not effectively capture the role of social and cultural processes in generating class divisions' (Savage et al., 2013: 220). That is, there is more to social class than simply occupation or income. Savage, a sociologist, and his colleagues propose a new model of identifying a person's position in the social class hierarchy. Their model draws on the work of Pierre Bourdieu (1984), a French sociologist, who argued that there are three kinds of capital. First, economic capital refers to wealth and income. Second, social capital describes the social connections an individual can profit from. This kind of capital is recognised in the aphorism 'It's not *what* you know but *who* you know'. Finally, cultural capital includes education, whether formal or related to other social practices. For example, a university degree enables you to apply for particular jobs. A recognised qualification in a foreign language may give you access to careers that were otherwise unavailable. Cultural capital gives you access to opportunities, people and lifestyles. It is a very durable kind of capital. A university degree doesn't diminish when a person 'spends' it in the way that money does. Competence in particular forms of language is a form of cultural capital; being able to speak Standard English may give a person opportunities they might not otherwise have. While cultural capital may be durable, it is not always portable. Standard English may be worth very little in some contexts.

In order to arrive at a more comprehensive social class model for Britain, they conducted a survey called the Great British Class Survey (GBCS). They asked over 160,000 Britons about aspects of their economic, social and cultural capital.

Table 9.3 Question categories for Great British Class Survey

Economic capital	Social capital	Cultural capital
Income, savings and value of home	The professions of social contacts	Leisure activities, including musical taste, hobbies and social activities

In the GBCS, cultural capital was assessed by asking about preferences in relation to food, clothes and leisure activities (Table 9.3). In Activity 9.1, you might have decided that while upper-class people attend the opera and listen to classical music, working-class people aren't so interested in these pursuits. These kinds of activities are often discussed in terms of 'taste' and include things like the kind of food you like to eat (foie gras or pizza), the kinds of clothes you wear (haute couture or mass produced) and the kinds of places you like to visit (museums or casinos). These different preferences are not a reflection of which preferences are inherently better than others. The theory of social and cultural capital simply recognises that some attributes give people power in the social hierarchy in which they exist.

Consumption is highly marked for class and economic status and is intricately linked with symbolic capital (see Bourdieu, 1984; Wallop, 2014). To take just one example, Freedman and Jurafsky (2011) compared the 'words and metaphors' used on expensive and inexpensive crisp (or 'potato chip' in other parts of the world) packaging. By comparing the text on expensive and inexpensive packages, they found that potato chips are strongly imbued with social class indicators. For example, the more expensive potato chip packaging featured longer sentences and words (e.g., savoury, culinary), while the inexpensive chips had fewer and more common words (e.g., fresh, light). They suggest this feature is perhaps meant to appeal to the educational capital that can vary with socio-economic status. There were other differences in the way that the text related to the healthiness, authenticity, uniqueness and so on of the chips in spite of the fact that the key difference in the twelve brands analysed was price and not type of chip. They concluded that the language of packaging they examined showed a relationship between the price of the chips and socio-economic status (2011: 53). The text on the packaging capitalises on the type of social capital that is valued by the consumer the manufacturers have targeted.

Activity 9.6

> Consider the consumption patterns identified in the *Stuff White People Like* blog https://stuffwhitepeoplelike.com/ (see Section 8.2). What social class are these consumption patterns associated with? How can we interpret the feature of ethnicity in this context?

Savage and his colleagues assessed the GBCS results, together with an additional representative survey, and suggested seven social class groupings (Table 9.4).

Table 9.4 Summary of social classes

Social class	Description
Elite	Very high economic capital (especially savings), high social capital, very high highbrow cultural capital
Established middle class	High economic capital, high status of mean contacts, high highbrow and emerging cultural capital
Technical middle class	High economic capital, very high mean social contacts but relatively few contacts reported, moderate cultural capital
New affluent workers	Moderately good economic capital, moderately poor mean score of social contacts, though high-range, moderate highbrow but good emerging cultural capital
Traditional working class	Moderately poor economic capital, though with reasonable house price, few social contacts, low highbrow and emerging cultural capital
Emergent service workers	Moderately poor economic capital, though with reasonable household income, moderate social contacts, high emerging (but low highbrow) cultural capital
Precariat	Poor economic capital and the lowest scores on every other criterion

Source: adapted from Savage et al., 2013: 230

The social class groupings in Table 9.4 are a very different picture to the traditional high, middle and low class hierarchy. In particular, the new model identifies a new group they call 'precariat'. Further, this new system reflects changes in employment opportunities and also allows for different combinations of different kinds of capital (economic, social and cultural) to be recognised as distinct social classes (e.g., new affluent workers, emergent service workers).

9.9.1 Power and access to symbolic capital

Sometimes groups do not have access to typical types of **symbolic capital**. Access to social capital depends on the position of the individual but also on the ideologies that structure society. The most dominant ideologies can structure the world in concrete ways that prevent some members from acquiring symbolic capital. For example, many societies believe that Deafness is a disability. This belief is called 'audism'. Because of audism, the Deaf community does not have access to the same cultural and symbolic capital. Sutton-Spence and Woll observe that, in Great Britain, 'Social class does not have the same linguistic defining features for the British deaf community as for British hearing people. Deaf people are more likely to have unskilled and semi-skilled jobs than hearing people . . .' (2004: 170). The fact that Deaf people are more likely to have lower paid jobs demonstrates that the opportunities for claiming economic capital are limited. This is indicative of the marginalised position that the Deaf community occupies in society. That is, because the hearing world privileges speech and hearing, accessing kinds of capital that rely on speech and hearing will also be difficult.

Activity 9.7

What other groups of people have difficulty accessing routinely recognised symbolic and cultural capital?

Sutton-Spence and Woll show that income is not a good way of defining social class among the British Deaf community (2004: 170). That is not to say that there is no social class system in the British Deaf community. In fact, social class in Deaf communities (in Great Britain) is linked to one's family. British deaf children born to deaf parents are more likely to 'have had early exposure to a good model of adult BSL [British Sign Language]' (2004: 170) and therefore are more likely to become members of a 'linguistic elite' in the British Deaf community. Sutton-Spence and Woll argue that in the US Deaf community, members of the 'recognised elite social class' (2004: 170) are those who attended the only university for deaf people in the world, Gallaudet University (an example of cultural capital) (Gesser, 2007). Gesser's account shows that what counts as symbolic capital is local and depends on what the members consider to be valuable.

9.10 SUMMARY

Social class is difficult to define yet it is nevertheless a concept with social reality. In spite of this reality, many people do not recognise classism when it is present. We have also seen that there is some correlation between social class (variously defined) and linguistic features. The associations with particular linguistic features may be locally managed, and what is esteemed in one community may be irrelevant in another. Therefore, models like social networks and communities of practice illuminate what social roles are available and what is valuable symbolic capital in a community. Finally, we described a new model of social class developed in the UK. This model takes account of the different kinds of capital (economic, social and cultural) and provides a nuanced picture of what comprises social class in contemporary Britain.

FURTHER READING

Ash, S. (2004) Social class, in Chambers, J. K., Trudgill, P., and Schilling Estes, N. (eds.) *The Handbook of Language Variation and Change*. London: Blackwell: 402–422.

Block, D. (2013) *Social Class in Applied Linguistics*. London: Routledge.

Gesser, A. (2007) Learning about hearing people in the land of the deaf: An ethnographic account, *Sign Language Studies*, 7(3): 269–283.

Kerswill, P. (2001) Mobility, meritocracy and dialect levelling: The fading (and phasing) out of received pronunciation, in Rajamäe, P. and Vogelberg, K. (eds.) *British Studies in the New Millennium: The Challenge of the Grassroots*. Tartu: University of Tartu: 45–58, www.teachit.co.uk/armoore/lang/dialect.PDF

Loughnan, S., Haslam, N., Sutton, R. M., and Spencer, B. (2013) Dehumanization and social class: Animality in the stereotypes of 'white trash', 'chavs', and 'bogans', *Social Psychology*, 45(1): 54–61.

Mallinson, C. (2007) Social class, social status and stratification: Revisiting familiar concepts in sociolinguistics, *University of Pennsylvania Working Papers in Linguistics*, 13(2). Article 12: 149–163.

Thurlow, C. and Jaworski, A. (2006) The alchemy of the upwardly mobile: Symbolic capital and the stylization of elites in frequent-flyer programmes, *Discourse & Society*, 17(1): 99–135.

CHAPTER 10

Global Englishes

10.1 INTRODUCTION

This chapter explores language and power by considering the use of Englishes around the world. It is important to note that we use the term in the plural form (English**es**, not English). While there have been some efforts to identify a single variety of English which would be known as 'global English' that is capable of functioning as an international **'lingua franca'**, linguists don't believe there is one variety of English that could or should be labelled as 'global English'. There are, nevertheless, strong opinions among non-linguists about which variety of English used around the world should be called 'global English' or a 'lingua franca'. This chapter explores what different perceptions of global English means and how society negotiates these ideologies.

We begin by considering how global English might be defined and the issues and ideologies that play a role in that definition. Different models for describing the multiple Englishes around the world are explored and the ramifications of these models, especially with regard to teaching and learning are considered. Examples of UK, Singlish and Indian English are presented to illustrate differences that exist among them. We then explore how different varieties of English play a role in social capital in the global linguistic marketplace, and perspectives on the position of English as a global language as active **linguistic imperialism** are presented. Finally, we consider variation and subjectivity in the meaning of English by considering English as it is used in linguistic landscapes around the world.

10.2 WHAT DOES GLOBAL ENGLISH MEAN?

In the first chapter of this book, we examined the question 'What is language?' To that end, we considered how language is a structured system that speakers inherently understand and learn along with linguistic and communicative competence. We also raised the topic of politics and power in relation to how languages are defined. That is, whether a variety counts as 'language' rather than simply a variety of another language is more a question of power and other ideologies than it is a question of linguistic structure or fact. These are key issues to keep in mind as we consider global Englishes.

In order to understand what global Englishes means, we begin with Kachru's model of 'World Englishes' (1985), which considers the different kinds of English around the world and provides a visual representation of these varieties that can be interpreted in different ways.

The concentric circles in Figure 10.1 outline the distinction that Kachru makes between inner, outer and expanding circle nations in the World Englishes context. Inner circle nations are countries where English is spoken as a first language ('mother tongue' or **L1**). They are very often nations to which very large numbers of people migrated from the UK. For example, the

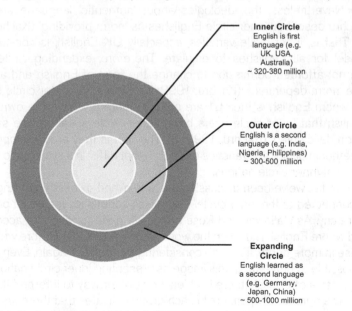

Inner Circle
English is first
language (e.g.
UK, USA,
Australia)
~ 320-380 million

Outer Circle
English is a second
language (e.g. India,
Nigeria, Philippines)
~ 300-500 million

Expanding
Circle
English learned as
a second language
(e.g. Germany,
Japan, China)
~ 500-1000 million

Figure 10.1 Kachru's Circles of English (1985)

US and Australia are inner circle nations. Outer circle nations are countries where English is often one of the official languages and may even be an L1 for a section of the population, but it isn't the only official language. Outer circle nations are often countries which have previously been colonised by the UK and the relatively smaller number of migrants brought with them the English language. The expanding circle includes countries where English is used in addition to other languages. English may well be widely taught and learnt in the expanding circle, but it tends to be neither official nor the L1 of a majority of the population.

Whether a country is in the inner, outer or expanding circle, then, has little to do with geography but more to do with history, migration patterns and language policy. The circles in Figure 10.1 may nevertheless suggest a transmission from one circle to the other. Seeing the image in this way suggests that inner circle nations are the 'origin' of English and the language reaches other countries through a kind of diffusion, like ripples in a pond of water. Such a reading implies a one-directional relationship between these nations with inner circle nations at the centre. This might suggest to some that inner circle nations are the originators of English. However, as Kirkpatrick observes, while Kachru's model does not suggest that one variety is better than any other (2007: 28), inner circle nations are, in fact, perceived as having greater ownership over the language, in that they have inherited English as their L1. Even among inner circle nations, not all nations can claim authenticity of the English language. The UK is widely perceived as being the 'origin' of the English language and is seen as the authority on what counts as 'standard' English. Inner circle nations tend to be regarded as 'authentic' speakers of English (Evans, 2005). However, as we show here, the English used even in inner circle nations is not homogenous.

Nevertheless, the ideologies about 'authentic' language are strong. Kachru describes inner circle Englishes as 'norm providing' (Kachru, 1992: 5). That is, inner circle varieties, especially UK English, is considered the model for all Englishes to emulate. Therefore, expanding circle nations are not afforded permission to change the form of English and are therefore 'norm dependent' (Kachru, 1992: 5). Even many outer circle speakers for whom English is their L1 are not considered to have the ownership of English that inner circle users have. Outer circle speakers are said to be 'norm developing' (Kachru, 1992: 5). The norms they are developing come together in distinctive varieties of English that differ in a systematic way from those of inner circle nations.

So far, we've been discussing the 'origin' and ownership of English as it is connected to the inner circle. This raises serious issues about power and hierarchy. As Galloway and Rose argue, we need to take into account how and where English is used in the world today (2015: 20). Before we consider these in more depth, it's worth considering Figure 10.1 again. Even though it is possible to understand this image as presenting inner circle nations as the originators of English, there is at least one other way to interpret it.

The number of speakers in each group indicates that there are far more expanding circle speakers of English than inner and outer circle speakers. The numbers could be interpreted as representing sets of speakers, where inner circle speakers are – numerically speaking – a subset of both outer and expanding circle speakers.

Acknowledging both the number of speakers not from the inner circle and the prejudice that can attach to outer and expanding circle varieties of English, Jennifer Jenkins (2009) suggests that we should cease making a distinction between speakers of English. Jenkins uses the term 'World Englishes' for any English – irrespective of which 'circle' it fits into. 'In other words, my interpretation does not draw distinctions in terms of linguistic legitimacy between say, Canadian, Indian, or Japanese English in the way that governments, prescriptive grammarians, and the general public tend to do' (2009: 200).

The power and prevalence of attitudes about different varieties of English are captured by Jenkins's inclusion of governments, prescriptivists and the general public. And while Jenkins's position is very attractive, as it acknowledges that all these varieties of English do count as 'English', it is nevertheless important to pay some attention to the attitudes to English that are so prevalent.

If all varieties of English are included in a visual model of World Englishes, the possible 'circles' can be redrawn.

Figure 10.2 seems to support Jenkins's interpretation of 'World Englishes' by including all varieties. Significantly, what this representation calls into

Figure 10.2 McArthur's Circle of World English (1987)

Source: McArthur, Tom (1987) 'The English Languages?' in *English Today* 11: 9–11

question is the possibility of talking about 'English' as unspecified. At best, 'English' is a convenient abstraction which hides a great deal of variation in terms of phonology, syntax and lexis and also in terms of domains of use and power.

What these two different representations suggest is that we can approach World Englishes from a number of perspectives. The perspective chosen depends very much on the argument one wants to make.

The idea that there is a global English that is the same all over the world is unfounded. If it could be developed, it is unlikely that it would remain unchanged. As Mufwene remarks, 'If WSSE [World Standard Spoken English] were to arise spontaneously, or could do so at all, it would be the first such evolution toward linguistic uniformity in the history of language spread and contact' (2010: 46). In a sense, there is no such language as English – at least, it exists only in the most abstract of conceptions. And if we focus on speakers of English, it is also extremely difficult to place individuals in any of these models (see Galloway and Rose, 2015: 23).

10.3 LEARNING ENGLISH

Learning English or any language as a second or additional language will usually mean that speakers will be found wanting when compared to the L1 standard. As we discuss here, linguists have argued that to use inner circle English norms as the 'standard' that all speakers should aim for is to create a goal that is both impossible and stigmatising.

10.3.1 Two models

In the case of English around the world, then, there are at least two competing models (see also Hilgendorf, 2015; Galloway and Rose, 2015). One is the English as a lingua franca model and the other a World Englishes model. Both have consequences for the kind of English that is taught.

Quirk argues for the importance of English teachers having English as their L1 (1990). Further, he argues that valuing regional ethnic and social varieties results in insufficient attention being given to the importance of teaching a standard variety (1990: 7). Despite the existence of other varieties of English, like Indian English, Quirk argues that students should also aspire to and be instructed in Standard English. 'It is neither liberal nor liberating to permit learners to settle for lower standards than the best, and it is a travesty of liberalism to tolerate low standards which will lock the least fortunate into the least rewarding careers' (1990: 9). Quirk's argument may seem unappealing in the sense that it values local varieties of English less than standard varieties. Kachru argues that Quirk's position is essentially 'deficit linguistics' (1991: 4) that portrays varieties that are not standard as deficient in some way.

Image 10.1 Learning English

Some varieties of English are rated more highly than others by laypeople (e.g., Bayard, Weatherall, Gallois and Pittman, 2002; Cowie, 2007; Deuber, 2013; Evans, 2005, 2010; Ladegård and Sachdev, 2006; Zhang, 2013); however, the context and the prevailing **linguistic market** (see Chapter 6) play an important role in the esteem of the variety:

> Certainly, if I were a foreign student paying good money in Tokyo or Madrid to be taught English, I would feel cheated by such tolerant plural-ism [of language varieties]. My goal would be to acquire English precisely because of its power as an instrument of international communication.
>
> (Quirk, 1990: 10)

Indeed, students are aware of the hierarchy of Englishes. Marr (2005) describes the attitudes of Chinese students studying English in London. He found that they had chosen to study in the UK because they believed it was a place where they could learn 'standard' English. One student stated that the 'English language in England is the pure and original' (Marr, 2005: 243).

If the goal is a high-power job in an inner circle nation, then standard English is precisely what is required. Until negative attitudes to outer and expanding varieties of English change, a local variety of English will not be as valuable as standard English. Research by Galloway (2013), however, suggests that attitudes can be changed. She found that exposing students to global Englishes as part of their teaching programme can have an effect on their perceptions of different varieties of English. While students still expressed a preference for native varieties, her results suggest that 'there is a slight openness about the position global Englishes should have in ELT [English Language Teaching]' (2013: 801).

It is also worth noting that the particular linguistic market in which Quirk assumes speakers to be using language is not that in which many speakers live. Most outer and expanding circle speakers are using English to interact locally rather than to compete for jobs with the global elite. Kachru notes that 'English has become the main vehicle for interaction among its non-native users, with distinct linguistic and cultural backgrounds – Indians interacting with Nigerians, Japanese, Sri Lankans, Germans with Singaporeans and so on' (1991: 10). As such, English is not simply used to interact with L1 English speakers nor to understand British and American values, nor with any goal of 'nativeness' in mind. Kachru urges a full consideration of language use, in its social and cultural context, while also attending to the dimensions of power that the deficit model at least implicitly condones. There is no reason why there cannot be more than one standard (see also Jenkins, 2009). The idea that there is, or should be, only one standard is an ideological exercise of power in which only those who 'own' the standard benefit. These benefits are both personal (in terms of what the variety gives speakers access to in the linguistic market) and also financial for those who produce materials using these standards for instruction.

Those who argue for more democratic standards acknowledge the current benefits of standard English. In order for a system of multiple standard Englishes to be accepted, however, there needs to be a paradigm shift (Kachru, 1991: 11) that takes seriously the social, cultural and linguistic context in which many speakers of English actually live and work. Canagarajah too argues that the teaching of English (or any language) must take into account the social, linguistic and cultural context in which it takes place. Rather than inner and outer circle, he refers to the 'core' or 'centre' and 'periphery'. This highlights the power differential among language varieties.

> My position, then, is that while we must recognise the contextual appropriacy of different Englishes and teach students as many variants as possible . . . This would lead to the pluralisation of standards and the democratisation of access to English.
>
> (Canagarajah, 1999: 181)

Canagarajah's position emphasises the importance of developing learners' critical language skills. This approach also pays attention to language as repertoire. Rather than focus on a 'standard' variety, looking at linguistic repertoires considers what speakers can do with the language resources they have. Further, if the paradigm of hierarchies of English is to be changed, it also needs to be addressed in the inner circle community.

Referring to varieties of English as 'better' or 'worse' is – of course – vexing and technically inaccurate. This is exactly what Jenkins's concept of 'World Englishes' aims to remedy. For Jenkins, 'world Englishes' 'refers to *all* local English varieties regardless of which of Kachru's three circles they come from' (Jenkins, 2009: 200). All these varieties are 'bona fide varieties of English regardless of whether or not they are considered to be "standard", "educated", and the like, or who their speakers are' (Jenkins, 2009: 200). She is particularly interested in the use of English as a lingua franca, 'the common language of choice, among speakers who come from different lin-guacultural backgrounds' (Jenkins, 2009: 200).

A person on Twitter writes that they are so fluent in their local English, 'Singlish' that they can't speak 'proper English' anymore. What does this tell us about how people think about their own language use? Do you think that this person should be worried about their 'proper English'? Do you think someone from an inner circle nation would be worried in the same way?

Activity 10.1

It is often the case that speakers of outer and expanding circle varieties accept the negative attitudes toward their English as accurate. This belief is referred to as **linguistic insecurity** (Labov, 1966). Lippi-Green (2011) suggests that by accepting that their own variety is inferior, speakers con-tribute to the marginalisation of their variety: 'When speakers of devalued or stigmatised varieties of English consent to the standard language ideology, they become complicit in its propagation against themselves, their own inter-ests and identities' (Lippi-Green, 2011: 68).

Wee (2005) argues that the defence of varieties of languages (like Singlish) is often forgotten in arguments about the protection of language. While there are many who support the protection of endangered and indig-enous languages (inter-language variation), he argues that we also need to pay attention to intra-language variation and the maintenance of these varieties. Wee reports that views like this led to the Speak Good English Movement (SGEM) in 2000, which endorses inner circle varieties as 'good' while arguing that Singlish is not (Wee, 2005: 58).

While the denigration of Singlish at first appears to be universal, there is evidence that speakers of varieties like Singlish want to protect these languages because of the way they express both culture and identity for Sin-gaporeans (Chye, 2000, TalkingCock website; Wee, 2005). Further, as it has meanings distinct from Standard English, speakers can use Singpororean English to demonstrate new identities (Brown and Jie, 2014).

For the purposes of English language instruction or teaching in English language medium, as indicated, the most important thing is to interrogate and investigate attitudes to language variation. Only then can learners make informed choices and – more important – perhaps start to shift the exchange rate on different varieties.

> Before teachers are likely to promote L2 inter-speaker variation in the classroom, they will need to experience a change of attitude towards it and, in turn, be equipped with the means of changing their students' attitudes (and this includes L1 students, possibly at secondary school level).
>
> (Jenkins, 1998: 125)

None of this is new. Williams, Whitehead and Miller (1972) show that debates about attitudes to language and their impact on teaching have been around for some time.

> To prevent language attitudes from serving as false prophecies, or worse yet becoming themselves self-fulfilled prophecies, teachers should be trained to be sensitive to the variations in social dialects and the variations in performance. Language evaluation, which incorporates the attitudinal side of the social dialect coin, should be included as part of the teacher training process.
>
> (Williams et al., 1972: 276)

10.3.2 'Lingua franca core'

The question remains, then, what variety of English should be taught to L2 learners? We saw above that Jenkins's concept of World Englishes seeks to remove the prejudice that attaches to some varieties. Jenkins also proposes a model for teaching that takes account of the linguistic difficulties of learning English as an L2 and attempts to create equality among dialects of English. Jenkins points out that British and American English can be very difficult to acquire as second languages (L2). Part of this is due to the sound systems of the varieties. For example, the pronunciation of 'th' by L2 speakers of English frequently creates misunderstanding. Jenkins therefore argues that pronunciation of English could be more achievable for those learning English (Jenkins, 1998: 119) if 'standard' pronunciation was ignored and more natural simplified forms were taught. Jenkins argues that 'Any neutral, universal forms of English pronunciation, simplified or otherwise, will therefore probably have to be unplanned, emerging naturally from "below" rather than being imposed from "above"' (1998: 120). Nevertheless, Jenkins has proposed a 'lingua franca core' (LFC) in relation to pronunciation models of English for learners. This model prioritises intelligibility over sounding like a native speaker of an inner circle variety. Features of the LFC are drawn from empirical examination of non-native speakers (NNS) and the variants that impeded intelligibility. In the case of 'th', substitution of 'v' or 'f' is acceptable in the LFC. We can't provide all the details here (see Jenkins, 2002: 96 ff); rather, we simply note that the LFC, by promoting intelligibility over prestige, provides a practical model for teaching EIL (English as an International Language) and therefore makes an important contribution to eroding the power differential among varieties of global Englishes.

Likewise, Canagarajah points out that in English language teaching contexts, especially in outer circle nations, learners should be permitted to develop a functional command of English (e.g., Canagarajah, 1999). Thus, instead of judging learners on how well they can command a legitimated construct of an inner circle variety, the focus is successful communication.

10.4 INSIDE THE INNER CIRCLE

As indicated in Figure 10.2, there is a great deal of variation in the forms of English used around the world. Despite the arguments that appeal to some 'pure' or 'original' form of the language described earlier, identifying a 'standard' form is not straightforward. This is clear when one considers variation in inner circle nations. Here, we consider an example from British English. Although McArthur's circle (Figure 10.2) acknowledges various 'British' Englishes, his representation is hardly the full picture. Just as English in outer and expanding circle nations is characterised by hybridity, contact and 'interference' so too is 'British English' (whatever that might mean).

As we noted, there is a perception that British English is somehow more correct, more logical and more beautiful than other varieties of English. We can question at least the first two of these claims by considering the stigmatised use of 'ain't'. According to prescriptive rules, 'I ain't' is not 'grammatical' (see Section 1.4). This form may be interpreted as indicating a lack of education or lower social class. However, if we consider the linguistic 'job' that 'ain't' is doing, this form doesn't seem illogical at all. Table 10.1 presents a paradigm for the English verb 'to be' in the negative.

Table 10.1 'To be' in the negative

	Singular	Plural	Singular	Plural	Singular	Plural
1st	I am not	We are not	I'm not	We're not	I _____	We aren't
2nd	You are not	You are not	You're not	You're not	You aren't	You aren't
3rd	She/He is not	They are not	She/he's not	They're not	She/he isn't	They aren't

---

What verb would fill the gap for the first person singular in Table 10.1? Would your suggestion be accepted by prescriptivists?

Activity 10.2

The gap in table 10.1 is known as the *amn't gap (Broadbent, 2009). The * indicates that the form is 'ungrammatical' in the linguistic sense. Following the paradigm, the form 'amn't' is logically what should fill this gap. Why do you suppose 'amn't' has not filled the gap?

Activity 10.3

Try saying 'I amn't' repeatedly and quickly. What happens?

Having gathered and analysed data from Yorkshire in England, Broadbent (2009) argues that 'ain't', having undergone a process of sound change, is actually a realisation of 'amn't' and thus fills the gap in the table (but see Liberman, 2014). This suggests that 'ain't' is, contrary to popular perception, in fact a logical solution to a gap in the English verb paradigm. This is more evidence of the arbitrariness of preferred prescriptive forms of so-called standard English ('ain't' is not a legitimate verb form).

10.5 'SINGLISH'

Having already mentioned 'Singlish', we now discuss it in more detail. Singaporean English (SgE) is composed of several varieties. There are a number of different Englishes spoken in Singapore because of the number of L1s that are used there. These include Mandarin, Malay, Tamil and a range of other languages (Leimgruber, 2012: 2). Most Singaporeans are multilingual, and English is encouraged because 'from an official perspective, [it] is solely meant to strengthen international competitiveness' (Leimgruber, 2012: 2). English is a medium of education and has become more common as the primary language used in the home (Leimgruber, 2012: 3). However, there is also anxiety that learning English may bring with it particular cultural values, like individualism, that are considered undesirable (ibid).

Standard English is advocated in education and by official language policy (Gupta, 2004). Singlish, then, functions as a local variety of English in the same way as regional dialects in English-speaking countries like the UK and the US. In places where standard English and Singlish exist, it is possible to say that it is a diglossic speech community. In a diglossic speech community, one language is considered the H (or high) variety and the other the L (or low) variety (Ferguson, 1959). Standard English, then, is the H while Singlish and other regional varieties of English are L. H and L varieties are used in different domains and for different purposes. Education, dealings with government and formal interactions take place in H while talk between friends and family is likely to take place in L. The belief that the L variety is not a language at all but rather a 'corruption' of the standard (Chapter 2) is common in diglossic communities.

Here, we explore a feature of the outer circle variety of English known as Colloquial Singaporean English (CSE), also referred to as Singlish. We focus on **discourse markers**. A discourse marker structures utterances, especially longer ones, but also provides important cues about the attitude of the speaker about what they are saying or responding to. It should be understood, though, that there are other ways CSE varies when compared to Standard English.

One of the many discourse markers found in Singlish is 'ah'. Deterding shows that this is used to mark the topic of an utterance. In addition to the discourse marker 'ah', topic marking is also accomplished by putting the topic at the beginning of the sentence. The Example 10.1 shows how both of these strategies are used together.

Example 10.1

a   Reading, ah, I guess, erm .... fictions

(Deterding, 2007: 72)

b   Magazines, ah, magazines ... er ... mmm ... all sorts lah, I guess I would try to read ... also kinds of magazines

(Deterding, 2007: 72)

Note that the examples in 10.1 put the topics ('reading' and 'magazines') first, followed by 'ah'. The rest of the information follows after this topic marking. As Deterding points out, something generally follows 'ah' (2007: 74). Leimgruber notes that 'ah' seems to be a discourse marker that is very frequently used. The second discourse marker we examine, 'lah', may be less commonly used, but it is closely associated with the idea of Singlish and is often used to index this language and the identity it conveys. 'Perhaps the one word that is most emblematic of Singapore English is the discourse particle lah' (Deterding, 2007: 66). The examples in 10.2 demonstrate how the particle is used as a discourse marker in Singlish.

Example 10.2

a   shopping-wise, nothing much to buy there lah, basically

(Deterding, 2007: 63)

b   a lot of things to do lah, so didn't really enjoy the three weeks there

(Deterding, 2007: 66)

c   I do enjoy talking to them at times lah, yah, er yup but ... OK lah I guess

(Deterding, 2007: 68)

In these examples, note that 'lah' comes at the end of clauses. Deterding notes that the particle 'serves to soften the tone of an utterance and build solidarity between speakers' (2007: 74). Given this function, and the meanings of Singlish itself, it is not surprising that this is considered its emblematic discourse marker. Leimgruber argues that CSE and Standard English in Singapore signal very different meanings. While Singlish is associated with localism, informality, closeness and community, standard English is linked to authority, formality, distance and educational attainment (2012: 56, following Alsagoff, 2007: 39). The different forms of these varieties are connected to very different functions. The distinction between these varieties is not only *when* they *should* be used but also *what they communicate*, over and above content.

10.6 INDIAN ENGLISH

According to the models presented in previous sections, Indian English is another outer circle variety which arose from a history of colonisation by the UK. While we have pointed out that some people in India use English as their L1, it is not the case that all people in India speak English. Sailaja notes that while few people report English as their 'mother tongue', over 64 million people use English (2009: 3). Nevertheless, it is generally accepted that there is a variety of English called 'Indian English', which bears traces of contact with other languages used in India, especially Hindi. Some of the syntactic and lexical features in Table 10.2 are found in Indian English (Sailaja, 2009, 2012).

Table 10.2 Examples of Indian English

Syntactic features	
'no' as interrogative tag	You will come, no? (Sailaja, 2009: 59)
Wh- questions no inversion?	When you will begin? (Sailaja, 2009: 57)
Use of progressive tense	I am having three books with me. (Sailaja, 2009: 49)
Additional prepositions	To accompany with, to combat against (Trudgill and Hannah, 2002: 132)
'itself' and 'only' as emphatic	We arrived today only;
	We will be required to have our classes here itself (Trudgill and Hannah, 2002: 132)
Lexical features	
Compound formation	key bunch (Sailaja, 2012: 362), time pass (a relaxing leisure activity Behra and Behera, 2012), good name (first name Behra and Behera, 2012)
Pluralisation of mass nouns	furnitures, aircrafts (Trudgill and Hannah, 2002: 130)
Borrowings from Hindi	'thali' – plate; 'bandh' – strike (Sailaja, 2012: 362)
Semantic variation from Standard English	drama – play; 'stir' – agitation (Sailaja, 2012: 362)
Hybrid constructions	Police-wallah; paper wallah – where 'whallah' means 'occupation' (Sailaja, 2012: 362)

While we can identify some unique features of Indian English, it is not a variety that lends itself easily to description. Nor does Indian English fit easily into first/second/additional language divisions. As Sailaja notes, 'while it is a second language to most of its speakers, many users, especially those who are displaced from their regions, claim it as their first language. It remains alien to many others' (2012: 360). Further, given the particular link of region, language and identity in India, it is not easy to get reliable self-reported figures of language use. People may still report their 'mother tongue' as the regional language regardless of their own proficiency (Sailaja, 2012: 360).

Sailaja also cautions against describing Indian English with feature lists (like Table 10.2), as they have 'the danger of creating the impression of homogeneity, uniformity and universality' (2012: 366). She argues that more research and documentation of this variety is needed. Indian English demonstrates the complexity and difficulty in attempting to define global Englishes.

10.7 PIDGINS AND CREOLES

In discussing global or world Englishes, however, attention is often given to varieties not found in the inner circle. When turning to other circles, the question of what counts as a language and what might be considered a variety of English becomes even more complicated. The wide range of **pidgins** and **creoles** that are used throughout the world contribute to this issue. Pidgins are used as lingua francas largely for trade or other practical interaction. A pidgin will draw on the languages of the **interlocutors** in order to bring together the linguistic resources necessary for these tasks but is not the L1 of speakers in the community. Because of the specific uses of pidgins, they may be 'little more than strings of nouns, verbs and adjectives, often arranged to place old, shared information first and new information later in the sentence' (Bickerton, 1983). The language providing vocabulary is called the **lexifier**, while the language which provides the syntactic structure is called the **substrate** language. After an extended period of use of a pidgin in a community, it becomes more fully developed, and serves as an L1 for the community. The language at this stage is called a creole. Note that the term 'Pidgin (with capital P)' is sometimes used to refer to a variety that is actually a creole. Activity 10.4 is a text in Hawai'i Creole English (HCE).

The following text in Hawai'i Creole English (HCE) is from the Bible (www.pidginbible.org/Concindex.html). Can you identify features that vary with respect to standard English?

Day numba one
3. Den God say, 'I like light fo shine!' an da light start fo shine. 4. God see how good da light. Den he put da light on one side, an da dark on da odda side. 5. Da light time, he give um da name 'Day time'. Da dark time, he give um da name 'Nite time'. So, had da nite time an da day time, az day numba one.

Activity 10.4

Vocabulary items in Activity 10.4 are identifiable as English, demonstrating that English is the lexifier language although the written form suggests that there are phonological differences. There are significant differences in syntax due to the number of languages (including Cantonese, Portuguese and Japanese) contributing to the form of HCE (Siegel, 2000). A translation of the Bible into HCE serves as evidence that HCE has a full range of functions and is in every sense a language. Table 10.3 demonstrates a few of the differences between HCE and English.

Table 10.3 Some features of Hawai'i Creole English (HCE)

Feature	HCE	English
'get' means both 'has/have' and 'there' is/there are'. (Sakoda and Tamura, 2008)	'They get three sons'. 'Get one student he bright'.	'They have three sons'. 'There is a student who's bright'.
Like in many other languages, no verb is required in some sentences (Hargrove, Sakoda and Siegel, n.d.)	Mai sista skini.	'My sister's skinny'.
'wen' is used before a verb to indicate past tense (Sakoda and Tamura, 2008)	Ai wen si om	'I saw him'.

Although creoles may draw on English as either a **lexifier** or **substrate** language, they are not simply varieties of English but fully functional languages. The distinction is not easy to draw, and there may even be a continuum in a speech community between an English-based Creole and a local variety of English. As we have seen, both will be stigmatised in relation to a standard variety, and this is the case with HCE (Drager, 2012; Ohama, Gotay, Pagano, Boles and Craven, 2000, and see Wassink, 1999 for Jamaican Creole).

10.8 LINGUISTIC MARKETPLACE

We have already encountered the concept of 'social capital' as developed by sociologist Pierre Bourdieu (Chapters 1 and 6). In relation to global Englishes, social capital is also relevant. The difference is the context, that it is a global linguistic marketplace rather than a local one. Local markets in the global context do not, however, cease to be important. Rather, these local markets need to be understood as situated in a broader linguistic economy. We have already discussed the importance of different attitudes towards varieties of English (Chapter 1). But it makes sense to consider attitudes to varieties in terms of social capital and global linguistic markets, as this highlights the power that accrues to speakers of esteemed varieties.

The metaphor of a linguistic market is particularly useful in the context of global Englishes. There is a great deal of research about attitudes to languages and what kind of capital one accrues on the basis of particular varieties of English (see Section 10.3.1). What people think about a variety will have an influence on what context they think it is appropriate for. Knowing the value of a variety of English on the linguistic market is crucial in understanding and deploying the linguistic resources you have. Some argue that the linguistic market is controlled by global elites and that their 'elite' variety of English becomes important as a symbolic resource (Bourdieu, 1977).

Which variety of global English do you think has the most value in the global linguistic marketplace?

Activity 10.5

You probably guessed that inner circle Englishes, particularly UK English, are the most highly valued in the global linguistic marketplace because of the complicated interaction of language ideologies and world political landscape we described earlier. This means that people who wish to enter the international job market cannot compete for jobs if they do not have a suitable level of fluency in the 'right' form of English (although it should be noted that this is also true on the local level – see Chapter 9).

Such attitudes, especially when linked to access to the labour market, can be understood in terms of changes in the labour market that are being brought by the globalisation of all types of markets.

10.8.1 Call centres and English

Many businesses rely on 'call centres' for a variety of services that they provide to their customers. In a call centre, employees of business provide service to customers over the phone. Because the service to the customers is provided over the phone, the call centre may be located in a place that is not near the customers or the company headquarters. Sometimes, companies will 'outsource' such labour to save money. That means that a call centre may even be located in a foreign country. In order to get hired in a call centre that serves English-speaking customers, an employee must have an excellent command of English.

Claire Cowie's (2007) research documents the demand from companies for employees working in call centres in India who have or can learn 'neutral' English accents. Cowie notes that it is difficult to know what 'neutral' means in this context, but she suggests it may refer to an 'unmarked' variety, a variety that is not easily identified in terms of place or status. As we have already seen, in the context of global English, whether an accent is marked or not is completely relative to the context in which the language is used and the individuals using it. Other research on call centres also documents the importance of employees having the 'right' type of accented English (Friginal, 2009; Rahman, 2009). Rahman studied the linguistic capital of a 'neutral accent' in the Pakistani call centre labour market: 'This accent is the scarce good, the salable commodity, which enables the [customer service representatives] to cross linguistic boundaries and, if successfully deployed, even pass as native speakers of English' (2009: 238). Further, Rahman notes, 'Call centre workers consider their acquired accent not only a business necessity but also "normal", thus implying the deficiency of all other accents and, hence, the desirability of changing them' (Rahman, 2009: 250). This demonstrates the deeply rooted ideology of the hierarchical organisation of varieties of English in Pakistan.

Heller (2003) describes the commodification of language in Francophone Canada to highlight the many tensions created by this commodification in the global economy. Such tensions may arise between the authenticity of L1 speakers and standardised varieties or hybridity versus a stable corporate image. All these tensions have ramifications for the global labour market.

The case of call centres also reveals the differences among different kinds of English and the beliefs and ideologies that people have about them. Research about the ideologies of the call centre workers has also been conducted in the Philippines (Tupas and Salonga, 2016). The Philippines has seen a large increase in the number of call centres it hosts: there were only two call centres in 2000, but over 1,000 in 2016 (Tupas and Salonga, 2016: 369). In their research, Tupas and Salonga studied call extracts but also interviewed the workers. They identified a number of ideologies in this data. The first is connected to a discourse of flexibility. Because the call handlers take 'phone calls from different places, they are aware of and take pride in the ability to accommodate to the caller's variety of English. One of the call handlers, Lloyd, says:

> Because we're catering to the global needs, we don't only take calls from the U.S. It's actually worldwide. You can speak with people with thick British accents, Welsh accents, with Arabic accents, with Indian accents, so we adjust in that particular aspect. If you talk to a non-native English speaker, we adjust our registers, we adjust our jargons. We speak slowly, and then we use very simple terms. The pace is changed and then we have to rephrase a lot.
>
> (Tupas and Salonga, 2016: 373)

It is worth knowing that for every 100 applicants for these call centre positions, only about five are considered to be qualified. They are therefore placed high in the social hierarchy in terms of 'education, class, urbanity and, of course, English language proficiency' (Tupas and Salonga, 2016: 370).

That is, the employees take pride in their ability to be linguistically flexible, and their linguistic ability is a marker of class and privilege. The discourse of flexibility is, therefore, an ideology of privilege.

As good as the workers' English is (especially when compared to the rest of the population in the Philippines), they nevertheless judge themselves against native speaker standards, especially American English. Lloyd, whom we saw earlier is proud of his language skills, expressed that this way:

> There are really customers who would make you feel like you do not deserve speaking that language [English]. I'm not a native speaker, sometimes I commit lapses, and sometimes it really makes you feel that you are different from them [customers]. They get to that point that they really had to say it, 'Okay, I'll repeat'. There are those markers that [are] really belittling of your personality.
>
> (Tupas and Salonga, 2016: 376)

This kind of statement suggests linguistic insecurity in the context of the call centre job where they compare their 'Filipino English' to inner circle varieties. Outside of the call centre context, however, where the workers can compare their English language skills to those of their national peers, they seem linguistically secure about their English.

10.9 LINGUISTIC IMPERIALISM

Some scholars focus on the **hegemonic** nature of English around the world. That is, because of the political and economic dominance of English-speaking countries, the English language is seen as dominant (Phillipson, 2003). While most scholars attribute the position of English to 'the particular history of the English-speaking nations' (De Swaan, 2010: 72), others are more specific than this, linking this history to a conscious project of expansion and acquisition of power. Phillipson and Skutnabb-Kangas argue that the spread of English is indicative of a more general neo-imperial project, one that seeks to encourage the growth and dominance of neo-liberal values, including freedom of trade, freedom of action for corporations and free movement of money. 'English can be seen as the *capitalist neo-imperial language* that serves the interests of the corporate world and the governments it influences' (Skutnabb-Kangas and Phillipson, 2010: 82). This perspective highlights the power, maintenance and spread of English. Evidence for this view can be found in a range of places, including the institutional infrastructure of the EU (European Union). There are 23 official languages in the EU (De Swaan, 2010: 69). While all of these are used informally, for official documents and public events, English is used most of all (De Swaan, 2010: 70).

In addition to an active project of expansion, some label English as a 'killer language' (e.g., Phillipson, 2003). That is, one could interpret the number of speakers of English and the way English is used around the world as correlated with the well-established death of many minority languages.

De Swaan characterises English as a 'hypercentral' language, 'the hub of the linguistic galaxy – like a black hole devouring all languages that come within its reach' (2010: 57).

What are the underlying assumptions in this quotation?

Calling English a 'black hole' or even a 'killer language' suggests that there is something about English itself which is a danger to other languages. But as De Swaan points out, the present status of English 'has nothing to do with the intrinsic characteristics of the English language; on the contrary, its orthography and pronunciation make it quite unsuitable as a world language' (2010: 72). Attributing human characteristics to a language overlooks the impact of activities of governments, corporations and other bodies and attitudes associated with that language.

Mufwene (2010) describes the reasons people acquire English, largely for professional advantage, and notes that such acquisition does not necessarily lead to abandoning one's first language. Language death, he argues,

occurs insidiously, when the socioeconomic structure of the relevant populations forces them to communicate more often in a dominant language other than their ancestral one, without them realising what the long-term effect of their communicative practice is, namely loss of capacity to use their respective heritage languages.

(2010: 50)

Socio-economic structure is the most relevant issue and it is impossible to disentangle the global economic structure from the status and future of languages. While it may make logical and economic sense for speakers to abandon their languages in particular contexts, how these conditions came about is also worth exploring.

Table 10.4 presents details on the language used at home for Chinese people in Singapore. What trends can you see? What might the trends suggest about language policy and the economic context?

Table 10.4 Language most frequently spoken at home among Chinese resident population in Singapore aged 5 and over

Home language	1990 (%)	2000 (%)	2010 (%)
English	19.3	23.9	32.6
Mandarin	30.1	45.1	47.7
Chinese Dialects	50.3	30.7	19.2
Others	0.3	0.4	0.4

Source: adapted from Lee Eu Fah, n.d.

Table 10.4 shows that Mandarin use at home among Chinese residents in Singapore is increasing (Lee Eu Fah, n.d.). Silver (2005) describes evolving language policy in Singapore, noting that while English has always been seen as important for global economic competitiveness, there is now also recognition of the importance of Mandarin in this context. It is perhaps not surprising then that there is a 'Speak Good Mandarin' campaign (Silver, 2005: 58) that is parallel to the 'Speak Good English' campaign (see Section 10.3.1.) and thus confirms the importance of Mandarin in this community.

The connection between economic power and language works in many ways. It is not simply that a language provides economic and symbolic capital once it has been acquired. As Mufwene notes, gaining a language 'comes at a cost ... the expense and effort of language learning itself' (2010: 66). If resources are limited, it makes sense to acquire only one language. Ammon notes, '[S]ets of competing languages function to some extent, like zero sum games: the rise of one can entail the fall of the other' (2010: 118). The relevant resources include not only those of the individual concerned but also of the nation in which they live. It is possible, for example, to produce multilingual individuals if the education system is set up to do so. Of course, this relies on education being affordable, accessible and well provided for in terms of teaching staff and materials. Under good conditions, the acquisition of another language can result in additive multilingualism.

There are many viewpoints on **linguistic imperialism** and the positive or negative effects of the position of English as a global language. The arguments made depend very much on the goal of the author. Some may want to emphasize injustice, lack of power and language death. This position highlights linguistic and other inequalities in the world. While accepting that there are inequalities, others seek to change this state of affairs, drawing attention to the relationship between language, trade, economics and language policy.

10.10 WHAT DO LANGUAGE VARIETIES MEAN IN THE GLOBAL CONTEXT?

As we've seen, there is no such thing as a singular global English. And we've discussed in this chapter and others the impact of language ideologies and how they lead to consistent perceptions of language variation. At the same time, it's important to be careful about making generalisations. In the global context, we must consider how English is transported around the world, how it is modified in local contexts and what it means to those who use it. Blommaert points out that it shouldn't be assumed that varieties will have the same effect when they are used outside their local context. In other words, if a local variety of a language is used outside of that local context, the audience may or may not notice the relative meaning associated with that variety. According to Blommaert:

> Values and functions of resources are attributed locally, and people construct meanings on the basis of codes, conventions, hierarchies and

> scales available to them . . . but the values and functions thus attributed
> to resources . . . are not necessarily transferrable to other environments.
>
> (Blommaert, 2003: 44)

Further, because language is an important aspect of how people construct their identities, the different meanings of a variety have consequences for the identity a person is able to construct. For example, Singlish is an important marker of local Singaporean cultural identity. The government programme of encouraging 'standard English' indicates that Singlish is valued in informal contexts but not in formal contexts, such as education and government. In terms of linguistic markets, Singlish provides a great deal of cultural capital for Singaporean identity but may provide very little in other English-speaking contexts. Singlish is very valuable in some contexts but in others doesn't count as a legitimate language (Blommaert, 2009: 565). Tupas and Salonga (2016) suggest we discuss these differences in terms of 'unequal Englishes'. They explain that 'some Englishes are still more acceptable and privileged than others' (2016: 368).

Blommaert notes that we can make sense of these different values, these different markets and contexts, in terms of Dell Hymes's 'second linguistic relativity' (2009: 565 ff). In Chapter 2, we outlined linguistic relativity, the idea that the language a person speaks has an effect on how they interpret the world. Second linguistic relativity takes into account what language is used for, the social context in which it is used. The associations that listeners have with a language depend on the variety used. Therefore, it is not possible for English to have a single affective association because the associations a listener or speaker makes with it depend on where it is used, in what form and by whom. This is second linguistic relativity; what the language denotes is relative to the form it takes and the context in which it is used.

> Whenever discourses travel across the globe, what is carried with them
> is their shape, but their value, meaning or function do not always travel
> along. They are a matter of uptake, they have to be *granted* by others, on
> the basis of the dominant [values].
>
> (Blommaert, 2009: 567)

In other words, not all varieties are equal. This inequality has consequences for the people who use these languages. As Blommaert notes, '[*D*]*ifferences* in the use of language are quickly, and quite systematically, translated into *inequalities* between speakers' (Blommaert, 2009: 567; see also Mufwene, 2010).

10.10.1 Repertoires

We noted that one way of thinking about the teaching, learning and use of English is to consider what people do with this language. Focus on language repertoires emphasises a functional command of English rather than being fluent in a 'standard' variety. This approach can also be connected to the discussion of languaging (see Section 7.3). That is, rather than distinguishing between different languages or language varieties, languaging invites us to consider them as resources. This difference in approach to understanding language use can be extended to code switching (see Section 7.7.1). The term 'code switching' involves a speaker moving from one code (or language) to another. If a 'languaging' perspective is taken, 'code switching' could be understood as translanguaging (see Sultana, Dovchin and Pennycook, 2013).

Dovchin takes a translanguaging perspective in a study of English used by Mongolian speakers on Facebook (2017). Dovchin explored 24 public community Facebook pages. Example 10.3 provides some examples from a page for a celebrity chef.

Example 10.3

Facebook text
1   Brie cheese sharsan yum uu?
     Brie cheese fried did you?
     'Did you fry the brie cheese?'
2   Tegeed salad, tomor aygand ni jam bgaa yum uu?
     And salad, steel bowl inside the jam to have there is?
     'And is there jam inside the salad and the steel bowl?'
3   Brie cheesee bread crumbs unhuruuleed tegeed sharna
     Brie your cheese bread crumbs is mixed and then is fried
     'Your brie cheese is mixed in the bread crumbs and then fried.'
                                                (Dovchin, 2017: 19)

The examples of 'brie cheese', the addition of 'e' to the end of 'cheese', or 'breadcrumbs' being mixed could be analysed as 'code switches'. Indeed, these examples are simply indicative of a more widespread localisation of English into Mongolian found on Facebook pages where English is 'meshed and mixed' with Mongolian as part of users' creativity (2017: 23). Dovchin argues that English 'can no longer be considered as [a] separate linguistic system but rather as part of local language' (2017: 23). This research shows that far from English 'belonging' to a particular place or a specific group of speakers, English is a resource from which speakers draw in order to 'enrich the modern Mongolian language' (2017: 23). Certainly, the way that Mongolian speakers use English on Facebook is not the same as the way other groups might. This is precisely because they have localised these resources.

10.10.2 Discourse in advertising and linguistic landscapes

As we have seen, English is widely used around the world. In fact, English can be found in contexts even where a consumer is not expected to know English. Discourse in advertising and linguistic landscapes in transnational contexts demonstrates the ideology of the valorisation of English. For example, Androutsopoulos (2013) describes how English is used in Germany in marketing brochures, commercials, webpages and magazines. He calls this usage 'a framing device that establishes, symbolically or indexically, frames of interpretation for the adjacent national-language content' (2013: 234). Piller (2001: 180) argues that in Germany, 'English has become thoroughly associated with a certain segment of German society as it appears through advertising discourse: the young, cosmopolitan business elite'. This means that the use of English in commercial contexts points the audience to a particular way of understanding a text. For example, the use of an English expression like 'hip-hop' in a heading for a story in a music magazine immediately evokes a set of meanings and representations of hip-hop musical culture for the readers. This set of meanings can only be evoked by an expression like 'hip-hop'. Thus, using English in this way may be a means for indexing a variety of meanings that help sell, persuade and inform. 'This leaves English to do mainly symbolic work, to work through stereotypical associations with the language, its speakers, and the cultures where it is spoken' (Piller, 2001: 180). This type of usage of English has also been studied in other countries. For example, Troyer (2012: 110) found that in Thai online newspapers:

> English is used to associate products and services (especially those related to media and technology) with concepts of modernity, globalisation, mass communication and media, commerce and wealth while Thai is used to initiate a closer connection between sponsor and audience in advertisements for organisations and events.

This type of symbolic meaning is found even in expanding circle nations, such as the Democratic Republic of Congo (Kasanga, 2012a) and Cambodia (Kasanga, 2012b). The symbolic usage of English around the world demonstrates the power and influence that English has. Nevertheless, it's important to remember that, as discussed earlier, the meanings that English may evoke are variable according to the locale and audience.

Vandenbroucke (2016) explores the linguistic landscapes (see Chapter 5) of different shopping areas in Amsterdam and Brussels. She examined the use of English on signage in three shopping areas (upscale, midscale and downscale) of Amsterdam and Brussels.

Figure 10.3 shows that the midscale shopping areas in both cities had the highest percentage of English signage. The midscale shopping areas had a predominance of stores that are international (e.g., River Island, Pull&Bear, H&M, The Body Shop, Esprit). These shops, therefore, have a higher presence of English in the language they use for advertising and brand identity. Vandenbroucke suggests that the presence and language choices of international franchises are a result of the homogenising forces of globalisation. In contrast, 'upscale and downscale consumption discourses imply more heterogeneity' (2016: 104). The lower percentage of English in linguistic landscapes of upscale shopping areas suggests that where there is

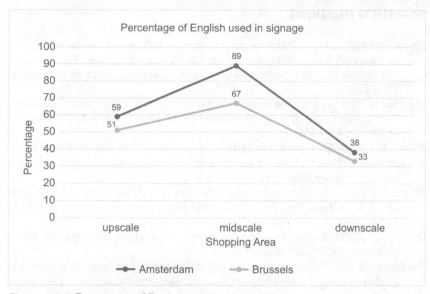

Percentage of English used in signage

Figure 10.3 Percentage of English used in signage in shopping areas in Amsterdam and Brussels

Source: adapted from Vandenbroucke, 2016: 93

a preference for eilteness, that this characteristic is not signalled by English in these areas. Further, because the downscale shopping areas chosen cater more to migrants, they therefore present their customers with signage in their L1 and there is a lower percentage of English in signage there.

This research again reminds us that English is not valued in the same ways around the world. It is used differently, carries a range of meanings and provides another example of second linguistic relativity. Vandenbroucke shows that the linguistic market is not only local and national; it is global 'with different values attributed to English in commercial discourse' (2016: 104).

10.11 SUMMARY

In this chapter, we have explored why global English cannot be considered a single way of speaking. It refers to many different varieties of English, and each has its own value and meaning associated with it, depending on the speaker and the context. This can be understood in relation to the complex forces that shape language use and understanding. Instead of thinking about English in the singular, it is important to remember that the meaning that English has depends on the repertoires of speakers, local linguistic markets and language ideologies. Language ideologies play a very important role in these meanings and therefore afford certain varieties a great deal of power and influence in the local and global linguistic marketplace.

FURTHER READING

Chew, P. G. (2007) Remaking Singapore: Language, culture and identity in a global-ized world, in Tsui, A. B. M. and Tollefson, J. W. (eds.) *Language Policy, Culture, and Identity in Asian Contexts*. Mahwah, NJ: Lawrence Erlbaum Associates: 73–93.

Dovchin, S. (2015) Language, multiple authenticities and social media: The online language practices of university students in Mongolia, *Journal of Sociolinguistics*, 19(4): 437–459.

Evans, B. (2010) English as official state language in Ohio: Market forces trump ideology, in Kelly-Holmes, H. and Mautner, G. (eds.) *Language and the Market*. London: Palgrave Macmillan.

Gupta, A. F. (2004) Singlish on the web, in Hashim, A. and Hassan, N. (eds.) *Varieties of English in South East Asia and Beyond*. Kuala Lumpur: University of Malaya Press: 19–38.

Jenkins, J. (2009) English as a lingua franca: Interpretations and attitudes, *World Englishes*, 28(2): 200–207.

Seidlhofer, B. (2009) Common ground and different realities: World Englishes and English as a lingua franca, *World Englishes*, 28(2): 236–245.

CHAPTER 11

Projects

11.1 INTRODUCTION

In this chapter, we provide some ideas about projects you could do to explore the topics introduced in this book. The best way to find out about what language is and what it means is to go and see how the language around you is being used. In the chapters so far, you have read about some of the research that sociolinguists do. The important thing to remember is that every language community, every text, every utterance can potentially tell us something new. The way that you use language, the way that communication occurs with your friends or in your family is all valuable sociolinguistic data. But as you may have realised already, a lot of this data passes us by. We're so accustomed to using language to do things that we don't normally pay much attention to how we do this. We seem to know instinctively what works and what is appropriate, but think about how difficult it would be to explain these rules to someone new to the language situations that you know.

The projects will give you some idea of what sociolinguists do when they conduct research. It should give you an understanding of the kind of work involved, how long particular kinds of investigations take and what kinds of questions we can ask. Most important, we hope that in doing some of these projects (or designing your own), you'll realise that the language you use or observe is just as interesting, complex and worthy of consideration, as the examples that have been given throughout the text.

Some of these projects are based on particular topics that have been covered. However, more often than not, it will be helpful to consider topics and approaches from a variety of perspectives rather than just those suggested by a particular chapter in the book. For example, transitivity analysis (Chapter 2) is useful in all kinds of contexts. Likewise, recording and transcribing conversation is an excellent way to examine the tiny details that we're not generally aware of when participating in, or even listening to, conversations.

11.2 THINGS TO BEAR IN MIND WITH DATA COLLECTION

11.2.1 What is data?

Data can be found everywhere in many forms

Sociolinguists work with spoken and written data. Obviously, written data can be easier to work with, as you don't need to transcribe it. You need to consider data as any language that is used by people, in all kinds of situations.

One easy way of collecting spoken data is to record the people you know. There are two advantages to this. Firstly, it will be easy for you to obtain permission from the people you record. It is imperative to inform your respondents that they are being recorded and obtain their permission to do so (see BAAL guidelines). Linguists never record anyone without their knowledge, as this is unethical.

Secondly, people you know might feel more comfortable being recorded by you. If people are self-conscious about being recorded, they're more likely to 'perform'. The problem raised by the presence of the researcher and the desire to get natural speech is usually spoken about in terms of the 'observer's paradox'. The paradox is that you want to observe, to be present, but exactly this presence may change the way people speak. There are a number of ways to minimise the effects of the paradox. One strategy Jennifer Coates used was to have respondents record themselves when she wasn't there (2002). William Labov suggests asking respondents to tell a story about an emotional event. Such an emotional story may reduce the amount of attention people pay to being recorded and to their speech performance. There might not be a good way, or even any way, of overcoming the observer's paradox. When you're analysing your data, you must remember the observer's paradox, especially in terms of what you can claim about the way your respondents use language. Sometimes, it is clear in the data that respondents are thinking about being recorded. There may be evidence that the speakers are or are not aware of being recorded. Do they constantly refer to the fact of being recorded? It's impossible to be inside someone's head and know for certain whether they are aware of being observed. This doesn't mean that you can't trust your data. It just means you have to think carefully about what you can trust it to tell you.

11.2.2 Transcribing

If you are working with recorded data, you need to transcribe it. That is, you need to construct a written representation of the spoken data. You can see some examples of transcription in chapters throughout this book. You may have noticed that some details of the talk are indicated with symbols and other typographic conventions. These details are explained in a 'transcription key'. There is a transcription key provided at the start of the book.

Transcription is a very time-consuming process. As a rule of thumb, it takes at least four hours to transcribe one hour of clearly recorded speech. Transcription time will increase if there is more than one speaker or if the quality of the recording is poor. But it is important to construct a good, detailed transcription. It is not possible to make claims about characteristics of a conversation without this level of detail. It can take a few times of listening to figure out what people are saying, so you need to be patient and listen to your data more than once. There are some tools that can help, especially if your data is digitally recorded. One example is oTranscribe, a web app that allows you to listen to your data and stop and start it by using keystrokes on your computer.

11.2.3 Data analysis

Analysing data requires spending time looking at and thinking about the material. Everyone has their own methods for working with data, and these projects should help you research and develop your own strategies by trying out different methods to see what works for you. Ideally, when you collect your data, you will have a clear question in mind or a particular feature you want to examine.

If you're not sure about what you expect to find, one way to begin is to look for surprising characteristics; sometimes things 'jump out at you'. Think about and speculate on why you noticed it. Is the characteristic something very unusual (for the speaker or the situation)? Is it something you don't understand, or is it something that appears in more than one place in the text or the conversation?

If this doesn't work, consider the kinds of variation we find in language that we have discussed in earlier chapters. For example, transitivity analysis (Chapter 2) is a good feature to consider when looking at written texts, particularly persuasive texts. With patience and attention to detail, you can discover and describe the data. Further, when you're working with data, it will usually be impossible to say *everything* about it. If you're going to say anything meaningful about what the patterns are, you have to focus on a small number of features. If you've spent enough time with your data, the analysis will always provide more than you can write up in a paper of reasonable length.

Different types of text will require you to look for different features. But the same general approaches that we have described will still be useful to get you started.

The following projects are suggestions for research to help you practice the skills and understand the theories in the previous chapters. The projects suggest features that you might look for and questions that you might ask about your data. It is important to remember that the data you have limits the questions you can ask about it. Your conclusions must be supported by sufficient evidence in your data. For example, if you have conversational data from men in their 20s, you obviously won't be able to say anything about how women behave in conversations, or about how older or younger men might behave. You also won't be able to say anything about what these same men might do in the presence of different people (women, older men and so on). Every data set has specific limitations. The goal of this kind of research is not to come to conclusions about the whole of the human race. You will learn something about how *these people* use language in *this situation*. Therefore, you must choose your data set carefully.

11.3 PROJECTS

Project 1 – mini dictionary

Your task is to compile a mini dictionary of novel lexical items in your speech community. Language changes all the time. While lexicographers constantly update dictionaries, the process is slow. In any case, some words or expressions don't stay around for very long. Over the course of at least a week, keep a notebook with you and write down all the words and expressions you suspect you wouldn't find in a dictionary. It may be the case that the word is common, but the particular meaning is not. Think about what the words on your list mean (their definition) and how they can be used. You might need to sit down with friends and test their intuitions about how terms can be used. If it's an adjective, can it be used only about people or also about things? If it's a verb, what kind of subject can it take? Does it need an object? Choose at least six words, and write as full an entry as you can for each one. Look it up in a good dictionary (like a full version of the *Oxford English Dictionary*). Does it appear there? Does it have the same meaning? See if other people also use the terms you found in your speech community. Can you find anything out about the history and origins of these terms or how long they have been in use? Some words are used in very limited contexts or in a particular way. For example, in British English, 'bang' can be used in specific collocations as an intensifier, e.g., 'bang on time', meaning exactly on time and 'bang up to date', meaning completely up to date. When the first author encountered this term, she tried it out as an intensifier in all kinds of situations. To express the shaggy nature of a toothbrush, she said 'bang old toothbrush'. A competent member of the speech community informed her that this was not how the intensifier is used.[1] 'Bang' can only be used as an intensifier in a very limited set of circumstances. Documenting the details of use and meaning of new words may require more thought than you would expect.

Project 2 – political speech

In this project, the task is to examine a political speech in detail in order to uncover strategies of persuasion, self-representation and conveying information. Choose a recent speech by a politician from your country or region. Then choose another speech, either from the same politician to a different kind of audience or on a different topic. You might also choose a speech from a different politician to compare it to, but choose a speech that is similar in some way to the first. You'll need the audio from each speech. Transcribe them, including pauses, stress on particular words, hesitations and false starts. You might also find it useful to make a note of speed if this varies throughout the speech. It's a good idea to transcribe any laughter or applause from the audience too. For national politicians, you can often find transcripts of speeches on a government website. Don't assume their transcripts will be accurate or include the information you need, but you can use it as a starting point to save some transcription time.

Examine each speech carefully. What is the goal of each speech? Is it intended to inform or persuade? Is it an emotional or a rational speech? How is the argument constructed? You will need to provide evidence from the specific linguistic choices made to justify your conclusions about the speech. For example, if you think that it is an emotive speech, you will probably look for particular word choices (recall the paradigmatic axis Chapter 2). What register is used? Is it formal or informal? There are any number of tools and concepts you can use for this project, but it's a good idea to look at Chapters 2, 3 and 4 for an idea of what might be appropriate. Compare the similarities and differences between the two speeches.

Project 3 – your own many voices

This project explores how your own use of language changes in different situations. Sociolinguists call this change 'style shifting'. Over the course of a week, record yourself in different situations. You may not be able to analyse all the data, but you should have a good selection of your speech in different contexts. Remember to be aware of sections of the data where you're aware of the recording. You'll need to focus on analysing only the natural, spontaneous data. It can be very difficult to be objective when analysing yourself so you might try to team up with a colleague and exchange data.

You will probably have conversations with friends, conversations with family, talk in a work context and talk in a service encounter. Choose a small amount from each of the different contexts, about a minute, and transcribe them. Are there any differences in the way you talk? Do you address people differently? Do you use different words? Do you speak in a more standard way in some contexts? Thinking about the different kinds of variables examined in the book (age, gender, ethnicity and so on), which are relevant in the way your language changes?

Project 4 – conversational politics

This project explores conversation in groups to find whether some participants have more power than others in the conversation. There is always a structure in conversations that to a greater or lesser extent, all participants contribute to. Very often, each person plays a particular role in a conversation. For example, who seems to be directing the conversation? Sometimes the most powerful participant in a conversation is a child or baby (or even the television). Record a conversation that involves a group of people. You might choose your family or a group of friends. Is there someone who interrupts more than other people? Who asks questions? Who chooses topics of conversations? Whose contributions are responded to or laughed at? Ochs and Taylor (1992) may be useful as a model for analysing conversations.

Project 5 – expertise in the media

This project explores representations of expertise in the media (see Chapter 4). Choose a media report on a scientific issue. This may be about scientific research, a health risk of some kind or even unusual weather. Gather other reports on the same issue from a number of different outlets. Analyse the use and representation of expertise. Are experts quoted? What is their expertise? How are they identified? Is there more than one expert identified? How much emphasis are their views given?

Project 6 – representation of women/men

This project explores the representation of women or men and involves written data. Narrow your data by choosing an issue and medium to focus on in the data. For example, you might want to look at news stories where a woman/man is involved, how a female/male politician or celebrity is written about or how health and fashion features aimed at women/men are constructed. You can collect data from newspapers, magazines, television, radio and the internet. What words are used to address and describe women/men? What adjectives are used? What values and ideologies underlie the representations you are working with?

Project 7 – titles around the world

The titles *Miss* and *Mrs*, because they are always followed by the family name of a father or husband, are historical reminders of a time when women were regarded as the responsibility, or indeed the property, of their fathers and husbands. While women's political and economic rights have changed considerably in many countries, the English language still allows us to mark the marital status of women in ways that do not exist for men. Is women's marital status marked in other languages? If so, how? It's important to examine a language you know well or to have a consultant who speaks that language natively. Do people try to avoid title and surname conventions when they get married? How can they do this with their language? You might investigate the use of titles and surnames in same-sex civil partnerships, which are frequently referred to as 'marriages'. One resource might be wedding announcements in newspapers or coverage of celebrity same-sex partners to gather the data here. How might labels for these new types of partnerships affect the language system?

Project 8 – identity

These days, when you apply for a job or a course of study, you are usually required to fill in a form about your ethnicity, age, nationality and disability status. Find several of these types of forms. What terms are used for indicating a person's identity? What categories are included? From the categories and the labels and language used, is it possible to tell what is considered 'normal' or unmarked? What does this reflect about this society? Are the forms for different purposes the same? Are there identities that aren't represented? A local careers office or job centre or national census survey would be a good place to find some.

Project 9 – digital detox[2]

Social media in all its forms is an important part of the online linguistic landscape (Chapter 5), for the communication of news (Chapter 4) and for the maintenance of relationships (Chapter 8). For this project, you will refrain from using all forms social media of any kind for one 24-hour period. That is, do not look at the internet, Facebook, email, texts, Twitter, Instagram or WhatsApp (or any other platforms you use). You may use your phone to make and receive calls, however. Keep a handwritten account of what this is like. Describe how often you feel the impulse to check your accounts and how not being able to check them feels. How does it affect your communication with your friends and family? How do you find out what is happening in the world? Do your friends comment on your absence? What do they say? This is a reflective project that encourages you to critically engage with your own social media habits and how they interact with your offline life.

Project 10 – little bits of data

A Facebook 'feed' (the posts that are presented to you when you look at your Facebook account) constitute what Michael Hoey identified as a 'discourse colony'. The discourse colony is a particular kind of text 'whose component parts do not derive their meaning from the sequence in which they are placed'

(Hoey, 1986: 4). Because the colonies have small component chunks, they provide a ready-made set of small texts that can be compared and contrasted. First, identify the discourse colony you want to examine (e.g., your own feed or that of a group you belong to). Can you identify patterns in the way that information is presented in the posts? Which features of Facebook do the posters use, and how do they use them? You'll need to analyse the texts closely, paying attention to their syntax, lexical choices and structure. What do you find, and why do you think the texts are structured in the way they are?

Project 11 – children's television

At certain times of the day, usually morning and afternoon, television channels broadcast programmes for children. These programmes are often composed of different segments joined together. In between segments, hosts of the programme conduct competitions, interview celebrities and so on. Focussing on the hosted sections, transcribe parts which are addressed directly to the audience (the camera/children). Is there anything distinctive about the way the audience is addressed? Is a specific vocabulary or tone used? Does language speed up or slow down? Are there any features of child-directed language (see Chapter 8)?

Project 12 – computer-mediated communication (CMC)

Save all your incoming and outgoing CMC for a period of time. How long this should be depends on how active you and your friends are in the CMC domain. How does the language differ from other kinds of written language? Are there differences in syntax, spelling and lexical choices? Are other symbols or images used? Finally, does CMC share any features with face-to-face conversations?

You might like to add a second component to this project. Once you have analysed your data and thought about why the use of language may be the same or different, interview some of your friends. You could ask them why they use CMC (instead of 'phoning'). Do they use language differently? Have they noticed CMC conventions? Has their language use in other areas changed because of CMC? You might like to take notes when interviewing, but it's also very helpful to record the interview. You may not need to transcribe all of it, but transcribing some of the interview conversation will give you very useful comparative material for deciding whether face-to-face conversations and CMC are similar or different.

Project 13 – blogs and vlogs

This project examines blogging and **vlogging** in order to explore the conventions of written and spoken language in this genre. Brown (2008) argues that blogs are a place where we find linguistic innovation. Identify a blog to analyse. You might like to choose comparable material (about the same subject) from different bloggers, or you might like to follow an individual blogger over time (there are usually archives on their sites). Alternatively, you could choose a vlogg (video blogging). Examine the structure of the texts and identify new lexemes or syntax. Are these features linked to the purpose of the blog? Do they succeed in portraying a particular identity? Are some forms of blogs more successful than others? To answer this last question, you'll have to think about what blogs are for.

Project 14 – linguistic landscapes

Many scholars have studied the significance of public signs, their legal significance and their linguistic force. Signs that detail legal rules are everywhere, from parking signs to conditions of entry to shopping centres. Collect as many examples of regulatory signs as you can. What you will find depends on your local area, though parking lots are excellent places, as the contractual terms are often detailed near the entry for the car park. Look at the kinds of syntactic choices that are made. Pay attention to pronouns and modal verbs. What kinds of transitivity choices are made? Are the notices clear? Would you say they constitute information, requests or warnings?

Project 15 – political agency

Identify a social campaign that has generated controversy (e.g., marriage equality, climate change, #blacklivesmatter, see Sections 5.6.2, and 7.4.1). Look for discussions of this campaign in a wide variety of platforms (e.g., in Facebook groups, Twitter hashtags or comments on news stories, see Section 4.10). Identify the dominant opinions and the groupings of people who are associated with those opinions. What kinds of arguments do they make for their position? Do different opinion groups rely on different kinds of tactics (e.g., ethos, pathos or logos, see Section 3.4)?

11.4 RESEARCH RESOURCES

11.4.1 Where to find published research

You might like to look at research being published in specialist journals. Your school or university may have access to these, but there are often some articles and issues that are freely accessible. Even reading the abstracts will give you a good idea of the kind of work that researchers are doing.

Communication and Medicine
Critical Discourse Studies

Discourse and Society
International Journal of Speech Language and the Law
Journal of Language and Politics
Journal of Sociolinguistics
Language in Society
Language Variation and Change
Text & Talk

11.4.2 Other resources

There are a great many resources available online which may be useful for your own research or project work. Some of them have been mentioned already. We have placed other resources on the companion website.

> *Ethics* – British Association for Applied Linguistics (2016). Recommendations on Good Practice in Applied Linguistics, 3rd edition. British Association for Applied Linguistics. https://baalweb.files.wordpress.com/2016/10/goodpractice_full_2016.pdf [accessed 6 March 2018]
> Transcription resource: http://otranscribe.com/ [accessed 5 April 2018]

FURTHER READING

Cameron, D. (2001) *Working with Spoken Discourse*. London: Routledge.

Carter, R., Goddard, A., Reah, D., Sanger, K., and Swift, N. (2007) *Working with Texts: A Core Introduction to Language Analysis*, Beard A. (ed.). London: Routledge.

Cukor-Avila, P. (2000) Revisiting the observer's paradox, *American Speech*, 75(3): 253–254.

Hillier, H. (2004) *Analysing Real Texts: Research Studies in Modern English Language*. Basingstoke: Palgrave Macmillan.

Mallinson, C., Childs, B., and van Herk, G. (2013) *Data Collection in Sociolinguistics: Methods and Applications*. London: Routledge.

van Leeuwen, T. (2004) *Introducing Social Semiotics*. London: Routledge.

Wray, A. and Bloomer, A. (2012) *Projects in Linguistics and Language Studies*, 3rd ed. London: Routledge.

NOTES

1   Thanks to Isobel Scott-John for her expertise and patience in inducting Mooney into the British speech community.
2   We read about this on social media but cannot recall who first came up with the idea. Thanks to whichever American professor created this project.

Glossary

AAE – African-American English

accent – a way of describing the set of features which characterise a speaker's language. Accent is about pronunciation and may provide social or regional information. See also **dialect**.

accommodation – adjusting the way one speaks to be more like a real or imagined interlocutor.

active/passive – verbs can be in the active or passive form. This changes the location of the agent of the verb. In active constructions, the agent is first; in passive constructions, the agent is last and can be deleted. 'Fido ate the biscuit' is active; 'The biscuit was eaten by Fido' is passive.

address forms – a word or phrase used when speaking to a person in order to identify them. The form used depends on the context and the relationship between the two people. Address forms include titles like 'Mr' and 'Ma'am' and also less formal terms like 'darling' or 'mate'.

adjective – words used to modify a noun or provide further information about it. For example, the underlined terms are adjectives: 'the <u>hungry</u> dog' or 'the <u>intelligent</u> woman'.

affective – related to affect, that is, emotion. Tag questions may have an affective function, that is, to signal concern for another speaker or invite them to participate in a conversation.

agency – agency can describe the role of the agent in a sentence (see active/passive). It can also be used to describe the power people have over particular actions, events or processes.

asymmetry see **symmetry**.

asynchronous communication – communication that takes place when interlocutors are not present in the same temporal location. In asynchronous communication, there is a lag between turns. Letter writing and email are asynchronous. See also **synchronous communication**.

back-channelling – the practices that listeners engage in to display they are paying attention to a speaker. This includes nodding, facial expressions and **minimal responses**.

bilingual – strictly, having two (bi-) languages but also used for someone who speaks more than one language.

binomial – a noun phrase that consists of two nouns placed together, usually separated by 'and'. For example, 'fish and chips' is a binomial.

child-directed language (CDL) – language used by adults to speak to children. CDL is characterised by slower and more explicit language that is perceived to facilitate language acquisition.

citizen journalism – a type of user-generated content, where people who are not professional journalists provide material for broadcast or publication in news outlets.

closed question – a question with a small number of answers predetermined by the form of the question. Questions that require a 'yes' or 'no' response are closed questions. This contrasts with open questions, which often begin with 'when', 'where', 'why'.

code – a general term that may refer to a language (linguistic code) or any other semiotic code, including colour, typeface, dress and so on.

code switching – when a speaker changes from one language or variety to another. This may occur in a variety of linguistic contexts, such as a word, a phrase or a longer stretch of talk.

collocation/collocate – combinations of words that frequently appear together, such as 'salt and pepper', often in a noun phrase. Frequent collocations can indicate the connotations of a word and other associations.

communicative competence – in contrast to competence and performance, communicative competence is the knowledge a speaker uses to construct utterances that are appropriate for a particular speech community.

community of practice – a group of people who come together for a common aim or activity. Communities of practice often develop their own ways of using language. Sociolinguistics has taken up this model of interaction to examine local language use.

competence and performance – competence is knowledge of the rules of a language, its syntax, semantics and so on. Performance is actual use of the language, how competence is exploited. See also **communicative competence**

connotations – the associations of a word, over and above its **denotative** meaning.

covert prestige – the assignment of positive value to a language or variety that exists only within a particular group. A variety that has covert prestige is valued within the community is it used but not the wider community. See also **overt prestige**.

creole – a language that has emerged from two or more languages in contact. In contrast to a pidgin, a creole functions as a first language for its speakers.

crossing – the use of a language variety by a person who is not a member of that variety's speech community in order to express a particular attitude stance.

cultural capital – see **symbolic capital**.

deictic – a word that depends on context in order to communicate meaning. Common deictics include 'here' and 'there'. A physical sign may also perform deictic functions by pointing to something. This relies on spatial context.

denotation – the literal meaning of something, that is, what a term refers to. See also **connotation**.

density see **social networks**.

descriptive/description – the approach to language that seeks to describe the features of language as it is used by speakers rather than to prescribe the form that should be used. See **prescriptivist**.

diachronic – examining a situation as it changes over time. See also **synchronic**.

dialect- a way of describing the varying features (e.g., syntactic, phonological, lexical) of a language. Dialects may be linked to region, social group or other identity. See also **variety**.

discourse – a term used in linguistics with a range of meanings. Firstly, it refers to various forms of communication, such as conversations among people, written texts and the like. Secondly, it refers to the ideology that underpins a text. For example, 'the discourse of romantic love' refers to a set of ideas about behaviour and conduct relating to love. Further, it refers to even larger ideological structures that are referred to as 'dominant' discourses.

discourse marker – a word whose function is to structure speech rather than provide meaning. 'So', 'well', 'now', 'really' and the like are all discourse markers.

dysphemism see **euphemism**.

epistemic modal forms – a form of modal auxiliary verb that expresses uncertainty.

ethnographic – a research methodology which seeks to describe a particular society or event through such methods as participant observation and interviews, usually over a long period of time.

ethos – one of three persuasive strategies. Ethos involves appealing to or relying on the credibility, status or reliability of the speaker. See also **pathos** and **logos**.

euphemism – a word to refer to something unpleasant or offensive in a more appealing or positive way. Dysphemism does the opposite, making something pleasant seem unappealing.

face threat – an action or utterance which either impedes a person's desire to do something or their own self-image. Face-threatening acts (like requests) may be mitigated in some way (for example, with 'please') to reduce the face threat.

foreground – to draw attention to something; this is a visual metaphor, that is, something that is put in the foreground is made more prominent. This can also be done linguistically, through the use of marked terms, stress in speech or other modes of emphasis.

given information – in contrast to new information, given information has already been explicitly introduced in a text or is assumed by other structures. See also **presupposition**.

hedges – linguistic devices or forms that minimise an utterance in some way. This may take the form of epistemic modals, tag questions or other discourse markers. For example, one might say 'I *think* she arrived' to hedge the claim that she did in fact arrive.

hegemonic (adj)/hegemony (n) – refers to the social, political or cultural dominance of one group or **ideology**.

ideology – an organised collection of values or beliefs.

imperative – a verb form which is both a command and the simplest verb form in English. 'Come!' or 'Speak!' are both imperative forms.

imply, to – a way of communicating something without directly saying it. This is very similar to **pragmatic presupposition**.

interlocutor – another way of describing an addressee.

interruption – variously defined as simultaneous speech and an utterance that stops the interrupted person speaking.

intertextuality – generally used to refer to the referencing of or allusion to one text by another. This may be done by obvious quotation, parody or borrowing a textual feature readily associated with another text.

intransitive – see **transitive**.

L1 and L2 – an abbreviation for Language 1 and Language 2, that is, a person's first language (L1) and their second language (L2).

langue – the language system or building codes, according to Saussure. The language people actually produce depends on langue but is called **parole**.

lexical item – a term used by linguists to refer to 'a word'.

lexicographer – a person who documents the changing meaning of words in a language and writes dictionaries.

lexifier – the language which serves as a lexical base for a **pidgin** or **creole**.

life stage (perspective) – this perspective considers age as defined by the various periods that people pass through as they get older rather than as determined by how old a person is in years.

liminal – a space or time that is between one thing and the other. An entrance may be a liminal space; it is neither completely inside nor completely outside.

lingua franca – A language that is not native to either speaker or listener but is used for communication.

linguistic determinism/relativism – also known as the Sapir-Whorf hypothesis, this is the idea that language influences thought. The strong version, linguistic determinism, holds that a person cannot conceive of things that are not expressed by their language. The weaker, and more accepted version, suggests that people are influenced by things that are expressed by their language.

linguistic imperialism – is the imposition of one culture's language upon another culture.

linguistic insecurity – refers to the belief that one's own language variety is somehow inferior to others, especially standard varieties.

linguistic market – The linguistic market can be understood as a metaphoric 'market' where people can 'spend and trade' their social/cultural capital. Integral to this metaphor is the metaphoric value of a particular language variety that is allocated according to the social/cultural capital that the variety is associated with.

linguistic variable: a linguistic feature (phoneme, morpheme, lexeme and so on), which has an identifiable alternative form which means the same thing but is associated with varying non-linguistic meaning. Negation in English, for example, can be expressed in different ways and these differences convey meanings to the interlocutor in addition to the negation (e.g., *I have no money* and *I ain't got no money*).

linguistic variation – refers to the inevitable differences across and within languages and dialects.

literacy – usually used to refer to the ability to read and write but can also be used to describe the ability to interpret and produce different kinds of texts and semiotic codes.

logos – one of three persuasive strategies. Logos involves appealing to or relying on the logic of an argument, including the use of verifiable facts. See also **ethos** and **pathos**.

marked – generally speaking, 'marked' means noticeably unusual. More specifically, linguistic forms that are marked reflect a deviation from what is perceived as the norm. This deviation can be signalled in a variety of ways (e.g., morphemically, lexically). Unmarked linguistic forms are neutral in so far as they represent the perceived 'norm'. For example, the unmarked form *nurse* is often assumed to refer to a woman. To refer to a nurse who is a man, the additional term *male* is often added: *male nurse* (the marked form).

metalinguistic/metalingual – literally, above (meta-) the linguistic, thus, the metalingual function of language describes how language can be used to talk about language. It is common when dealing with comprehension issues.

metaphor/metaphorical a metaphor is a type of figurative way of describing something by comparing it to something else. It may be compared to something abstract or concrete. Unlike simile, metaphorical expressions make an implicit comparison. Metaphors have the structure 'x is y' as in 'John is a bear'. It should be noted that metaphors in Lakoff and Johnson's model (1980) are slightly different as it refers to metaphors that exist at a cognitive level and result in metaphorical expressions in language. For example, the metaphor used in the phrase 'Bob attacked Jane's statement' is understood because of the existence of an unspoken cognitive metaphor 'ARGUMENT IS WAR'.

minimal responses – in conversations, the contributions that speakers make to show that they agree or that they are listening; for example, 'mm hm', 'yeah' and so on. See also **back-channelling.** .

modal (auxiliary) verb – the modal auxiliary verbs of English include 'will', 'shall', 'can', 'may' and so on. Modal auxiliaries have several meaning functions, including the indication of certainty or uncertainty (epistemic modality). For example, compare '*I will be coming*' and '*I may be coming*'. Tag questions ('isn't it?') may also have a modal function and express uncertainty.

modality – this refers to the different possible modes of communication, including speech, writing and visual modes, including sign language. The term is also used to discuss texts which combine modalities, 'mutli-modal' texts, which are common in computer-mediated communication.

morphology – refers to the function and forms of morphemes, the smallest meaningful parts of language.

multimodal – see **modality**.

multiple negation – refers to the use of more than one form of negation in an expression in English. For example, the phrase *I didn't eat anything* has one negative form (*didn't*) while the phrase *I didn't eat nothing* has two (*didn't* and *nothing*). Multiple negation is also referred to as 'double negatives'. Prescriptivists argue that multiple negation is non-standard.

narrative – 'narrative' may be used in different ways. In sociolinguistics, it generally refers to a text (written or spoken) which relates events, in the past tense, with a temporal relationship between them. For example, 'Tom went out. Tom came back' is a minimal narrative. Both clauses are in the past tense, and the ordering suggests he first went out and then came back. Narrative can also be used as a partial synonym for **discourse**.

new information – something used for the first time in a text. See also **given information**.

nominalisation- the process of making a noun from another kind of word. Nominalisations may have the suffix '-tion' or '-ness'. For example, 'facilitation' is a nominalisation of the verb 'to facilitate'; and 'cleverness' nominalises the adjective 'clever'.

noun phrase – a term that linguists use to refer to a noun. A noun phrase may consist of a noun and other words, such as *the* and *blue* in *the blue book*, or it may be 'bare' such as *book*.

overlap – an overlap is an instance of simultaneous talk which does not result in a speaker stopping what they were saying; it is distinct from **interruption**.

overt prestige – the positive value overtly associated with linguistic forms of language through the public acknowledgement of them as 'correct' by users. See also **covert prestige**.

paradigmatic – The paradigmatic axis of language refers to the notion that words that are used are chosen from among all possible choices, and such choices can be said to be meaningful. For example, to call a woman a 'girl' rather than a 'lady' depicts her as young. This is part of the structuralist view of language. See also **syntagmatic**.

parallelism – when there is the same or similar syntactic structure in two or more parts of a text. This similarity asks the reader to understand the two parts in relation to each other. This is a stylistic choice common in persuasive speech.

parole – the language we actually produce, according to Saussure. Parole acts depend on **langue**.

passive voice see **active voice**.

pathos – one of three persuasive strategies. Pathos involves appealing to or relying on the emotion. See also **ethos** and **logos**.

performance – see **competence**.

personification – to describe an entity that is not a person as though it is a person. For example, the weather may be described as 'angry', attributing it human emotions and thus personifying the weather.

phatic – one of Jakobson's six functions of language. The phatic function involves building or sustaining relationships. 'Small talk' is an example of the phatic function of language.

phonetics/phonetic – the study of individual speech sounds. This includes attention to how these sounds are made as well as to variation among speakers with respect to these sounds.

phonology/phonological – phonology is the study of the organisation of sounds, or sound systems, of languages.

pidgin – a simplified language that arises in a situation where speakers who do not know each other's language are in long-term contact. A pidgin borrows from a **lexifier** for words and a **substrate** language for syntactic structure. A pidgin is not the L1 for any speaker. A **creole** may develop from a pidgin, when it becomes the L1 for speakers in the community.

plexity see **social networks**.

pragmatic presupposition see **presupposition**.

prescription/prescriptivist – the belief/people who believe that there is a 'correct' form of the language, including specific syntactic and semantic rules that should be followed.

presupposition- there are two kinds of presupposition. Semantic presupposition is embedded in an utterance or phrase and remains true even if the utterance is negated. For example, 'My mother is coming to the party' presupposes that I have a mother and there is a party. Pragmatic presupposition is something that is implied by the utterance. For example, 'I forgot my umbrella' implies that it is raining.

pronoun – a class of words which can replace a noun or noun phrase in a sentence. Pronouns in English include 'I', 'me', 'she', 'her' and so on.

repetition – a particular kind of **parallelism** where content is repeated.

rhoticity- refers to the 'r' sound in language. For example, in the English language, the word *fourth* has an 'r' after a vowel sound. This linguistic variable is relevant to the concept of language variety because some varieties of English pronounce this 'r' (e.g., US English) while others don't (e.g., UK English). Thus a rhotic variety pronounces the 'r' while a non-rhotic variety does not. In addition, this linguistic variable is associated with language ideology because it has different values associated with it.

semantic derogation – process in which, over time, a word can take on a second or new meaning and/or connotations which are negative or demeaning. For example, the word *spinster* in English referred to a profession, spinning yarn, in the 14th century. In modern English, it is a negative word that refers to an older woman who is not married.

semantic presupposition see **presupposition**.

semantics – the study of the meaning of words.

semiotic – something that is meaningful as a sign; semiotics is the study of signs. Language is a semiotic, but so too are colours, typefaces, layout and so on.

sexism – the unequal treatment of people on the basis of their sex.

shared floor – in conversations, if more than one person is allowed to speak at a time, it can be described as a shared (conversational) floor. The norm is generally considered to be the one-at-a-time floor, where only one speaker has speaking rights at any given moment.

sign- the combination of the **signifier** and the **signifed**. The relationship between the signifier and the signified is arbitrary.

signified – the concept represented by the **sign**.

signifier – the form representing the **sign**.

simile – an explicit comparison made between two things usually employing the word 'like'. For example, 'her eyes are like stars' is a simile. In contrast, 'her eyes are stars' is a metaphor.

social network – a way of describing a person's social connections in a community in terms of the type and frequency of interactions they have with other members. Relations can be described in terms of plexity (uniplex or multiplex) and density (dense or loose). For example, if A is a work associate and cousin of B, their relationship is multiplex because they know each other in more than one capacity. If they only know each other in one context, their relationship is uniplex. Density refers to the relationships between members of a particular person's network. If many members of A's network know one another, A's network is dense. If very few people in A's network know one another, A's network is loose.

standard language – refers to the variety of language that is perceived to be the most correct version of that community's language. The definition of 'correct' varies according to the community; thus, there is not a single standard variety of a language.

stratified/stratification – division into layers, where a layer can be 'above' or 'below' another layer. In terms of social stratification, people in any one layer share certain social characteristics and are 'equals' but differ from and are not 'equal' to people in other layers. One example of social stratification by social class is upper, middle and lower or 'working' class.

structuralism – for linguistics, the idea that the system of signs is structured and that the meaning of signs depends on their position relative to other signs.

style – a particular meaning conveyed by the use of a set of linguistic forms that are associated with that meaning.

substrate language – see **pidgin**.

symbolic capital – symbolic (or cultural) capital refers to intangible assets that individuals accumulate or inherit, which, like real capital (money), can be used to procure things. Such intangible assets might take the form of self-presentation, language, relationships, education and so on. In this book, we use 'symbolic capital' to include cultural and social capital. See also **linguistic market**.

symmetry – as used in linguistics, symmetry refers to a balanced distribution of related expressions. For example, standard English shows symmetry between the first person singular and plural pronouns *I/we*, that is, there is a different pronoun for singular and plural. However, the relationship of second person singular and plural pronouns is not symmetrical. There is only one second person pronoun, *you*, and it has a singular meaning. There is no second person plural pronoun in 'standard' English (note that many varieties of English have resolved this asymmetry with forms such as *y'all* and *youse*). Asymmetry can be seen in lexical relationships as well. For example, address forms for women *Mrs*, *Miss* and *Ms* while there is only *Mr* for men.

synchronic – to examine something at a particular point in time. See also **diachronic**.

synchronous communication – communication that happens when both interlocutors are in the same time frame. A face-to-face conversation is synchronous communication. See also **asynchronous communication**.

syntagmatic – as opposed to **paradigmatic**. The syntagmatic axis of language describes the way words are ordered in relation to each other, from left to right.

syntax – describes the rules and structures of a language at the level of clauses, phrases and sentences (i.e., word order). Different languages have different syntactic 'rules'. In English, for example, the typical word order is subject-verb-object.

tag questions – a question that is added to the end of a declarative statement that turns the statement into a question. For example the addition of *isn't it?* to the end of the statement *the weather is nice* results in the question *the weather is nice, isn't it?*.

text – text may refer to a piece of writing, a spoken utterance (especially an extended one) or an act of computer-mediated communication. 'Text' provides a single word to refer to a piece of language in a range of **modalities**.

three-part list – a common feature of persuasive language. This is a particular form of parallelism involving three components. For example, 'ready, willing and able' is a three-part list.

transitive – a type of verb. A transitive verb requires a direct object in order to make sense, whereas an intransitive verb does not. For example, the verb *to buy* does not make sense without an object; *Frank bought* is meaningless but *Frank bought a book* is meaningful. An intransitive verb, such as *vote*, does not need a direct object to make sense: *Sarah voted*.

transitivity (model) – a way of analysing the structure of sentences that includes semantics as well as syntactic structure. It considers the actors, their actions and the objects of their actions rather than only the positions of nouns, verbs and other parts of speech.

turn/turn taking – a turn is a contribution to a conversation; turn taking describes the way these conversational contributions are ordered, that is, who is allowed to speak and when.

unmarked see **marked**.

user-generated content – material contributed by the audience and viewers to media outlets.

variety – a form of language used by a group of speakers; although similar to the term 'dialect', 'variety' is preferred because it avoids the negative associations of 'dialect'.

vlogger – a video blogger. Video bloggers produce online videos to express their opinions and ideas. Vlogs and vloggers are found on sites like YouTube.

vocative – the vocative case is a grammaticalisation of socially directed speech. It is a special marker that tells the named person they are being searched for or spoken to.

References

Agerholm, H. (2016) North Korea bans sarcasm because Kim Jong-un fears people only agree with him 'ironically', *The Independent*, 8th September, www.independent.co.uk/news/world/asia/north-korea-bans-sarcasm-kim-jong-un-freedom-speech-a7231461.html [accessed 9th January 2018].

Agress, L. (2016) Why are we so grammatically incorrect?, *Baltimore Sun*, 26th December, www.baltimoresun.com/news/opinion/oped/bs-ed-agress-grammar-redux-20161226-story.html [accessed 9th January 2018].

Aisch, G., Huang, J., and Kang, C. (2016) Dissecting the #PizzaGate conspiracy theories, *New York Times*, 10th December, www.nytimes.com/interactive/2016/12/10/business/media/pizzagate.html [accessed 2nd February 2018].

Allcott, H. and Gentzkow, M. (2017) Social media and fake news in the 2016 election, *Journal of Economic Perspectives*, 31(2): 211–236, www.aeaweb.org/articles?id=10.1257/jep.31.2.211 [accessed 6th April 2018].

Alsagoff, L. (2007) Singlish: negotiating culture, capital and identity, in Vaish, V., Gopinathan, S. and Yongbing. L. (eds.) *Language, Capital, Culture*. Rotterdam: Sense Publishers: 25–46.

Al-Rawi, A. (2017) News organizations 2.1, *Journalism Practice*, 11(6): 705–720.

Ammon, U. (2010) World languages: Trends and futures, in Coupland, N. (ed.) *The Handbook of Language and Globalization*. Oxford: Blackwell: 101–122.

Androutsopoulos, J. (2013) English 'on top': Discourse functions of English resources in the German mediascape, *Sociolinguistic Studies*, 6(2): 209–238.

Aristotle (1991) *The Art of Rhetoric*, Lawson-Tancred, H. C. (trans.). London: Penguin.

Ash, M. (2013) South Africa: Karoo fracking debate triggers legislative overhaul, *Mondaq*, 20th November, www.mondaq.com/southafrica/x/276232/Oil+Gas+Electricity/Karoo+Fracking+Debate+Triggers+Legislative+Overhaul [accessed 22nd January 2018].

Ash, S. (2004) Social class, in Chambers, J. K., Trudgill, P., and Estes, S. (eds.) *The Handbook of Language Variation and Change*. London: Blackwell: 402–422.

Attwood, F. (2007) Sluts and riot grrrls: Female identity and sexual agency, *Journal of Gender Studies*, 16(3): 233–247.

Austin, J. L. (1975) *How to Do Things with Words*. Oxford: Oxford University Press.

Baer, D. (2016) English could use Swedish's untranslatable words for relationships, *The Cut*, 19th October, www.thecut.com/2016/10/english-could-use-swedishs-words-for-relationships.html [accessed 14th January 2018].

Bailey, G., Baugh, J., Mufwene, S. S., and Rickford, J. R. (eds.) (2013) *African-American English: Structure, History and Use*. London: Routledge.

Baker, P. (2010) Will Ms ever be as frequent as Mr? A corpus-based comparison of gendered terms across four diachronic corpora of British English, *Gender & Language*, 4(1): 125–149.

Balantrapu, M. (2016) How a ban on sarcasm is a protection of free speech, *The Hindu*, 10th September, www.thehindu.com/thread/reflections/article9094244.ece [accessed 9th January 2018].

Banda, F. and Peck, A. (2016) Diversity and contested social identities in multilingual and multicultural contexts of the Western Cape of South Africa, *Journal of Multilingual and Multicultural Development*, 37(6): 576–588.

Baranowski, M. (2002) Current usage of the epicene pronoun in written English, *Journal of Sociolinguistics*, 6(3): 378–397.

Baron, D. (1981) The epicene pronoun: The word that failed, *American Speech*, 56: 83–97.

Barrett, D. (2013) Edward Snowden leaks could help paedophiles escape police, says government, *The Telegraph*, 6th November, www.telegraph.co.uk/news/uknews/terrorism-in-the-uk/10431337/Edward-Snowden-leaks-could-help-paedophiles-escape-police-says-government.html [accessed 12th June 2014].

Bateman, J. A., Delin, J., and Henschel, R. (2006) Mapping the multimodal genres of traditional and electronic newspapers, in Royce, T. D. and Bowcher, W. L. (eds.) *New Directions in the Analysis of Multimodal Discourse*. Mahwah, NJ: Lawrence Erlbaum Associates: 147–172.

Bayard, D., Weatherall, A., Gallois, C., and Pittman, J. (2002) Pax Americana? Accent attitudinal evaluations in New Zealand, Australia and America, *Journal of Sociolinguistics*, 5(1): 22–49.

BBC (2015) What is fracking and why is it controversial?, *BBC News*, 16th December, www.bbc.co.uk/news/uk-14432401 [accessed 17th March 2018].

Beal, J. (2009) Three hundred years of prescriptivism (and counting), in Tieken-Boon van Ostade, I. and van der Wurff, W. (eds.) *Current Issues in Late Modern English*. Bern: Peter Lang: 35–55.

Bebout, L. (1995) Asymmetries in male/female word pairs: A decade of change, *American Speech*, 70(2): 163–185.

Becker, K. (2009) /r/ and the construction of place identity on New York City's Lower East Side, *Journal of Sociolinguistics*, 13(5): 634–658.

Bednarek, M. (2016a) Investigating evaluation and news values in news items that are shared through social media, *Corpora*, 11(2): 227–257.

Bednarek, M. and Caple, H. (2014) Why do news values matter? Towards a new methodological framework for analysing news discourse in Critical Discourse Analysis and beyond, *Discourse & Society*, 25(2): 135–158.

Behra, A. K. and Behera, R. (2012) Indian English: Linguistics and social characteristics, *International Journal of English and Education*, 1(1): 53–60.

Bell, A. (1991) *The Language of News Media*. Oxford: Blackwell.

Bell, A. (2014) *The Guidebook to Sociolinguistics*. Oxford: Wiley Blackwell.

Bennett, J. (2012) 'And what comes out may be a kind of screeching': The stylisation of chavspeak in contemporary Britain, *Journal of Sociolinguistics*, 16(1): 5–27.

Benor, S. B. (2010) Ethnolinguistic repertoire: Shifting the analytic focus in language and ethnicity, *Journal of Sociolinguistics*, 14(2): 159–183.

Ben-Rafael, E., Shohamy, E., Mara, M. H., and Trumper-Hecht, N. (2006) Linguistic landscape as symbolic construction of the public space: The case of Israel, *International Journal of Multilingualism*, 3(1): 7–30.

Berman, E. (2014) Negotiating age: Direct speech and the sociolinguistic production of childhood in the Marshall Islands, *Journal of Linguistic Anthropology*, 24(2): 109–132.

Bever, L. and Phillips, K. (2017) Michelle Carter, who urged her boyfriend to commit suicide, found guilty in his death, *Washington Post*, 16th June, www.

washingtonpost.com/news/true-crime/wp/2017/06/16/shes-accused-of-pushing-him-to-suicide-now-a-judge-has-decided-her-fate/?utm_term=.c229c395a202 [accessed 9th January 2018].

Bickerton, D. (1983) Creole languages, www.ohio.edu/people/thompson/Creole.html

Biressi, A. (2011) 'The Virtuous Circle': Social entrepreneurship and welfare programming in the UK, in Wood, H. and Skeggs, B. (eds.) *Reality Television and Class*. London: British Film Institute/Palgrave Macmillan: 144–155.

Blommaert, J. (2003) Orthopraxy, writing and identity: Shaping lives through borrowed genres in Congo, in Martin, J. R. and Wodak, R. (eds.) *Re/Reading the Past: Critical and Functional Perspectives on Time and Value*, Vol. 8. Amsterdam: John Benjamins: 177–194.

Blommaert, J. (2009) A sociolinguistics of globalization, in Coupland, N. and Jaworski, A. (eds.) *The New Sociolinguistics Reader*. Basingstoke: Palgrave Macmillan: 560–573.

Blommaert, J. (2013) *Ethnography, Superdiversity and Linguistic Landscapes: Chronicles of Complexity*, Critical Language and Literacy Studies. Bristol, UK: Multilingual Matters.

Bloxam, A. (2010) Students vow to continue rioting over fees, *The Telegraph*, 11th November, www.telegraph.co.uk/education/universityeducation/8125050/Students-vow-to-continue-rioting-over-fees.html [accessed 12th June 2014].

Bodine, A. (1975) Androcentrism in prescriptive grammar: Singular 'they', sex-indefinite 'he', and 'he or she', *Language in Society*, 4(2): 129–146.

Boletta, W. L. (1992) Prescriptivism, politics, and lexicography: A reply to Jane Barnes Mack, *ILT News*, (October): 103–111.

Bonilla-Silva, E. and Forman, T. A. (2000) 'I am not a racist but . . .': Mapping white college students' racial ideology in the USA, *Discourse and Society*, 11(1): 50–85.

Borden, S. L. and Tew, C. (2007) The role of journalist and the performance of journalism: Ethical lessons from 'fake' news (seriously), *Journal of Mass Media Ethics*, 22(4): 300–314.

Boroditsky, L. (2001) Does language shape thought? Mandarin and English speakers' conceptions of time, *Cognitive Psychology*, 43: 1–22.

Boult, A. (2016) Salford City Council outlaws swearing in public, *The Telegraph*, 3rd March, www.telegraph.co.uk/news/uknews/12182309/Manchester-council-outlaws-swearing-in-public.html [accessed 9th January 2018].

Bourdieu, P. (1977) *Outline of the Theory of Practice*, Nice, R. (trans.). Cambridge: Cambridge University Press.

Bourdieu, P. (1984) *Social Critique of the Judgement of Taste*. London: Routledge.

Bourdieu, P. (1991) *Language and Symbolic Power*. Cambridge: Polity Press.

Boyce, T. (2006) Journalism and expertise, *Journalism Studies*, 7(6): 889–906.

boyd, d, Golder, S., and Lotan, G. (2010) Tweet, tweet, retweet: Conversational aspects of retweeting on twitter, *System Sciences (HICSS), 2010 43rd Hawaii International Conference on IEEE,* Honolulu: 1–10.

Boyle, S. (2013) Barbies for girls, cars for boys? Let toys be toys and get them gender neutral presents this Christmas, *The Independent*, 17th December, www.independent.co.uk/voices/comment/barbies-for-girls-cars-for-boys-let-toys-be-toys-and-get-them-gender-neutral-presents-this-christmas-9011155.html [accessed 12th June 2014].

Branigan, T. (2014) China bans wordplay in attempt at pun control, *The Guardian*, 28th November, www.theguardian.com/world/2014/nov/28/china-media-watchdog-bans-wordplay-puns [accessed 9th January 2018].

Branum, J. and Charteris-Black, J. (2015) The Edward Snowden affair: A corpus study of the British press, *Discourse & Communication*, 9(2): 199–220.

British Association for Applied Linguistics (2016) *Recommendations on Good Practice in Applied Linguistics*, 3rd ed. British Association for Applied Linguistics, https://baalweb.files.wordpress.com/2016/10/goodpractice_full_2016.pdf [accessed 6th March 2018].

Broadbent, J. M. (2009) The* amn't gap: The view from West Yorkshire, *Journal of Linguistics*, 45(2): 251–284.

Brown, A. (2018) What is so special about online (as compared to offline) hate speech?, *Ethnicities*, 18(3): 297–326. doi: 10.1177/1468796817709846

Brown, D. W. (2008) Paris Hilton, Brenda Frazier, Blogs, and the Proliferation of celebu-, *American Speech*, 83(3): 312–325.

Brown, D. W. and Jie, T. S. (2014) Singapore English and styling the Ah Beng, *World Englishes*, 33(1): 60–84.

Bruno, N. (2011) *Tweet First, Verify Later: How Real-Time Information Is Changing the Coverage of Worldwide Crisis Events*. Oxford: Reuters Institute for the Study of Journalism, University of Oxford: http://reutersinstitute.politics.ox.ac.uk/fileadmin/documents/Publications/fellows__papers/2010-2011/tweet_first_verify_later.pdf

Burridge, K. (1996) Political correctness: Euphemism with attitude, *English Today*, 12(3): 42–43.

Cameron, D. (1995) *Verbal Hygiene*. London: Routledge.

Cameron, D. (2007) *The Myth of Mars and Venus*. Oxford: Oxford University Press.

Cameron, D. (2011 [1997]) Performing gender identity: Young men's talk and the construction of heterosexual masculinity, in *Language Society and Power: A Reader*: 179–191, first published in Johnson, S. and Meinhof, U. (eds.) *Language and Masculinity*. Oxford: Blackwell.

Cameron, D. (2014 [1990]) Demythologising sociolinguistics: Why language does not reflect society, in Joseph, J. E. and Taylor, T. J. (eds.) *Ideologies of Language*. London: Routledge: 79–93.

Canagarajah, A. S. (1999) *Resisting Linguistic Imperialism in English Teaching*. Oxford: Oxford University Press.

Canagarajah, A. S. (2012) Migrant ethnic identities, mobile language resources: Identification practices of Sri Lankan Tamil youth, *Applied Linguistics Review*, 3(2): 251–272.

Carlson, H. K. and McHenry, M. A. (2006) Effect of accent and dialect on employability, *Journal of Employment Counseling*, 43(2): 70–83.

Carrington, V. (2009) I write, therefore I am: Texts in the city, *Visual Communication*, 8(4): 409–425.

Chambers, J. K. (1992) Dialect acquisition, *Language*, 68(4): 673–705.

Chambers, J. K. (2009) *Sociolinguistic Theory*, rev. ed. Oxford: Blackwell.

Chan, F. (2017) 8 men deported from Singapore released after Indonesian police found no ties to ISIS, *Straits Times*, 13th January, www.straitstimes.com/asia/se-asia/eight-deported-indonesians-released-after-police-found-no-ties-to-isis [accessed 14th January 2018].

Chang, J., Lefferman, J., Pedersen, C., and Martz, G. (2016) When fake news stories make real news headlines, *ABC News*, 29 November, http://abcnews.go.com/Technology/fake-news-stories-make-real-news-headlines/story?id=43845383 [accessed 2nd February 2018].

Charteris, J., Gregory, S., and Masters, Y. (2018) 'Snapchat', youth subjectivities and sexuality: Disappearing media and the discourse of youth innocence, *Gender and Education*, 30(2): 205–221.

Chilton, P. (1982) Nukespeak: Nuclear language, culture and propaganda, in Aubrey, C. (ed.) *Nukespeak: The Media and the Bomb*. London: Comedia Publishing Group: 94–112.

Chomsky, N. and Herman, E. S. (1988) *Manufacturing Consent: The Political Economy of the Mass Media*. New York: Pantheon.

Chye, D. Y. S. (2000) Standard English and Singlish: The clash of language values in contemporary Singapore, in Treis, Y. and de Busser, R. (eds.) *Selected Papers from the 2009 Conference of the Australian Linguistic Society*, www.als.asn.au

Coates, J. (1996) *Women Talk: Conversation between Women Friends*. Oxford: Blackwell.

Coates, J. (2002) *Men Talk: Stories in the Making of Masculinities*. Oxford: Blackwell.

Coates, J. (2004) *Women, Men and Language: A Sociolinguistic Account of Gender Differences in Language*, 3rd ed. London: Routledge.

Coates, J. (2014) Gossip revisited: Language in all-female groups, in Coates, J. and Cameron, D. (eds.) *Women in Their Speech Communities*. London: Routledge.

Coates, J. and Sutton-Spence, R. (2001) Turn-taking patterns in deaf conversation, *Journal of Sociolinguistics*, 5(4): 507–529.

Cohen, A. (n.d.) Advanced style, www.advanced.style [accessed 20th February 2018].

Cohn, C. (1987) Slick'ems, glick ems, Christmas trees, and cookie cutters: Nuclear language and how we learned to pat the bomb, *Bulletin of the Atomic Scientists*, 43(5): 17–24.

Conley, J. M., O'Barr, W. M., and Lind, E. A. (1978) The power of language: Presentational style in the courtroom, *Duke Law Journal*, 6: 1375–1399.

Cormack, L. and Singhal, P. (2017) Big stores to ban plastic bags, *Sydney Morning Herald*, 15th July 2017, p. 2.

Coughlan, S. (2011) Is the student customer always right?, *BBC News*, 28th June, www.bbc.co.uk/news/education-13942401 [accessed 17th January 2014].

Coupland, N. (1997) Language, ageing and ageism: A project for applied linguistics, *International Journal of Applied Linguistics*, 7(1): 26–48.

Coupland, N., Bishop, H., Evans, B., and Garrett, P. (2006) Imagining Wales and the Welsh language: Ethnolinguistic subjectivities and demographic flow, *Journal of Language and Social Psychology*, 25(4): 351–376.

Cowie, C. (2007) The accents of outsourcing: The meanings of 'neutral' in the Indian call centre industry, *World Englishes*, 26(3): 316–330.

Croom, A. M. (2015) Slurs, stereotypes, and in-equality: A critical review of 'how epithets and stereotypes are racially unequal', *Language Sciences*, 52: 139–154.

Crowley, T. (2003) *Standard English and the Politics of Language*, 2nd ed. Basingstoke: Palgrave Macmillan.

Crystal, D. (2005) *How Language Works*. London: Penguin.

Crystal, D. (2006) *Language and the Internet*. Cambridge: Cambridge University Press.

Curzan, A. (2014) *Fixing English: Prescriptivism and Language History*. Cambridge: Cambridge University Press.

Cutler, C. A. (1999) Yorkville crossing: White teens, hip-hop and African American English, *Journal of Sociolinguistics*, 3(4): 428–442.

Danet, B. (1980) 'Baby' or 'Fetus'? Language and the construction of reality in a manslaughter trial, *Semiotica*, 32: 187–219.

D'Arcy, A. (2007) Like and language ideology: Disentangling fact from fiction, *American Speech*, 82(4): 386–419.

D'Arcy, A. (2010) Quoting ethnicity: Constructing dialogue in Aotearoa/New Zealand, *Journal of Sociolinguistics*, 14(1): 60–88.

Dashti, A. A. (2009) The role of online journalism in political disputes in Kuwait, *Journal of Arab & Muslim Media Research*, 2(1–2): 91–112.

Davis, B. (2013) Hashtag politics: The polyphonic revolution of #Twitter, *Pepperdine Journal of Communication Research*, 1(1): 4, https://digitalcommons.pepperdine.edu/pjcr/vol1/iss1/4

Deccan Chronicle (2016) Sikh man shot dead by suspected militants in Afghanistan, 2nd October, www.deccanchronicle.com/world/asia/021016/sikh-man-shot-dead-by-suspected-militants-in-afghanistan.html [accessed 14th January 2018].

DeFrancisco, V. L. (1991) The sounds of silence: How men silence women in marital relations, *Discourse and Society*, 2(4): 413–424.

Denis, J. and Pontille, D. (2010) Placing subway signs: Practical properties of signs at work, *Visual Communication*, 9(4): 441–462.

De Swaan, A. (2010) Language systems, in Coupland, N. (ed.) *The Handbook of Language and Globalization*, Oxford: Blackwell: 56–76.

Deterding, D. (2007) *Singapore English: Dialects of English.* Edinburgh: Edinburgh University Press.

Deuber, D. (2013) Towards endonormative standards of English in the Caribbean: A study of students' beliefs and school curricula, *Language, Culture and Curriculum*, 26(2): 109–127.

Deumert, A. (2014) *Sociolinguistics and Mobile Communication.* Edinburgh: Edinburgh University Press.

Deuze, M. (2003) The web and its journalisms: Considering the consequences of different types of newsmedia online, *New Media & Society*, 5(2): 203–230.

de Vos, D. (2014) Why fracking in the Karoo will never happen, *Africa Geographic*, 18th March, https://africageographic.com/blog/why-fracking-in-the-karoo-will-never-happen/ [accessed 22nd January 2018].

Diaz, D. (2016) Obama: Why I won't say 'Islamic terrorism', *CNN Politics*, 19th September, http://edition.cnn.com/2016/09/28/politics/obama-radical-islamic-terrorism-cnn-town-hall/ [accessed 9th January 2018].

Divita, D. (2012) Online in later life: Age as a chronological fact and a dynamic social category in an Internet class for retirees, *Journal of Sociolinguistics*, 16(5): 585–612.

Dovchin, S. (2015) Language, multiple authenticities and social media: The online language practices of university students in Mongolia, *Journal of Sociolinguistics*, 19(4): 437–459.

Dovchin, S. (2017) The role of English in the language practices of Mongolian Facebook users: English meets Mongolian on social media, *English Today*, 33(2): 16–24.

Drager, K. (2012) Pidgin and Hawai'i English: An overview, *Journal of Language, Translation, and Intercultural Communication*, 1(1): 61–73.

Dubois, B. L. and Crouch, I. (1975) The question of tag questions in women's speech: They don't really use more of them, do they?, *Language in Society*, 4(3): 289–294.

Eades, D. (2000) 'I don't think it's an answer to the question': Silencing Aboriginal witnesses in court, *Language in Society*, 29: 161–195.

Eades, D. (2003) The politics of misunderstanding in the legal system, in House, J., Kasper, G., and Ross, S. (eds.) *Misunderstanding in Social Life: Discourse Approaches to Problematic Talk.* London: Longman: 199–226.

Eckert, P. (1988) Adolescent social structure and the spread of linguistic change, *Language in Society*, 17(3): 183–207.

Eckert, P. (1989a) *Jocks and Burnouts: Social Categories and Identity in the High School*. New York: Teachers College Press.

Eckert, P. (1989b) The whole woman: Sex and gender differences in variation, *Language Variation and Change*, 1(3): 245–267.

Eckert, P. (1997) Age as a sociolinguistic variable, in Coulmas, F. (ed.) *The Handbook of Sociolinguistics*. Oxford: Blackwell: 151–167.

Eckert, P. (1999) *Language Variation as Social Practice: The Linguistic Construction of Identity in Belten High*. Oxford: Blackwell.

Eckert, P. (2003) Language and adolescent peer groups, *Journal of Language and Social Psychology*, 22(1): 112–118.

Eckert, P. (2004) Adolescent language, in Finegan, E. and Rickford, J. R. (eds.) *Language in the USA: Themes for the Twenty-First Century*. Cambridge: Cambridge University Press: 360–375.

Eckert, P. (2005) Stylistic practice in the adolescent social order, in Williams, A. and Thurlow, C. (eds.) *Talking Adolescence: Perspectives on Communication in the Teenage Years*, Vol. 3. Oxford: Peter Lang: 93–110.

Eckert, P. (2009) Ethnography and the study of variation, in Coupland, N. and Jaworksi, A. (eds.) *The New Sociolinguistics Reader*. Basingstoke: Palgrave Macmillan: 136–151.

Eckert, P. (2014) The problem with binaries: Coding for gender and sexuality, *Language and Linguistics Compass*, 8(11): 529–535.

The Economist (2017) What to call the time of life between work and old age?, 6th July, www.economist.com/news/leaders/21724814-get-most-out-longer-lives-new-age-category-needed-what-call-time-life [accessed 9th January 2018].

Edelsky, C. (1981) Who's got the floor? *Language in Society*, 10: 383–421.

Eisikovits, E. (2011) Girl-talk/Boy-talk: Sex differences in adolescent speech, in Coates, J. and Pichler, P. (eds.) *Language and Gender: A Reader*. Oxford: Blackwell: 38–48.

Estes, A. (2017) Vaccines do not cause autism; they save lives, *Seattle Times*, 23rd June, www.seattletimes.com/opinion/vaccines-do-not-cause-autism-they-save-lives/ [accessed 21st August 2017].

Evans, B. E. (2005) 'The grand daddy of English': US, UK, New Zealand and Australian students' attitudes toward varieties of English, in Langer, N. and Davies, W. (eds.) *Linguistic Purism in the Germanic Languages*, Studia Linguistica Germanica. Berlin: Mouton de Gruyter: 240–225.

Evans, B. E. (2010) English as official state language in Ohio: Market forces trump ideology, in Kelly-Holmes, H. and Mautner, G. (eds.) *Language and the Market*. London: Palgrave.

Evans, V. (2017) *The Emoji Code*. London: Michael O'Mara Books.

Fairclough, N. (1995) *Critical Discourse Analysis: The Critical Study of Language*. London: Longman.

Fairclough, N. (1999) Global capitalism and critical awareness of language, *Language Awareness*, 8(2): 71–83.

Fairclough, N. (2001) *Language and Power*, 2nd ed. London: Longman.

Ferguson, C. (1959) Diglossia, *Word*, 15: 325–340.

Fernández Fontecha, A. and Jiménez Catalán, M. (2003) Semantic derogation in animal metaphor: A contrastive-cognitive analysis of two male/female examples in English and Spanish, *Journal of Pragmatics*, 35(5): 771–797.

Ferrara, E. (2017) Disinformation and social bot operations in the run up to the 2017 French presidential election, *First Monday*, 22(8), http://dx.doi.org/10.5210/fm.v22i8.8005

Figueroa, L. (2016) Cuomo, de Blasio and the 'semantics' of saying 'terrorism', *Newsday*, 18th September, www.newsday.com/news/new-york/cuomo-de-blasio-and-semantics-of-saying-terrorism-1.12334779 [accessed 9th January 2018].

Fishman, P. M. (1980) Interactional shitwork, *Heresies*, 2: 99–101.

Fletcher, P. and MacWhinney, B. (eds.) (1996) *The Handbook of Child Language*. Oxford: Blackwell.

Foges, C. (2015) Britain needs to smash the cut glass ceiling, *The Times* (London), 27th October, p. 29.

Forbes (2016) The fracking future fades, *Forbes Africa*, 1st July, www.forbesafrica.com/focus/2016/07/01/fracking-future-fades/ [accessed 22nd January 2018].

Fought, C. (2002) Ethnicity, in Chambers, J. K., Trudgill, P., and Schilling-Estes, N. (eds.) *The Handbook of Language Variation and Change*. Oxford: Blackwell: 265–290.

Freedman, J. and Jurafsky, D. (2011) Authenticity in America: Class distinctions in potato chip advertising, *Gastronomica: The Journal of Critical Food Studies*, 11(4): 46–54.

Friginal, E. (2009) Threat to the sustainability of the outsourced call center industry in the Philippines: Implications for language policy, *Language Policy*, 8: 51–68.

Galloway, N. (2013) Global Englishes and English Language Teaching (ELT): Bridging the gap between theory and practice in a Japanese context, *System*, 41(3): 786–803.

Galloway, N. and Rose, H. (2015) *Introducing Global Englishes*. Abingdon, UK: Routledge.

Garthwaite, K. (2011) The language of shirkers and scroungers: Talking about illness, disability and coalition welfare reform, *Disability and Society*, 26(3): 369–372.

Gendron, T. L., Welleford, E. A., Inker, J., and White, J. T. (2016) The language of ageism: Why we need to use words carefully, *Gerontologist*, 56(6): 997–1006.

Georgakopoulou, A. (2006) Thinking big with small stories in narrative and identity analysis, *Narrative Inquiry*, 16: 129–137.

Gesser, A. (2007) Learning about hearing people in the land of the Deaf: An ethnographic account, *Sign Language Studies*, 7(3): 269–283.

Gibson, C. (2013) Welcome to Bogan-ville: Reframing class and place through humour, *Journal of Australian Studies*, 37(1): 62–75.

Giles, H. and Reid, S. A. (2005) Ageism across the lifespan: Towards a self-categorization model of ageing, *Journal of Social Issues*, 61(2): 389–404.

Gill, C. (2010) Hijacking of a very middle class protest: Anarchists cause chaos as 50,000 students take to streets over fees, *Daily Mail*, 11th November, www.dailymail.co.uk/news/article-1328385/TUITION-FEES-PROTEST-Anarchists-cause-chaos-50k-students-streets.html [accessed 10th July 2014].

Gill, M. (2016) Angela Rayner called 'thick as mince' in abusive emails about her accent, *The Huffington Post*, 27th October, www.huffingtonpost.co.uk/entry/angela-rayner-hits-back-at-abusive-emails-over-her-accent_uk_5811d990e4b04660a438156a [accessed 21st February 2018].

Gillen, J. and Merchant, G. (2013) Contact calls: Twitter as dialogic social and linguistic practice, *Language Sciences*, 25: 47–58.

Gonzalez, T. (2017) How to hygge: The Danish secret to a happy home, *San Francisco Chronicle*, 6th January, www.sfchronicle.com/homeandgarden/article/How-to-hygge-The-Danish-secret-to-a-happy-home-10840502.php [accessed 14th January 2018].

Gorwa, R. (2017) *Computational Propaganda in Poland: False Amplifiers and the Digital Public Sphere*, Computational Propaganda Project Working Paper Series 2017

(4), http://trybun.org.pl/wp-content/uploads/2017/06/Comprop-Poland.pdf [accessed 2nd February 2018].

Gottfried, J. and Shearer, E. (2017) Americans' online news use is closing in on TV news use, *Pew Research*, www.pewresearch.org/fact-tank/2017/09/07/ americans-online-news-use-vs-tv-news-use/ [accessed 31st January 2018].

Guardian (2013) HSBC 'demises' jobs: Another absurd business euphemism, *The Guardian*, 23rd April, www.theguardian.com/business/nils-pratley-on-finance/2013/apr/23/hsbc-demise-job-cuts-euphemism [accessed 9th January 2014].

Gupta, A. F. (2004) Singlish on the web, in Hashim, A. and Hassan, N. (eds.) *Varieties of English in South East Asia and Beyond*. Kuala Lumpur: University of Malaya Press: 19–38.

Hamblin, J. (2013) Some Americans say they support the Affordable Care Act but not Obamacare, *The Atlantic*, 1st October, www.theatlantic.com/health/ archive/2013/10/some-americans-say-they-support-the-affordable-care-act-but-not-obamacare/280165/ [accessed 3rd January 2014].

Hargrove, E., Sakoda, K., and Siegel, J. (n.d.) Hawai'i Creole, www.hawaii.edu/ satocenter/langnet/definitions/hce.html#grammar-hce [accessed 13th June 2014].

Harris, R. and Rampton, B. (2003) Introduction, in *The Language, Race and Ethnicity Reader*. London: Routledge: 1–14.

Hartigan, J. (1997) Unpopular culture: The case of 'white trash', *Cultural Studies*, 11(2): 316–343.

Hartley, J. (2010) Silly citizenship, *Critical Discourse Studies*, 7(4): 233–248.

Hastie, B. and Cosh, S. (2013) 'What's wrong with that?' Legitimating and contesting gender inequality, *Journal of Language and Social Psychology*, 32: 369–389.

Hayward, K. J. and Yar, M. (2006) The 'chav' phenomenon: Consumption, media and the construction of a new underclass, *Crime Media Culture*, 2(1): 9–28.

Hazenberg, E. (2016) Walking the straight and narrow: Linguistic choice and gendered presentation, *Gender & Language*, 10(2): 270–294.

Heller, M. (2003) Globalization, the new economy, and the commodification of language and identity, *Journal of Sociolinguistics*, 7(4): 473–492.

Heller, M. (2006) *Linguistic Minorities and Modernity: A Sociolinguistic Ethnography*, 2nd ed. London: Continuum.

Herbert, J. (2000) *Journalism in the Digital Age: Theory and Practice for Broadcast, Print and On-Line Media*. London: Taylor & Francis Ltd.

Hermida, A. (2012) Tweets and truth, *Journalism Practice*, 6(5–6): 659–668.

Herring, S. C. (2010) Who's got the floor in computer-mediated conversation? Edelsky's gender patterns revisited, *Language@ Internet*, 7(8): 8.

Herring, S. C., Johnson, D. A., and DiBenedetto, T. (1992) Participation in electronic discourse in a 'feminist' field, in *Locating Power: Proceedings of the 1992 Berkeley Women and Language Conference*. Berkeley, CA: Berkeley Women and Language Group: 250–262.

Higgins, C. (2016) The hygge conspiracy, *The Guardian*, 22nd November, www. theguardian.com/lifeandstyle/2016/nov/22/hygge-conspiracy-denmark-cosiness-trend [accessed 14th January 2018].

Hilgendorf, S. K. (2015) Plurality and world Englishes: The social realities of language use, *World Englishes*, 34(1): 55–67.

Hines, C. (1999) Rebaking the Pie: The woman as dessert metaphor, in Bucholtz, M. (ed.) *Reinventing Identities: The Gendered Self in Discourse*. Oxford: Oxford University Press: 145–162.

Hitchens, C. (2010) The other l-word: On language, *Vanity Fair*, 13th January, www. vanityfair.com/culture/features/2010/01/hitchens-like-201001 [accessed 16th June 2014].

Hlavach, L. and Freivogel, W. H. (2011) Ethical implications of anonymous comments posted to online news stories, *Journal of Mass Media Ethics*, 26(1): 21–37.

Hoey, M. (1986) The discourse colony: A preliminary study of a neglected discourse type, in Coulthard, M. (ed.) *Talking about Text*. Birmingham: English Language Research Discourse Analysis Monographs No. 13: 1–26.

Hoffman, M. F. and Walker, J. A. (2010) Ethnolects and the city: Ethnic orientation and linguistic variation in Toronto English, *Language Variation and Change*, 22(1): 37–67.

Holmes, J. (1984) Hedging your bets and sitting on the fence: Some evidence for hedges as support structures, *Te Reo*, 27: 47–62.

Holmes, J. (1986) Functions of *you know* in women's and men's speech, *Language in Society*, 15: 1–22.

Holmes, J. (1987) Hedging, fencing and other conversational gambits: An analysis of gender differences in New Zealand speech, in Pauwels, A. (ed.) *Women and Language in Australian and New Zealand Society*. Sydney: Australian Professional Publications: 59–79.

Holmes, J. (1998) Women talk too much, in Bauer, L. and Trudgill, P. (eds.) *Language Myths*. Harmondsworth: Penguin: 41–49.

Holmes, J. (2008) *An Introduction to Sociolinguistics*, 3rd ed. Harlow: Pearson.

Horner, J. R. (2011) Clogged systems and toxic assets: News metaphors, neoliberal ideology, and the United States 'Wall Street Bailout' of 2008, *Journal of Language and Politics*, 10(1): 29–49.

Hu, Y., Manikonda, L., and Kambhampati, S. (2014) What we Instagram: A first analysis of Instagram photo content and user types, *Eighth International AAAI Conference on Weblogs and Social Media*: 595–598, www.aaai.org/ocs/index. php/ICWSM/ICWSM14 [accessed 6th April 2018].

Hudson, R. A. (1996) *Sociolinguistics*. Cambridge: Cambridge University Press.

Hughey, M. W. and Daniels, J. (2013) Racist comments at online news sites: A methodological dilemma for discourse analysis, *Media, Culture & Society*, 35(3): 332–347.

Hutchby, I. and Woffit, R. (2008) *Conversation Analysis*, 2nd ed. London: Polity Press.

The Idler (n.d.) Bad grammar awards 2015: Amazon win (Or is that wins?), https:// idler.co.uk/article/news-harry-styles-wins-our-first-ever-good-grammar- award/ [accessed 9th January 2018].

Irvine, J. and Gal, S. (2000) Language ideology and linguistic differentiation, in Kroskrity, P. V. (ed.) *Regimes of Language: Ideologies, Polities and Identities*. Santa Fe: School of American Research Press: 35–83.

Jenkins, J. (1998) Which pronunciation norms and models for English as an International Language?, *ELT Journal*, 52(2): 119–126.

Jenkins, J. (2002) A sociolinguistically based, empirically Researched Pronunciation syllabus for English as an international language, *Applied Linguistics*, 23(1): 83–103.

Jenkins, J. (2009) English as a lingua franca: Interpretations and attitudes, *World Englishes*, 28(2): 200–207.

Jensen, T. (2014) Welfare commonsense, poverty porn and doxosophy, *Sociological Research Online*, 19(3): 3, www.socresonline.org.uk/19/3/3.html [accessed 1st October 2015].

Joemat-Pettersson, T. (2014) Policy budget speech by the Minister of Energy Ms Tina Joemat-Pettersson, MP Good Hope Chambers, Parliament, Cape Town, 21st July 2014, www.energy.gov.za/files/media/speeches/2014/2014-Budget-Vote-Speech-by-Minister.pdf [accessed 22nd January 2018].

Johnson, S. and Finlay, F. (1997) Do men gossip? An analysis of football talk on television, in Johnson, S. and Meinhoff, U. H.(eds.) *Language and Masculinity*. Oxford: Blackwell: 130–143.

Johnstone, B. (2009) Pittsburghese Shirts: Commodification and the enregisterment of an urban dialect, *American Speech*, 84(2): 157–175.

Johnstone, B., Andrus, J., and Danielson, A. E. (2006) Mobility, indexicality, and the enregisterment of 'Pittsburghese', *Journal of English Linguistics*, 32(4): 77–104.

Johnstone, B., Bhasin, N., and Wittofski, D. (2002) 'Dahntahn Pittsburgh: Monophthongal /aw/ and representations of localness in southwestern Pennsylvania, *American Speech*, 77: 148–166.

Jones, D. (1980) Gossip: Notes on women's oral culture, *Women's Studies International Quarterly*, 3(2): 193–198.

Jones, R. H. (2005) Sites of engagement as sites of attention: Time, space and culture in electronic discourse, in Jones, R. H. and Norris, S. (eds.) *Discourse in Action: Introducing Mediated Discourse Analysis*. London: Routledge: 141–154.

Jones, T. (2015) Toward a description of African American Vernacular English dialect regions using 'Black Twitter', *American Speech*, 90(4): 403–440.

Jones, T. (2016) AAE talmbout: An overlooked verb of quotation, *University of Pennsylvania Working Papers in Linguistics*, 22(2): 11, http://repository.upenn.edu/pwpl/vol22/iss2/11

Jost, J. T., Federico, C. M., and Napier, J. L. (2009) Political ideology: Its structure, functions, and elective affinities, *Annual Review of Psychology*, 60: 307–337.

Jucker, A. H. (2003) Mass media communication at the beginning of the twenty-first century, *Journal of Historical Pragmatics*, 4(1): 129–148.

Kachru, B. B. (1985) Standards, codification, and sociolinguistic realism: The English language in the outer circle, in Quirk, R. and Widdowson, H. G. (eds.) *English in the World*. Cambridge: Cambridge University Press: 11–30.

Kachru, B. B. (1991) Liberation linguistics and the Quirk concern, *English Today*, 7(1): 3–13.

Kachru, B. B. (1992) World Englishes: Approaches, issues and resources, *Language Teaching*, 25(1): 1–14.

Kasanga, L. A. (2012a) English in the Democratic Republic of the Congo, *World Englishes*, 31(1): 48–69.

Kasanga, L. A. (2012b) Mapping the linguistic landscape of a commercial neighbourhood in Central Phnom Penh, *Journal of Multilingual and Multicultural Development*, 33(6): 553–567.

Kautsky, R. and Widholm, A. (2008) Online methodology: Analysing news flows of online journalism, *Westminster Papers in Communication and Culture*, 5(2): 81–97.

Kemper, S. (1994) Elderspeak: Speech accommodations to older adults, *Aging, Neuropsychology, and Cognition: A Journal on Normal and Dysfunctional Development*, 1(1): 17–28.

Kennedy, R. L. (1999) Who can say 'Nigger'? And other considerations, *The Journal of Blacks in Higher Education*, 26: 86–96.

Kiesling, S. F. (2004) Dude, *American Speech*, 79(3): 281–305.

Kiesling, S. F. (2005) Variation, stance and style: Word-final – *er*, high rising tone and ethnicity in Australian English, *English World Wide*, 26(1): 1–42.

Kirkpatrick, A. (2007) *World Englishes*. Cambridge: Cambridge University Press.

Knobel, M. and Lankshear, C. (2007) Online memes, affinities, and cultural production, in Knobel, M. and Lankshear, C. (eds.) *A New Literacies Sampler*. New York: Peter Lang: 199–227.

Knox, J. (2007) Visual-verbal communication on online newspaper home pages, *Visual Communication*, 6(1): 19–53.

Koutonin, M. R. (2015) Why are white people expats when the rest of us are immigrants?, *The Guardian*, 13th March, www.theguardian.com/global-development-professionals-network/2015/mar/13/white-people-expats-immigrants-migration?CMP=fb_gu [accessed 18th February 2018].

Kress, G. and Hodge, R. (1993) *Language as Ideology*. London: Routledge.

Kress, G. and van Leeuwen, T. (1996) *Reading Images*. London: Routledge.

Kristiansen, T. (2010) Attitudes, ideology and awareness, in Wodak, R., Johnstone, B., and Kerswill, P. (eds.) *The Sage Handbook of Sociolinguistics*. London: Sage: 265–278.

Kristiansen, T. (2017) The hows and whys of language-related stereotypes: A discussion based on Scandinavian examples, in Dabrowska, A., Pisarek, W., and Stickel, G. (eds.) *Stereotypes and Linguistic Prejudices in Europe*. Budapest: EFNIL-European Federation of National Institutions for Language: 247–272.

Kuiper, K. (1991) Sporting formulae in New Zealand English: Two models of male solidarity, in Cheshire, J. (ed.) *English around the World: Sociolinguistic Perspectives*. Cambridge: Cambridge University Press: 200–212.

Labov, W. (1966) *The Social Stratification of English in New York City*. Washington, DC: Center for Applied Linguistics.

Labov, W. (1970 [1969]) The logic of nonstandard English, in Alatis, J. (ed.) *Georgetown Monographs on Language and Linguistics*, Vol. 22. Washington, DC: Georgetown University Press: 1–44.

Labov, W. (1972a) *Sociolinguistic Patterns*. Philadelphia: University of Pennsylvania Press.

Labov, W. (1972b) Academic ignorance and Black intelligence, *The Atlantic*, 72, June: 59–67.

Labov, W. (1982) Objectivity and commitment in linguistic science: The case of the Black English trial in Ann Arbor, *Language in Society*, 11: 165–201.

Labov, W. (1989) The child as linguistic historian, *Language Variation and Change*, 1: 85–94.

Labov, W. (2008) Mysteries of the substrate, in Meyerhoff, M. and Nagy, N. (eds.) *Social Lives in Language: Sociolinguistics and Multilingual Speech Communities*. Amsterdam: John Benjamins: 315–326.

Ladegård, H. J. (1998) Assessing national stereotypes in language attitude studies: The Case of class-consciousness in Denmark, *Journal of Multilingual and Multicultural Development*, 19(3): 182–198.

Ladegård, H. J. and Sachdev, I. (2006) 'I like the Americans . . . but I certainly don't aim for an American accent': Language attitudes, vitality and foreign language learning in Denmark, *Journal of Multilingual and Multicultural Development*, 27: 91–108.

Lagerwerf, L., Boeynaems, A., van Egmond-Brussee, C., and Burgers, C. (2015) Immediate attention for public speech: Differential effects of rhetorical schemes and valence framing in political radio speeches, *Journal of Language and Social Psychology*, 34(3): 273–299.

Lakoff, G. and Johnson, M. (1980) *Metaphors We Live By*. Chicago: University of Chicago Press.

Lakoff, R. (1975) *Language and Woman's Place*. New York: Harper and Row.

Lansley, S. and Mack, J. (2015) *Breadline Britain: The Rise of Mass Poverty*. London: Oneworld.

Laserna, C. M., Seih, Y. T., and Pennebaker, J. W. (2014) 'Um . . . who like says you know': Filler word use as a function of age, gender, and personality, *Journal of Language and Social Psychology*, 33(3): 328–338.

Lawton, C. A., Blakemore, J. E. O., and Vartanian, L. R. (2003) The new meaning of Ms.: Single, but too old for Miss, *Psychology of Women Quarterly*, 27: 215–220.

Leber, R. and Schulman, J. (2017) Yes, the mainstream media does publish fake news, *Mother Jones*, 5th July, www.motherjones.com/environment/2017/07/timeline-climate-denial-nows/ [accessed 2nd February 2018].

Lee Eu Fah, E. (n.d.) Profile of the Singapore Chinese dialect groups, *Statistics Singapore Newsletter*, www.howardscott.net/4/Swatow_A_Colonial_Heritage/Files/Documentation/Lee%20Eu%20Fah.pdf [accessed 11th April 2018].

Leeman, J. and Modan, G. (2009) Commodified language in Chinatown: A contextualized approach to linguistic landscape, *Journal of Sociolinguistics*, 13(3): 332–362.

Leimgruber, J. (2012) Singapore English: An indexical approach, *World Englishes*, 31(1): 1–14.

Leonhardt, D. and Thompson, S. A. (2017) Trumps lies, *New York Times*, 14th December, www.nytimes.com/interactive/2017/06/23/opinion/trumps-lies.html?mcubz=0 [accessed 2nd February 2018].

Levison, C. (2013) *Cultural Semantics and Social Cognition: A Case Study of the Danish University of Meaning*. Amsterdam: De Gruyter.

Lewis, P., Vasagar, J., Williams, R., and Taylor, M. (2010) Student protest over fees turns violent, *The Guardian*, 10th November, www.theguardian.com/education/2010/nov/10/student-protest-fees-violent [accessed 12th June 2014].

Liberman, A. (2014) Three words of American interest in a prospective new etymological dictionary of English: *Ain't*, *alairy* and *alewife*, *American Speech*, 89(2): 170–189.

Liberman, M. (2006) Sex-linked lexical budgets, *Language Log*, 6th August, http://itre.cis.upenn.edu/~myl/languagelog/archives/003420.html [accessed 31st May 2014].

Lippi-Green, R. (2011) *English with an Accent*, 2nd ed. London: Routledge.

Loftus, E. (1975) Leading questions and the eyewitness report, *Cognitive Psychology*, 7: 550–572.

Lou, J. J. and Jaworski, A. (2016) Itineraries of protest signage, *Journal of Language and Politics*, 15(5): 612–645.

LSA (1996) The LSA Guidelines for Nonsexist Usage, *LSA Bulletin*, (December): 68, www.linguisticsociety.org/resource/lsa-guidelines-nonsexist-usage [accessed 12th June 2014].

Lucy, J. A. (1996) The scope of linguistic relativity: An analysis and review of empirical research, in Gumperz, J. J. and Levinson, S. C. (eds.) *Rethinking Linguistic Relativity*. Cambridge: Cambridge University Press: 37–69.

Lucy, J. A. (2005) Through the window of language: Assessing the influence of language diversity on thought, *Theoria*, 54: 299–309.

MacFarlane, A. E. and Stuart-Smith, J. (2012) 'One of them sounds sort of Glasgow Uni-ish': Social judgements and fine phonetic variation in Glasgow, *Lingua*, 122: 764–778.

MacFarquhar, N. and Rossback, A. (2017) How Russian Propaganda spread from a parody website to Fox News, *The New York Times*, 7th June, www.nytimes.

com/interactive/2017/06/07/world/europe/anatomy-of-fake-news-russian-propaganda.html [accessed 2nd February 2018].

Machin, D. and van Leeuwen, T. (2009) Toys as discourse: Children's war toys and the war on terror, *Critical Discourse Studies*, 6(1): 51–63.

Makoni, S. and Pennycook, A. (2005) Disinventing and (re) constituting languages, *Critical Inquiry in Language Studies: An International Journal*, 2(3): 137–156.

Mallinson, C. (2017) Language and its everyday revolutionary potential, in McCammon, H. J., Taylor, V., Reger, J., and Einwohner, R. L. (eds.) *The Oxford Handbook of US Women's Social Movement Activism*. Oxford: Oxford University Press: 419–439.

Marcus, R. (2014) Edward Snowden, the insufferable whistleblower, *Washington Post*, 1st January, www.washingtonpost.com/opinions/ruth-marcus-snowden-the-insufferable-whistleblower/2013/12/31/7649539a-7250-11e3-8b3f-b1666705ca3b_story.html [accessed 12th June 2014].

Marr, T. (2005) Language and the capital: A case study of English 'language shock' among Chinese students in London, *Language Awareness*, 14(4): 239–253.

Marsden, S. and Holmes, J. (2014) Talking to the elderly in New Zealand residential care settings, *Journal of Pragmatics*, 64: 17–34.

Marwick, A. E. and boyd, d. (2011) I tweet honestly, I tweet passionately: Twitter users, context collapse, and the imagined audience, *New Media & Society*, 13(1): 114–133.

Mather, P.-A. (2011) The social stratification of /r/ in New York City: Labov's department store study revisited, *Journal of English Linguistics*, 40(4): 338–356.

Matley, D. (2018) 'This is NOT a #humblebrag, this is just a #brag': The pragmatics of self-praise, hashtags and politeness in Instagram posts, *Discourse, Context and Media*, 22: 30–38, https://doi.org/10.1016/j.dcm.2017.07.007

Mautner, G. (2007) Mining large corpora for social information: The case of elderly, *Language in Society*, 36: 51–72.

Mautner, G. (2010) *Language and the Market Society: Critical Reflections on Discourse and Dominance*. London: Routledge.

Mautner, G. (2012) Language, space and the law: A study of directive signs, *International Journal of Speech Language and the Law*, 19(2): 189–217.

May, S. (2011) *Language and Minority Rights: Ethnicity, Nationalism and the Politics of Language*, 2nd ed. London: Routledge.

McArthur, T. (1987) The English languages?, *English Today*, 3: 9–13.

McCarthy, T. (2013) NSA whistleblower Edward Snowden says US 'treats dissent as defection', *The Guardian*, 1st November, www.theguardian.com/world/2013/nov/01/nsa-whistleblower-edward-snowden-letter-germany [accessed 12th June 2014].

McCulloch, G. (2014) A linguist explains the grammar of doge, *The Toast*, 6th February, http://the-toast.net/2014/02/06/linguist-explains-grammar-doge-wow/ [accessed 12th June 2014].

Mendoza-Denton, N. (1996) 'Muy macha': Gender and ideology in gang girls' discourse about makeup, *Ethnos: Journal of Anthropology*, 6: 47–63.

Mendoza-Denton, N. (2011) The semiotic hitchhiker's guide to creaky voice: Circulation and gendered hardcore in a Chicana/o Gang persona, *Journal of Linguistic Anthropology*, 21(2): 261–280.

Mills, S. (2008) *Language and Sexism*. Cambridge: Cambridge University Press.

Milroy, J. and Milroy, L. (1999) *Authority in Language: Investigating Standard English*. London: Taylor & Francis Ltd.

Milroy, L. (1987) *Language and Social Networks*, 2nd ed. Oxford: Basil Blackwell.

Milroy, L. and Gordon, M. (2003) *Sociolinguistics: Method and Interpretation.* Oxford: Blackwell.

Mitchell, A., Gottfreid, J., Barthel, M., and Shearer, E. (2016) The modern news consumer: Pathways to news, *Pew Research Centre*, 7th July, www.journalism. org/2016/07/07/pathways-to-news/ [accessed 2nd February 2018].

Montgomery, M. (2008) *An Introduction to Language and Society*, 3rd ed. London: Routledge.

Motschenbacher, H. (2013) Gentlemen before ladies? A corpus-based study of conjunct order in personal binomials, *Journal of English Linguistics*, 41(3): 212–242.

Mufwene, S. (2010) Globalization, global English, world Englishes, in Coupland, N. (ed.) *Handbook of Language and Globalization.* Chichester: Wiley Blackwell: 31–55.

Mullany, L. (2007) *Gendered Discourse in the Professional Workplace.* Basingstoke: Palgrave Macmillan.

NCTE (2002) Guidelines for gender-fair use of language. *NCTE Position Statements on Language*, www.ncte.org/positions/statements/genderfairuseoflang [accessed 12th June 2014].

Ndhlovu, F. (2013) Language nesting, superdiversity and African diasporas in regional Australia, *Australian Journal of Linguistics*, 33(4): 426–448.

Nero, S. (2006) Language, identity, and education of Caribbean English speakers, *World Englishes*, 25(3/4): 501–511.

Newman, N. (2017) Digital news report: Overview and key findings of the 2017 report, www.digitalnewsreport.org/survey/2017/overview-key-findings-2017/ [accessed 2nd February 2018].

Nguyen, L. and McCallum, K. (2016) Drowning in our own home: A metaphor-led discourse analysis of Australian news media reporting on maritime asylum seekers, *Communication Research and Practice*, 2(2): 159–176.

NPR (2017) Obamacare and affordable care act are the same, but Americans still don't know that, *All Things Considered*, 11th February, www.npr.org/2017/ 02/11/514732211/obamacare-and-affordable-care-act-are-the-same-but-americans-still-dont-know-that [accessed 2nd February 2018].

O'Barr, W. and Atkins, B. (1980) 'Women's language' or 'powerless language'?, in McConnell-Ginet, S. et al. (eds.) *Women and Languages in Literature and Society.* New York: Praeger: 93–110.

Ochs, E. and Schieffelin, B. (1984) Language acquisition and socialization: Three developmental stories and their implications, in Blount, B. G. (ed.) *Language, Culture and Society: A Book of Readings*, 2nd ed. Long Grove, IL: Waveland Press: 470–512.

Ochs, E. and Taylor, C. (1992) Family narrative as political activity, *Discourse & Society*, 3(3): 301–340.

Ohama, M. L. F., Gotay, C. C., Pagano, I. S., Boles, L., and Craven, D. D. (2000) Evaluations of Hawaii creole English and standard English, *Journal of Language and Social Psychology*, 19(3): 357–377.

O'Neill, B. (2011) A critique of politically correct language, *The Independent Review*, 16(2): 279–291.

Osborne, P. and Roberts, T. (2017) *How Trump Thinks: His Tweets and the Birth of a New Political Language.* London: Head of Zeus.

Overell, C. (n.d.) Waleed Aly praises Melbourne coke dealers for bold transition to recyclable baggies, *The Beetota Advocate*, www.betootaadvocate.com/uncategorized/ waleed-aly-praises-melbourne-coke-dealers-bold-transition-recyclable-baggies/ [accessed 2nd February 2018].

Oxford English Dictionary, www.oed.com

Palosaari, N. and Campbell, L. (2011) Structural aspects of language endangerment, in Austin, P. K. and Sallabank, J. (eds.) *The Cambridge Handbook of Endangered Languages*. Cambridge: Cambridge University Press: 100–119.

Parkinson, J. and Jaffe, M. (2011) What's in a word? The debate over 'ObamaCare': The name & the law, *ABC News* (US), 18th February, http://abcnews.go.com/blogs/politics/2011/02/whats-in-a-word-the-debate-over-obamacare-the-name-the-law/ [accessed 12th June 2014].

Parks, J. B. and Roberton, M. A. (2004) Attitudes toward women mediate the gender effect on attitudes toward sexist language, *Psychology of Women Quarterly*, 28(3): 233–239.

Paterson, L., Coffey-Glover, L., and Peplow, D. (2016) Negotiating stance within discourses of class: Reactions to *Benefits Street*, *Discourse and Society*, 27(2): 195–214.

Pavlenko, A. (2017) Superdiversity and why it isn't: Reflections on terminological innovation and academic branding, in Breidbach, S., Küster, L., and Schmenk, B. (eds.) *Sloganizations in Language Education Discourse*. Bristol, UK: Multilingual Matters: in press.

Payne, A. (1980) Factors controlling the acquisition of Philadelphia dialect by out-of-state children, in Labov, W. (ed.) *Locating Language in Time and Space*. New York: Academic Press: 143–178.

Peccei, J. (1999) *Child Language*. London: Routledge.

Peterson, L., Radebe, K., and Mohanty, S. (2016) Democracy, education, and free speech: The importance of# FeesMustFall for transnational activism, *Societies without Borders*, 11(1): 10, https://scholarlycommons.law.case.edu/swb/vol11/iss1/10

Phillipson, R. (2003) *English-Only Europe? Challenging Language Policy*. London: Routledge.

Pickles, E. (2013) Eric Pickles: Immigrants must learn English, *The Telegraph*, 13th November, www.telegraph.co.uk/news/uknews/immigration/10445883/Eric-Pickles-Immigrants-must-learn-English.html [accessed 13th June 2014].

Pilkington, J. (1998) 'Don't try and make out that I'm nice!' The different strategies women and men use when gossiping, in Coates, J. (ed.) *Language and Gender: A Reader*. Oxford: Wiley Blackwell: 254–269.

Piller, I. (2001) Identity constructions in multilingual advertising, *Language in Society*, 30: 153–186.

Pini, B. and Previte, J. (2013) Gender, class and sexuality in contemporary Australia: Representations of the boganette, *Australian Feminist Studies*, 28: 348–363.

Portero, C. M. (2011) Noun-noun euphemisms in the language of the late 2000's global financial crisis, *Atlantis*, 33(2): 57–137.

Prendergast, C. (2015) Ghosting: What to do if you've been a Victim, *Independent*, 22nd July, www.independent.co.uk/life-style/love-sex/ghosting-what-to-do-if-youve-been-a-victim-10408043.html [accessed 9th January 2018].

Preston, D. R. (1996) Whaddayaknow? The modes of folk linguistic awareness, *Language Awareness*, 5(1): 40–74.

Preston, D. R. (2010) Language, people, salience, space: Perceptual dialectology and language regard, *Dialectologia: Revista Electronica*, 5: 87–131.

Pullum, G. (1991) The great Eskimo vocabulary hoax, in *The Great Eskimo Vocabulary Hoax and Other Irreverent Essays on the Study of Language*, Chicago: University of Chicago Press.

Purnell, T. C., Idsardi, W. J., and Baugh, J. (1999) Perceptual and phonetic experiments on American English dialect Identification, *Journal of Language and Social Psychology*, 18(1): 10–30.

Quirk, R. (1990) Language varieties and Standard Language, *English Today*, 6(1): 3–10.

Rahman, J. (2008) Middle class African Americans: Reactions and attitudes toward African American English, *American Speech*, 83(2): 141–176.

Rahman, J. (2012) The N word: Its history and use in the African American community, *Journal of English Linguistics*, 40(2): 137–171.

Rahman, T. (2009) Language ideology, identity and the commodification of language in the call centres of Pakistan, *Language in Society*, 38: 233–258.

Rampton, B. (1995) *Crossing: Language and Ethnicity among Adolescents*. London: Longman.

Rampton, B. (1997) *Language Crossing and the Redefinition of Reality: Implications for Research on Code-Switching Community*, Working Papers in Urban Language and Literacies, Paper 5, Kings College London, www.kcl.ac.uk/schools/sspp/education/research/groups/llg/wpull.html. Also in P. Auer (ed.) (1998) *Code-Switching in Conversation, Language, Interaction and Identity*. London: Routledge: 290–317.

Rampton, B. (2011) Style contrasts, migration and social class, *Journal of Pragmatics*, 43: 1236–1250.

Remeikis, A. (2017) Pauline Hanson says Islam is a disease Australia needs to 'vaccinate', *The Sydney Morning Herald*, 24th March, www.smh.com.au/federal-politics/political-news/pauline-hanson-says-islam-is-a-disease-australia-needs-to-vaccinate-20170324-gv5w7z.html [accessed 18th February 2018].

Rendle-Short, J. (2009) The address term 'mate' in Australian English: Is it still a masculine term?, *Australian Journal of Linguistics*, 29(2): 245–268.

Richinick, M. (2013) Obama defends health care law – and delays it, *MSNBC*, 26 September http://www.msnbc.com/morning-joe/obama-defends-health-care-law-and-delays-it [accessed 12th June 2018].

Riordan, M. A. (2017) Emojis as Tools for emotion work: Communicating affect in text messages, *Journal of Language and Social Psychology*, 36(5): 549–567, doi:10.1177/0261927X17704238

Roberts, J. (2004) Child language variation, in Chambers, J. K., Trudgill, P., and Schilling-Estes, N. (eds.) *The Handbook of Language Variation and Change*. London: Blackwell: 333–348.

Robson, D. (2013) Middlesbrough school urges parents to correct pupils' Tees dialect, *The Gazette*, 5th February, updated 13th May, www.gazettelive.co.uk/news/local-news/middlesbrough-school-urges-parents-correct-3666192 [accessed 21st February 2018].

Romaine, S. (1978) Postvocalic /r/ in Scottish English: Sound change in progress?, in Trudgill, P. (ed.) *Sociolinguistic Patterns in British English*. Baltimore, MD: University Park Press: 144–157.

Romero-Figueroa, A. (1985) OSV as the basic order in Warao, *Lingua*, 66(2–3): 115–134.

Rosa, J. D. (2016) Standardization, racialization, languagelessness: Raciolinguistic ideologies across communicative contexts, *Journal of Linguistic Anthropology*, 26(2): 162–183.

Rosman, K. (2015) Me, myself and mx, *New York Times*, 5th June, www.nytimes.com/2015/06/07/style/me-myself-and-mx.html?mcubz=0 [accessed 16th February 2018].

Rutter, T. (2013) #Barf: How Twitter can reduce the spread of norovirus, *The Guardian*, 11th December, www.theguardian.com/public-leaders-network/2013/dec/11/twitter-reduce-spread-norovirus [accessed 9th January 2014].

Saatchi, C. (2017) Women speak 12,000 words a day, men speak 4,000, *London Evening Standard*, 27th July 2017, p. 36.

Sacks, H., Schegloff, E. A., and Jefferson, G. (1974) A simplest systematics for the organisation of turn-taking for conversation, *Language*, 50: 696–735.

Sailaja, P. (2009) *Indian English: Dialects of English*. Edinburgh: Edinburgh University Press.

Sailaja, P. (2012) Indian English: Features and sociolinguistic aspects, *Language and Linguistics Compass*, 6(6): 359–370.

Sakoda, K. and Tamura, E. H. (2008) Kent Sakoda discusses Pidgin grammar, *Educational Perspectives*, 41: 40–43.

Salford City Council (n.d.) Salford quays public spaces protection order, www.salford.gov.uk/crime-reduction-and-emergencies/anti-social-behaviour/public-spaces-protection-orders/salford-quays-pspo/ [accessed 9th January 2018].

Sankoff, D. and Laberge, S. (1978) The linguistic market and the statistical explanation of variability, in Sankoff, D. (ed.) *Linguistic Variation: Models and Method*. New York: Academic Press: 239–250.

Sankoff, G. (2005) Cross-sectional and longitudinal studies in sociolinguistics, in Ammon, U., Dittmar, N., Mattheier, K. J., and Trudgill, P. (eds.) *An International Handbook of the Science of Language and Society*, Vol. 2. Berlin: Mouton de Gruyter: 1003–1013.

Sapir, E. (1958 [1929]) The status of linguistics as a science, in Sapir, E., *Culture, Language and Personality* (ed. D. G. Mandelbaum). Berkeley, CA: University of California Press.

Saussure, F. de (1966) *Course in General Linguistics*, Bally, C. and Sechehaye, A. (eds.) with Reidlinger, A. and Baskin, W. (trans.). London: McGraw Hill.

Savage, M., Devine, F., Cunningham, N., Taylor, M., Li, Y., Hjellbrekke, J., Le Roux, B., Friedman, S., and Miles, A. (2013) A new model of class? Findings from the BBC's Great British class survey experiment, *Sociology*, 47(2): 219–250.

Schellhase, J. (2012) Fracking it in South Africa: An argument for shale gas production in the Karoo, *African Arguments*, 15th November, http://africanarguments.org/2012/11/15/fracking-it-in-south-africa-an-argument-for-shale-gas-production-in-the-karoo-by-john-schellhase/ [accessed 22nd January 2018].

Schilling-Estes, N. (2004) Constructing ethnicity in interaction, *Journal of Sociolinguistics*, 8(2): 163–195.

Schleef, E. (2008) Gender and academic discourse: Global restrictions and local possibilities, *Language in Society*, 37(4): 515–538.

Schulz, M. (1975) The semantic derogation of women, in Thorne, B. and Henley, N. (eds.) *Language and Sex: Difference and Dominance*. Rowley, MA: Newbury House: 64–75.

Schwarz, J. (2003) Quantifying non-sexist language: The case of Ms, in Sarangi, S. and van Leeuwen, T. (eds.) *Applied Linguistics and Communities of Practice*. London: Continuum: 169–183.

Scollon, R. and Scollon, S. W. (2003) *Discourses in Place: Language in the Material World*. London: Routledge.

Scotsman (2015) Scots language found to have 421 words for snow, 22nd September, www.scotsman.com/lifestyle/scots-language-found-to-have-421-words-for-snow-1-3895100 [accessed 14th January 2018].

Sealey, A. (2000) *Childly Language: Children, Language and the Social World.* Essex: Harlow.

Shale Stuff (2014) The process of fracking, http://shalestuff.com/education/fracking/fracking [accessed 22nd January 2018].

Shankar, S. (2008) Speaking like a model minority: 'FOB' styles, gender, and racial meanings among Desi teens in Silicon Valley, *Journal of Linguistic Anthropology*, 18(2): 268–289.

Sheldon, P. and Bryant, K. (2016) Instagram: Motives for its use and relationship to narcissism and contextual age, *Computers in Human Behavior*, 58: 89–97.

Shenk, P. S. (2007) 'I'm Mexican, remember?' Constructing ethnic identities via authentication discourse, *Journal of Sociolinguistics*, 11(2): 194–220.

Shildrick, T. and MacDonald, R. (2013) Poverty talk: How people experiencing poverty deny their poverty and why they blame 'the poor', *The Sociological Review*, 61(2): 285–303.

Shohamy, E. and Ben-Rafael, E. (2015) Introduction linguistic landscape: A new journal, *Linguistic Landscape*, 1(1): 1–5, doi:10.1075/ll.1.1.001int

Shon, P. C. H. (2005) 'I'd grab the S-O-B by his hair and yank him out the window': The fraternal order of warnings and threats in police-citizen encounters, *Discourse & Society*, 16(6): 829–845.

Siegel, J. (2000) Substrate influence in Hawai'i Creole English, *Language in Society*, 29: 197–236.

Silver, R. E. (2005) The discourse of linguistic capital: Language and economic policy planning in Singapore, *Language Policy*, 4(1): 47–66.

Simon-Vandenbergen, A.-M., White, P. R. R., and Aijmer, K. (1999) Presupposition and 'taking-for-granted' in mass communicated political argument: An illustration from British, Flemish and Swedish political colloquy, in Fetzer, A. and Lauerbach, G. (eds.) *Political Discourse in the Media: Cross-Cultural Perspectives*, Pragmatics and Beyond New Series. Amsterdam: John Benjamins: 31–74.

Simpson, P. (1993) *Language, Ideology and Point of View.* London: Routledge.

Skutnabb-Kangas, T. and Phillipson, R. (2010) The global politics of language: Markets, maintenance, marginalization or murder?, in Coupland, N. (ed.) *The Handbook of Language and Globalization.* Oxford: Blackwell: 77–100.

Smitherman, G. (1977) *Talkin and Testifyin: The Language of Black America*, Vol. 51. Detroit: Wayne State University Press.

Snow, C. (1977) The development of conversation between mothers and babies, *Journal of Child Language*, 4: 1–22.

Soffer, O. (2016) The oral paradigm and Snapchat, *Social Media + Society*, 2(3), https://doi.org/10.1177/2056305116666306

Spender, D. (1980) *Man Made Language.* London: Routledge.

Squires, P. and Lea, J. (2013) Introduction: Reading Loïc Wacquant-opening questions and overview, in Squires, P. and Lea, J. (eds.) *Criminalisation and Advanced Marginality: Critically Exploring the Work of Loïc Waquant.* Bristol, UK: Policy Press: 1–18.

Stanford, J. N. (2008) Child dialect acquisition: New perspectives on parent/peer influence, *Journal of Sociolinguistics*, 12: 567–596.

The Star (2017) Indonesia releases eight IS suspects deported from Singapore, 13th January, www.thestar.com.my/news/nation/2017/01/13/indonesian-men-released-after-questioning/ [accessed 14th January 2018].

Starbird, K. (2017) Examining the alternative media ecosystem through the production of alternative narratives of mass shooting events on Twitter, *11th International AAAI Conference on Web and Social Media (ICWSM)*: 230–239.

Starbird, K. and Palen, L. (2010) Pass it on? Retweeting in mass emergency, *Proceedings of the 7th International ISCRAM Conference*, www.cs.colorado.edu/~palen/starbirdpaleniscramretweet.pdf [accessed 12th June 2014].

Stuart-Smith, J., Timmins, C., and Tweedie, F. (2007) 'Talkin' Jockney? Variation and change in Glaswegian accent, *Journal of Sociolinguistics*, 11(2): 221–260.

Stuff White People Like (2010, March 14). #132 Picking their own Fruit [blog post]. Retrieved from https://stuffwhitepeoplelike.com/2010/03/14/132-picking-their-own-fruit/

Sulleyman, A. (2017a) Here is Facebook's guide to fake news, *The Independent*, 9th May, www.independent.co.uk/news/facebook-fake-news-guide-articles-curate-stop-take-down-lies-russia-donald-trump-us-politics-a7726111.html [accessed 2nd February 2018].

Sulleyman, A. (2017b) Twitter could roll out 'fake news' button on Tweets, *The Independent*, 30th June, www.independent.co.uk/life-style/gadgets-and-tech/news/twitter-fake-news-button-flag-tweets-offensive-content-a7816466.html [accessed 2nd February 2018].

Sultana, S., Dovchin, S., and Pennycook, A. (2013) Styling the periphery: Linguistic and cultural takeup in Bangladesh and Mongolia, *Journal of Sociolinguistics*, 17(5): 687–710.

Sutton-Spence, R. and Woll, B. (2004) British sign language, in Davies, A. and Elder, C. (eds.) *Handbook of Applied Linguistics*. Oxford: Blackwell: 165–186.

Tagliamonte, S. A. (2005) So who? Like how? Just what? Discourse markers in the conversations of young Canadians, *Journal of Pragmatics*, 37(11): 1896–1915.

Tagliamonte, S. A. (2008) So different and pretty cool! Recycling intensifiers in Toronto, Canada, *English Language & Linguistics*, 12(2): 361–394.

Tagliamonte, S. A. (2016) *Teen Talk: The Language of Adolescents*. Cambridge: Cambridge University Press.

Tagliamonte, S. A. and Denis, D. (2008) Linguistic Ruin? LOL! Instant messaging and teen language, *American Speech*, 83(1): 3–33.

Talbot, M. (1992) 'I wish you'd stop interrupting me': Interruptions and asymmetries in speaker-rights in equal encounters, *Journal of Pragmatics*, 18: 451–466.

Talbot, M. (2010) *Language and Gender*, 2nd ed. Cambridge: Polity Press.

Thomson, K. (2014) Edward Snowden, Russian agent?, *Huffington Post*, 2nd January, www.huffingtonpost.com/keith-thomson/edward-snowden-russian-ag_b_4531020.html [accessed 12th June 2014].

Thornborrow, J. (2001) Authenticating talk: Building public identities in audience participation broadcasting, *Discourse Studies*, 3(4): 459–479.

Thurlow, C. (2006) From statistical panic to moral panic: The metadiscursive construction and popular exaggeration of new media language in the print media, *Journal of Computer Mediated Communication*, 11(3): 667–701.

Thurlow, C. and Brown, A. (2003) Generation txt? The sociolinguistics of young people's text-messaging, *Discourse Analysis Online*, 1(1), http://extra.shu.ac.uk/daol/articles/v1/n1/a3/thurlow2002003-paper.html

Times of India (2016) Sikh man shot dead in Afghanistan, 2nd October, http://timesofindia.indiatimes.com/world/south-asia/Sikh-man-shot-dead-in-Afghanistan/articleshow/54641284.cms? [accessed 14th January 2018].

Townes, C. (2015) Obama explains the problem with 'All Lives Matter', *Think Progress*, 22nd October, https://thinkprogress.org/obama-explains-the-problem-with-all-lives-matter-780912d54888/ [accessed 18th February 2018].

Troyer, R. (2012) English in the Thai linguistic netscape, *World Englishes*, 31(1): 93–112.

Trudgill, P. (1972) Sex, covert prestige and linguistic change in the urban British English of Norwich, *Language in Society*, 1(2): 179–195.

Trudgill, P. (1974) *The Social Differentiation of English in Norwich*. Cambridge: Cambridge University Press.

Trudgill, P. (1999) Standard English: What is isn't, in Bex, T. and Watts, R. J. (eds.) *Standard English: The Widening Debate*. London: Routledge: 117–128.

Trudgill, P. and Hannah, J. (2002) *International English*, 4th ed. London: Routledge.

Tupas, R. and Salonga, A. (2016) Unequal Englishes in the Philippines, *Journal of Sociolinguistics*, 20(3): 367–381.

Tyler, I. (2008) 'Chav mum chav scum': Class disgust in contemporary Britain, *Feminist Media Studies*, 8(1): 17–34.

Underhill, R. (1988) Like is, like, focus, *American Speech*, 63(3): 234–246.

United Nations (1979) *CEDAW, Convention on the Elimination of Discrimination against Women*, www.un.org/womenwatch/daw/cedaw/text/econvention.htm [accessed 12th June 2014].

United Nations High Commissioner for Refugees (1951) *Convention and Protocol Relating to the Status of Refugees*, www.unhcr.org/uk/3b66c2aa10 [accessed 18th February 2018].

University of Washington School of Information (2017) Professors aim to fight for truth by 'Calling Bullshit', 17th January, https://ischool.uw.edu/news/2017/04/professors-aim-fight-truth-calling-bullshit [accessed 2nd February 2018].

Urwin, R., Cecil, N., and Dex, R. (2017) BBC pay? Women let it happen, *London Evening Standard*, 27th July, p. 1.

Vandenbroucke, M. (2016) Socio-economic stratification of English in globalized landscapes: A market-oriented perspective, *Journal of Sociolinguistics*, 20(1): 86–108.

van Dijk, T. A. (1993) *Elite Discourse and Racism*. Newbury Park/London: Sage.

van Dijk, T. A. (2004) Racist discourse, in E. Cashmere (ed.) *Routledge Encyclopaedia of Race and Ethnic Studies*. London: Routledge: 351–355.

van Dijk, T. A. (2006) Discourse and manipulation, *Discourse & Society*, 17(3): 359–383.

Varis, P. and Blommaert, J. (2015) Conviviality and collectives on social media: Virality, memes, and new social structures, *Multilingual Margins: A Journal of Multilingualism from the Periphery*, 2(1): 31–31.

Vatvani, C. (2017) Indonesian police free 8 men deported from Singapore over IS images, *Channel News Asia*, 13th January, www.channelnewsasia.com/news/singapore/indonesian-police-free-8-men-deported-from-singapore-over-is/3435914.html [accessed 14th January 2018].

Vertovec, S. (2007) Super-diversity and its implications, *Ethnic and Racial Studies*, 30(6): 1024–1054.

Vessey, R. (2016) Language ideologies in social media, *Journal of Language and Politics*, 15(1): 1–24.

Vosoughi, S., Roy, D., and Aral, S. (2018) The spread of true and false news online, *Science*, 359(6380): 1146–1151.

Vriesendorp, H. (2016) The internet's (new) usage problems, *English Today*, 32(3): 18–19.

Waddell, K. (2016) Facebook and Google won't let fake news sites use their ad networks, *The Atlantic*, 15th November, www.theatlantic.com/technology/archive/2016/11/facebook-and-google-wont-let-fake-news-sites-use-their-ads-platforms/507737/ [accessed 2nd February 2018].

Wagner, S. E. (2008) Linguistic change and stabilization in the transition from adolescence to adulthood. Unpublished PhD dissertation, University of Pennsylvania.

Walker, L. (2014) Pun no more: China bans wordplay in broadcasts and advertisements, *Newsweek*, 28th November, www.newsweek.com/pun-no-more-china-bans-wordplay-broadcasts-and-advertisements-287947 [accessed 9th January 2018].

Wallop, H. (2014) *Consumed: How We Buy Class in Modern Britain*. London: Collins.

Walton, S. and Jaffe, A. (2011) 'Stuff white people like': Stance, class, race, and internet commentary, in Thurlow, C. and Mroczek, K. (eds.) *Digital Discourse: Language in the New Media*. Oxford: Oxford University Press: 199–219.

Wardle, C. (2017) Fake news. It's complicated, *First Draft News*, https://firstdraftnews.com/fake-news-complicated/ 16th February. [accessed 17th July 2017].

Wassink, A. B. (1999) Historic low prestige and seeds of change: Attitudes toward Jamaican Creole, *Language in Society*, 28(1): 57–92.

Wassink, A. B. and Dyer, J. (2004) Language ideology and the transmission of phonological change changing indexicality in two situations of language contact, *Journal of English Linguistics*, 32(1): 3–30.

Waterson, J. (2017) There's no evidence Theresa May actually said this quote about lesbians, *Buzzfeed*, 5th June, www.buzzfeed.com/jimwaterson/theres-no-evidence-theresa-may-actually-said-this-quote?utm_term=.rcPxzK4EP6#.ospAgQzNZd [accessed 2nd February 2018].

Wee, L. (2005) Intra-language discrimination and linguistic human rights: The case of Singlish, *Applied Linguistics*, 26(1): 48–69.

Whorf, B. L. (1954) The relation of habitual thought and behaviour to language, in Hayakawa, S. I. (ed.) *Language, Meaning and Maturity: Selections from Etc., a Review of General Semantics, 1943–1953*. New York: Harper and Row: 197–215.

Wierzbicka, A. (1997) *Understanding Cultures Through Their Key Words*. Oxford: Oxford University Press.

Williams, F., Whitehead, J. L., and Miller, L. (1972) Relations between language attitudes and teacher expectancy, *American Educational Research Journal*, 9(2): 263–277.

Wilmot, K. (2014) 'Coconuts' and the middle-class: Identity change and the emergence of a new prestigious English variety in South Africa, *English World-Wide*, 35(3): 306–337.

Wineburg, S., McGrew, S., Breakstone, J., and Ortega, T. (2016) Evaluating information: The cornerstone of civic online reasoning, *Stanford Digital Repository*, http://purl.stanford.edu/fv751yt5934

Wittgenstein, L. (1963) *Tractatus Logico-Philosophicus*, Pears, D. F. and McGuinness, B. F. (trans.). London: Routledge/Kegan Paul.

Wolfram, W. A. (1969) *A Sociolinguistic Description of Detroit Negro Speech*. Washington, DC: Center for Applied Linguistics.

Wolfram, W. A. (1998) Language ideology and dialect, *Journal of English Linguistics*, 26(2): 108–121.

Wolfram, W. A. (2009) African American English, in Kachru, B. B., Kachru, Y., and Nelson, C. L. (eds.) *The Handbook of World Englishes*. Malden, MA: Blackwell: 328–346.

Wolfram, W. A. and Schilling-Estes, N. (1998) *American English: Dialect and Variation*. Oxford: Wiley Blackwell.

Women's Agenda (2016) The 'best' sexist remarks of 2016, 22nd September, https://womensagenda.com.au/latest/the-best-sexist-remarks-of-2016/ [accessed 16th February 2018].

Woods, M. (2007) Unnatural acts: Nuclear language, proliferation and order, *Journal of Language and Politics*, 6(1): 91–128.

Woods, N. (1989) Talking shop: Sex and status as determinants of floor apportionment in a work setting, in Coates, J. and Cameron, D. (eds.) *Women in Their Speech Communities*. London: Longman: 141–157.

Wray, A., Evans, B., Coupland, N., and Bishop, H. (2003) Singing in Welsh, becoming Welsh: 'Turfing' a 'grass roots' identity', *Language Awareness*, 2(1): 49–71.

Yale Environment 360 (2011) *Forum*: Just how safe is 'fracking' of natural gas?, 20th June, http://e360.yale.edu/features/forum_just_how_safe__is_fracking_of_natural_gas [accessed 22nd January 2018].

Ylänne-McEwan, V. (1999) 'Young at heart': Discourse of age identity in travel agency interaction, *Aging and Society*, 19(4): 417–440.

Young, R. F. and Bayley, R. (1996) VARBRUL analysis for second language acquisition research, in Bayley, R. and Preston, D. R. (eds.) *Second Language Acquisition and Linguistic Variation*. Amsterdam: John Benjamins: 253–306.

Zhang, Q. (2013) The attitudes of Hong Kong students towards Hong Kong English and Mandarin-accented English, *English Today*, 29(2) (June): 9–16.

Zhang, X., Myhrvold, N. P., and Caldeira, K. (2014) Key factors for assessing climate benefits of natural gas versus coal electricity generation, *Environmental Research Letters*, 9(11): 114022, http://iopscience.iop.org/article/10.1088/1748-9326/9/11/114022/pdf [accessed 17th March 2018].

Zhang, Y. B., Harwood, J., Williams, A., Ylänne-McEwan, V., Wadleigh, P. M., and Thimm, C. (2007) The portrayal of older adults in advertising: A cross national review, *Journal of Language and Social Psychology*, 25(3): 264–282.

Zimmer, B., Solomon, J., and Carson, C. E. (2014) Among the new words, *American Speech*, 89(1): 89–110.

Zimmer, B., Solomon, J., and Carson, C. E. (2017) Among the new words, *American Speech*, 92(1): 52–80.

Index